BEGINNINGS AND BREAKTHROUGHS

MY JOURNEY TO MIDLIFE

THOMAS KANNATTUMADOM

INDIA · SINGAPORE · MALAYSIA

ISBN
Paperback 979-8-89544-803-8
Hardcase 979-8-89699-296-7

"The mind should be like a reflector that reflects memories. Childhood memories should come and go. Even a small ray of light should make so much awakening. I long for that transparency, that it should not hurt anyone and that nothing should be untrue."

CONTENTS

At the beginning (Preface) *9*

1. My Lineage 14
2. The Reading Room and My Father's Occupation.......... 22
3. Paternal Relations.......... 31
4. The Mischiefs 43
5. The Stories from Grandpa 55
6. Reading, Tahkli And Quiz Competition.......... 66
7. Situation in Kuttanadu And Arrival Of Peter And Paul 77
8. The Teenager Deeds 92
9. Mother's Relations 105
10. Learn Values 115
11. Tribulations and Happiness.......... 125
12. School Results 136
13. Village Life.......... 142
14. Pre-University.......... 152
15. Services, News and Articles.......... 166
16. New Circumstances and Lessons 176
17. Fever During the Onam Season.......... 182
18. The Tribulations 191
19. Where Can I Earn My Bread?.......... 199

20. Engineering Marathon 206
21. First Attempts for a Job 221
22. I Got a Job 228
23. A Journey with Confidence 234
24. Job at Home State 246
25. Another Start 252
26. Official Life Begins 258
27. To Know More 264
28. Personal relations 268
29. Complexities 274
30. Began Higher Study 285
31. New Pastures 291
32. Diversity in the City 296
33. All for Progress 311
34. Life Partner 322
35. Sari & Dhoti 329
36. Saraswati Yamam at Sengottai 337
37. Arranging Lives 350
38. Mutual Relations 355
39. A Cow That Gives Milk Whenever It Is Milked 363
40. Get Ready, Come Back to Win 378
41. Being Lonely is Not Good 387

42. Life Problems 393

43. Chandran 401

44. Tour with Raju 409

45. Separation and Compassion 417

46. Yes, I do 431

47. The New Families 441

48. In Your Hands 455

49. Honeymoon - Through the Monuments 465

50. The Pulse of New Life 478

51. Love Letters 484

52. On the Anniversary 498

53. Survival in the Emergency 506

54. Change of Residence 513

55. The arrival of Ann Nita 521

56. New Residences 529

57. New Horizons and Chain of Successes 538

AT THE BEGINNING (PREFACE)

My dear brothers and sisters,

It's been long since I've seen you in person, talked, and written to you. Authorities have imposed lockdowns and other restrictions across the country due to the epidemic of COVID-19. When the immunisation vaccine became available and the controls were gradually phased out, it relieved the people. Yet, the crisis continues. We can move forward only when the restrictions are lifted, as our everyday life includes travel. We should do things beautifully under all circumstances, then only our journey ahead will have meaning and purpose.

Even in the control of an epidemic, optimists see signs of good. Vehicle traffic decreased; thus, carbon emissions were reduced, and the harmful blanket of pollution that once obscured the beauty of nature began to change, making the air cleaner and more transparent. Restrictions on social contact and travel restrictions helped prevent the spread of the disease.

Schools started online classes for students. It changed the routine of some people who woke up earlier and rushed to their offices. People were forced to sit at home and work—adequate sleep helps the body boost its immune system and fight off deadly viruses. More time and attention were given to health care at home. Family unity increased. Spending time with family members is a healing method that calms many ailments! While the precaution of keeping social distance and wearing a mask seems to test our patience, it has also been able to bring back many of the simple life experiences we lost earlier. We realised the increasing importance of hygiene and a disciplined lifestyle.

Fifteen years after retiring from the Central Government, my main job was to audit the quality system until the outbreak of COVID-19 and travel restrictions. The practice of travelling, going to commercial enterprises, looking around, seeking information from employees, and auditing documents and records ceased altogether. There were only a few online remote audits. There is a lot of idle time, and being sedentary is the most unbearable.

Attitudes that are acceptable to us will increase the positive energy and make the unhealthy ones fail. Suppose we adapt our lifestyles, thoughts, and actions to the current situation in this restricted age. In that case, we can transform our perspective into a completely healthy state of mind.

Then, into thoughts, into more reviews. Thoughts become memories, memories are life, and more life evokes memories. Life is good when I am happy. But I think life is so much better when others are happy! Who benefits from NRE thoughts if not shared?

All good deeds are born due to the stress that thoughts create in the mind. Whether creation happens or not, this emptiness, this indifference created by unemployment, can only be overcome by cultivating positive, creative energy and overcoming this personal crisis. After reading a lot more, you may not be able to achieve it. Then, you must be faithful to your promises and keep trying to fulfill them.

Thanksgiving is upon us, so the holiday season is complete. With a slight change in my attitude, I became increasingly excited over time. I have increased my energy. One by one, I began achieving goals I could not reach.

There is plenty of time to talk to you alone. The best medium for that is writing all that on a laptop. It takes a lot of time, time, correction and typing to be satisfied with what the printed script and the language we understand have to say.

I intend another journey through the memories with the same paths I have walked. What's coming with it? You may have sometimes wondered about my reaction to them, even in things. You may have wanted my clarity, even for something I have not told you before. Some things I have never even told my children before. I walk with memories in my heart. They can be left astray and lose the right path if left unmanaged. Good memories are the timeless treasures of the heart. I could write them down before they left my mind. During the global catastrophe of Corona, I was forced to stay home, and my family and time continued to encourage me and my writing.

Is there anyone who has no memories? Man lives forever in memories. Without memories, we would be living human beings. Happy memories move people forward. Memories that do not bring so much happiness come back occasionally, even if you try to erase them from the mind. Wouldn't there be things to remember and rejoice in ordinary life and be comforted by the thought of what life's mental struggles have gone through?

Is it possible to evaluate things equally at all ages? Each decision was based on the knowledge and circumstances of the day. Over time, abilities and circumstances changed, and we acquired new knowledge and expressions. Science and technology grew. Changes came. Is it possible today that some decisions considered proper at a young age were incorrect? He thought it was right then, believed, and acted sincerely. Individually, I could do nothing. Everything has happened. I took full responsibility for the events. God rewarded me for that, too. I am forever indebted to everyone. It will be the same tomorrow.

As I begin to write, I must narrate the 75 years of life, the ups, and downs of happiness, the puny sorrows, the satisfactions, the thoughts, the lessons, the mental conflicts, the confusions, the views of ignorance, the thoughts of what I have done. Things that were always thought unnecessary should also be written down here.

I should write without exaggeration, without creating anything out of the imagination, only the memories of the events that took place, the events of the everyday life of an ordinary person. Memoirs inherently show a feeling of vague or melancholic longing; therefore, if someone sees any aberrations, kindly consider that those are not intentional. Also, do not expect an extraordinary life or experience here. That's all I meant by everyday life. Man is born, tries to learn something for a long time, learns little, gets a job, gets married, gets into family life, raises children, and flies away when they grow up. Then we waited for them, for the grandchildren. It's time to dump her and move on. We leave behind for the living on departure, which is the legacy of the rest of our lives.

Every ordinary life story is extraordinary.

In the evenings of life, one of the most important things you can do when you have completed most of your duties and responsibilities and assessed yourself as having lived a satisfying and productive life is to thank your contemporaries. It can be through any communication or thought process; Only you should be happy and satisfied.

The primary purpose of this essay is to express gratitude. My sincere and profound thanks go to the Creator who first gave me life. Thanks to my parents, who loved me the most and caused me to be born on this earth in this family. Let me offer a bouquet of thanks to a hundred people whose names are written and a thousand who are not named.

I'm worried about how acceptable these posts will be for today's generation. I hope the next generation will not miss reading these posts as eagerly as they would like. It would be a great pleasure if you could read the whole article and share your thoughts. I will take comfort in the fact that my effort was not in vain. Because I was so naughty, the main character was named after me!

Yours sincerely,
Thomas Kannattumadom

My Family in 2020: (From Top) Families of Tony, Nita, Seema

1. MY LINEAGE

My childhood memories revolve around the Valayamchira house. I was the only child of Achayan (father) and Ammachi (mother). It remained so until the age of eight. Even as a child, when I was growing up and going to school, the locals called me 'Ottaprakkadi' (solitary) because I was a lonely child!

The house in the hamlet was a two-room house with a thatched roof made of coconut tree leaves. The house had a kitchen, a sloping thatched roof on the east side, and a closed verandah on the south side of the hut. The south side faced the ravine, and water was in the frontal view. Madhavan Nair's provision shop was on the other side of the canyon. The creek ends on the west side. Walking along the ridge near the gorge, you can see a motor floor where an engine runs on crude oil. The gorge narrows when you pass the motor floor and walk south, becoming a small stream flowing further west. The ridge extends west and passes to the next row of houses on a broad bank. The stream, a bit further west, joins the Pookaitha River.

There is a large pit at the back of the motor floor. The water reaching through the narrow drainage of the paddy field gets collected in the large pit near the motor box. All the water should drain out to begin cultivation in the paddy field. Once the water reaches the pit, the engine pumps the water through the wooden box to flow into the ravine.

A flatbed was at the southern end of the paddy field to collect the harvested paddy. The paddy sheaves are arranged and stacked in a pile after harvesting. On the west side of the Valayamchira backyard was the paddy field of about 16 acres, known by the measure of paddy seeds. It is known as the 'ninety-six 'para' measures, and the domain is at the southern end of Kavilpadam. The motor floor is adjacent to the paddy field area. The field is harvested in sheaves during the day. Threshing is the method of separating the paddy from the bundle. That activity goes on during the early daytime and at night. Winnowing is done with a natural west wind. The lanterns were there at night until very dark or early morning. In those days, cultivation and harvesting were possible only once a year. During the off-season, people searched for other jobs that were rarely available.

'Ninety-six para measures of paddy field' belonged to Valiyaparambil Outhakutty. Later, Kavalackal Ettinchira Outhakutty bought it. When my peer Chandappan grew up, he got the farm property as his family share.

Nanu and Narayaniamma of Attiyil lived in a hut on the eastern side of the Valayamchira house. Their son Maniyan was a friend and peer of the Ottaprakkadi. Thankappan was Maniyan's elder brother. At a young age, I used to call him 'Thampakkan' by the twist of my tongue. We used to come together to play head ball- throwing a ball made of coconut leaves. We also played kabaddi. We had a lovely time on swings during the Onam season; Thankappan helped us tie the rope on tree branches for a swing. 'Kaikottikkali' is a dance form like 'Thiruvathirakali'. The women dressed in traditional Kerala attire sing in a unique rhythm, clapping their hands and playing in circles. Onam was also a time of multiple games. Thiruvathirakali, Thumpithullal, Pulikali, and Kabaddi competitions were all held in a festive atmosphere. We children used to watch every match and enjoy the festival keenly.

My mother used to warn me to "go home" and run away from the scene sometimes. I would ignore the inappropriate words Attiyil

Nanu and Narayani used when they occasionally quarreled and raised their voices.

During the rainy season, I used to climb a bench on the verandah of the Valayamchira house and look out of the window at the front stream through the uncovered window. I saw the pupae-like raindrops falling on the stream's water level and happily sang –

> "Paddy sprouts, paddy sprouts, paddy grows, Droplets fall,
> drizzle and paddy drizzles, and drizzles…, paddy sprouts".

Later, I learned that the raindrops helped us grow and harvest the crops.

Even when it was not raining, I climbed the bench on the hut's verandah and watched outside. One day, when I looked out of the window, I saw a ripe mango -yellow in colour -on a branch leaning onto the stream just in front of me! There were lots of ripe green mangoes, too. When I looked at the ripe mango, I saw one mango sticking out and falling— as if I desired to get the mango and the tree readily obliging me. The mango fell into the water. Following it, I watched it until the water droplets splashed on the surface. By the time I called my mother "Amme" and ran to the shore of the ravine, the mango had gone down into the water and disappeared!

The stream is of good width. I am unsure whether a stone will reach the other side when thrown. At the eastern end of the stream is the intersection of the four streams—a bridge to cross over made of coconut trunk. People walk across the bridge—for everything: school, church, and other houses. No one is known to have fallen off the bridge. The only library in the village, which started 67 years ago, is currently located on the bridge's north end. The bridge is also modified to allow travel with cycles and autos.

Agriculture and fisheries were the most suitable sources of livelihood in the waterlogged Kuttanad habitat. My father's family or anyone else in the Kannattumadom family did not own any farmland or paddy fields. They made a living by catching fish that grew in rivers and lakes in a natural environment. However, everyone said their job was related to farming. Nature and the environment have changed over time, or man has neglected them, and fish stocks in rivers and lakes have dwindled. Over time, as fishing became the only means of subsistence, people began to look for alternatives for a living. Engaging in agricultural work has become a natural occupation. Success in life is always motivated by adaptation to change over time in any activity.

Like some of the disciples of Christ such as James and John (the sons of Zebedee), Simeon Peter and his brother Andrew - the four sons of Kuruvila Thomma of the Kannattumadom family – Ouseppachan, Vavachan or Vavachi, Kuriako and Anthonichan (KT Antony) had been fishing with their father at some point in their childhood and adolescence. It is undeniable that the family considered fishing as a means of subsistence.

My grandfather's name is Kuruvila Thomma, and I called him Appan-Grandpa. Achayan's mother is Kathrina, and I called her Amma- grandma. Before I was born, my grandfather, besides fishing, also worked as an occasional "Merchant towards the East." He used to go to Kottayam, Pala, and Changanassery in the East in a big boat, bring the necessary groceries to Kuttanad and the western areas, distribute them in the provision shops, etc. He went back in two weeks for further mercantile; that was life.

In the early stages of development and reforms, someone might have asked my grandfather - "Why don't you adopt modern fishing methods to get more fish? More fishing means more money and will bring more prosperity. You can have a big house, agricultural properties, and comfortable living. "What do you say, 'Thommaple?"

Grandfather would have immediately given his reply in a flash of wit and wisdom- "I am already happy and living happily."

That was Kuruvila Thomma, the head of the family, my grandfather. No one in Appan's (my grandfather's) family had the misconceptions of today's generation who think that happiness comes when we acquire possessions and own lots of wealth and money.

Kannattumadom was where Kuruvila Thomma found a place far from his ancestor's home, Anjiliparambil. That was after the marriage of his younger brother Varkey, the youngest in the family. Life went on as 'go for the trade towards the East, with farming labour and net fishing. Someone would dry the harvested paddy for someone else and carry it to some barn. The grandfather and the eldest sons in the family - Ouseppachan, Vavachi, and Kuriako - did the same fishing and farm labour once they crossed adolescence. The youngest was Anthonichan, who attended school.

My mother used to tell me to call my father's sisters 'Ammayi' (aunty) and aunty's husband 'Achen.' Achayan had two sisters – Kavalackal Ammayi (Rosamma- Pet name Mammikunju) and Thathampally Ammayi (pet name Pennamma). Mammikunju was the eldest daughter of the Kannattumadom family. Pennamma Ammayi was Achayan's younger sister who lived in Thathampally near Alappuzha. Another Ammayi of Maramkunnil was the cousin of Achayan- the daughter of his mother's elder sister. In my college days, we lived as her neighbour in Maramkunnil.

There were four streams at the east intersection of the ravine in front of Valayamchira's house. Kavalackal Ammayi (Rosamma, Pet name: Mammikunju) was my father's elder sister who stayed at the canyon junction. I always mentioned her as the mother of Kuriachan and addressed her as 'Ammayi.' Kavalackal house was – a palace-like house at the intersection on the way to my schools. Ammayi married Chacko in the Kavalackal family, the house on one of the four corners at the ravine junction. It was her second marriage after her first husband died. When the wealth of the Kavalackal family dwindled due to the loss of most of the agricultural lands and property over a short period in history, the natives renamed the house 'Kudilil' – meaning a hutment. Ammayi was one of the most loved mothers, as much as my mother. I was the most mischievous 'Ottaprakkadi,' according to her. She always smilingly offered me black coffee in a small cup whenever I saw her at the Kavalackal house. And there was a genuine reason for it, but it was never revealed or said in words.

The grandfather and grandmother lived at Kannattumadom with their eldest son, Ouseppachan, Kuriako, and the youngest son, Anthonichan. Achayan was the second son, and nearly three years after his marriage, he moved to Valayamchira's house for an independent living. Until then, he was with his parents at Kannattumadom.

Grandfather and the head of the Kannattumadom family (Appan) married off his children when they became of marriageable age. After her first wedding, Appan's eldest daughter Rosamma (pet name: Mammikunju) gave birth to a baby boy in Mithrakari. Soon after, her husband died of illness, and she became a widow. Her husband's brothers evicted the widow when they distributed their family property. Appan went to Mithrakari, took his widowed daughter and grandson (Kuttappan), and brought them to Kannattumadom. Kavalackal Chacko, farmer, and widower, chose Rosamma for his remarriage. Chacko had four children in his first marriage (Ambalappuzha Chechy, Thrissur Chechy, Kunjachan Chettan, and Kunjappi Chetan). Chacko and Rosamma lived in Kavalakkal house with their five children from earlier marriages. The couple subsequently had seven more children: Thommikunju, Kuriachan, Kunjamma, Kuttappan, Thommachan, Lillykutty, and Aniyappan. Kuttappan was of my age.

Ouseppachan (I used to call him Perappan), the eldest son of Kuruvila Thomma in Kannattumadom, lived in a hut on the other side of the Pookkaitha River; the property was owned by a farmer who acquired many real estates. After selling the tenancy, Ouseppachan and his family moved to a separate hut constructed on the north side of the Kannattumadom main house. As 'the trade towards the east' ceased, Ouseppachan had no regular work except local casual farm labour and culinary skills.

I have not heard of my grandfather taking Achayan for 'the trade towards the east.' The father, mother, and the other three adult sons were living in Kannattumadom as a joint family after the marriage of Ouseppachan.

The father arranged the marriage of the following two children from known families, as the familiarity developed while dealing with the 'trade towards the East.' Achayan married Annamma from the Arackal family in Kainakari. Kuriako (Chittappan) married Theyyamma from Pala.

Pennamma Ammayi was married off to the Kottaparambil family in Thathampally. In Kottaparambil, Achen (Joseph was his name) worked as a grocery merchant near the Alappuzha Shavakkotta Bridge. When my mother gave birth to a baby boy, she told me that Kottapparambil Achen and Ammayi were called upon to be the baby's godfather and godmother during her son's baptism. After the marriage, Achayan (Vavachi) owned a pair of bullocks and joined the team which ploughed the paddy fields. Ouseppachan was a brilliant culinary professional for the neighbourhood. Others would go fishing. No matter what work was done, the family had no significant progress. They could manage their daily life. The marriage of Anthonichan, the youngest son of Kannattumadom, occurred when I was growing up as the eldest son of my parents and developing memories.

After puncha cultivation of paddy, there was no other cultivation until the following season. This was because there were no irrigation facilities to repeat the paddy cultivation in the Kuttanadu region. After the harvest, the field was dry, and after ploughing, the outer bund was breached open to allow water to enter the field. Saltwater was also allowed to enter the paddy fields. The field, the stream, and the backyard will all be flooded with the same water level. Puncha cultivation was done by pumping out the water in the area. It was ploughed again before the paddy field dried up, and the land was prepared for sowing paddy seeds. It has been going on for several generations. Since no other work was available, everyone would go fishing alone or in groups.

Many insects, birds, and pests affect the growth of paddy plants at various stages. One of the agricultural jobs Achayan did was to protect the paddy from worms in case such problems occurred in the paddy field. He went around the paddy field swinging a basket to catch the worms/pupae from every plant. After the harvest and threshing, they enthusiastically did the subsequent work on the paddy. Achayan was thus enthusiastically involved in various agricultural and non-agricultural activities. For Kuriako, farming did not seem lucrative, nor did he get engaged with others. But he was ready to do agriculture if he had his farmland.

2. THE READING ROOM AND MY FATHER'S OCCUPATION

The first significant event in the village that comes to mind is the library movement and how the convenience of reading was facilitated. Dramas were rehearsed and staged publicly to raise funds for the library. CYMA Library was established and organised by KT Antony and his friends like Mathew Vanchikkal and Mani Valezhath. In the backyard at Valiyaparambil, Owner Joseph permitted the starting of the reading room facility with a library.

A reading room was a space set up for casual browsing. A library was the whole building wherein books or materials were collected and preserved for easy distribution to interested readers. Funds were necessary to set up the facilities for the benefit of all, and arranging cultural shows was a means of collecting adequate funds.

Rehearsals for the play occurred in the evenings in Valayamchira Vavachi's (Achayan) house courtyard. A rectangular tent in the yard was made of coconut leaves and bamboo. Preparations were made for staging the play by setting up a large pandal and a stage on the west side of the pandal.

The year was 1953. I was a seven-year-old then, watched the rehearsals, and stood in the house's yard until I got tired, went to bed at night, and fell asleep. My mother made black coffee and gave it to the performing artists. Three or four young and enthusiastic 'Appachans' were there with names like - Thuruthichira Appachan, Valiyathara Appachan, and Panakkezhath Appachan. Anthonichan and his brother Vavachi were there to complete the list of all the male and female performing artists in the plays.

The play 'Calvaryile Kalpapadapam,' written by Kainikkara Padmanabha Pillai, was the first play staged for the benefit fund of the library. The drama team later became famous for performing plays like 'Two plus Two Make Five' (by TN Gopinathan Nair) and 'Beheading of John the Baptist'(Bible drama).

Thuruthichira Appachan was a good comedian. He would give much love and warmth and be active in the group. Amidst the chores of watering and weeding the plants in the emperor's garden in the play, the gardeners- coworkers with a pitcher and sat by leaning on each other's back, singing "Domdamiko, Domdamiko - Uriaryikku Shappad, Urathile Vilayatt." (Eat well, and do percussion and play). There were good jokes and good deeds - in the play. There were good, explosive scenes that everybody enjoyed.

Thuruthichira Appachan would hold me, watching the rehearsals close to him, and ask–

"Whom do you like, your Mom or your Dad?"

I used to answer soon – "I like both".

Then Appachan continued his questions: "What was the reason?"

There must have been something wrong with the answer I gave. The actors all laughed together. They also gave me the name 'Mahakusruti' in that drama training tent. Even at seven, I did not have a sibling, which must have made them call me a loner boy - 'Ottaprakkadi.'

The playing group later rehearsed and performed in several plays and raised funds for the village library. The dramas were performed repeatedly at Vaishyambagam School and Chempumpuram Primary School. Anthonichan won the 'Best Actor award in all the plays, and Achayan won the 'Best Actress trophy. The awards were given by prominent villagers who appreciated the plays. Valiyathara Appachan picked me up, the seven-year-old boy, laughing and clapping when I saw my father performing shyness in a female role.

Achayan danced to the song -

"Anathalayolam venna tharaamedaa,
Ananda Sree Krishna vaay murukku"

(Malayalam Film "Jeevitha Nauka": Jeevitha Nauka, Singer: Kunju Kunju Bhagavathar, Pushpa, Music: Dakshinamoorthi, Lyrics: Abhay Dev)

He performed graceful movements with his hands, eyes, and facial expressions. The seven-year-old must have slept through the night in the rehearsal tent of the play after he had bought that butter and put it in his mouth as a response to his father's performance.

The dagger used in the play 'Calvary' - a blade made of delicate wood carvings on the handle with sharp edges and a coat of aluminium paint for the shine - was always a big attraction for me. I would take it and preserve it after the rehearsal was over. I would run and fetch them when needed during the play. Appachan once agreed to give the dagger to me after the play was staged. The only condition he stated was that I must perform the role of Judas committing suicide, as it was in the play.

A group of young people from the village neighbourhood and the locals came together as a team to plough the paddy field using bullocks. Achayan, Ottathyckal Thomachi, Puthiyaveettil Appachan, Ezhupathil Vavachan, Valiyathara Appachan, and the Muttunkal brothers, etc., were the members, colleagues, and co-workers in the ploughing team.

Vavachi and Thomachi have been doing agricultural work together for a long time. The fellow travellers in various engagements had many similarities in between. They had a similar family background. They were sympathetic supporters of each other. Their eldest sons grew up together and went to school together. Thommachi carried on with his job of working on the farmlands for a long time and later switched to running a provision shop.

Once a week or two, if Achayan carried two (para) measures of paddy from the farmer's paddy barn and brought it home, then there was prosperity and happiness at home for two weeks. My mother boiled the paddy in a large pot, spread it on a mat in the courtyard, dried it in the sun, pounded it in a mortar using a long pestle, and made it into rice for cooking. Achayan used to do these logistics for our daily needs, and during his spare time, he did the work for the village library.

Before the cultivation, the team ploughed the fields. Once the paddy was harvested, it was dried, weighed, carried in sacks, loaded onto a boat, brought to the barn, and stored for a long time. As requested by someone, Achayan must have transported the haystacks to Kollam (Quilon) on a slow-moving barge boat known as the 'Kettuvallam' - a houseboat without roofing, pushed by bamboo poles. He used to return with charcoal purchased from Kollam after all the struggles and bargains of merchandise at Kollam.

The whole bundles for haystacks were tied up and put into a boat, and the stalks and stalks were carried back to Kollam. After four to five days, the burned cashew shells ('Kari'- the black charcoal) were loaded onto the boat and returned. On the way, the 'Kettuvallam' remained moored by the backwaters to prepare food and sleep at night. All other times, the boats were pushed forward and navigated using Bamboo poles from the fore and aft ends.

There were many cashew processing factories in Kollam. After separating the shells and husk from the whole cashew nuts and collecting the oil, the nuts are segregated, and the black charcoal remains. This charcoal processes Calcium Oxide (Neettu Kakka) and Lime Powder. Sometimes, the charcoal is replaced by Neettu Kakka loaded onto the barge boat. Suppose you transport haystacks, charcoal, Neettu Kakka, or lime, whatever it may be. In that case, the customer will be charged for transportation in cash.

If you come with any supplies from Kollam, the next trip will be three or four days later, returning to Kollam with a load of haystacks. It is impossible to say how often they went on these mercantile trips to Kollam, perhaps until the subsequent paddy cultivation started.

After the charcoal transportation work was reduced, 'company trading' was a job opportunity in a small way. On the other side of the Pookkaitha river in Kanjippadam, two months before harvest, along with Puthiyaveettil Vakkan, Achayan organised a wayside tea and snacks shop, mainly catering to the harvest workers. After the harvest, the trade had to be wound down when the field bund was cut off and water allowed to enter the field.

That was the non-agricultural livelihood of some of the people of Kuttanad at that time. With modern developments, the mercantile barge boats were ultimately overtaken by trains and motor vehicles. And then Achayan was jobless.

In the evenings at home, the mother and son would light a kerosene lamp and pray that Achayan would get a suitable job and make us feed. Achayan may not have returned from the library.

"It is evening now. We have lit the lamp. Come, Jesus, and raise me to be a good boy forever." With her son sitting on her lap with folded hands, Ammachi continued the prayer.

That was a prayer my mother taught me when I was a child - she would sing and pray that I would be raised as a good child forever!

When my siblings - Babu and Leelamma - grew up, my mother taught them the same prayer.

Anthonichan, my uncle, whom I always called 'Kochuppappan,' was a degree student in Changanassery during drama rehearsals and library activities. He worked as the secretary of the library. He turned the library into a building that grew from a leafy shed into an important cultural institution that stood tall as the village's pride. But he did not have a lucrative career then. He got a job as a journalist in Alappuzha after he had passed his degree. Kochuppappan took charge as the Alappuzha correspondent of the daily Deepika (in 1960). He had to hand over the library responsibilities, the secretary's position, and duties to his brother. At the behest of the working committee, Achayan happily took over the responsibilities. He was also interested in reading books and periodicals and was constantly engaged in library activities.

Whatever job Achayan did and activities he got involved in, overcoming hunger in those days was not easy. There was hardly any regular job giving adequate compensation to meet both ends. When he had a nuclear family to support, he separated from his ancestor's home, Kannattumadom, and started living separately at Valayamchira.

When Achayan had no farming or other related agriculture work and passed through a difficult period without a specific job, Anthonichan (Kochuppappan) came to the rescue. It was a godsent idea that Kochuppappan called Achayan to give him a small job distributing a few newspapers in the village. Kochuppappan aimed to increase the circulation of the popular newspaper Deepika, of which he was the Alappuzha representative. Out of the bundles of newspapers that came to him, Anthonichan gave twenty-five copies to Achayan for distribution to interested readers in the nearby villages. Achayan travelled from Ambalapuzha West Gate to Mathur -Thaicherry in the north via Kanjippadam, Vaishyambhagom, and Chempumpuram.

"God bless - if there are natives interested in reading, want to grow and gain knowledge, this will become a way of life for you, Vavachi. Look for a while."

Anthonichan said while handing over twenty-five copies of the Deepika newspaper. He knew that it was a field that no one quickly dared to undertake as none had a good sense or judgment in tackling an unknown situation that even the wisest would avoid.

"The monthly subscription is two rupees per copy of a newspaper. An agent gets a commission of twenty percent. If all goes well, your monthly income will be ten rupees. Three stomachs may not feel the hunger at the price of a sack of paddy."

Educated, knowledgeable, and loving brother was advising with good intentions - Achayan determined within a few minutes and said,

"Let's see what Anthonichan said may be true. Let me see it for a few days."

The newspaper was initially sent by line boat from Alappuzha to Kanjippadam. At first, he walked that distance and then rowed in a rented small canoe. After two or three months, he would paddle the canoe to Ambalapuzha. Every day, he did the same work. He should go in the morning and can only return home in the afternoon. Although Achayan reluctantly said delivering the newspaper to every door was a shame, Anthonichan insisted on continuing the daily work for some time.

The locals loved to read. Every month, the number of newspapers increased by five or ten to reach one hundred. After working as a newspaper distributor, agent, and reporter for a year, Achayan realised that it was a dignified job. The local information was occasionally written as news and printed in the next day's newspaper! So, he became more interested in writing and sending reports. The locals were happy to read the newspaper about what happened in the neighbourhood. Achayan took over the 'Malayala Manorama' agency from Ambalapuzha and started functioning. Copies of Manorama were received, along with copies of Deepika.

He bought a log of Anjili wood, and Kunjayyappan, the village carpenter, carved a small canoe. The journey to Ambalapuzha then took place in the tiny canoe. He would go early in the morning before sunrise. He would row everywhere, deliver the newspaper, and return home at two or three o'clock. He would have lunch at home after all the work.

Anthony Kochuppappan's pride was immense because the seed he sowed by sending a mere bundle of newspapers had yielded a good harvest and was adequate for the survival of Vavachi's family. It continued for years later. When Achayan's children came to know him, they had so much love and respect for Anthony Chittappan, which increased over time.

Achayan hired an assistant to deliver the newspapers when the business got better. As a schoolchild, I developed a habit of reading the Manorama newspaper. I went to the village library and read other newspapers and magazines. I took books from the library and read them.

Meanwhile, Achayan attended small public meetings in the neighbourhood and continued participating in the democratic movements, extending the struggle for freedom. Since the country's independence, he has adopted khadar/ khadi- an Indian homespun cotton cloth, as his garment to proudly proclaim his involvement in the freedom struggle and preserve it as his display of patriotism. He always wore a white khadi dhoti and a white khadar Jubba, a long one with sleeves rolled up above the elbow. Achayan was still wearing a Khadar dhoti even while resting at home.

Achayan developed a national interest and political consciousness through journalism. He has worked with the Indian National Congress. Although he did not desire any position, he reached the block leadership level. His colleagues and friends respected him. He acted as the booth agent for Congress in all the general elections.

When journalism emerged as a way of life for him, public relations improved, and thus, he gained a good name and prestige. 'Journalist Vavachi' has been an integral part of all social activities in the region and has continued uninterrupted for years.

Uthaman from Kanjippadam took Vavachi and went to Thiruvananthapuram one day and met K. Sukumaran, the then-editor of Kerala Koumudi daily. That was the beginning of a long-term relationship. Achayan took charge of the Kerala Kaumudi daily in the Ambalapuzha region.

Achayan started that journey in 1953 and continued for more than 35 years. As an agent for the Ambalapuzha region, he had three or four dailies and associated periodicals for regular distribution. He became Manorama's correspondent, an active journalist, a prominent librarian, and a social reformer. He became the most acceptable public figure among the natives and the perfect social reformer and philanthropist who saw everyone equally regardless of caste or creed. The people gave him a lot of love and respect.

3. PATERNAL RELATIONS

Growing up in Kannattumadom, Anthonichan was the first to graduate from college. The first in the family, perhaps the second most educated person in the village after Kochukutty Ezharayil (Kavalackal).

While he was the Alappuzha correspondent for the Deepika Daily, he also assisted Fr. Gilbert CMI in the initial efforts to establish the Carmel Polytechnic at Punnapra. He was involved in social work with Fr. Gregory Kalluparambil, the vicar of Punnapra St Gregorios Church and the founder of St Joseph's Old Age Home. I learned of this information much later, after I entered adolescence. Until then, my Kochuppappan (Anthonichan) was the hero in my village as he established a library, performed well in several plays, and was a generally accepted and educated person.

My parents had a great love and affection for Anthonichan and great pride in his activities and achievements. It must be assumed that his college education, work in the town, and loving demeanour were the reasons for this. Anthonichan, who was well-liked by the locals because of his work related to library and theatre, was the first English-educated youngest son in the Kannattumadom family.

The first of the celebrations I remember at the Kannattumadom ancestor home was the wedding of Kochuppappan, the youngest son in the family. His marriage at Kannattumadom was the most significant festival and event I remember vividly.

There was a big pandal in the courtyard of the Kannattumadom house for Kochuppappan's wedding. On the west side, there was the cooking house. Mike's set with speakers was tied to the coconut trees at a height. Film songs were playing loudly. The mike set was routine for large ceremonies and public meetings in the village on those days.

My playmates were Kunjamma, the daughter of Perappan (Ouseppachan), and Marykutty, the daughter of Thathampally Ammayi. None of the other siblings had grown up as much as these cousins. None of the aunts' sons, who were older than me and had grown up, had included me as their playmate since they lived in separate houses in the nearby villages.

Eagle-eyed Marykutty was very smart, and she would look at my eyes and occasionally say -

"Why are you looking at me? I will pierce your eyes" –

Her index finger would come so close to my nose. And then she would laugh out loud!

Anthonichan married the daughter of the elder brother of Fr. Gregory Kalluparambil.

Achayan invited the couple to visit Valayamchira for a feast after the marriage. Achayan had prepared a proper reception for the couple. An annex was made to the west side of our palm leaves hut, which was covered with more palm leaves and bamboo palms. During the visit of the couple who came over for the reception, I remember sitting on the bench with the newlyweds to have Kozhukattai (steamed rice flour stuffed with grated coconut and jaggery), Ethapazham, and coffee.

Kuriako Chittappan later started the egg trade from that annex on the west side of the Valayamchira palm leaves house.

Kuriako Chittappan brought Theyyamma Aunty from Pala after marriage. She went to Pala for the first banquet party after their wedding. Chittamma never went to Pala again to meet her parents or siblings. She did not have the time to go! No one ever came and took her also. Even when Theyyamma Chittamma's father and mother died, no one came from Pala or informed her, and no one came looking for them later. I have not even heard Chittamma say anything about her parents or siblings. She showed no remorse for it. She must have tucked inside everything in her mind, and it was visible in her teary eyes.

My Kuriako chittappan was never at home during the day. He used to go out in the mornings and come late in the evenings. He used to go by canoe for the egg trade.

Chittappan used to go to Pulimkunnu or Changanacherry market with his baskets of collected eggs, sell them there in the wholesale market, and buy groceries and stationery in bulk. He had a few varieties of Aluminium utensils, Jaggery packs, candy jars, and other groceries stacked in a tiny four-seater canoe while going around for daily eggs. He bought chicken eggs from the houses near the ravine shores. Sitting on the canoe, he sold the utensils and groceries to needy people.

Chittamma was the only one who looked after their children, the grandfather and grandmother, all day and did all the household chores alone. Grandfather and grandma lived with Kuriako uncle - or Kuriako uncle lived with his parents at Kannattumadom. Anthonichan (Kochuppappan) and Kuriako Chittappan used to pay for all the domestic expenses. It was because Ouseppachan (Perappan) was in trouble without much work. He would bring all the fish if he went fishing in the boat.

The grandfather and grandmother never had to ask or buy anything from their children. They were always satisfied and happy when their daily needs were met. Whenever Anthony Kochuppappan came from Punnapra, he would give them some maintenance. He would also provide some amount for his elder brother (Ouseppachan) and say to him in confidence - "If Kochayan (eldest brother) comes to Punnapra, you can live happily there and do some work or trade in the local market."

After the harvest, when the field and the pond were dry, it was challenging for the Theyyamma Chittamma in Kannattumadom. She had to walk about a mile through the paddy field, fill a large mud pot with water, and carry it on her head to bring it home, almost eight to ten water pots daily. Occasionally, Chittamma used to suffer from Bronchial asthma. But the smile on that face when she saw everyone in the family was beautiful! Joy and Celinamma were small children then and younger than me. Chittamma, who worked hard on all the household chores, never got a day off. Later, they had six more children: Sicily, Mathukutty, Susamma, Sunnychan, Salimma, and Manoj.

Kuriachan, one of my cousins in Kavalackal, used to come to Valayamchira every morning to load Kuriako chittappan's stationery and grocery items onto the canoe for his egg trade. After finishing the job, Kuriachan had to walk up to the High School at Champakulam. After loading the goods, Chittappan would get on the canoe's stern. Kuriachan would give the oar to him. After receiving the oar, Chittappan would wrap a spoonful of tea leaves in a torn newspaper. A bamboo basket with haystacks spread inside was the method of bulk packing jaggery moulds secured with ropes for lifting. He would pack a few small broken fragments of palm jaggery that fell off the bamboo packing case onto another piece of paper. Whether it was called the gift or the wage in kind for the support services, it was packed in the paper; Kuriachan gladly brought it to his Kavalackal house. Coming from the school, he would take tuition for the children at the new Kavalackal house across the ravine, studying in small classes. One 'Para' measure of paddy for two months of tuition per student – was the meagre income - but it was the only income for the Kavalackal family of six or seven. After the 10th class,

Kuriachan started going to Kakkazham to study Survey and Civil Engineering Certificate Course. Then Kuriachan's younger brother Kuttappan took over the responsibility of loading and unloading for Chittappan's trade, and the family received the gift of tea powder. I saw Kuriachan or Kuttappan coming to work and going away after work every morning. When Chittappan returned after the egg trade, it was after nightfall on most days. That's why I remember seeing them only during rush hour in the morning.

Kuriachan's elder brother, Thommikunju, went to school and was very interested in learning Hindi to get a job.

Kuriachan had another elder brother, Kuttappan, born to his mother in her first marriage. I called him Kuttappan Chettan, who stayed at Kannattumadom and used to come to Valayamchira's house during my childhood. Kuttappan Chettan was the only son from his mother's first marriage. He was born in Mithrakari. While growing up, he was in his mother's house before her second marriage, i.e., Kannattumadom, where his grandfather and uncles also lived.

When Kuttappan Chettan came to Valayamchira, laughter, games, and jokes were aplenty, and the mischiefs of the little boy there (myself) also increased with joy. He was tall and handsome. Chettan used to grab my legs with his right hand, slowly lift me, and then hang my head down, "Ammo!" I would shout and cry aloud with fear. My body still shivers! Then, I would climb onto his back to play mahout with Chettan as the elephant. Everyone loved Chettan, as he loved everyone else equally. His little stammering when speaking did not hinder the continuous flow of love to others at times. He always considered it as a different ability. Others gave him back more love in kindness and deeds.

I was in the sixth standard in middle school then. One day at lunchtime, four of us friends were sitting down and were about to open our lunchboxes and start having lunch. Standing on the verandah, my peer Maniyan called me outside the classroom window.

"Please come down here."

"Come inside. Let's have lunch," I replied.

Maniyan waited. He was sad. But he did not say anything until we finished our lunch.

Maniyan came with us to wash my hands while we walked out to the ravine shore. Maniyan said: -

"Kuttappan Chettan is no more, and his body has been brought home."

It was a great shock, and I silently sighed with grief, and nothing was seen and heard.

Maniyan confirmed the death in silence and depression. Nothing more was said. I took the books, left the school, and ran home in front of Maniyan. Tearful eyes had blocked the view, but I ran through the familiar path. I heard the mothers of Muppathinkalam and Marymangalam asking me -

"Why are you crying, Mone (my son)?" "Why are you running?" –

"My Chettan (elder brother) is dead," I cried. He was taken to Alappuzha by boat yesterday due to a fever. Are you coming, Ammayi ..."?

Maniyan confirmed the information to everyone as I was still crying.

There was no one at the Valayamchira house. My running race continued to the ancestor home - Kannattumadom.

Lots of people were gathered there. Chettan was lying on the bed in the verandah and fully covered with white clothes.

At that time, his mother was living at Kavalackal. Chettan's body was not taken there. No one wanted to say whether the information was passed on to his paternal relatives in Mithrakkary. Why was it so?

No one asked explicitly.

I heard someone say, "Let them be happy as much."

"Someone had rolled a fishing hook inside a rice ball and gave him to eat, to kill him!".

How could the villagers or his relatives be so cruel?

My goodness! Why kill such a good Chettan?!

As the library activities became more efficient, people gathered every evening. The number of books has exceeded two hundred. Many types of newspapers and magazines were available for reading. A bench for people to sit on and a desk arranging newspapers were added as facilities. The continuous efforts of Anthony Kochuppappan as the secretary and the selfless cooperation of others contributed to the prosperity and popularity of the library. The nightfall will be by the end of the evening's radio news. Everyone who came to the library would return to their respective homes. The secretary also closes the library and goes home.

Just as Achayan returned home from the library one evening, I, his seven-year-old son, was called out.

"Eda… Come here."

I saw my father's face tremble with grief and anger. He grabbed his son's tiny hand palms together. I was frightened and numb.

"Hey ...did you…, Tell me the truth, Tell the truth., Did you take it?"

Several lashes were given with a cane. Usually, rattan is applied to my clothed buttocks or below the calf muscles.

My mother grabbed the rattan, asking him to stop beating her child.

"You stand aside," He repeated with sadness and anger. He hated himself for not being able to bear the humiliation, pulling the stick and throwing it away without hearing anyone's cry -

He went to the kitchen and looked for a sickle (scythe knife), "Where is it?". One side of the hut, which segregated the extension to the west side, was partially cut open and pushed out. Kuriako chittappan's belongings in the shed, such as the Aluminium utensils and the empty egg storage baskets, were overturned. All other noises mingled with the screaming of the mother and her son. Throwing out the sickle and deciding on something, Achayan called his brother upsettingly.

"Eda ... Kuriako .... you ..."

When the day's egg trade was over, Chittappan had put the goods back in the shed, and it was time for him to close it. He stood there staring at Achayan without saying anything.

"Better you shift your egg trade, and it is enough to be here, today itself, change it or take it somewhere" - without saying that he meant it.

Achayan took the oar for the canoe in his hand. He closely held the hands of his son, and I looked at my mother. We both were sobbing uncontrollably, and tears were rolling down our cheeks. As we were pushed into the canoe, Achayan called out -

"Get into the canoe, quick... Eda Kuriako, I need this canoe. I'll take it for a while."

Without waiting for an answer, he untied the knots that tied the canoe to the shore, sat at one end of the canoe, and rowed. He was determined. The mother and son cried and held on to the canoe's sides. The canoe crossed the motor floor and passed through the small ravine towards the west, slowly passed the row of houses on the ridge, Thattara house and the Kanjiramchirayil house, and headed straight towards the west. Anyone could hear only the sound of the canoe rowing and the sighs of the mother and son. There were only another hundred metres to the Pookaitha River. Suddenly, the rowing stopped. The night was frozen with mixed emotions and terrible silence.

Achayan said quietly and firmly to his family-

"Let's go to the river and die... get finished there, t-o-g-e-t-h-e-r."

It was a voice of determination, unafraid, challenging the terrifying silence the night provided. But at the last word, the father sounded a feeble melancholic whimper. The mother and son heard it. Mother's face rose to the sky. "Oh my God!" Mother silently offered her last prayers to the sky amidst the sighs, begging and praying with hands together with a hopeful expression on her face, very emotional and worried. The canoe tilted and jolted everyone literally. I felt that something wrong was happening. Or then, why did I cry out so loud again and again?

"No ... don't go ...... Achayan, don't go "?

You could barely see the Pookaitha River a stone's throw away. In the dim light, the ridge - the outer bund of the paddy field on the right - was visible; it had a breach allowing the water to seep into the field, and the water did flow through the breach. The cry of sorrow and grief by the only child sitting in the canoe had more power than the water flowing into the field. That loving father must have called, "Mone..." The man realised that his love for his son was more than his love for his creator!

The son, who loved his parents so much and rowed the boat, stopped rowing and said in a low voice that he was talking to himself as if his loving parents had called from the Kannattumadom family to return home.

"Then, let us go home and tell Ammachi and Achayan we can do this afterward. That's enough."

He wondered for a moment. Will suicide wash away the stigma of crime unjustly imposed on us by others?

Slowly, the boat rowed back through the breach on the ridge and onto the water-filled paddy field. Kavilpadam is across the northern division of the paddy field. Our ancestor's home is a hundred feet north into the Kavilpadam -Kannattumadom, where my Grandparents lived. It is an island-like land in the middle of the flooded field.

I remember jumping out of the canoe and running towards my grandfather. The Grandpa took me in his arms and hugged me lovingly. The poor child might have cried and slept wearily; that is all I could remember. How good it is, not to remember!

The poor child might have cried, gotten tired, slept, and no longer remembered anything. Is it not better not to remember such an alarming increase in blood flow rate to the brain as the uncontrolled water flow through the breach on the ridge of a paddy field?

Will the scars left in the irreproachable innocent's mind ever disappear?

This life results from the call, the consolation, and the touch the grandfather and grandma gave their grandson. After a lot of experience and enjoyment, this life, which allowed me to write this, is to untangle a bit out of the nerves of some memory! The life of this person and those raised in the family later are the results of the rethinking of my parents. They lived in peace, without failure in any crisis, and with malice towards no one.

✧ ✧ ✧

The family returned to stay at Valayamchira after being consoled by the parents. The extension shed of the Valayamchira hut, which would have been a reminder of the nightmare, no longer remained. The west wall of the demolished room was refurbished with coconut tree leaves and bamboo. Woven bamboo-mat-covered walls remained motionless like unbreakable human relationships. It remained so until the site owner, Kuruppachan, demolished the hut and built a brick wall house with a stone foundation a few years later.

No one ever told or heard about how much money I had stolen.

"A boy from the nearest house took away your money." A priest who dwelt in the countryside and practised witchcraft in a northern church had said that. Achayan was outraged when he heard this rumour spread by his brother Kuriako after losing money from his egg store or elsewhere. It was a deep wound to Achayan's self-esteem and pride. If he knew that someone in the family had done that wrong, Achayan would have given a double refund and apologised, even if the family had to stay hungry. Although nobody believed Kuriako's interpretation, he did not use the discretion of kindness to his brother. He had the audacity, cunningness, or 'expert advice' to blame his brother and family. Whatever the amount, if he handed over some money to Kuriako, he would have received it happily! But that gesture would amount to a false confession after making no mistake by any of his family members. Any little thing, especially rumours, spread very fast in the village. It affects the near and dear ones. One who initiates the rumour does not realise that. A sincere man thought it was better not to live in shame than to be accused. He did not quarrel with anyone and did not hate anyone. He pardoned everything and attempted to dissolve his life and belongings in the flowing water of the river.

The egg store quietly moved away. Kuriako moved with his Aluminium utensils and jaggery packs to another location, and another egg storehouse was erected near the east junction. He operated his mercantile from there.

4. THE MISCHIEFS

Valayamchira had a long, narrow stretch of vacant land on the eastern side of our dwelling. Before the first communist regime came to power in Kerala, leaders like Varghese Vaidyan and TV Thomas participated and spoke at the village meetings held in Valayamchira. After the sessions, there used to have performances by singer K.S. George -

"പാമ്പുകൾക്കു മാളമുണ്ട്, പറവകൾക്ക് ആകാശമുണ്ട്

മനുഷ്യപുത്രനു തല ചായ്ക്കാൻ, മണ്ണിലിടമില്ലാ...മണ്ണിലിടമില്ലാ...

(Snakes have burrows and birds have skies"...)

Samba Sivan's kathaprasamgam (singing and storytelling performance) was sometimes heard.

I was studying in standard one or two at that time. I used to go to the government primary school with Markos and Maniyan as my companions. I remember the day I joined the primary school. After receiving the gurudakshina offering of betel leaf with areca nut, Vasupillai Sir asked me, "What is the child's name?"

I looked at my father, seeking his help to answer the question.

He replied to me by saying, "KT Thomas." I said –"It is my father's name".

"He's his father's son," said Thuruthichira Appachan, who had come with Achayan to seek admission for his friend's son to the government primary school.

The guru's words were encouraging, which he said, smiling at me.- "You are smart."

It was well understood that Vasupillai sir would be good in the fifth-grade mathematics class. Vasupillai sir held the ear lobes of all my friends and made them spin around for two minutes as if he were drawing circles on the blackboard with chalk. He pulled the ear lobes of the children one by one when they moved up their heels from the ground, and the heels dropped down when he finished drawing the circles by holding on to their ear lobes.

Though naughty, I do not remember Vasupillai sir catching my ear lobes in the mathematics class. I remember him saying, "You're good," more than once. This love for Vasupillai sir must be the context for why I liked mathematics more than all the other subjects of my studies.

When I was five and a half years old, I went to school, and until then, there was no other heir or claimant to jump onto his mother's lap. "He would suckle his mother's breast milk, as Kavalackal Ammayi would always tell, and that "He was such a little thief."

After joining the primary class at five and a half years old, I used to go to my mother's lap to drink my mother's breast milk every time I came home from school. It did not matter to me while the mother was chopping for the curry, cooking the rice, boiling it, or weaving the coconut leaves in the courtyard.

I was like that even after my mother often commented, "Enough, stop it, I'm going to buy the 'chenninayakam' (Extracted from Sun-dried aloe vera with a bitter taste) and apply. Then only you will stop doing this."

As the paddy field was drained and prepared for cultivation, I used to go to the motor installation site and watch the engine being filled with crude oil and the belt loaded onto the wheel. The valve's rising and falling back as a tuk-tuk and the "chuck chuck" roar of smoke billowing out at one end of a large tube were gripping. The miraculous phenomenon of water flowing into the stream does not get you bored, no matter how long you look at it. And you will become a mechanical engineer later in life! It was never a thought that flashed in my mind.

Once the water level falls, many fish run in the pits and ditches. Fishing could be done by going down the channels with a fishing net. Sometimes, it was possible to catch fish even by hand. I would come home with the fish in my hand, hand over the fish to my mother, swim in the ravine, and get ready for school with friends. Markos was my group's tallest and healthiest friend, always helping me with something. He would be close to me, protect me in adverse situations, and defend me from adversaries.

Thamarakath Sir was the most loved and respected teacher in primary school. He was tall, fair, and handsome. "Thamarothe Kaimal Sir" always wore a white dress and stretched his legs long. He grew a thick black moustache on his face. His love and interest for 'Vavachi,' the journalist, my father, might have given me some special consideration from him.

One day, on my way back from school, I saw a wristwatch on the property's sidewalk while walking through the backyard of Thamarakath's house. I did not know what to do, whether to pick it up or not. I did not know who had lost the watch. I entered Kavalackal Ammayi's house at the junction on my way home. I told my aunt about the watch I got on the way. Kuriachan's father searched for the owner, walked up to the backyard in Thamarakath, found the owner, and returned the wristwatch to the owner. It was Kaimal sir's watch. He lost it somewhere outside his house but did not know where. After that, Kaimal sir was given special consideration and a particular interest in me, Vavachi's son. He was my class teacher in the fifth standard.

Achayan once put me in a canoe and rowed me for the Ambalapuzha Sri Krishna temple festival. We returned after watching the Malayalam movie 'Nalla Thanka'. There were good songs in the film as well. I can only remember a scene in the movie where the hot rice porridge was overturned onto the ground in front of the children who sat down to eat food. The small children were crying. Or was such a scene my nightmare? I do not know.

We should graze the roof of our thatched hut every year before the arrival of the monsoon season. About a hundred pairs of dried halved leaves of the coconut tree were necessary to redo the thatching. The owner of the land, Perumaparambil Kuruppachan, used to come to Valayamchira to oversee the plucking of coconut fruits from the trees there. The Vannan (the coconut tree-climber) was told to cut down one or two coconut palms each from every coconut tree, "according to Vavachan's wishes." My mother would tear up the palms into two halves, put them in water for seasoning, and take them out after ten days. After weaving them into palm fronds, she dried them in the sun and stored them till it was time to thatch the roof. My mother worked all day in the fields, picking up the fallen rice ears with grains and walking behind the harvesters. She was busy raising some chickens at home, selling eggs, processing cow dung, and buying groceries from Madhavan Nair's shop across the river, not to mention the daily routine of cooking and feeding everyone in the family.

When any hen was tired of laying eggs, the hen would tremble like having a severe fever. It is then called the hen with a fever or something like that. Once the fever subsides, the hen starts laying eggs again every day. Sometimes, my mother had shown me that the fever would go away quickly if the hen was dipped in water and given bathing.

It was the day of grazing the thatched roof. There were elders – the Appachans to help. Two of them were sitting on the roof above, and one below was fetching the woven dry coconut leaves to the top. Achayan had gone to Ambalapuzha, and Ammachi was busy preparing food for the guest workers in the kitchen. There was not enough height for me to pick up and throw the dry coconut leaves. I was moving around looking for some engagement or entertainment. What to do next? Then, I noticed a hen with a fever, shivering and moving in the courtyard here and there.

It was thought that catching and dipping the hen in water would quickly relieve the fever, and there was no better fun and enjoyment. Perhaps the habit of preparing for adventure with self-confidence grew inside me, the naughty one. I was confident that if the hen were submerged in the water for longer, the fever would go away today itself. If it were fed, it would start laying eggs from tomorrow! I did not waste any more time and sincerely dipped the hen into the water. Was it adequate or a little more time than necessary? When I lifted the hen out of the water, it was a surprise that the head of the hen was still hanging down and was not moving at all!

I must have panicked and called out loud, "Ammachi" (Mom) ... Appachan, sitting on the roof, saw it. Appachan, also called my mother.

"Chedathi (Elderly sister)…., let's make chicken curry for the roof grazers today!"

My mother ran and looked eagerly without knowing what was going on. Poor little boy, poor chicken!

Appachan remembered the name 'Kusruthi,' laughed, and called me such names again!

Valayamchira house had a small window lined with bamboo on the north side of the kitchen. There was adequate wind and light to the rooms from the north side. Next to the window was a box of a long bench-like one-meter width, enough to accommodate a lifting cover on the top. The wooden box was used to store all the rice and provisions inside. The top surface was enough for my mother to lie down and straighten up for a nap in the afternoon after lunch.

The mother would light a small kerosene lamp with an open flame on the porch and a six-inch-tall kerosene lamp she had purchased from an egg vendor in the kitchen box. Kusruthi entered the kitchen just as his mother left for something outside.

You will find something to eat inside the box: sugar, jaggery, or ungrated coconut halves. I lifted the lid of the box. I did not notice the kerosene lamp on it, and as I lifted the lid, it got tilted and fell to the backside coconut leaf wall of the house. It was sudden; the fire broke out! Frightened by the fire, I closed the box, called "Amme," and ran out. The fire spread very fast. The people standing in front of Madhavan Nair's shop on the opposite side of the canal could see the smoke and fire reaching the top of the house. They all jumped into the water and swam across to the front of the hut, nearshore. Kusruthi's mother would call out, "Oh, my God." Those on the other side all reached, and the fire was extinguished by pouring water with their effort. Part of the house, which had been subjected to the fire, was razed to the ground and brought burned - light at dusk hours, northerly winds, and air circulation in the house. Smoke and burning smell spread all over the place and in the neighbourhood.

Before returning, the rescue men investigated what happened and why the fire happened. There was nothing wrong in their findings, but they gave Kusruthi another more prominent name – 'Maha-Chattambi.' He has been Chattambi for a long time. In addition to the chicken drowning, anyone passing by, irritating me, smashing me alone, and calling the seven-year-old - "Eda, Ottaprakkadi," inviting reaction from me, I was sure to have a bite on their hand or wherever I could catch hold of their limbs. Thus, I was Chattambi and 'Katiyan' (who bites), and I am Mahachattambi now! What to say - some breeds are like that!

It cannot be said whether the box where the rice and other items were kept remained in the kitchen. My mother said something to Achayan before he went to the library. However, he left without any reply.

We used to play kabaddi and ball games on the ground near Valayamchira in the evenings. After the game, I did not see my mother at the usual place when I came home. Usually, my mother would cook rice and curry by lighting a fire in the kitchen, hearth, or firepit. The fire was not burning, nor was the smoke from a damp oven due to wet logs, palm leaves, or husks. I saw my mother sitting in the fireplace again after a while. Just sitting there, there was no fire, no smoke!

"What, mother?". I must have asked. That was enough! Those eyes were full of tears. The eyes must have filled with water without smoke from the firepit!

When Achayan returned from the library, he had a paper cone and a newspaper instead of a book or a magazine. I heard Achayan saying this after handing over the pack to my mother-

"Aikkarachira Gopalan was kind, and he gave this. Don't go hungry anyway!" My mother unpacked the cone -It was rice! She looked up, smiled, and went to the kitchen. After that, we saw the smoke spreading from the kitchen.

Although it was a little late, I did not hear Achayan say anything during dinner that day. I do not remember. When I got up, he was staring at me and sobbing. I know today what he might have said on that day!

Aikkarachira Gopalan was later identified as a farmworker, a communist, the elder brother of Chellappan, who ran a tea shop, and Gopi, a communist martyr in my village. I often remember Achayan saying sometime later that the rice wrapped in the newspaper he brought was the goodness of Aikkarachira Gopalan.

Once, during a long walk through the village's alleys in the first week of the New Century, I met Palathittachira Kuttappan, my peer. While talking to him, he introduced one young man to me, saying, "This is late comrade Gopalan's son - working in the police."

I had money in my purse; I thought, what if I take a few notes and compliment the police officer? No, don't pay; some loans are never repaid. When alone, I often think about where I came from and let out relief or sob. How much food for how many people do we need to buy to pay off that debt? Can a thousand rupees be sufficient for an invaluable cone of rice?

Holding the hands of Gopalan's son and wishing him all the best, he must have been wondering why I had tears in my eyes. I said, "Oh, you are Gopalan's son. May good things happen to you?" I walked away, wiping my tears. He will never know how much we are indebted to his father. My chest would have swelled if I had stood there for more moments. No one will ever forget the one who removes your hunger!

"The seed of the righteous will not beg bread." That is what Achayan often used to say. He who is hungry knows the hunger of others.

Psalms 37:25: "I have been young, and [now] am old; yet have I not seen the righteous forsaken; nor his seed begging bread."

I particularly remember Dominic, the most lovable of my friends, when I was in standard four or five in primary school. His house was right next to the school. After having lunch wrapped in banana leaves, I sometimes accompanied Dominic to his home. He had only his mother there. She had been selling ground nuts for a living. Dominic wanted to study, grow up, and earn a good job. That desire was seen as one of Dominic's best qualities, and for me, it was a great thing to associate with him. Dear Dominic, where are you today? Behind the curtain of time? Everyone is hiding somewhere. How much do I desire to meet you?

I was the eldest boy of the youngest generation in the family of Kannattumadom. I had a good friend in Dominic when I went to school. When I returned home, I was waiting to go to school the next day to meet Dominic. When another boy was born into the ancestor family, I, his elder brother, named him Dominic. Everyone called him the name for some time. Later, I realised that I was the only brother who continued to call the baby Dominic. That was until I grew up, completed my studies, and moved to the ancient city of another state in search of work. It was all forgotten. Perhaps the boy himself did not like to be called Dominic. As I grew older, the name Dominic faded from my memory. According to my wish, no one, including his parents or siblings, was eager to remember that name and call him the name.

There were only classes to study in the government primary school until the fifth standard. When I passed out from the fifth standard, I was enrolled in a middle school affiliated with our church. Vasupilla Sir retired. That was realised when I went to the government primary school with my father to get the transfer certificate. Kaimal Sir of Thamarakath issued me the transfer certificate. He caressed my head and shoulders so much, saying I should continue studying hard.

On the eve of the Passover (Pessaha), everyone gathered at Kannattumadom. Everyone was busy. To help the elderly ladies, Kunjamma and I, the Kusruthi from Valayamchira, organised coconuts and machetes and placed three or four coconuts near the stone on the front (east) side of the yard. First, the husk must be removed. I took a coconut and held it with my left hand so it did not roll. I cut the husk with a machete, which was a heavy cut! I saw blood on the husk and the machete. There was no pain at all. When Kunjamma looked, the index finger of my left hand was cut into two pieces, and one piece was hanging on the skin. Kunjamma and I cried in tandem. Someone came running. My grandfather quickly peeled the powder from the tender coconut leaf and wrapped it around my finger with a cloth. Since the cut was on my left finger, I could eat the special meals on the festival days. When writing this, the incision is still visible as the diagonal of a rectangle extending from the nail to the knee of my left index finger.

After joining the Sixth Standard, I met Sebastian (Thambichan), a friend who came to school to attend the same class, and we walked back through the village lanes together. Thambichan is the son of Thommachi, who is part of Achayan's ploughing group. Thambichan was an excellent, loving friend like Dominic.

It's incredible to know what life's experiences and friendships lead us for later life! I shall write more about it chronologically as it unfolds.

On his way to school one day, Thambichan saw his friend fishing in the narrow irrigational canal – a narrow water passage of the 'ninety-six – para' paddy field with a fishing net. He went to Valayamchira's house, kept the books there, removed his shirt, and joined me for fishing. When the pot was full of fish, we took it and handed it over to my mother, went down to the stream, washed our bodies in the ravine, and went to the sixth standard class. This association was the beginning of permanent lifelong cooperation and cohabitation.

No one has ever consoled by saying that naughty young people later become good, respectable, and responsible citizens when they grow up!

I joined and cooperated with my father's non-agricultural activities during the harvest season. I waited for Achayan's return after a trip to Kollam. I spent more time at local games, the library, and school and forgot about breastfeeding. My mother never bought Chenninayakam. The locals kept calling me the Kusruthi, or the Chattambi, and the Ottaprakkadi, till the birth of a sibling for me. As a boy, whenever I got an opportunity, I chased the people who called me names and bit them, not looking at precisely what I got to hold on to or what the person's body part was – arm, wrist, or finger! Time has passed on.

My Grandfather Kuruvila Thomma and Grandmother Kathreena (1970)

Pennamma Ammayi

5. THE STORIES FROM GRANDPA

When the fields were flooded, and all the farmlands were underwater, it was time to wait for the next crop. The Kannattumadom house looked like an island in the middle of the water. Perappan was preparing to live in a small reclaimed land by filling the pond on the north side of the Kannattumadom property. He was a tenant of a wealthy property owner at Thuruthichira. It was his second return to his parent's family with his own.

In 1957, under the leadership of EMS, the Communists formed the first ministry in Kerala state. Five cents of land were the property size Perappan received as his entitlement as a tenant under the Land Reform Bill passed by the first Communist government. The property owners had to divide most of the land accumulated over the years into the hands of farm labourers and tenants. Ouseppachan and his family came to live in their original ancestral home, thinking that living with their parents would be a relief rather than being away without any proper job. On the eastern side of the Pookaitha River, there were more opportunities to work in the paddy fields and on the land.

When the pond on the north side at Kannattumadom was filled up with mud and an extension of the land was made, Grandfather decided to fill in the pakkalli- swampy and uncultivable land - on the south side of the island also over time. He saw that the filled area was good land and level. He had raised four or five spots with mud from the agricultural field where coconut trees were planted. One day, when I was in Kannattumadom to give the betel leaves and areca nut that my father had sent, Grandpa was planting the coconut trees.

"Eda -Mone, come and get this sapling and plant it here."

Holding my hand, the coconut sapling planted by my grandfather grew bigger and bigger. Whenever I went to Kannattumadom, I would go under the coconut tree. My mind was full of memories of the flowering of the coconut tree and taking its first fruit to our holy cross parish church.

A large ditch was on the west side of the backyard at Kannattumadom. There was a stream and a pond at the southern end of the ditch to collect potable water. It was a significant relief for Chittamma when she could collect drinkable water from the pond during the summer season.

When the paddy fields were flooded and remained for a month or two, Grandfather blocked the creek and isolated the ditch to farm fish there. He provided shade by placing large coconut leaves and planting them upright in the water. When the water in the area dried up, they would tie up the overflowing ditch, pull out the shades for fishing, cast their nets, and catch large prawns, Karimeen – (Pearl Spot - the green chromide), Varaal (Snake Head), and Kaari –(Catfish). The eldest grandson, myself, was always called to pick up the fish that fell from the net and put them in the fish pots and bags.

Grandfather had a great affection for my father ('Vavachan'). Grandpa sent him to a school in Champakulam to read up to the fifth grade and encouraged him to row a small canoe while going to school. My Grandpa went fishing in a large canoe at Karumbavalavu and Pandarakkalam Lake in the north. Ouseppachan (Perappan), or Vavachan -was always there with my Grandpa. The boat used could carry four or five people. Grandpa used to sit and row in the stern seat and Achayan in the bow seat. After two hours of rowing, they would reach the riverbank, where they could cast their net. Only giant prawns, Karimeen, Manjakkoori (Yellow Catfish), and Attu Walah, could be found in the lake. If they threw the net in the Karumbavalavu, they would get Attu Walah and Kanampu. They would be going very early in the morning. They would return at nine or ten o'clock before noon. They would sell the fish to needy people and return home with the rest.

He often told me, his grandson, these stories when fishing in the nearby Pookkaitha River. He narrated the heroic stories of when he went fishing in the lake. The Grandpa was with his grandson whenever he went to cast the net into the river. Grandson used to pick up the fish, put it in the fish pot, carry the pool, and walk with him.

"Your father was frightened sometimes. On the way to the lake while rowing in the boat, or when the canoe was stopped, or when I got up and began to cast the net - whenever it may be – if he happened to see the common water hyacinth or Kaitha (thorny green palm) floating in the water, in the dim light - it was enough for him to start crying and be afraid of."

"But he never hesitated to row the canoe and do the work as long as he wanted. You must see that and learn from him." "You see! He is still rowing in a canoe - you must grow up to support and shade him".

"Once upon a time, when he was a kid, I thought everything was finished!" Grandpa stood straight and took a deep sigh of relief without lifting the net from the ground!

"When we laid the foundation stone for the house at Kannattumadom, the middle room was set aside for the barn. The paddy barn, which holds one thousand para measures of paddy, was made of wood. It was placed in the middle of the house when you view it from the verandah. Haven't you seen a small carved door that is not too high? We wanted to move the barn to the middle and lay the stones below, which the barn needed to lift and move.

Your father was four or five years of age then. No one saw him running around and crawling like this. I realised the danger when I heard the baby's cries from under the wooden barn. Oh, my God!

"Come on, lift… lift, the baby is under the barn." That was when we all stopped breathing, "Lift, lift". Someone came and pulled the baby out from the bottom of the barn!"

The grandfather sighed a long sigh of relief, took the net, and put it on his shoulder.

"Ever since then, everyone has called your father 'Pathayam Thangi' (Barn Lifter!)

You are the son of that 'Pathayam Thangi'! Grandpa stooped and smiled at me, wiping tears from his eyes.

"Then there was the accident when the stage was built at Valiyaparambil to stage a play for the fund-raising for the library. Planting poles, tying bamboo poles, and grazing on top, there was a seating capacity for five hundred people to watch the play and another raised stage for performance. While making the big tent, your father climbed onto the roof to tie the bamboo pole. He slipped "Ayyo" (Oh! my God), see he was down on the floor! Somebody picked him up, put him in a canoe, rowed it, and took him to the Vaidyan (doctor) Varghese at Muttar. There were no fractures or bruises. He fell on his chest—he had difficulty in breathing. The physician gave him all the tinctures and medicines for three months. There was one additional medicine for burning on his chest. It was necessary to apply that once. That mark can still be seen on your father's chest. The smell on his vest was not of sweat alone. There was the odour and colour of the medicine the Vaidyan gave that day. You will still see the virtue of the 'Ashtanga Hrudayam."

After the fifth class, Grandpa sent him to an Ayurvedic physician (Vaidyan) to study 'Ashtanga-Hrudayam.' Gurukul's type of education was provided at Vaidyan's house. The first lessons of Ayurveda are summarised in 'Ashtanga-Hrudayam'- a work that reflects the purpose and quality of life. To study the four ways of life- the Purusharthams are the inherent values of the Universe: Artha (economic values), Kama (pleasure), Dharma (righteousness), and Moksha (liberation). The Purusharthams are the blueprint for human fulfillment - the obedience required to attain the goal- the four ways of life prescribed by the ancient Indians to improve human life. Achayan learned all this for about a year and stayed at Vaidyan's house. When the nostalgic thought of being away from his father and mother increased, he returned home. The grandfather had gone to the Vaidyan's place to meet his son.

I used to go to Kannattumadom and spend some time there with Grandpa and Grandma at least once a month and once a week during the school holidays. My Grandpa would sit next to me and tell me stories. He would take me to work and teach me farming lessons. He would slowly tell stories by laughing without taking his eyes off the net while fishing.

"Our Annakutty teacher told us about the flood of Noah's time. What is this flood of the year ninety-nine Appa? Which is this year, ninety-nine? Tell me about that, Appa..."

In July 1924, the catastrophic floods of Kerala took place - commonly called the "Great Flood of 99", which our ancestors termed the most frightening memory. It was the worst flood in our part of the country in the twentieth century. The largest one in history. The torrential rains and floods that lasted for three weeks wholly submerged the lower parts of Kerala. Most of the districts in central Travancore were submerged for days. Three-fourths of Ernakulam district was submerged. Floods engulfed Travancore with seawater from the west and mountain water from the east.

I heard Grandpa discussing his days on a 'Kettuvallam' for the "Great Flood of 99". "It was still raining. And by removing water from the boat. The stern was tied, and the wind kept the ship afloat. At the bottom of the boat-house, we laid the wooden planks on the boat and sat there, talking, weeping, praying, sleeping, and waking up, until the water receded" -

The highlands were all filled with refugees. People fled in droves from the lowlands, and thousands of refugees arrived in the hills in two days. Thousands fled for their lives. Many huts made of firewood, palm fronds, and mud were washed away, and traffic was disrupted. The trains stopped running. The postal system stopped. The bridges were flooded. The landslide caused massive destruction and uprooted trees. The carcasses of men and the corpses of cattle and wild animals flowed everywhere.

Rains, floods, and famine plagued the people. Central Kerala was the worst hit by the floods.

Unable to withstand the mud and water that flowed in the floodwaters, the bunds collapsed and destroyed all roads. A little bit of road traffic that was there earlier came to a complete standstill. The railway station and railroads were lost forever. The flood disrupted postal systems.

The landslide near Munnar turned an acre of land into a vast lake. The dam burst on the sixth day of the monsoon. The floods ended with the simultaneous clearing of 200 acres of land in Pallivasal. The very appearance of Pallivasal has changed. At Pallivasal, generators generating electricity were submerged in water, services were stopped, and people and pets sought shelter on the roofs of houses and buildings. The highlands were filled with refugees. The people were starving because they did not have enough food and water. Many buildings collapsed. Some villages were wiped out. Towns and villages have permanently been disfigured by mud.

The floods, which claimed thousands of lives, caused the extinction of many species of birds and crops. Many lost their homes, property, and pets. Rivers and streams overflowed, roads were blocked, wells and ponds were filled with mud, and giant trees were uprooted.

The highest rainfall was recorded in the catchment areas. Mullapperiyar was the only dam in Periyar at that time. The floods in Central Kerala were so severe that the Periyar, which has many tributaries, was also flooded.

"It was the greatest flood in Kuttanad since Noah's day. What troubles did our God save us from?"

Grandpa said this, keenly overseeing his grandson and listening to him.

"Where was I then, Appa?"

"Your father was not yet married before that day, boy!"

Before the floods of the nineties, only the eldest daughter (Mammikunju Ammayi) was married off and sent to Mithrakari. Grandpa told me that sometimes. At that time, Achayan was studying in school. He was ten or eleven years old. That means Achayan must have been 30-31 years old when I was born.

My grandchildren will also tell their grandchildren the story of today's COVID-19, the country's state at the time of the story, and the family's life.

Grandpa was a farm manager of one of the branches of the New Kavalakkal family- Ezharayil- and worked for a long time after all his children were settled down. First, for the elder brother, then for the younger one, Kunjomma, and later for Kochukutty, he was the steward who looked after their crops for two generations. A steward looking after all the paddy fields in various areas occasionally applies fertilisers and employs labourers. Grandpa worked as a farm manager for all the elders in the Kavalackal family and their grandchildren in its branches for a long time. It was my grandfather who sweated the most for their prosperity. The love and respect they gave in return for my Grandpa always displayed sincerity and great self-respect in his deeds, which was a testament to that. Grandpa's humble and unwavering moral stand prevailed in the face of the selfishness and arrogance of the capitalists of the day. My grandfather earned all the love and respect of the farmworkers who worked in their fields.

Grandpa stayed home and did miscellaneous work when their farm work was not there. He would water the backyard, dig the bed for coconut trees and banana plants, weave a net out of cotton threads, and cast his nets into rivers and ravines to catch fish.

Kaithatra Kunchariya and his children were known for hard farming, coconut drying, and net fishing in our neighbourhood. I remember Kuriachan going to Kakkazham to study civil engineering with Philip, alias Peelichan. Philip's brother Ouseppachan was very good at fishing with nets. When caught in a net trap, fish like Eel would be bitten and cut with his teeth. Mathen was the "prodigal son" who went to school, wandered somewhere else, and returned as a young man a few years later. Anthonichan was my peer. He was mainly interested in drying coconuts to make copra. I watched him remove the coconut husk, cutting and pouring the water into a bowl to drink or drain it. Occasionally, we found the coconut apple inside and ate it with pleasure. If you cut coconuts, stack them, and look at the copra field, you never know how the time will pass. I went to buy the coconut husk or shells to light a fire in the kitchen for my mother. Blowing the spark when smoke spreads through the eyes without burning firewood was a rare remedy.

Mid-summer vacations in primary and middle school were when cattle grazed and roamed in the fields after the harvest. During the day, when there was nothing else to do, Kaithatra Anthonichan or someone else would come to call me. We carried a small basket of palm fronds on our heads and went out into the field to fill the basket with cattle dung.

We used to search the field and pick up the dung until we could bear the load. The dung was dried, powdered, and sold as manure for plants. The ashes and waste were bought at retail and sold in bulk, and those who traded on the boat collected manure for the plants to help the farmers. With the help of a cow my mother had raised at home for an anna (1/16 of a rupee), she would sometimes earn three or four annas. About half or more of the cattle dung would be collected in the basket on some days. When it was time to go to the library, come back and bathe in the ravine. That's how vacations were sometimes spent. After attending high school for higher studies, I never went for such a field job. No family member had ever gone for fieldwork or a manure gathering!

Kochuppappan and Chittamma lived in Punnapra after their marriage. I remember going there with my father on vacation and seeing a vibrantly coloured bract of bougainvillea, full of flowers in front of the house, spread out on poles and terraces. It is beautiful to see the flowers surrounded by three or six bracts with the bright colours associated with the plant, including pink, magenta, purple, red, orange, white, or yellow.

Perumaparambil Kuruppachan had cultivated ten paras of paddy sowing and farming land toward the front of Kannattumadom. One day, Kuruppachan said to my Grandpa -

"If you are interested, the paddy land may be yours, 'Thomma Mappilay."

Grandpa replied that it was a good thing.

"If Anthonichan takes interest, it could happen. We can get it?" It was a word of encouragement from his father that Anthonichan was happy to have it, and he bought it. And then requested his father-

"Just write it in Achayan's name."

"Let's measure it, and we can write the documents accurately since it is a property transaction." Kochuppappan took me along to measure the boundaries of the paddy land before writing the document.

Kochuppappan came from Punnapra and chose me to assist him in surveying the property. The area was calculated by walking, measuring, and drawing the plan with a hundred-foot-long measuring tape. The confidence and the encouragement that Kochuppappan had instilled in me were immense.

(A typical measure prevalent in the area: 10 Para=approx.160 cents=1.6 acre, the 1-acre area is 43560 sq. ft.)

Anthonichan had no time to cultivate, fertilise, clear the weeds, or harvest.

He used to say, "Achayan should do everything yourself, " and paid the required amount in his hands. Appan (Grandpa) did farm work, especially when he did not need to go for the supervisory job at Kavalackal.

In traditional agricultural farming, farmers had to irrigate their paddy fields by treading a large wooden water wheel over a small stream that could be directed to the area. One day, when Appan was walking on a water wheel by his footsteps, I wanted to see the water flow and the wheel's rotation. Grandpa said after seeing me there -

"Then, you stay here. I'll go home and have some coffee and come back soon."

"Appa, let me ride the wheel." Grandpa's silent consent to the question encouraged me. I had gained some confidence from him.

I climbed the scaffolding for the water wheel, sat on the bamboo strips, pedalled, and turned the wheels with my legs.

Water gushing out made me happy. There was great excitement as more and more water kept flowing out. Grandpa came back too quickly!

The farm labourers collect the sheaves and pile them up high in the yard during harvesting. On the day of the harvest, they ran all over the field and gathered the paddy ears. They were harvesting paddy from our land! The woman who harvested and cut the ears gave me some, and I collected all the ears and kept them in my memory as some achievement. Grandpa showed me practical farming lessons while walking on the ridge and supervising the harvesting.

The Theyyamma Chittamma would boil and dry the paddy in the sun. One or two sacks of rice would be delivered to Kochuppappan's house in Punnapra. Grandpa would call me to accompany him while going there. On the way back with Grandpa, my feet burned in the hot sand in the open space near the school at Punnapra. I quickly ran across and crawled among the bushes, saw the green lawn, stepped on it, and cooled my feet. When Grandpa slowly walked in, my whole body was itchy and fat with red streaks on the skin with poison ivy (Toxicodendron family of plants). Grandpa uprooted some 'Thumba' plants (common Leucas zeylanica: native herb) from the ground. He gave me to rub on my body. He took some and showed me how to use it until we returned home when all the rashes would have gone.

6. READING, TAHKLI AND QUIZ COMPETITION

Achayan used to go to the library in Valiyaparambil every evening. The library should be opened, and books should be distributed. Some days, he would take his son, too. The children's club had started in the library. All the friends studying in the school celebrated Independence Day on August 15 by planting a bamboo pole in front of the library and hoisting the national flag. On invitation, Damodaran Pillai sir hoisted the flag. Keshava Pillai of Chandiram, the principal, had gone to hoist the flag at the North Primary School. That was why Damodaran Pillai sir was invited.

As secretary of the library, Achayan was responsible for distributing books. Most of the time, Achayan's son would write the name of the distributed book, the member reading's name, and other details in an issue register. He would also take the books, write them in his name, and take them home to read. That was the beginning of extracurricular reading.

The first book I read was 'Nirapara' (symbol of prosperity), a book of poems by P. Kunhiraman. The book was the number one book in the library's stock register. Why was such a small book added as number one in the library? I still remember Achayan's answer to that question.

"This library should be filled with books. The book 'Nirapara' was added as the first number to the register. It's like saying that the list of groceries for a feast (sadya) should start with turmeric powder while writing the names of the condiments."

The Chattambi also wrote the name of another book, the detective story- 'Hands that Held the Dagger' by Tatapuram Sukumaran. He thought that historians might point out later that this was the first book read by an investigation expert!

Kainikkara Padmanabha Pillai's play 'Calvariyile Kalpa Padapam' is one of the first books I read. That was the play for the theatre that Achayan, Kochuppappan, Valezhath Mani, and other local youth rehearsed and prepared at Valayamchira yard, performed, and presented to raise funds for the library.

It is unknown if anyone had owned a radio at that time. Everyone heard about it and wanted to buy one for the library. A handful of people listen to the radio, read newspapers, and read a few books. The library was initially housed in a one-room hut.

C. Y. M. A. was the name for the library initially. They raised funds by performing theatre. The foundation was made of stone, cement, and sand mortar, used for walls and plastering, and the hut was turned into a two-room building. A youth club and children's club were started. The youth held a boat race, and the children celebrated Independence Day and Onam.

It was the day P.N. Panicker Sir came to inspect the library. He was satisfied with the list of members, book distribution registers, magazines, and reading facilities. Panicker sir was told about the children's club, and he liked a separate section in the library for children's literature, with a board with the name 'Children's Library' displayed.

"This is my son, and he's the secretary of the Children's Club here."

Panicker Sir was told. He called me nearby.

"In which class are you studying?" I answered.

"What's your son's name?" he asked Achayan. When I said my name, he laughingly interrogated me, saying it was the library secretary's name. Before he could complete the laugh -

I remember being asked, "Okay, Can you give a short speech? Let me hear it. "I did say a few words, including some I heard during the Independence Day celebrations.

Experience and courage brought out two or three sentences relating to what I heard on Independence Day.

He must have loved it. Achayan said something to Panicker, sir, and after hearing that, his voice was choked with emotion.

Panicker sir responded by saying - 'Bless you."

That was the norm regarding Achayan expressing happiness or sorrow with emotion. A condition in which words block the throat. He showed it on his face and voice.

The first lesson, the first blessing, and the courage to live a life by teaching as much as possible to a small audience- learning and teaching- must have sprouted from there. I learned that elocution is the art of public speaking that gives us self-boost and confidence to speak in front of a large audience.

Panicker Sir and Achayan have travelled extensively together to grow the library movement in Kuttanad. The library receives a lump sum grant every year. The secretary's son and others could choose the books he liked.

The newspapers in the reading room, the radio, and the books in the library all created a great revolution in the village. People expanded their knowledge and transformed their lives. They learned their duties and rights and became more responsive and responsible citizens. The ideas of democracy and communism became widespread.

Thekkekalathil Kunjachan was a relative, contemporary, and good friend of Achayan. He had good observation skills and an interest in political affairs. He was always waiting for the newspaper to arrive at the library in the morning. After lunch and a nap at his residence across the ravine, he would return to the library and wait for the radio to wake up for a news programme broadcasted from the Thiruvananthapuram radio station. Valiyathara Appachan and

Kannattumadom Kuriakose would come to listen to the radio news and movie songs from 6 p.m. onwards.

Once, a unique programme was broadcast from Kozhikode radio station, especially for the islanders (i.e., for the people of Lakshadweep islands, a Unior Territory, and the spoken language there is Malayalam). Appachan and Kuriakose were very interested in knowing what the event was about.

Unfortunately, the broadcast from Kozhikode was the same as the news program from Thiruvananthapuram. Kunjachan insisted on the news broadcast and turned down the offer to listen to the schedule for the islanders.

The problem was severe—a slight political turnaround as well. No one was willing to give up. The secretary of the library intervened and negotiated a truce. Kunjachan's interest in the news is justified. The information includes political analysis that creates good awareness and knowledge; therefore, the news should be listened to regularly. Appachan and Kuriakose argued that the program was mainly for the islanders and was also designed and explicitly broadcasted for them - "We need to hear it - because we are the islanders. We, the islanders, permanently live in the middle of a flooded paddy field, and our residence plot is surrounded by water; therefore, we are islanders!"

No one paid attention to the islanders' news and programme amidst the sounds of laughter!

An unoccupied property was in the paddy field of BBM UP School. It was full of mango trees, and every tree was full of mangoes, some ripe and entirely red. My friends, Krishnankutty, Vithupurakkal Gopi, and Thambichan, used to throw stones and get at least three or four mangoes daily.

I particularly remember working with bamboo to protect the coconut saplings during 'Labour Week' at school. Spinning cotton was a craft in the school during craft class. The teacher gave us training on the use of a Tahkli spindle. Some even thought spinning cotton on a Tahkli was more efficient than spinning cotton on a spinning wheel. We learned to spin with a Tahkli and cotton in the craft class at the Upper Primary School. We made a few bath towels using the threads spun by us. In those days, the craft class taught it to spin yarns using cotton on Tahkli and spin in charkha.

I won prizes and certificates for the long jump, three-legged race, and bread-biting competitions at the annual games. Krishnankutty was my partner for the race, which was on three legs. We were of a similar height. We moved our legs simultaneously and practiced a synchronous movement after tying my left leg with my right one, Krishnankutty.

I always wanted to be sitting on the front bench in every class. Leaning on the desk and looking straight ahead was an outstanding achievement that no one in front was obstructing my view forward. When studying in the sixth standard, I was on the front bench. Purushothaman was my friend from the Paruthikalam house, and we used to call him Purushan. He was sitting on the bench just behind me. Purushan gave me an unforgettable memory of my school life. That's what everyone sang for a long time. The song was -

"Kettie Thomas, Aare (whom) Kettie (hit) ?, Purushane Kettie, Enna (what) Kettie?

Tahkli Kettie, enthinu kettie (Why), chumma kettie (carelessly), eppol (when) kettie, classil (in class) kettie; Evide (Where) kettie, muttel (On the knee) kettie, Ennittooriyedukkaan pattiyathumilla ! (Then he was stuck; he could not remove it.)"

I was leaning on the back desk and attending the class. When the class teacher turned to the blackboard to write something, someone in the back slowly pulled back the desk. With careful attention to the teacher, I did not precisely know how much I was reclining. Suddenly,

I got a hit on my back as someone sitting behind me moved the desk forward and pushed. It hurts on the back. Sometimes, I looked back and smiled at those who pretended it was "not me" who drove and broke my back. There was no such thing as a big joke; when there was pain, a fierce look on the backbenchers, and gnashing of teeth, that was the norm. But today, it has been repeated three or four times. Nobody repeats good jokes. Tahkli, the spinning tool, was in the middle of my notebooks. I grabbed it, turned, and gave a sting somewhere under the desk. I did not know where it had caused a wound to someone. The sting was on Purushan's knee! Suddenly realising that it must have wounded him, I tried to retrieve it, but it was not coming out. It was hurting him more. The hook at the tip of the Tahkli penetrated his skin, ruptured the skin, and the blood was slowly oozing out. Altogether, I panicked!

Frightened, I ran out of the classroom, called the teachers, and cried. Purushan also cried when the craft teacher who used to teach spinning cotton to Tahkli came with a piece of cotton and pulled Tahkli off his knees. He gave him a nice, clean gauze bandage.

I do not remember having received any punishment for my misbehaviour. However, the song has become popular among the students since then, and they used to tease me sometimes. Name and fame as 'Kusruthi' have been associated for over three years, even in Upper Primary school.

"Eda Tahkli, Edo Tahkli," Purushan called me once when I met him on the way after several years, which saw him as a transport bus conductor and head of a family, now retired and taking rest at home.

"Are you still up to your old tricks?"

We hugged and were speechless for some time before sharing our welfare and goodwill.

In the seventh class, I continued to sit on the front bench. 'Pulling back the desk and quickly pushing it forward' was a pastime and entertainment for many of my friends. This time, when my back got hurt, I got up and gave a slap on the cheek of the boy sitting at my back. I did not look to see who that boy was. After a second, I found my close friend was holding his face and looking stunned. It was Thambichan! Everyone in the class saw it. I was sorry but did not do anything to console him. No one said anything. Thambichan did not say anything and did not respond. There was no quarrel when we walked home from school together in the evening; he asked nothing, and I replied nothing. If you understand the mistakes and the misdeeds, then whom to apologise to or what to apologise for? In friendship, everyone ought to understand the other's feelings and perspectives.

In almost every academic studies class, Vithupurakkal Gopi and I were at the top among the boys, and Ammini Amma and Leelamma were among the girls. Most of us got the highest marks in most subjects. For mathematics, it was always me taking the top positions. While studying in the seventh standard, Kattampally Mathew Sir congratulated me for getting 100 marks for the Onam and the Christmas examinations. It was general information all over the school. DB Kurup Sir taught us General Science and Social Studies. Annakutty Arakkaparambil was the teacher who taught us Malayalam in all the classes. Kurup Sir and Annakutty Teacher were taking lessons with great interest, which helped us remember things we learned.

Teacher Annakutty, after teaching some lessons in the eighth standard Malayalam class, used to organise a quiz competition among the students in the course itself. The match was between the boys and the girls, who had approximately equal strength in numbers. The children asked questions alternately, and the teacher was the quiz master who would judge the correctness of the questions and give marks for the team delivering the correct answers—no marks for mistakes or answers not given. I remember preparing for the quiz competition after learning about pigeons. Among the boys, Gopi and I used to ask more questions. The girls who answered more questions were Amminiamma and Leelamma. Before the end of a tense contest, it was my chance to ask a question, and it was Leelamma's turn to answer.

The Kusruthi shot an arrow of flowers! The teacher and the boys laughed aloud when they heard the question. It was all noisy and had mysterious smiles!

The question was, "Describe a dove's mating habits/courtship rituals." That was the last lesson taught in the Malayalam class. Doves are kept as pets in some churches. Female doves have a distinct "rosy" colour about their neck and cheeks, giving them an overall feminine appearance. I had no intention of comparing that girl with doves, but surely, I thought it was a strategic question that would win the quiz contest for the boys.

Leelamma knew the answer well but was so shy that she was reluctant to stand up and answer. Even after a lot of persuading by her friends, she stood up amidst the din of the boys. She was stunned and embarrassed by the boys' commotion. Meanwhile, the boys even demanded - "We would like to see the romantic antics acted out by your performance!"

Leelamma sat down without answering. She was on the verge of crying. The boys had won the quiz competition. They made me a hero. Despite her knowing the answer, she made the boys win. Her friends pushed her to be my hero. They spread a rumour telling me that Leelamma and I were in love. Thambichan was the one who kept on associating my name with that girl often while nit-picking over tiny matters or when annoyed with me!

No matter how much love or mutual respect and consideration were there between us, even in class, we refrained from looking at each other or talking or smiling out of fear. Shortly after changing our schools - me to Champakulam and Leelamma to Karumady for high school education, we had not met for many years. The fear of not knowing how to fall in love stayed in my mind. I do not know about that girl. When I found courage, life changed its course and moved far forward.

After the regular classes, catechism classes were expected in the school. One hour of worship with twenty-four hymns was recited every Thursday after school in the church. I read the entire prayer during the worship hour. "You just have to read it" - that was the suggestion from Annakutty's teacher. Adoration was performed at the end of the hour-long prayers.

After the reading, I was to assist the priest and be along with the priest at the altar -as the altar server. Annakutty teacher persuaded me to perform on the altar, too.

After seeing my zeal in worship and prayers, Fr George of the Holi Cross church once requested my father - "Let him go to become a priest. " Without beating around the bush, Achayan told the father - "Acha, I have only this school-going child, and the whole future of my life depends on how fast he can fly away. The younger one is too small to attend school yet. !"

Achen did not insist further.

It was customary to elect a secretary to the literary association of the school. A new student was needed to take responsibility every year. While studying in the eighth standard, Keeppada Joy and Gopi took the initiative to nominate me for the post. Kattampally, Mathew Sir, and Kurup Sir gave permission. Annakutty's teacher said, "If you are contesting, you should read the annual report on the school's anniversary."

I gave the nomination papers and contested the election. I went around to various classes, asking for votes. Amminiamma, from the girl's side, was the opposing candidate. The support of the students was mainly for that girl. Then Rosamma of Arakkaparambil, Unda Shantha, Leelamma, and her sister Kunjamma declared their support for me. Since Kunjamma did not complete her studies last year, she had to stay in the same class that year. Everyone must have voted for me; I was the favourite for at least a few girls. Perhaps that was why I won the contest by a slim margin.

Gopi participated in the kathaprasamgam programme, which is storytelling through poems, held after the annual general meeting.

I was more interested in telling the story of "Manishada." Annakutty's teacher decided who should say to the story. Gopi organised a finger-tapping percussion instrument known as Khartal ('chaplankatta'), played the song well, and told the story. After hearing the story presented by both of us, the teacher said, "Let Gopi tell the story. You just read the annual report." Gopi also wore a long, knee-length collarless kurta for the 'kathaprasamgam' programme.

Friends came to know that I had become proficient in the kabaddi game. The captain would call my name first and add me to his team. The technique of bending down due to my short physique and catching hold of the opponent's leg to force him out of the attack was enough to win the game.

I had mastered that technique and did not bother about my meagre physical strength. As a result, I also gained some adversaries. The day was selected when all the opposing arguments and quarrels were settled amicably or otherwise. It was the day when the school closed for the mid-summer vacation. Everyone leaves school on that day. It was difficult to escape from their eyes. How many blows Vanchikkal Kurian and Krishnan Kutty gave their opponents was not countable. I, too, got a few from them while defending myself, and I did not tell anyone or seek help from anyone. I was silently bearing it. If it came to my parents' knowledge at home, the punishment would be severe, and hence, I was not even crying. I was ready to celebrate the holidays the next day, and everything was forgotten!

Markos was my guardian in primary school and the UP school J Chacko. They could not score good marks in the class they studied. They were neither excellent at studies nor the games we played in school. Academic years and time elapsed. In the complexity of growing up, they went on their ways.

The period was when electricity never reached any house in our village. If I saw a digging to put a post somewhere and pulling the long wire, I would keep watching it. In the backyard of Muppathinkalam, I saw a teak wood post laid, and aluminum wire was being pulled out. Electric lights were lit in some homes on the way to school. I had no idea when it was going to reach our homes! The radio was purchased in the library when electricity arrived there. If I had urinary incontinence on the way to school, finding a place below a coconut tree or under a bush was common to find relief. One day, I felt like passing the urine to the bottom of a new electric post, into a small pipe where the earth wire was passing down to the earth to hit a bull's-eye, and – 'Hummo' – total blackout in the eyes, I did not miss too many heartbeats! It could have caused some tissue or organ damage! Thank the heavens, and it did not happen for the sake of my children! After high school, I learned that urine is alkaline and allows the current to pass through!

7. SITUATION IN KUTTANADU AND ARRIVAL OF PETER AND PAUL

Familiarity with the political environment of the place at that time is relevant to understanding the subsequent events.

Our region is between the valleys of the Eastern Ghats and the relatively high plains of Alappuzha in the west. Four rivers flow through Pampa, Achankovil, Manimala, and Meenachil. During the monsoon season, the water collected by these rivers flows into Kuttanad and into the Arabian Sea through Lake Vembanad.

Excess water from Upper Kuttanad and Lower Kuttanad flows into the Arabian Sea through the Vembanad Lake in the north. Therefore, floods were periodic events that were uncontrollable. Thottapalli spillway was completed in 1955 to allow the excess water from the Kuttanadan rivers to flow into the sea. After the construction, the authorities realised that the water could not flow as intended through the spillway due to the topography and ecological inadequacies.

A more detailed study was required before the design.

Kuttanad is an area where paddy and coconut are mainly cultivated. Many tributaries of the Pampa River flow through Kuttanad below sea level. The site is an ideal hub for agriculture and allied industries. Houseboats attract tourists. The monsoon season is the best season for backwater fishing.

Tourist places are in and around Kuttanad. Seen from the outside, it is a beautiful, scenic place and rich in rice yield. Many overflowing rivers, houseboats, and boat races add to the scenic beauty. There are plenty of river-fishing resources in Kerala - Giant prawns, Karimeen

(Pearl Spot), Manjakkoori (Yellow Catfish), Attu Walah, and Kanampu; Ducks, coconut toddy add to tasty food.

You can see full-day agricultural labourers working in the fields in one of the rarest areas with no air pollution. It was one of the rare areas where the mountains, rivers and the Arabian Sea's shores are in the same district.

Everything, including the people's lives in Kuttanad, is washed away during the rainy season or when it rains heavily. Ordinary life becomes a flood of misery. Home, land, and agriculture are in the water. There is no dry place to rest.

The general condition of Kuttanad is no different even now. The environment and the situations are not diverse, and development, if any, is limited to travel and communication. In all other areas, the problem continues to be pathetic.

Although surrounded by water, potable water is scarce here. The flowing river water is causing floods in Kuttanad. Farms are usually flooded, and crops are destroyed. The sharp decline in water quality and the environment makes people's lives more miserable.

In other seasons, the uncontrolled growth of weeds in stagnant water creates a shortage of fresh water and inconveniences water transport. Proliferating mosquitoes cause health problems. The lack of adequate transport facilities, including roads and water transport, hinders Kuttanad's development.

The State of Kerala was formed on November 1, 1956. On April 5, 1957, Shri. EMS was Sworn in as the Chief Minister. In 1958, India adopted and implemented the metric system of currency. Since then, one rupee has become 100 paise. Earlier, there were 16 annas for one rupee. With the new system coming into effect, the price of an anna has increased to 6 paise. Plans were afoot to build a road parallel to the artificial AC (Alappuzha-Changanassery) canal. The AC

Road was opened in 1958 to facilitate commercial development and tourism.

The main bridges across the three tributaries of the Pampa River, which flows through Kuttanad, are Pallathuruthy, Nedumudi, and Kidangara. The bridges were later built in the 1980s. The Alappuzha-Changanassery Road was constructed through the paddy fields in the Kuttanad area, where paddy is cultivated below sea level. Almost every year during the monsoon season, whenever floods occur, most of the Alappuzha-Changanassery Road is submerged by floods in Upper Kuttanad. The media have always expressed the hardships and lack of travel facilities for the public in Kuttanad.

The liberation struggle was a political agitation that started in 1958 against the first Communist government in Kerala, headed by EMS. The uproar resulted in the dismissal of the ministry in 1959.

The reasons for starting the liberation struggle were -

Concerns about communist ideology felt by community organizations such as the Christian Church, the Nair Service Society, and the Muslim League;

Doubts in Opposition on the Education Bill introduced by Mundasseri, the Land Reforms Bill introduced by KR Gauri, and the Agriculture Relations Bill;

Allegations of corruption in connection with the steps taken to fill the food deficit in the state

These were the main factors that helped the agitation.

The early liberation struggle, known as the Boat Strike, also occurred at our school. It was a strike by students blocking the boat service and disrupting traffic. The riverboats were stopped by a rope tied across the Pookaitha river at Kanjipadam, demanding that students be charged only one Anna (6 paise) for the journey.

The strike was led by Kavalackal Josekutty, Keeppada Joy, and Attiyil Mohanan. A few classes were cancelled. Gopi and Sebastian were not interested in the adventures, so they did not participate in the struggle. No student from our school was travelling in a boat, which prompted the students to oppose the boat strike. Still, the strike was carried out by declaring solidarity with the students from other schools.

According to family traditions, my mother was taken to her parent's home in Kainakari two months before her first delivery. When the time came, she was taken by boat to a hospital on the beach at Alappuzha. I do not know how many years I came into my parents' life. I think it's about two years after their marriage.

"Is it because of you that I have suffered the most pain…., then you are the same… troubling me again ..." My mother used to say this when she was angry with me or sad.

The pain must have plagued my mother's subconscious for a long time. Perhaps that is why the years of sobriety went on. God blessed the mother with the blessing of having another child again about eight years later. I did not understand anything.

So, when the mother starts to feel sad, I will go closer and ask her what the matter is, and then she will put aside her sadness or anger and put me in her lap and tell a story. Stories were everyone's life and love relationships at various levels; Mother has said it all!

My mother went to study with friends at Kainakari church-owned catholic school. When my mother's elder sister (Peramma) married, my mother cried and could not sleep alone for several days.

One day, while I was running around at Valayamchira alone as kusruthi and Ottaprakkadi, a Valavara boat – a typical Kuttanadan small-sized houseboat with a single-room facility came. My father and grandfather took my mother in that boat to Alappuzha.

Valiyathara Appachan came to row the boat. Then Appachan stopped the Chattambi and said to him –

"It's time for you to finish your mischiefs and solitary wayward ways, and when your mother returns, your Ottaprakkadi position will go away!"

My mother was brought back to Kannattumadom in the same boat four or five days later.

My mother shook my head with her hands, laughed, put her face to my cheeks, and hugged me. My mother's stomach was deflated. My grandpa and grandma, whom I called my Valyammachi or Amma, brought two small kids out of the Valavara boat and put them on the bed beside my mother. The grandfather called his grandson nearby and said to him, pointing to the kids-

"This is Peter, and this is Paul" (Babu, January 14, 1954)

"Both came out into the world prematurely by about a month - before they attained full growth in pregnancy - so I baptized them at the hospital when they were fed the gold and honey and called them names." The grandpa said.

Traditionally, Swarna bhasma, raw gold, is rubbed on a washed stone with a bit of water in very minute quantities. It is then churned with honey before being given to the newborn for licking. It is believed that Swarna bhasma, or raw gold in kids, boosts the disease-fighting capacity, boosts immunity, and prevents frequent recurrent infections, asthma, and other allergic conditions. It also helps improve memory, attention span, concentration, and learning ability, making the kid more intelligent. If taken regularly for six months, the child will have excellent grasping power and improved speech, hearing, and visual acuity.

There were separate cradles for the two babies. Like two small sparrows, they could be kept in your hand regardless of size or health. Yet the two cried, opened their eyes, and clenched their fists simultaneously. Two brothers came together for the Ottaprakkadi.

Is this what Appachan said? If I had siblings, no one would call me a loner!

Peter was a little more agile and active than Paul. Both were given drops of medicine and breast milk. Yet, one morning, Peter did not wake up, drink milk, or cry. I saw my mother crying. Valiyathara Appachan brought a small box of wooden planks, which were short in length and width. It was filled with cloth and flowers, and Peter was put in it, and the box was put in a small canoe and taken away. One of the two kids went back in a hurry!

When everyone returned home to Valayamchira in a canoe two months later, Ottaprakkadi disappeared. No one called me 'Ottaprakkadi' anymore. When my younger brother (baptismal name: Paul) grew up, Achayan called him 'Babu.' Babu's elder brother occasionally accompanied Babu, played with him, and took him for a walk. Once, the elder brother held the baby's legs together like Kuttappan Chetan and slowly lifted him with the head pointing downwards -

"Ammo..." I do not know, I do not know the truth, what happened?

Babu fell from my hands and cried.

"Oh, my baby!" said the mother, who came and took the baby in her hand, rubbed his head, and soothed him. She looked at the elder boy pathetically and warned-

"Runaway, you big- 'Kochayan' do not get a hit from me !" Said mother. I was stunned, and I did not run. When I saw the baby crying, I did cry in unison.

Achayan and his brothers called him 'Chettan' - the son of Achayan's Peramma (mother's elder sister) in Maramkunnil.

Achayan's chettan (elder brother) is Perappan for me. 'Perunnekkaran Chettan' used to come from Perunna and stay at Vavachan's house twice a year. This visit was mainly during the harvest season. He won't go to any other relatives' homes in Kannattumadom. He was in love with Vavachan, or Vavachan was the only man who saw him compassionately as an elderly human being and brother. Parappan always had a little soda powder wrapped in a small piece of paper on his lap, a side flap of his dhoti folded. He was of good height and health, oily black, and wearing a loincloth and a shoulder towel. He sat on a bench or chair for long hours whenever he came, putting one leg over the other for hours together. He occupied the same seat again after the meal. He was just too lazy to work on anything. He would buy hot water, mix it with soda powder, and drink it three times a day before every meal. He used to eat food and go to bed immediately after meals in the afternoon and the evening. However, when my mother occasionally told him to cast a net to catch fish, he threw the net into the stream, taking me with him. In those days, one could hear many 'Vazhappally Veeradiyaan' stories (writings about St. Thomas, who established a church at Nilakkal.) during the fishing intervals or after the meal - sometimes, folk songs and 'Njanappana' enlightenment songs in Malayalam. Example-

> "കണ്ടുകണ്ടങ്ങിരിക്കും ജനങ്ങളെ കണ്ടില്ലെന്നു വരുത്തുന്നതും ഭവാ"
> രണ്ടു നാലു ദിനംകൊണ്ടൊരുത്തനെ തണ്ടിലേറ്റി നടത്തുന്നതും ഭവാൻ
> മാളിക മുകളേറിയമന്നന്റെ തോളിൽ മാറാപ്പു കേറ്റുന്നതും ഭവാൻ"
> "എണ്ണിയെണ്ണികുറയുന്നിതായുസ്സും മണ്ടിമണ്ടി കരേറുന്നു മോഹവു"

(Poonthanam Nambudiri)

After a week or two, Perappan would go away, and I forget about it. If he had been to other relatives' houses, he would be there for a few minutes and never for more than a cup of tea. After staying at Vavachan's home for days together, he would request a small sum for a shirt and dhoti from Achayan. He happily ate enough rice with any curry available without any hesitation. Parappan had unique personal qualities and physical figures, ate well, fell asleep, sat down, and returned to Perunna eight to ten days later.

Achayan called and wrote in his register that it was not 'Leelamma' but 'Lailamma.' When she grew up, she would say her name was 'Lailamma Somas.' I remember it was so until she married, and it's the same in her school certificates. Inside the front cover of Achayan's account book, he wrote the names of his children. The family she went into after her wedding called her name - "Leelamma is enough."

She must live there in that house; let them call her. That was what we finally determined. "Lailamma, born: August 12, 1956", was recorded in Achayan's account book. I do not know what the reason was. It may be because we could not get a 'Valapura' boat, or we did not get a man to row, or we were afraid that my mother's pain would be unbearable even before she reached Alappuzha Beach Hospital.

"Mone, run and tell Bhadran's mother to come here soon." Valyammachi (Amma) of Kannattumadom – Achayan's mother - went to holy cross church every morning. As a Syrian Christian woman, she used to wear chattayum mundum, the traditional attire, and kavani (neriyathu) to cover her head while in church.

("Chatta" is a seamless white garment consisting of a white blouse covering the whole upper part of the body. "Mundu" is a long white garment wrapped around the waist and reaches below the ankles.)

While returning from church, she used to come to Valayamchira to see her grandson. Valyammachi said - "Go quickly, Mone, go and tell her she will come."

I ran and crossed the motor floor through the western ridge, and after the next row of houses, there was the house of the toddy tapper Bhadran. Bhadran's mother was a well-known midwife, not very tall, a little fat, with a brassiere alone on the upper body, always smiling and having a chewy mouth. She was a mother who comforted those becoming mothers with labour pain.

Achayan and Ammachi were happy that a girl child was born after two boys. Bhadran's mother announced that she got a girl born in the Chithira star.

Even before the baby girl was one year old, when we had to move out of the house and return to Kannattumadom house, someone had already predicted that – "Isn't that a girl born in Chithira star? That's sure to happen! When Chithira is born, ... will dig the floor, ("ചിത്തിര പിറന്നാൽ അത്തറ മാന്തും") is the folklore".

Some predictions do come true.

When Kuruppachan told Grandpa that the people living there at Valayamchira had to move out since he had decided to give the property to his daughter after her marriage, Kuruppachan, and Grandpa were perfect friends, Grandpa thanked him for allowing his son and family to stay in Valayamchira for so long. The foundation was not dug up. There was no need to level the base. Grandpa instructed his son to vacate the house without demolishing the foundation or house, take clothes and utensils, and return to the parental home. That is how we left Valayamchira forever. Leaving Valayamchira was like going behind something invaluable there, the whole of my childhood- the most beautiful part of life- never returning.

Kuruppachan dug up the foundation made of mud from the paddy field. He demolished the hut, which was made of clay and coconut leaves. He made a stone foundation. Before asking his daughter and family to stay there, the walls and roof were made with bamboo and coconut leaves.

The blessed son of Grandpa obeyed his father's instructions. Temporarily, he and his family stayed with his parents. Achayan talked to his 'Aliyan' (brother-in-law) in Maramkunnil while looking for another place to stay. The mother of Kannattumadom and the mother of Annakutty at Maramkunnil were sisters. Annakutty is Maramkunnil's mother's only daughter. Varghese came from Kelamangalam, married Annakutty, and lived in Maramkunnil since no other male members were there. Plenty of land was near the ravine banks, surrounded by farmland, another 108 para measures (approx. 16 acres) of farmland in the Muttanaveli paddy field, and everything else for a comfortable living.

Varghese and Annakutty had their children studying in various classes at the same school. They are Appachan, Thommikunju, Lillykutty, Kunjamma, Thankamma, Lucy, Unni, Sunnychan and Sabukuttan. Sunny died of an illness before he was ten years old. Achayan's Varghese Aliyan was an expert in agriculture and interested in public affairs. In the evenings, after farming and work, he would lie in an armchair in the living room of his house, talk about household chores, drink a bottle of toddy, eat and sleep peacefully.

Grandfather would say, "Annakutty is the same age as Ouseppachan." As Achayan's cousin Annakutty got older, Varghese Aliyan saw the brothers in the Kannattumadom as his younger siblings. When such a young brother came and asked for a site to stay in his backyard, Maramkunnil Achen immediately replied. "Am I not happy about that? Why do you want to ask me permission to do that? Vavachan, you are welcome. Come to my neighbourhood and stay there after making a new hut."

Nothing more was sought. The countryside was rich in virtues. Everyone in the village knows everyone else's concerns. Everyone responds amicably. Achayan swore he would not claim or buy anything under the new land reform law. There was no need to say that. No one expressed any fear. That was Achayan's sincerity and his integrity that no one could question.

Achayan's Varghese Aliyan once went to the far eastern market to buy timber wood logs and build a set of new shops near his house in Maramkunnil. The largest wholesalers of timber were in Kottayam, Pala and Changanassery. He took Ottathyckal Thomachi to help bring the wood through the river like a ferry. Many people in the village used to say that when they bought all the timber, tied the raft, and went back through the boat, they could not control the raft in the stream and fell into the river. Thommachi had a providential escape in that incident. When the wooden door frame was first cut with a chisel, Damodaran, the carpenter, said – "I don't see anyone living or trading in the new building, Vakkan (Varghese) Mappile". Even fifty years after the building was erected for shops, it is unknown if it had been used for anything other than some storage until it was demolished last year. Predictions of village folks, too, sometimes come true!

As the sequence of events unfolded, another house came up in the same backyard of Maramkunnil. The new family weaved dreams of a new place to live. They quickly adapted to the unique circumstances. Chavelithara Madhavan lived on the north side. On the south side, a small streamlet, the water flowing into the ravine in front, etc., are closed with a bund, making it possible to walk through. To the south of the streamlet was the cattle shed of Maramkunnil, then the yard, the house, and the barn. Walk along the west side of the house, and you are under the shade of a camphor-smelling Karpoora mango tree, the fruits of which are top-rated for their taste, aroma, size, and quality.

On the south side of that house is a paddy field. When the water got filled in the paddy field, only a step down was needed to reach the water from the backyard. It was convenient to moor the canoe close to the shore.

The Chavelithara family was on the north side of Madhavan's house. Chakkiamma and her sons lived there. At that time,

Chakkiamma's elder son, Asankutty, was a middle-aged man but not married. When he was young, he tapped toddy from coconut trees, collected toddy, and ran a toddy shop. He did not go for a tap after he had started the shop. There were others as tappers. A grocery and provision shop was near the house, handled by his youngest brother, Kunju Pillai. Asan Kutty's younger brother - Gopalan - was a srank in the state boat service. He lived at Madathiparambil with his wife and children. Around that time, Chavelithara Kunju Pillai brought his wife from Punnapra.

After dusk, Asankutty was busy at the toddy shop and Kunju Pillai at the grocery store. After drinking toddy, those who go out from the shop would come to Kunju Pillai's grocery store, buy beedis, smoke, and walk satisfied for the day towards the south or north. On the south side, if the walks were a bit bumpy or topsy turvy, Madhavan sitting on the verandah of his hut would make a fizzing or miaow sound between reading his greatest epics. The one who hurried to his own house but went in circles would hear that strange sound, turn around, remove his shoulder towel, and tie it onto his head, "Araada... Who is making a cricket screech sound there !" he murmured and walked away without seeing anyone around. That, too, is part of the virtues of the countryside!

The shop and grocery store will be closed on Mondays. There will be no rush after dusk. Kunju Pillai goes to Alappuzha to buy goods in bulk, and it gets very dark at night for him to return. Asankutty will collect all the toddy on Mondays and hide it in the cowshed at Maramkunnil to make it more potent. The focus is on farming during the day. There was no greeting or political discussion from the locals. There was no quarrelling with anyone, no worries. When you see a new neighbour building his hut, watching the house building and progressing, you may laugh while looking at it but say nothing.

Between Madhavan's house and the left bank of the streamlet, Perappan drew a line 20 feet in length and ten feet wide, in which he made a firmer block from the paddy field than the mud of the stream, planted sand, planted coconut tree stems as pillars, split the areca nut tree, and made a house out of sticks, coconut dry leaves, and bamboo. As a team, Parappan, Valyathara Appachan, Thuruthichira Appachan, and Chennatt Outhakutty completed the housebuilding work in two weeks. The foundations were laid with sandstone, and the floor was levelled. Kunjayyappan Panikkan (carpenter) made the door with coconut stem and mango tree planks. After finishing two rooms under the roof of the main building, a verandah was made on the east side. A curtain made of bamboo and palm leaves was used to cover the patio, and now it looks like a whole house. The thatched-roof huts are almost identical. Suppose the carpenter makes the triangular joints at either end of the prominent load-bearing member. In that case, he will see a high triangular face at the junction of the three sides at both roof ends. Without a carpenter, everything would be fine and flat. An extension was arranged to the north side, and the kitchen was made. Bricks and a fireplace were there, ready to cook. A beautiful house was completed, sturdy, and safe, with a comfortable bedroom, hall, and kitchen – all-inclusive. You must stay with your parents and children and start a family.

"Quality toilet makes the house a home of its own," I read somewhere. The suitable toilet for the new house was five hundred feet away, a pit covered all around with coconut leaf, in the southwest corner of the Maramkunnil estate. A flat stone to climb onto the twin bridge made of coconut stems split horizontally across its long axis. When you return with a small water jug, you see someone else waiting. If the paddy field next to it is flooded, there is no need to carry the jar of water!

The wind from the west was sometimes foul-smelling. The sewage

The disposal facility was established recently at one end of the 'newly filled landfill site,' a little far away. The people living in the

Maramkunnil backyard did not have any difficulty. New residents also used the same facility. You only needed to enter it with a jug of water sufficient to clean your body and hands and return comfortably. Occasionally, there was a need to communicate between people inside and outside through nasal or throat-clearing sound transmissions, which was common in the countryside. Chavelithara Madhavan and his children did not have that facility, so we sometimes had to tolerate a foul smell.

My mother planted bananas and a small horticulture garden on the west side of the house. Beyond that, she built a roofless rectangular shed with coconut leaves for women to bathe in. Not only in the huts but in most homes built of stone, there was no room for men, women, or couples. There are not even doors for all the rooms, let alone door locks. No electricity, no electric lights. It was very dark when you turned off the evening lamp or the lantern. Sleep came soon. I could never sleep in such darkness when I lived in the city.

I started my high school education while living in a house in Maramkunnil. I walked four or five kilometers along the country roads with my friends to Champakulam. In the corner of Achayan's room, I had a small table with books and a small stool for sitting, reading, and writing. I was sleeping on the top of the rice box. Get up in the morning, return from the 'newly filled landfill site,' swim, jump into the river, and bathe. Appachan from Maramkunnil was studying in class X in high school. Appachan was known to participate in swimming competitions and win prizes. Appachan taught a student of three classes below to swim across the ravine. Swam with competition, drank water, and did not know how time had passed. My eyes reddened as I climbed ashore, dressed, picked up the books, and went to school with friends from the northern villages.

When his grandson grew up, he could lift and cast a net to fish. When he began to live at Maramkunnil, near the ravine, his grandfather made a net for him to fish. So, for many holidays, he released nets in the gorge. Babu followed me with a small jug to collect the fish. When the courtyard was flooded, throwing nets in the submerged yard and catching Varaal and other fish was fun. These are special good memories that the floods have given me. I remember having water in the bedroom and on the porch and using a small canoe tied to the verandah of the house. How did my mother cook food in the kitchen below the foundation level? I do not remember, but we ate daily, thanks to her incredible efforts.

8. THE TEENAGER DEEDS

There was only an old rice box as furniture when we moved from the Kannattumadom family home to the Kannattumadom at Maramkunnil. I remember lying on a mat on top of it and dreaming and eating food sitting on it. There was a wooden box for clothes my Ammachi got from her brothers as a wedding present. The furniture, utensils, and household items had to be loaded onto a small boat.

Manorama, Deepika, and Kerala Kaumudi were the newspapers and several other periodicals that Achayan distributed. The number of newspapers and journals increased over a period. People became more literate and became more enlightened. Achayan got recognition for his services. Achayan's popularity grew. Achayan was always very proud of his work.

So, life got greener step by step. In four to five years, Achayan got a wooden single cot bed, a table, chairs, and a bench to put on the verandah. Kunjayyappan Panikkan and his elder brother Neelakandan Panikkan also built a small Anjili canoe in our courtyard. My mother did not need more firewood to light the fire in the kitchen until the canoe work was finished. Otherwise, it was enough to pick up the coconut leaf or leaf stems that had fallen in the area surrounding the house or sidestep. There was nothing like what was in Valayamchira, with only one or two coconut trees and the remaining swamp-filled land.

The canoe was built by cutting and polishing from the trunk of a large Anjili (wild jack) tree. One can row and travel. The size of the canoe makes it difficult for the small waves in the river to enter the canoe, but one can sit inside and row fast in it. That's good enough.

There were many children from that area going to school in Champakulam. Many friends will meet in the library when they arrive early and indulge in games, laughter, jokes, and storytelling. The Balajanasakhyam was formed and grew up there in connection with the library.

"Amme, I'm going home." I would go to Kannattumadom at least once a week. Go west to the paddy field, walk along the ridges in the paddy field, along the northern or southern hill, and climb up to Madathiparambil, then west. You can walk through the range of 'ten paras' and climb into the backyard of Kannattumadom. If water is in the field, you must go to Chennattu property and wave your hands towards Kannattumadom. Kunjamma or Animma will be rowing in a small canoe and will come to pick you up. When Achayan comes from Ambalapuzha, he brings a big packet of betel leaves, areca nuts, tobacco leaves, and another bag of coffee beans and jaggery at least once a month.

Bundles of newspapers regularly come and drop in front of Keshavan's tobacco shop on the west side of the temple. The Ambalapuzha newspaper office was also inside Keshavan's shop. Achayan regularly buys those packages from that store once a month. And then he would say to me -

"Take it home and give it to your grandma."

Valyammachi would gladly receive it when I went to Kannattumadom with the package. She would laugh so heartily that the traditional mekkamothiram ('kunukku') worn by Valyammachi on her upper ear lobes would be dancing. Kunukku was two inches in diameter and with a cross-section of a pencil.

Shaking her head and laughing, she would sit on the verandah, open the package, and call Theyyamma to hand over things belonging to the kitchen. Betel leaves and tobacco would go to the box earmarked for that purpose.

As I watched her, I realised that the same grandma took care of me when the Chinese flu affected us, and we were confined in the ancestor's home for a few days. It was a type of fever that came from China. I said something while half-asleep with the severity of the fever. I woke up in shock and was crying, and it was the same grandma who consoled me. I remembered that Amma helped me and cared for everything. *Covid-19, an infectious disease caused by the Coronavirus, was more deadly than the flu. When writing this, I see that the Covid epidemic is sweeping across the globe. Health experts look for effective remedies. All the people moving around take precautions to prevent its spread by protecting themselves.*

It happened on the day when I went to Kannattumadom with coffee beans and tobacco. The following incident proved that even though I was a grown-up boy, the kusruthi and associated mischiefs had not left me yet. The whole yard was covered with fine gravel and small pieces of rock. To the south of the yard was a Kilichundan Mango tree. There were many mangoes in it, and it looked ripe. It was mid-May, the peak season of mangoes. People in our village were feasting on mangoes. Womenfolk in every household were busy preparing pickles and salted mangoes. Kids enjoy their summer break climbing on mango trees, plucking mangoes, and having them while sitting on comfortable seats on the branches with thick barks, staining their shirts and trousers.

It was a great desire to see the mango fruit. I was always fascinated by the 'king of mangoes'- the Kilichundan mango, for its taste, fragrance, and vibrant colour. I desired to have it somehow.

If I had jumped up, I might not have reached there to pluck the mangoes or hold a branch by hand as I was not tall enough.

I looked around and saw no stick or bamboo long enough. I threw a stone from below, aiming at a bunch of big mangoes. The rock went straight to the forehead of the Valyammachi (Amma), walking along the south side! Kusruti was trembling and could not open his mouth when he saw blood coming from her skin on the forehead!

"I did not see Amma…please; I did not know; Pardon me, sorry! Sorry!"

I sat down involuntarily. Grandma did not cry out loud. She walked with her forehead covered and came to the verandah of the house. Grandpa took some water and rubbed over the injury. He saw a lump like a small mango on her forehead when he removed his hand. While walking to Maramkunnil, I remembered an incident like this one almost only a week ago. That, too, was due to the desire to have mangoes. I assumed no one knew about that incident because it showed my madness!

In the backyard of Valiyaparambil, Kilichundan mangoes were ripe and big. I did not find a stone to throw at it. While standing there, an acquaintance with a bow and arrow ('thettali') in his hand walked towards me, and I came forward. It was Sreenivasan.

Everyone will affectionately call him Cheeni, the son of Cherukkaaman, who ran a toddy shop on the west side of Kavalakkal house. Sometimes, he was laughing, and sometimes, he remained silent. He laughed at himself. Cheeni said something without making a sound or good stability to his head. He used to carry a bow and arrow and looked through the shore for fish. He will catch the fish if found by shooting the arrow sent from his bow. He was in front of me. I went straight to Cheeni and asked, "Can you give me that 'thettali' ?"

Without asking why I needed it, as there were no fish or pond nearby, Cheeni handed over the 'thettali.' Bow and arrow were set.

I did aim at the mango I saw nearby on the tree. The trigger worked correctly, the arrow went exactly where it was to go, and the mango looked at me and laughed! Total panic! Only the bow was in my hand, and I returned it to Cheeni, and without thanking him at least once, I quickly left the place. No one saw it, or so I thought. They would have known whose head was unstable if anyone had seen it! Who knew the innumerable dimensions of the mischiefs of a naughty one? Even as a high school student, and after fourteen years of age, the misdeeds did not diminish. I am still counting the increased misconduct that comes to my memory!

Did the arrow hit anyone in the forehead? What a misery and tragedy it would have been! Bowing down and walking with fear was self-loathing. The fear that someone would come looking for me was a burden on my mind!

Today, Valyammachi's forehead was also broken by throwing stones.

It must have been that year that Grandma fell on the way to the church. She slipped and fell. A radius bone below the knee of the left arm had a crack. The little finger was also bent down and broken. The hand had laid inside a plaster for two to three months. When the dressing was removed, that hand's physical capability was diminished. The little finger and ring finger did not straighten up. She was taken to Pulinkunnu on a canoe for two months, where she was treated with a combination of oil, kuzhambu (an ayurvedic nerve tonic), and massage. Someone had come to paddle the boat. The high school student suggested going with his grandma during the school holidays. He would leave in the morning and return in the afternoon. That's fine. If he had returned in the evening, he would not have had much time to play ball or kabaddi with his friends during the day.

The hand regained some relief and capability, but the little finger remained folded. Kusruti used the engineering technique of gently stroking the little finger-like straightening of a curved bar.

"No, ah ... "ങാഹാ, അയ്യോ ... അയ്യോ, എടാ, വിടടാ, തേ ഒരു വീക്ക് വച്ചു തന്നാലുണ്ടല്ലോ" *(Oh no!. Leave me, Do I give you a hit?)*

Valyammachi may scream.

"Then what.., How will you hit me with this swollen and curved finger -?" Grandma laughed, and both Kunukku hanging in her ear lobes swung back and forth.

Whenever Kochuppappan came from Punnapra, he used to go to Maramkunnil and take his brother's eldest son to Kannattumadom. Especially if the field were filled with water, I would row the boat to Kannattumadom and simultaneously respond to inquiries about my studies. Chittamma would make strong coffee in the evenings and give it to her mother-in-law and father-in-law in large Chinese bowls (Koppa). Chattambi would also get a share along with Kochuppappan.

I used to go with fishing hooks to the Pookkaitha riverside on the ridge of the 'Six Hundred Para' (measure) paddy field - near the house of Dani and Markos during the holidays. Fishing seemed a more familiar profession than farming for the entire family. I was aware that I, too, had joined the bandwagon. It was mentioned earlier, what I heard, that the grandpa and his children all went to the river or lake to catch fish by throwing nets or bait on hooks.

I used to get up in the morning, carry a mixture of the cake and rice that my mother had ground as the bait in my dhoti lap, and walk to the ridge by the bank of the Pookkaltha River. Some friends, too, had come along. The bait mixture was rolled to the size of a pearl, hooked onto the fishing hook, and the lead was tied to the rod, thrown into the river, and paid attention keenly to the bait being pulled away. The float will show that. There were days when I could catch eight to ten Karimeen (pearl spot) or an eel of one to two kilograms. But there were days when we returned without joy. Parayanattuthara Kuttappayi, Thattuthara Appayi, and Kavalackal Kuttappan used to say, "The sun rays are intense. Let us go back." When Kalanchi (Asian sea bass) Attu Walah or Manjakkoori carved the bait and dragged it away, Kuttappayi pulled the rod and broke the lead on the fishing rod. He slid into the river, which was a lot of fun! I searched and walked to find a fishing rod of bamboo that was lightweight and strong! Finally, I went to Thamarakath's house, where I found a cluster, and from that, I cut out one or two.

I studied at Champakulam High School for three years. The monthly tuition fee was six rupees.

Because of the name kusruti, some geniuses deliberately attached their mischievous behaviours to the famous kusruti. That is how I was punished during the drill period. I would gladly accept it! I only prayed that nobody at home would know. Achayan's sharp words or thrashing blows below the leg knee were sure at home. I was afraid of that.

The incident took place at Champakulam High School.

"Left Right, Left Right," we were marching on the school grounds. Some girl walked past the compound wall. "Left-right," and a rare sound in between was not the usual whistle the drillmaster blew for marching. It was like a goat crying; twice, it was heard, "the... Mnhe... "— The drill master's whistle came after six steps.

"Stop."

"Attention."

Who ... made the sound "Mnhe... Mnhe.... Mnhe.."? Who cried like a sheep?

No one answered. The drillmaster asked again. No one answered.

Walking to the class after the drill -

"You, Kusruti, do not go to the next class. Stand outside ..."

Everyone went up to the verandah of the Ninth class ... Everyone went into the class except me. Someone was laughing loudly!

The one who mimicked the sound of the sheep must have pointed to this fellow student. I did not see who he was.

Pappachan Sir came from the verandah and watched the class through the window. He had a cane in his hand.

Would you agree if I said "not me"? I was already a mischief-monger!

Pappachan Sir asked - "If you see girls, you must blow the whistle. Do you feel like crying like a goat, don't you?

He gave three beatings on my right broad palm. I did not cry, fearing it would be like a sheep if I had cried! I learned that all emotions, such as sadness, disappointment, frustration, worry, and anger, are expected and need not be avoided, suppressed, or feared in adverse situations and when the chips are down.

"Okay, get in the class."

I was very much relieved.

While studying in that class, when someone adds something else that can also be punishable like this in the name of regular mischief -

I looked helplessly through my wet eyes into George's sympathetic eyes. George came from Amichakari and was always sitting on the backbench, occasionally greeting and smiling at me. George was an excellent and mature classmate. Someone like my Kuttappan Chettan spoke well like an adult, was good-natured, and always discussed a subject of mutual interest.

This time, things slipped. George of "Amichakari" intervened and saved me from that ordeal.

I felt great love and gratitude from someone who compassionately saw the helpless. This was the first time with such recognition. Friendship, for me, was showing kindness.

"Thank you." In that moment of relief and contentment, I asked George -

"Should I call you George Chetta?"

He agreed! Indeed, he was an elder to me, like an elder brother, for a long time.

It was so until the end of the schooling, the next two years. How many times have I reached out to those hands of compassion?

After Kuttappan Chettan had passed out his survey and civil engineering studies, Kuriachan left home to work. That was the reason perhaps I could not see him often. Kunchacko was also away and had no daily interactions, while I desired to get the shadow of an elder. George, the "saviour", gave it to me for a while.

Memories of Onam ball games and boat races often come to mind. Ball games were played at Nanatt Chira and Palathittachira. Onam season is frequently considered to start from the beginning of the Nehru trophy boat race on the second Saturday of August every year. Before that, the traditional boat race, also known as the Champakulam' Moolam' boat race, used to be celebrated. It used to be a school holiday on that day at Champakulam.

The small boat races were held in the ravine in front of Valayamchira and the canyon next to the Pulikkalkavu temple on the north side of the village. The Balajanasakhyam, Yuvajanasakhyam, and the locals organised the boat race. Nanattu Pachu Pillai, Kavalakkal Joy, Babychan, and Maramkunnil Appachan were at the forefront of the youth club. We competed in a two-row boat race with Vazhayil Gopi as my companion and won first place in one of the races. Gopi used to paddle from home to Kanjipadam every morning, distribute milk, and come back ready to go to school. Narakathra Kuttappan's boat was found after searching for a vessel of a suitable size to compete for the two paddlers category. Before the competition, the canoe was brought home, dragged to the shore, dried, and applied with beaten eggs on the outer side. We defeated Kavalackal Chandappan and Sunny at the finishing point, and the Narakathara boat defeated their boat. Celebrating the victory, Gopi went to all the shops in Kanjipadam, where he used to distribute milk with the trophy we won. They encouraged us.

After watching all the snake boats in the Nehru Trophy Boat Race, boating was still exciting. That was the first time we saw the Nehru Trophy boat race. The boat race at Champakulam used to have a boat rowing the course and completing it. The winner was determined by measuring the time taken to complete the course. Here, four snake-boats advance parallelly, fighting side by side, sometimes winning by a single row length. The visitor's pavilion and the photo finish came much later.

It happened once when Grandpa had to be rushed to the hospital. He was taken to Alappuzha and then to Shankar Ram's hospital in Pathirappally by car. He had a heart condition. Two days later, when Achayan came back from Ambalappuzha, Achayan was sad while saying -

"Father - is ill. Anthonichan said community prayers were happening in the churches and monasteries in Alappuzha and Punnapra.

Achayan took me along to the Pathirappally hospital, and we saw him. Anthonichan was right there to take care of Grandpa.

"Shankar Ram came this morning and woke up Achayan. Now he is very relieved. He said he would send us back home in a week."

Grandpa was quite exhausted. Still holding his grandson close by, he touched my cheek and smiled.

During that visit to the hospital, Kochuppappan showed me the foetus of two, three, and four-month-old babies in a glass bottle with some liquid in front of the first room of the hospital. He said this was how a baby grows in its mother's womb.

The day my grandpa returned to Kannattumadom was a great occasion. He was brought by a boat. When I heard that he had come, I went to the parental home with my mother. Lots of people came to see my grandpa.

The doctor told him that there was a lot of medicine to consume, so he should not eat salt for some time and not do any farming work.

"There is always water in the mouth like this; how can I drink porridge with no salt and chilli?" Grandpa expressed disappointment.

Two or three months later, the water in the field had not yet dried up. He tied the Anjili canoe at Chennatt, and leaving it there, he walked and came to see his grandson.

"Oh, Achayan has come," said my mother.

"Grandpa, how did you come, and who brought you here ?" wondered the grandson.

"How long, without doing anything like this, how long could I sit idle, without going anywhere? Happy that I could come and see you all."

Years later, the exhausted father returned - surely there would be something special when Grandpa came to see his grandson.

My mother made his strong coffee.

My mother said, "Go with Grandpa and take him home as he leaves."

We got on the boat, and I started to paddle.

"Mone… You give me the rowing paddle; let me …."

"No, Grandpa. I can row. I know it."

"No, Mone. One day, I want to put your son in this boat and paddle, and only I will die. I am still strong, you see…."

Like the consolation words from the prophet, it cooled my mind and made it fragrant. Then, I could not answer anything, and Grandpa paddled the boat himself.

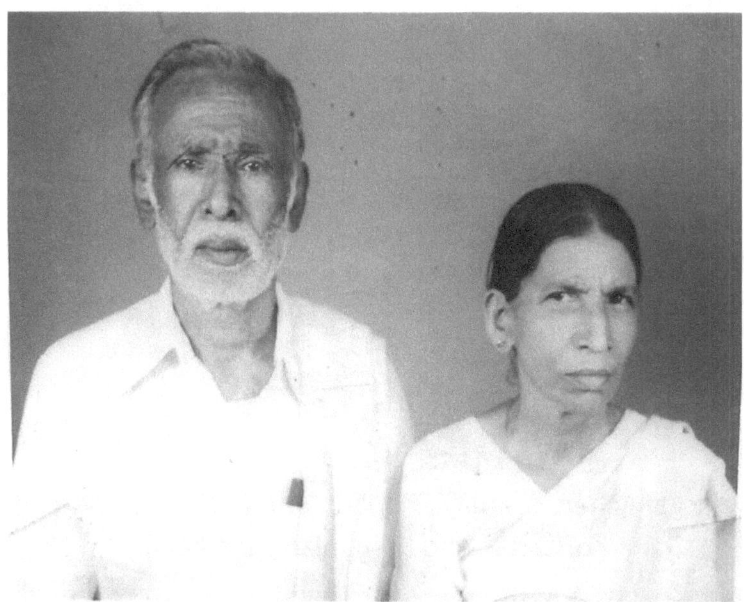

Ouseppachan Perappan and Peramma

Kuriako Chittappan and Theyyamma Chittamma

Kavalackal Achen, Ammayi, Appan, Amma after the marriage of Kuriachan and Kunjunjamma Chechi

KT Antony Kochuppappan and Marykutty Chittamma

9. MOTHER'S RELATIONS

A patriarchal system prevailed in a society where the father was the head of the household. In most Christian families, males dominate all social, political, economic, legal, and cultural roles. After their marriage, women always consider their husbands the head of the family, and the house where they stay together is the permanent home for them and their children. Gender equality and involvement of women in all the fields commenced and have been happening more since my school days. The male members in that family also dominated matriarchal systems. The system weakened over a while, or it was discarded by some people and societies who came across the modern way of living. The fathers were considered the heads in every branch of our ancestral family, Anjiliparambil, which we saw when we grew up in the Kannattumadom family. We remain in our father's house most of the year. Children usually get a chance to visit their mothers' houses during school vacations or while gathering for family-friendly events or social events. The children use the opportunity to nurture their mothers' existing direct and indirect relationships before marriage.

After school was closed for vacations, my mother wanted to go to the Arackal ancestral family, which was raised by her parents in Kainakari. As Achayan used to go to Ambalappuzha every day for work, my mother could not go to her parent's home and stayed there for more days. After leaving her son for a month's vacation, the mother would return in a day or two.

Achayan will arrange a 'Valapura' boat for the mother and son to visit Kainakari. Dani, or Markos, steered the boat with oars, short or long. You could reach Kainakari Arackal house at about 10 am, provided you left early. The journey and the views along the ravine or river were incredible. Anything carried for parents at Kainakary would be wrapped and placed inside the 'valapura' boat. Ammachi sat inside the valapura under the shade. The mother's son liked sitting in the Sun and on the boat's steps. Markos would have joked something, forgotten the fatigue, and paddled the boat. Sometimes, Dani, Markos' older brother, came along.

The countryside along the route is full of streams and small canals. The field consisted of paddy with coconut, banana, areca nut trees and shrubs, and occasional houses at the ravine banks. Men are engaged in work in the areas and out in the fields. Streams connect rivers. There are narrow ridges between the stream and the paddy field, and the banks are widened by putting the mud from the area. Small and large houses next to each other on the broad ridges, coconut leaf thatched-roof cottages, with only the foundations paved with stone or bricks and thatched houses. The small wooden bridges across the river are high enough to allow a smooth passage without any roadblocks for boats going under the bridge. Sometimes, when we reached the bridge, Dani would lean on one end of the ship, leaning against the canoe. Once he crossed the bridge, he got up again, relied on the oars, and moved forward. When the boat passes under the bridge, the Kusruti sits on the boat and enjoys the view till the bridge is fully passed. I would have remembered if I had ever seen any vehicle passing by on a dusty road somewhere—the geography and the environment of my hometown, Kuttanad, in the Nineteen fifties and sixties.

When we arrived at Arackal house, the hero was always Annamma's son. Appappan, Ammammachi, Kochachan, Aunty, Kunjommachayan, Kunchacko, and Kuttachan Chettan would call me near embrace and caress. Appachi and Joy, Vakkachan and Ammini, Joychan, Kunjumon from Ayiraveli, and George from Chempil all would get together to play. My mother's brothers were together at Arackal house. Only her eldest brother, Vakkachan (Valyachayan), lived on an island, like Kannattumadom, in the middle of a paddy field near Arackal. He moved to the middle of the paddy field on the east side, away from the joint family. Hence, they marked the end of the joint family. After some time, Valyachayan moved to Kochi, where he found it convenient to auction cash crops such as pepper and cardamom and trade through commission agencies.

I stood watching the volleyball at Chempil. Sometimes, the ball bounces away. The Arackal yard was full of mangoes. Kunjumon, Appachi and Joy played Kuttiyum kolum (Gilli-danda), a traditional game with me. Sitting with the grandpa there, we prayed, who marked a cross on our forehead. We had lunch together with Grandpa. Grandpa spread a mat in the south-side room and looked north towards the door. The grandma must provide the food by herself. Grandpa's meal ends with a ball of rice mixed with curry, rolled up and taken in his hand while he gets up.

A bowl is kept on the verandah, and behind it is awaiting the pet dog. The dog stood up near the bowl when the dog saw Grandpa coming out the door. Grandpa would

tell his pet dog while holding the rice ball in his hand-

"Go round the house and come back; make it three times. ."

The dog ran around the house quickly. After running around the house three times, the dog returned and stood behind the bowl. Grandpa put the ball into the bowl. The dog ate with gratitude and love, shaking its tail vigorously. The daily training made sure to see it all the time – 'thank you, remember it.

In the early days, my grandpa and Kochachan went to Alappuzha for business and returned in the evening. After Kochachan's trade was shifted to Chennamkari, only Appappan and Valyachayan worked at the Alappuzha auction centre of spices.

Then Kunjommachayan got a job in an ice factory in Kochi. The ice factory manager, the supervisor, and such a responsibility were given to him by the ice factory owner who moved there. It was a significant relief from the heavy work of processing paddy into rice in the backyard and selling it in Alappuzha. That is why Kunjommachayan took a job in an ice factory and went to Kochi. A career with a steady income and a monthly salary was better than carrying a sack of paddy on the shoulders, rowing a boat, and so on, and such an opportunity came after a long wait. He also got married after going to Kochi.

Kunjommachayan found a rented house and asked his elder brother and family to go to Kochi to improve their lives. The children, Joy and Ammini, were in school. The ones below were very babyish. Valyachayan decided to move to Kochi as he had experience in the market. In a big city like Kochi, he had better jobs and trade opportunities in the spices market. When Valyachayan moved to Kochi, Grandpa was left alone.

Kochachan, Kunjommachayan, and Kunchacko are used to process

paddy into rice in Arackal's backyard and sell it in the Alappuzha market once. Tired of carrying paddy sacks on their back and tired of carrying several bags, Kunjomma and Kunchako could not go to school on time. Unable to even write the examinations well for so many years!

After Kunjomma got a job and went to Kochi, the hustle and bustle of paddy processing came to Kunchacko. Kochachan and Kunchacko carried the paddy, boiled it, dried it, put it in a boat, took it to Alappuzha, and sold it. With Kunchacko's enlistment in the military service, paddy processing at Kainakari Arackal ceased. Thankachan resumed the old grocery business in Chennamkari.

Whenever we went to Arackal's house, we used to go to her elder sister's house in Kainakari, who lived in a field on the west side of the Elankavu temple. Before marriage, there was so much love between these two sisters, who lived in their husband's houses after marriage. Peramma's son Vakkachi was at least two years older than me. Daughter Ammini was of the same age.

The two sisters were always there to make windmills using coconut palm leaves, run around, cast the nest, and catch fish from the ravine. The elder sister was enthusiastic about making kappa, fish curry, and rice and fed her younger sister and son! On the way back, Peramma would hug me and bid me bye.

"Now, when are we meeting again?"

The sisters and their children have not seen each other for a long time after the elder sister and family moved to Thovala in the south.

Ammachi's younger sister, Kunju-Mariya, married Devasyachan of Chekkidikkad South. She was older than their youngest brother, Kunchacko, and this is what my mother told me - "Do you remember, you were small and, on my shoulder, for the wedding of Kunjumariya? When you saw her husband putting the mangal sutra around her neck, you were disturbed and made a big noise while sitting in my hand. You did ask -

"What do they do, Amma? Say, what are they doing?"

Before getting selected for the Army and after his eldest sister moved to Thovala, Kunchacko sometimes came to Maramkunnil house. My Ammachi was there for him to love, have a quick visit, and tell jokes most of the time. Although he was called Kunchacko, he was affectionately known as Kunjunju. Others used to call him Kunchako, but I wonder why I called him Kunjunju, probably because my mother called him such or because I had a lot more affection towards my maternal uncle than the other uncles. The youngest son of the Arackal ancestor family was Kunchacko himself.

We laughed a lot when he came, were happy, and quickly passed our time in the playful moments. Together, we used to go fishing.

The only age difference is three years with Kunchacko. However, he was my uncle, the elder sister's son, who was still like his younger brother. Ammachi considered Kunchacko as her eldest son, too!

Kunchacko will associate with me for any deed. He was good at playing volleyball. (Later, when he served in the Army, he became an outstanding player in the battalion volleyball team.)

Even during his younger days, when he was the uncle of the naughty one, Kunchacko's misdeeds would not be as great as that of his nephew. But Chavelithara Madhavan's son Dharmadevan had a tiff with him. He said something, ending in a brawl going back and forth. Dharmadevan's lips broke, and blood came out. His mother and siblings came running and uttered many words that were not in the dictionary. They did not listen to what Ammachi pleaded with them. Eventually, Achayan talked to Madhavan, Dharmadevan's father, and negotiated the truce. Kunchacko stood like a warrior - unmoved by provocations. "To say the least, insulting anyone is to get a beating, whoever it may be!"

Dharmadevan's estrangement from Kunchacko later became a fear or respect for the brave.

Isn't it often Ammachi hears the unusual conversations in that house so loudly, especially when Madhavan rebukes his wife or children and enters into arguments?

That was his usual style. He had to stroll because he had a fungal disease on his feet. In addition to the uneasiness caused by it, vulgar language comes out quickly, even loudly. After all, you can always read the Ramayana and the Bhagavad Gita for forgiveness- that was his attitude.

Even if you sit on the verandah of non-functional shops at Maramkunnil, you can hear Madhavan reciting Bhagavata, reading it so loudly. Sometimes, he gets angry with Kamalakshi, his wife, and often rebukes Vishwambharan and Dharmadevan at intervals of reading the epics.

When Dharmadevan beats, he grits his teeth and becomes silent. The younger Vishwambharan will take the stick back. The youngest Rohithashwan was a revolutionary. He would take the rattan back, break it, throw it away, and walk out. Those who come to buy groceries from Kunju Pillai's provision shop may witness those scenes. Those sitting in Kuttiyasan's toddy shop will not pretend to have seen or heard of it. Neighbours saw and heard all these, considered them incorrigible, and lived quietly without getting involved in entertainment.

My grandfather (Maternal) worked as an agent for the wholesale trade at the Alappuzha spices auction centre, which was an arrangement for importing mountain goods such as cardamom, pepper, and ginger from the East and auctioning them off to traders. I saw it when I went to Arackal during the summer holidays. He used to put his lunch in a box and go to the spices auction centre in a small canoe early in the morning. On days when he did not take the lunch box, he would come back at two or three o'clock in the afternoon.

Everyone must be accessible and readily available to participate in the prayer meeting daily at dusk hours. Everyone should come and kneel on the porch and attend the 'marking of the cross on the forehead' prayers in the evening. The daily work and games are all over before that. Almost all the children who came to celebrate the holidays must be present, including my cousins - Joy, Appachi, Ammini, and Thankamma.

A wooden, altar-shaped structure was at one end of the closed verandah of the Arackal house facing east. There were separate images of the Holy Family, Jesus, Mother Mary, St. Joseph, St. Antony, and St. Sebastian. The altar was decorated with candles, beads, and flowers. All children should kneel in front of it for the evening prayer.

Grandpa himself will lead each of the prayers. Everyone else should recite the prayer and say the rest of the prayers. More than two hours will pass when the intercession- pleadings to all the saints were done after the rosary of five mysteries and the litany of the Blessed Virgin Mary. Theyyamma Aunty would sometimes run out of the kitchen and participate in one sacred mystery of the rosary, get up quickly, and return to the kitchen. She would ask someone looking at her why she got up and went.

"The rice is being cooked in the open fire; it must boil now. '

Those kneeling in front will sit flat on level ground after a while. Sometimes, they get tired and would fall asleep.

Grandpa comes to the evening prayer with a small rattan that is short and thin. If anyone in the congregation happens to have a sleep hangover more than once, a small blow will make him alert again.

Once found leaning down due to sleep, he can get up and wash his face. The beating, the beaten one is turning to grandpa for mercy, grandpa's piercing glance, and the child's plea with his face and eyes that he will no more do as such. All these do not prevent the chanting of prayers from going on uninterrupted. Probably every day, it all became an integral part of the evening prayer - 'marking the cross on the forehead.'

If the grandpa's return from Alappuzha is delayed, it confuses the children after dusk. The evening prayer should be said, but who will lead the prayers? Should I go to the verandah and kneel or not? Or let me sit there because I do not know when Grandpa will come. The moment he arrives and enters the courtyard, we can kneel fast!

One day, Grandpa suggested that Kunchacko should lead the prayer in his absence, whether Kunjomma was home. With that, the confusion was removed.

Accordingly, one day, when Grandpa was late to return from Alappuzha, all the children prayed for Kunchacko's leadership and presidency. No one else could pray as precise and enduring as Grandpa did. It was common for everyone to recite and pray together. At the end of the prayers and before saying, "Remember, O most loving Virgin Mary, that it is a thing unheard of that anyone who had recourse to your protection…..", an extraordinary prayer to invoke each of the saints through their intercession- viz; One our father in heaven, one Hail Mary and One Glory be to the father - was to be presented to each of the saints. That somewhat confused Kunchacko. What he did was innovative!

Countless 'Our father in heaven…, Hail Mary… and Glory be to the father… were recited - altogether, and he presented them all to all the saints and pleaded-

"It's for the intercession of all the Saints because I do not know how much is due to each of you - Achayan may come late - so let me do this: let every one of you please share and take our prayers for the intercession, without quarrelling ... Amen.

Remember, O most loving Virgin Mary......."

Laughing until every stomach ached, everyone got up and retired from the place with laughter instead of 'Glory to Jesus... "

Over a period, Arackal's house, backyard, and Kunchacko's share of the family property were sold. Thus, Arackal's house and the land became alien. Only a few memories of my mother's home linger in my mind.

Kunchacko soon escaped. Kunchacko joined the Army, and he got a job. One day, Kunchacko attended an Army recruitment camp in Kochi, showed his educational qualifications, and provided his fitness for a job. When the order to join the Army came, he immediately ran everywhere, told the information, prayed, and left for Deolali after seeking blessings from his parents. There was one year of uninterrupted training. He could return on leave only after the training period.

While seeking blessings from his father, Kunchacko was heavyhearted and sad. That's what Kunchacko told me -

"Later, I couldn't see Achayan alive." When I remember Kunchacko's old days, I can still see his chest moving up and down and silently sobbing.

For those who have drifted away from deep family ties to their way of life and its mysteries, perhaps the same emotion, fear, and hope - may all be a combined mental state. The separation's emotional intensity may diminish and fade away as time passes. Warm memories live on forever. My mind would say, "Look at all this now and learn, and your turn will come!"

10. LEARN VALUES

Theyyamma Aunty Kainakari, who did not get time to leave the kitchen, was married by Kochachan from her Veluthedathu house in my native village, Chempumpuram. Marrying into a typical joint family in those days was troublesome for many women. That was why mainly married women preferred to settle separately and have their own nuclear family, away from their joint family. How many people need to be served? How long would it take to boil water to cook rice or make coffee? Lunch after three o'clock in the afternoon and dinner after ten o'clock at night, no one deliberately delays it; It happens as such.

Below Appachi, there were six more kids- Vakkachan, Tomichan, Thankamma, Mariamma, Boban, and Binoy. When I got married, Boban was a small boy who touched and played in my room with the statue of the rooster-hen made in the 'plaster of Paris.'

When Grandpa died in 1964, Kunchacko in the Army did not get leave to come because it was training time. The instructor told him to toughen his mind despite the sad news. I came to Alappuzha with James Achen from Polytechnic. I bought a wreath, boarded a state water transport boat, and went to Kainakari. I placed the wreath, looking at Grandpa's thick, frozen, bright face. I liked the unique rashes of blisters that formed on his face while he was recovering from smallpox at a younger age. I talked to him alone, but I did not hear anything back. I don't remember what I told him about making the dog run around the house or saying the evening prayers while kneeling too long.

The grandma was always with grandpa, giving us love and affection, just as the mother hen would hold the chicks close to her wings. We were cousins - the kids were together with me, Appachi,

Ammini, and Joy that day. Younger children wandered around in their world with their peers.

The death of Grandma shattered the family. Valyachayan and Kunjommachayan settled in Kochi. Kochachan and his family, with six children, were left alone in Kainakari. Appachi was sent to Changanassery to study at the seminary after completing SSLC. School and household work were in trouble for Vakkachan, Thankamma, Tomichan, Boban, Mariamma, and Rosamma. After much suffering, Kochachan relocated to Kochi like the other brothers.

Joy and Ammini were in school, and the others were very young - Molly, Kunjachan, and Anto.

Joy and Ammini used to play together with me during their vacations at their father's house in Kainakari. I went fishing in the Pumpa River. I went to play at Chempil.

After all of them settled in Kochi, such gatherings became rare. "Kochayan" was how Ammachi, her younger sister and brothers, addressed their eldest brother. Occasionally, when he walked in to see his sister and family, I only saw him treated with love and respect.

Thankachan, - Job – Ammachi's second brother worked as a grocery merchant at Chungam in Alappuzha. It was later relocated to Chennamkari. He set up a paddy processing plant home with his brothers when the trade was not lucrative. Harvested threshed paddy was boiled, dried in the sun, de-husked in the mill, weighed and packed in sacks, and sold in the Alappuzha market. Physical activity was much needed for the job. The work done by the brothers together drove a joint family forward for a long time.

Thankachan, also known as Job or Thankan, as Ammachi called her younger brother, was married to Theyyamma, the sister of Veluthedathu Kuttappan and Appachan. Ammayi hardly had time to hand over a sizeable joint family's day-to-day running and housekeeping, even for a short time - when the younger brothers were not married. The eldest brother married and stayed away from the joint family. "No time to rest or be out, kids and elderly parents – how can we plan a journey together?"

That must be why Thankachan came alone whenever he came to see his elder sister and returned quickly.

"I came up to Veluthedathu's house. Let me go, and after return, I have to boil the paddy for drying tomorrow."

Thankachan was affectionate toward his children and his nephews (sisters' children).

Johnny and Josekutty were my Peramma's sons. Johnny was in the shop at Chennamkari to help Kochachan, and sometimes it was Josekutty. Appachi, Vakkachan, and Thankamma, Kochachan's children, continued their Kainakari School education.

Initially, Vakkachi, the elder sister's first son, then Josekutty, the second son, after they stopped studying, and later Johnny, the elder sister's children, were all given training at the grocery shop taught to trade. Their sister Ammini, who stopped schooling, was given training in domestic work. Thankachan helped the family. What else can be done to those who study in the same class for consecutive years? They had no interest in doing anything else. Thankachan looked after them until they left Kainakari and settled in Thovala with their parents. Then, everyone had to travel long distances to see their suffering. That seldom happens. No one in that family learned to trade. Growing up working in the hilly terrain, everyone lived their way.

How hard is it for everyone in a family to move on with life, eat, grow up, and be satisfied? How can even small families be able to stand on their own feet? How much time can be spent on friendly visits and social interactions? But isn't life a mixture of the correct proportions of good and not-so-good?

After the harvest and the threshing, the field is separated, and all the paddy is dried and processed and stored in barns - while the paddy was still in the Kettuvallam - during such an abundance, once-

"Paddy is available reasonably, and a good profit can be expected if processed and sold as rice."

Someone told Achayan about this rare opportunity and its possibilities. Achayan remembered Thankachan and asked him to come and have a look.

He did not say that the paddy was for sale. Achayan was skeptical about it, as it was not a familiar field for him; therefore, he was apprehensive- if it did not happen.

"Just come here once and go. "

Thankachan came. Late at night, after bargaining, trade did not take place. He returned home with his brother-in-law, ate the dinner my mother had served him, and went to bed.

Just as Achayan was preparing to leave for Ambalappuzha for the daily newspaper work, Thankachan was also ready to return to Kainakari in the morning.

"Aliya (Brother-in-law), let me go. The sale did not take place. I just lost one day. I would have gained fifty rupees profit if I had not come here.

There was a surprise on Achayan's face. Compensation for the lost bargain? What should be done by the person who tried to help? Is there compensation after failing to help get the business?

Achayan just looked at the face of Thankachan, who was holding his hand thoughtfully, with a fixed smile. Thankachan, suffering from a lack of money, must have realized the loss of a night's work. Achayan opened the table drawer, took fifty rupees, and handed them to Thankachan. Only then did Achayan take a deep breath.

My mother and I stared at each other without understanding anything. Achayan smiled and bid bye to Thankachan. Then he got into his canoe and paddled to Ambalappuzha.

When Achayan returned in the afternoon and had food, Ammachi said something and choked on some words. "However, what Thankachan did was….."

"Yeah, some people are like that! After all, it's your brother. It does not matter." Achayan consoled my mother.

Besides ploughing the field, Ouseppachan (Perappan) was involved in farming, baiting, and cooking for public feasts on special days. But it does not always work. At such a difficult time, a rented house was set up in Punnapra, and a shop was set up in the market to sell coir, palm leaves, and baskets. Younger brother (Kochuppappan) came forward, ready to arrange things. All amenities were done, but that trade and stay did not last long. The cost of living and debt increased, and he returned with his family to live in a pool-filled area on the north side of Kannattumadom. He did so because his father had agreed to give him a place to live in the backyard and walk around in Ouseppachan's name.

Because of the hardships of life, he thought it could be an increased burden to go somewhere else and rent a house, find a place to live, and so on.

Kuriakose uncle developed the egg trade into a stationery business, and things moved on quickly. He bought two acres of land in the nearby area and cultivated it. The younger brother had agreed with his elder brother Vavachi to segregate a plot of cultivable land and reclaim it to make a small house in the northeast corner of the land. Those sweet words he said when he borrowed some money from Vavachi. After writing the sale deed, I heard Achayan tell his father that Kuriakose was not interested in discussing such a subject as sharing a piece of land with his brother.

"No matter, he's like that, don't worry," Grandpa reassured him. After that, Ouseppachan told Kuriakose about another idea.

"You live with our parents in the family, so this house and this place are likely to come to you as your own. It's not right for me to stay on the north side of the house next to your kitchen. If you take that place and give me some amount, I'll do some work. I've told Achayan about it." Achayan told me to consult you ..."

Kuriakose uncle (chittappan) was happy.

"I will give cash that everyone decides together for the property."

So, he invested some money as capital, went to Punnapra, and started a coir and palm business. This is how he returned to Kannattumadom with more debt and hardship after losing his investment within a year.

Kuriakose said, "That's right, Kochayan (elder brother) does not need my permission to come back and stay here; I gave the money without writing any document."

The father came down from the yard and heard his two adult children say something loud. He listened to it for a while without saying anything.

"Children, call everyone. My time is running out. I must find a solution, close my eyes peacefully, and see that everyone is at peace."

He initiated a suggestion as to the solution for what he heard.

This is the first time in the history of Kannattumadom that there was a conversation about family property - about residence itself. There was no complaint when no one owned anything.

A small island was in the middle of the field, and the backyard became more spacious. The southern side was filled with sand and mud and planted coconut seedlings. The pool on the north side was filled. The father always worked for all the children, praying their hardships, misfortunes, and sorrows would not be heard. Kuriakose bought the land. Anthonichan purchased the land. Everyone can stay at home here if they want. And yet? What are they like?

The father thought- Ouseppachan had not made any document. And yet he sold his property and got the money, and now he, too, is out of the ownership, and no one else is asking or telling, but they are my children. I love them equally, and no one has less love for me.

"Call, call everyone."

Everyone was called. Everyone came. The two daughters were sent away with their share of assets they could have been given at marriage. None would claim ownership of the rest of the family's property. They are all satisfied with their circumstances. That is why there was no need to call them.

When Achayan was getting ready to go to Kannattumadom, Kochuppappan came from Punnapra.

Achayan said, "See, now Anthonichan has come, so why don't you also come with us."

Am I the fifth son of the grandfather's children? – He has two daughters and four sons. Is this a special invitation because I am the eldest of the current generation - the new generation? 'Isn't it a great honour for a junior staff member to have the rare opportunity to attend a board meeting as a special guest? We arrived at Kannattumadom.

The division of the family property was rapid and peaceful, without calling out anyone's interests. No one complained or panicked. Parents loved their children equally and were willing to give more but shared what they had with everyone. My grandfather said all things calmly and lovingly –

The family home and place of residence are for Kuriakose. The north side was already given to Ouseppachan for staying. Let it be so. Ouseppachan only had sold it to Kuriakose without any further ado. The ten-para measures of cultivable land on the quay were for Anthonichan, and the south side extension recently reclaimed is earmarked for Vavachan (Achayan).

The saplings planted there began to bear fruit. The coconut saplings I planted were also there.

Everyone felt a great deal of mental anguish was left for that father, who had happily divided all his assets. Only one problem was left out. Everyone knew that. The stumbling block in his father's voice marked it. - Where will Ouseppachan live?

Ouseppachan was the only one who looked at the future emptiness with sadness and fear. My father was also sad when he saw that. To comfort him, Grandpa approached and asked, "Ouseppachan, what are you doing?"

Every member of his family has two or three children. Can anyone tell who should live with whom? Today, there is no such thing as a nostalgic joint family. There are only nuclear families.

The silence lasted for four or five minutes. A heavenly force is needed for a peaceful consensus decision. Like the most critical moments of prayer, we await the unique moments of divine realization.

Any rare moment when the God who gives us everything asks for something in return from us. Humanitarians - those who know brotherly love - wait for the intercession of the holy spirit. A rare moment when the Almighty appears in any form!

When I looked at Achayan's face, I saw that spirit. The language of Achayan's heart is the language of emotion that radiates from his face. Words are hard to come out due to emotions and sentiment.

Then he walked straight to his son and held out both his hands. Unsure of what Achayan was going to do, the son stared blankly. Is this the moment for which he brought me here with him? I could hear the answer-

"Without asking you, I make a decision. May you forgive me".

Separating his son's hands steadily, Achayan turned and walked away and approached his father.

Some words came out of Achayan's eyes, nose, or lips. The spirit has no light, no sound or language. But this is what everyone understood -

"Give the place that Achayan gave me to Kochayan. Kochayan, I can do this much! Kochayan, stay after building a house there! "

That is brotherly love, the ideal life of Achayan. Nothing happened, as seen in some dramas or movies. Nobody expressed their thanks or words of dissent. Everyone happily departed.

A fortnight later, when I went to the Kannattumadom house and saw Grandpa and Grandma, I went to Perappan's new house. I drank the black coffee Peramma had lovingly given me and saw the flowering coconut trees. I returned to the home at Maramkunnil to share my grandparents' welfare with my parents.

Achayan asked-

"Did you know why I did so on that day?"

I keenly listened.

"If you love your brother, you must love him while he is alive, or you will have to grieve it later. You are my children; there will be no shortage for you because of this."

Finally in their own house

Achayan and Ammachi's daily routine with the Manorama newspaper

11. TRIBULATIONS AND HAPPINESS

Achayan came back from Kottayam very late at night. He did not get up even after waking up early. He also had a fever and was trembling all over his body.

I heard my mother telling Ouseppachan.

"He went to the Manorama office in Kottayam yesterday morning. The boat landed on the 'Six hundred Para' wing on the riverside. It was past midnight. He walked up to the CMS church and, through the uninhabited Madathiparambil, came here and called me. When I opened the door, it was like he was petrified. He got scared and saw something terrible. "

"Take care of that church. I've seen it, too, like the fire walking without touching the ground."

In the evening, the rashes appeared like sand all over his body. Ouseppachan came again and saw.

"It's not sand; it's like gravel. It's the bigger one. It's perilous. It's better to move him quickly."

"It's not the measles fever. It's smallpox," Perappan said in a low voice.

"Isn't this the public footpath right in front of your house? Avoid contact with people."

Achayan was taken in a boat to Kannattumadom. The MMR (measles, mumps, and rubella) vaccine is currently being given to children, and it is unlikely that Achayan was given that vaccine at his younger age. This pandemic takes two weeks to recover without special treatment if there are no complications like pneumonia. But since it is spread through the air, isolation is mandatory.

It is just like the current Coronavirus. Many patients die suddenly. There is no natural cure. The vaccines are all in the research phase.

Some friends, in turn, took over newspaper distribution. They went by boat. Palathittachira Mathamma used to help Achayan distribute newspapers for a long time.

Achayan stayed in the south room of the Kannattumadom for two weeks - on the south side of the room where the pathayam (grain storage silo) was sitting - 'Pathayam Thangi' stayed there for two weeks! We sought information daily but did not allow anyone to go and see Achayan in person. When he finally washed himself, he saw that his whole body was covered with gravel, black spots like the peeled outer shell of black gram. Grandpa always served boiling water with neem leaves, cooling and bathing him. Achayan was exhausted. He was growing a beard and moustache. Anyway, there were not many scars on his face.

Thuruthichira Appachan and Valyathara Appachan came to see Achayan, who returned after smallpox and a bath. He was taking a rest at home without rowing to Ambalapuzha every morning. Thuruthichira Appachan was a local leader then but had no other job. Sometimes, a pack of cards helped to keep Achayan conversing. It did not happen like that for many days. My mother used to prepare tea or coffee and sometimes lunch for everyone who came at lunchtime. I have heard under her breath about the difficulty of treating guests properly and the problem of preparing and serving them together with Achayan. Achayan did not give much attention to the limitations of the routine nature of the villages.

And then there were no more playing cards and conversations. There was another reason for this change. A few days ago, behind Chavelithara Madhavan's house, there used to be groups playing cards with stakes. Madhavan and a few other people were indulging in that. As I walked through watching it - a high school student named myself looked on curiously for some time - to find out the unique attraction of these playing cards. Achayan saw that. He called me. Poovarasu stick was in Achayan's hand when he entered the house. Below the knees, the high school student got three beatings on his legs. "Why divert your attention when you have enough to study and work? No more watching… okay?" "No, no."

The usual quota was two beatings. The place was correct. The number was wrong. Why? Mother reminded him of that and did not say it in many words, just the logic alone. "Why did you beat your son that day? If you hadn't beaten him, he would have joined you to play cards at home."

That was how the card games at home ceased.

"The younger ones learn by watching, the older ones. They must set a good example. My children should not do such deviant activities without reading, studying, or doing anything useful at home."

"Is there still no decrease in the number of kusruti? Don't you want to know that even when you grow big? Will you treat your teacher as if he is your teammate? I did get the news. What did you say to Pappachan Sir?"

The day the school closed for the mid-summer vacation after the ninth-grade examination. Pappachan Sir, the high school principal, was seen in the back of the church as I forgot everything about school and went out with my friends. I walked Straight up to him and wished him. He smiled.

"Two months' vacation, eat well, come back a little stronger," Sir advised affectionately. Instead, with a false laugh, I, too, gave a piece of advice to Pappachan Sir-

"Sir, please make your moustache a little longer, bigger, and curly to keep lemons on both ends ..." Like the moustache of Sreekandan

Nair, the RSP leader, it was so famous then. That's what suddenly flashed in my mind.

"Eda - you... I will give it to you. "Sir did not laugh. With one look, my whole body trembled. I turned, ran away, and hid.

That's the news. Achayan has come to know of it.

Achayan said - "That third beating was for that prank."

Babu will play with Sabukuttan in Puthuval- the reclaimed land at Maramkunnil. Leelamma walked around, played, and often cried with her mother - she was only four years old. It was a little tricky for the mother to lift the baby girl and walk, and it was even difficult for her to lie down.

One afternoon, as soon as Achayan came from Ambalappuzha, he said -

"You go home and call Ammachi and Achayan and come quickly."

Didn't ask the reason. The water dried up, and the paddy field was prepared for new cultivation. The information was told as Achayan wanted me to convey it. The grandpa must have understood. Wasn't that what he immediately asked me-

"Mone, go and call Sarasan's mother. Tell her to come quickly. Just tell her that she was needed."

Ran to the place. I saw Sarasan's mother and spoke. Sarasan's mother was a well-known midwife, just like Bhadran's mother. Sarasan and his mother lived on the north side of the house in a banana field across the river.

"Mone, go ahead. Here I come."

As soon as the mother said this, she came along quickly. Ayurveda says they regularly provide postpartum care and assistance, unlike hospital nurses. That is the goodness of the countryside.

"Girl child is three years old, so it must be a boy," she said.

Everyone waited until the evening. Sarasan's mother and some other women were in the labour room. At night, I spread a mat on the verandah and slept with my grandpa, and the high school student fell asleep fast.

In the morning, the grandpa himself woke up his grandson.

The grandma gave a baby to the grandpa. A baby wrapped in a white blanket cried, "Nga, Nga ...!". There was a smile on Grandma's face. Amma shook her head, and the golden 'kunukku' on her upper ear lobes also synced. She tried to stop the baby from crying.

The grandpa touched the honey in which the gold ring was rubbed and put it in the baby's mouth. The baby stopped crying, stuck out its tongue, and licked the honey with good taste.

"Look, you have a brother too, so touch and give honey to him too."

I touched the honey and gave it. The slender baby with soft skin responded equally without thoroughly opening the eyes.

In his accounts book, Achayan wrote in the middle notes on the inside of the cardboard cover:-

Serial number 4. Raju - was born on June 14, 1960.

On top of that, there were already three names in three different lines.

Three years later, Achayan added another name to the same book. That day, I was studying at SD College and waiting for the results after the pre-university exam.

Serial number 5. Babychan - was born on July 14, 1963.

The above events, beginning with "As soon as Achayan came from Ambalappuzha in the afternoon," were repeated for twelve hours- The father, the grandmother, Sarasan's mother, and it is dawn; the grandpa wakes me up and gives the baby a touch of gold with the honey.

That must be why Babychan and Raju walked together and played like twins most days. When they grew up together—they studied in school and college and got employment in the same government department.

Was it so the college student in that house was looking after his affairs and comforts during these years? What guidance or assistance service have I provided to my younger siblings? Why were such things not remembered and written here? Suppose the service provider does not recognize it. Do the receivers of such services remember anything and any factual matter deserving special mention? What is the benefit of growing up together and sleeping under the same roof? Otherwise, how does a human being nurture brotherly relations?

I remember wrapping my siblings' school books in comfortably sized white newsprint paper and labelling them before the school re-opens in two or three years. What else is brotherly love?

The two to three years just before and after my parents raised the two siblings in the family were, in many ways, a remarkable period in my life.

It was my final year at Champakulam School. The year-end public examination was the school's final in the eleventh standard. The studies of the subjects were considerable. Youth Festival was conducted for three days at school. There were various art and literary competitions. Sports competitions were held separately. The competitors were of different age groups, as the classes for students were different. I watched all the sports but did not participate because I was short and physically not built for "faster, higher, and stronger" achievements in the competitions. I did not participate in any art shows either. I wanted to join literary competitions in essay writing and short story writing. My interest in reading library books and periodicals helped. There was a poetry recitation and an *Aksharaslokam* competition. Gopalakrishnan was a classmate and friend. He used to memorize a lot of poems. The hymn begins with the first letter of the third line of the verse recited by one person, and similarly, the next one recites another hymn. Gopalakrishnan was encouraged to compete in the recitation, and I was to listen to it carefully. Today, Mankombu Gopalakrishnan is a well-known writer and film lyricist.

While writing the essay and the story, I remembered how little I had read in the library books and periodicals.

Joy Meppuram wrote as he came prepared for a story and ready to join the writing competition. All my friends were invited to read. The story's first line begins with, "Slowly the clouds in the sky were moving like cotton wool..." I remember, and it remained in my mind.

The theme of the story writing competition was- 'An educated person experiences difficulties and ultimately succeeds.'

When we got the subject for the storytelling competition, Joy Meppuram and many others left the classroom without writing the story. Only eight of us were left behind.

I spent a few minutes thinking about what story to write and how to write it.

Kochuppappan came to my mind as the first educated person. Kochuppappan, who went to college for the first time from Kannattumadom and graduated in science, was the Alappuzha representative of the Deepika newspaper and oversaw the administration of the Punnapra Polytechnic College. He was popularly known as Antony sir. But when I thought about the story,

I did not know much about the hardships he experienced before starting a career. Besides, after marriage, he was successful in his job.

Does one experience difficulty in getting married? Will success come after passing through the difficulties? What are those difficulties? If you do not know the problems and challenges one passes through, how can one be happy, and what is so great about success? And how can I write about it without direct or indirect knowledge?

The educated person who came to mind next was Kuriachan. Little has been heard of the sufferings of that person while seeking a job. Now that he has succeeded and got a job, he has relocated to the capital. Let me expand on the theme and write as much as possible!

For the first time, I started writing a story.

"It was a moonlit night. Some clouds were moving slowly across the sky like cotton wool. Chacko and Mammikunju were without sleep, walked around in the yard, and spent the night thinking about what to do in the morning.

Their son was learning the lessons the hard way. He was interested in learning and was taught the hard way by providing minimum facilities and bearing the expenses. The boy had a creditable pass in his final exams.

Now, getting a job has become possible, but far away in Assam, with the help of a philanthropist. You must board a train and travel for three days to get there. (I may re-write the story later.)

When the result of the story writing competition was announced, the first prize went to the story '*That Kuriachan Went to Assam.*' I received an award for the school anniversary- It was a literature review book by Ullattil Govindankutty. A famous writer, a special guest at the School Anniversary, gave the award. Thomas Sir, who taught me Malayalam in high school, congratulated me profusely. Achayan told everyone he met that his son had won a prize in story writing. Although he wrote a story in the competition, Keeppada Joy received no awards. Joy kept on telling everyone, without reading my story -

"What he wrote was not a story, but an event that happened somewhere."

I was reminded of an article by S. Krishnan Nair, "Children, you learn to lie." It's a good story if you can tell a lie properly. The lie arises in

the imagination. The way the story is told attracts people and makes the lie believable.

Thomas Sir taught me Malayalam in high school. English was taught by Joseph Sir Arathil, Mathematics by Mathew Sir, and Varkey Sir taught Hindi. Pappachan Sir was the Head Master. Every teacher taught very well. They have worked on an excellent success percentage. The students tried their best to grow into good citizens with talents. Thomas Sir's Malayalam verse recitation and grammatical commentaries inspired me to develop my love for the language and read more. Hindi, English, Mathematics, and Science were my favourite subjects. They expected me to be at least first-class in the school's final exam as I got high marks in almost all the subjects. As a high school student, I was convinced that only hard work and reasonable efforts would help me meet my expectations.

I tried sincerely. It was the mathematics exam on the last day. I couldn't do as well as expected. Something rang in my head as I was writing the answers to the mathematics exam in the afternoon. I was similarly scared in the Malayalam exam. No matter how well you write the grammar, literature, and verse commentary in Malayalam, the marks will be reduced if the teacher who evaluates them is unsatisfied. That was the fear. No matter how much you learn to read and write, you must register with specific ingredients to satisfy the evaluating teacher and nurture the writing. Are these ingredients called Guru's blessings? Isn't that the constant prayer and blessings of parents? Indeed, I had that. Still, what else?

I remember going home after all the exams, lying on Achayan's bed, eating nothing, and not hearing anyone's call. I woke up the following day after ten o'clock.

The boys in the Balajanasakhyam all grew up. In Nanatt Thundiyil, the head ball grew into volleyball. We organized retail pocket money and bought balls and a net. Bamboo poles were laid by digging and tying the net and drawing the length and width of the volleyball court. Every day from 4 pm, we had a volleyball game; friends arrived on time. We used to play volleyball until the dusk hour.

My mother's savings box was sometimes helpful in organizing pocket money. When I bothered Ammachi for pocket money, she would tell me -

"Break the bamboo and take what you need. Please give me the rest. If we get some fish tomorrow, I can give it to Kunjachan."

The mother knew the compounding effect of saving money better than anyone by keeping small amounts in the savings box.

Mother's Retail Savings Box was unique. Our kitchen walls were made of bamboo and coconut palm leaves. Below one of the bamboo pole nodes there, she made a slit longitudinally, a short length and width adequate for a coin to enter. Usually, nobody will notice it. Once you push a coin through the slit inside, it cannot be taken back. Small savings are deposited when convenient. The funds deposited over a period rested in the internode stem cavity above the bottom node of the bamboo. After a while, when there is such a critical need to break the bamboo and recover the coins - the bamboo is broken, the savings will be counted, and the demands will be partially met. Again, a split below the node of another bamboo will form a savings box to save money for another feast!

12. SCHOOL RESULTS

On May 25, 1962, SSLC results would usually be declared, and the winners' register numbers would be published in the newspaper. The name will appear on the school noticeboard later. When Achayan left for Ambalapuzha, he put his son's number in Jubba's pocket. He will look for the registration number in the newspaper after the newspaper bundle is dropped off the bus on the road. If you have seen the number, you know you have passed.

Early in the morning, I went to Chellappan Nair's shop, where he runs a tea shop at the western end of the holy-cross churchyard. Mathamma would be coming in the canoe with the newspapers. I was eagerly looking at the stream to the west. Chellappan Nair asked me to have a hot cup of tea as I had arrived earlier than usual to pick up the newspaper. While waiting for the opening of future studies, not even hot tea can usually warm the heart inside or make it beat. So, politely declined- "No, Nair uncle."

Mathamma came, pushing the oar forward and throwing the water backward. He saw me. The call came - "You have won. It is first-class for you".

I also got a package of chocolates that day and the newspaper bundle for distribution. Achayan had bought it from Ambalappuzha and sent it along.

All the subscribers got a chocolate toffee with the Manorama, Deepika, or Kaumudi newspaper. Even before reading the headline in the newspaper, everyone understood the main news - "You have won. Oh! First-class, brilliant. God bless you."

60% pass rate was there at Champakulam school. Only two first classes were there. The weekdays were filled with celebrations, certificate collection, etc.

Achayan was happy to tell everyone that his son had become eligible for a college education. The statement was adequate evidence for a satisfactory and proud accomplishment of such a great thing.

After distributing newspapers, collecting subscriptions, going to the bank, and paying the bills, Achayan returned in the canoe at about 2 p.m. The son's job is to fasten the canoe by attaching it by rope to the shore, park it, and carry the paddle. My mother would be in a hurry to serve him lunch.

When he had finished washing his hands and face and started eating food, Achayan would tell many jokes, among other things, in the passing.

"Today, there are three or four types of curry - chilli chutney, chilli squeezed, and chilli cut into three, chilli fried." Mother would listen carefully and then smile,

"On the way, why did you not buy and bring something to cook the curry?

I did not go fishing with a net. I had no time either. When you leave in the morning, how can I remind you? Okay, then you have this amount. Did you ever give me an amount and tell me to manage to buy fish or meat? You don't do that. Tomorrow, I will make aviyal (a mixture of vegetables) or Sambar, using various chilli. Is it okay?"

After a pause, she will reiterate. I must give Rs. 4 to Kunju Pillai's shop. I forgot the day I saw a fish vendor selling fish. She will keep saying something or other. By that time, Achayan would have finished his lunch.

Why did they find happiness in those situations they found themselves in? Has the glorification of poverty become a habit? Or was all this self-limiting patience anticipating a better, prosperous tomorrow?

Achayan would finish his meal, wash his hands, pick up the newspaper, and read in the canvas chair until four. What kind of stories of life struggle to tell and not to tell! Where you come from, where you go, where you look back, if you want to do something right in life, such a look is essential to yourself. No one is a little kid to tell and make him understand! Let our children also know the paths we have traversed and our struggles.

How calm were Achayan's mind and body when sitting on the armchair reading the editorial in the newspaper? He will sit until it's time to go to the reading room. Occasionally, he had a short nap.

Achayan was busy with newspaper distribution, social activities, library activities, and political thinking and participation.

My mother got ready and went to church on a Sunday morning. Achayan went to Ambalappuzha in the morning. It is customary for Achayan to come and attend the second Mass on Sundays at the holy-cross church. The children usually went to the second Mass since they had to attend catechism classes after the second Mass.

"Leelamma and Rajukuttan are sleeping. You keep a watch ."

When my mother went to the church, she told me and left. She added before leaving - "When Achayan returns, he has to go to a meeting in the afternoon. Jubba is washed, dried, and kept ready for ironing. If you can…."

Achayan has two or three Jubba, and that too was Khadi. Recently, he only wore Khadi. Dhoti and Jubba should be of the same colour, white. If one is a little bluish, if the dhoti is a little dull, it is difficult for Achayan. He hesitates to wear it.

Kunjukuttan of Kanjipadam was the regular-special tailor for Achayan. Whenever he brought the khadi cloth for stitching, he used to say,

"It is easy to sew two Jubba together, from 5 yards long cloth, without cutting into two pieces, and if you cut into two, some cloth will be lost. It isn't easy to sew a Jubba from two and a half yards. It will become small sometimes."

It was rare for Achayan to sew two Jubba together. You will have to buy two dhotis, which will be difficult due to the lack of funds. That's what my mother used to wash his dhoti and Jubba every day.

A cast-iron charcoal iron box with a wooden handle must be hot. We were having one. It was necessary to search for coconut shells all over the house, burn them to make charcoal, and put them in the box without extinguishing the fire. Spread one or two blankets or dhoti on the table, spread the Jubba on top of it, and put it straight and press, adding heat to the cloth. (Searching a synonym for the iron box, I got to eBay describing the exact antique piece for £56.25!). That was when Babu got ready to go to church. The shirt he was wearing with sleeves looked fully wrinkled on the back and everywhere on the shirt.

"Give me the shirt, and I will iron it and remove all the wrinkles."

Babu did not remove his shirt; he stood and looked at me. Time was short. My thoughts went haywire. Even if the shirt is not stretched out on the table and you put it on, the wrinkles can be smoothened without removing it!

Babu ran screaming, "Ayyo!" And the box fell! The idiot did not realize what he did.

When he took off his shirt, the skin on Babu's back was slightly burnt and was shining red. He stopped crying when I poured a little water and felt terrible. Babu went to church wearing a crumpled shirt.

When Ammachi returned from church, I recited a line of a poem from G's Perunthachan, which I learned in school.

'ഊർന്നു കൈയറിയാതെ, യറിയാതെയാണുളി'

(I do not know, do not know, how the chisel fell!)

What's that? Isn't it an act that has no justification? Can you escape by saying it is stupidity? It is excellent mischief! It has come close to smelling violence!

"Didn't you burn my baby's skin, you devil incarnate!" Ammachi sighed and whined.

When Achayan came - " Haven't you abandoned your mischiefs yet – How do you say you are a college student?"

It was afternoon. In any case, kusruti - or the indiscreet - did not get a beating. Was it because I was a college student?

Babu was a simpleton, and he was always like that. He never quarrelled with me or had any ill-feeling towards me. He was pious and very obedient.

After my mother went to church on Sundays, Babu and Leelamma regularly visited the verandah. They recited church songs and old Christian hymns. A long bath towel hanging behind the shoulder was tied in front of the neck. He sang the hymns with a book in his hand - must be Syriac - I don't know what they sang. The priest's style, rhythm, and rituals were repeated. Leelamma was kneeling behind and praying. She would put another towel or some small cloth on her head and make a kavani as Ammachi does in the church.

Raju was crawling and playing all around or not yet woken up.

The rituals continued for some time. Their Kochayan gazed there for a time, sometimes getting angry, arguing, disputing, and wrangling, pretending he was not there. And so, it went on.

"Hello, Mr Oommen Mathew. Can you iron out my shirt, too?"

Parayanattuthara Chackochayan, six and a half feet tall, was another older adult laughed and called out my name loudly. The name is after a contemporary local leader who looked like me and was known as Oommen Mathew. The incident was already known to many. No matter how unusual an event may be in any home, no matter how small, in the small village, in the community, the word is spread out fast and transparent, and everyone comes to know of it quickly as if the countryside west wind passes all over in an instant.

Meanwhile, Chackochayan once saved the kusruti from being beaten up by the local revolutionary youth. They were not the ones who had become the guardians of the environment, though.

13. VILLAGE LIFE

The ideal season for rearing fish and prawns in the rice fields of Kuttanad appears to be March to October. Kuttanad was rich in fish, prawns, and carp at that time.

There is no special fish cultivation in rivers, streams, lakes, and irrigated ponds. Fishing gear with nets, hooks, and baits was everywhere. Vayalattuthara Kuttappan, Chennatt Kuttappan, Appayi, and Outhakutty worked day and night to collect the food resources from the water. They are exported abroad and traded to companies' agents that help earn the foreign exchange. It was the way of life of most youth during the breaks when there was no farming. Native fish were unavailable in the countryside, and the price went up. Another resource, the frog, was then identified as an aquatic amphibian that lives on land and in the water and can earn foreign exchange.

At night, two young men set out to catch frogs, carrying torches, petromaxes, and torches for lighting. It quickly grew into a foreign exchange earning method. A significant doubt arose for young people even after a few days. We eat prawns and Karimeen with a taste of good curry and roast. So should the foreigners, too. They use a little tiny chilli, spices, and oil, though. But how will they eat this frog? None of the natives has cooked a frog. Is it fish or meat? If it is meat, it can be cooked like chicken or duck. Or you can add spices and fry in oil. Who knows? Who will cook? How to eat?

Two adventurous young men met in a house for a night. Two or three other close friends were also present. The frogs they got that day were prepared for cooking. Someone must have acquired technical knowledge and culinary skills from somewhere. It was another adventure for those who were watching. They climbed onto a nearby coconut tree. They located the earthenware pot, which was tilted and kept to fill the toddy from the coconut flower blossom, prepared by cutting the bloom. It was lifted, unbroken, and brought down without spilling toddy from the pot.

The flesh of frog legs is one of the favourite foods of foreigners. The Jews forbade the eating of such unclean amphibians. However, frogs, high in protein, omega-3 fatty acids, and vitamin A, are cooked in French cuisine in Thailand, Vietnam, Indonesia, France, Spain, and South America. It is eaten desirably with good taste.

It must have been the first time some of the compatriots in our village had cooked and eaten frog in a way they knew. Good toddy was poured into a glass and drank, accompanied by laughter and jokes!

The game's duration might have been extended a little more, or the torches (dry palm leaves tied up and fired for light) walking on the village walkways without touching the ground might have overheard the peals of laughter.

How could many folks in the village know when the sunlight came about these environmental atrocities done at night and in secret?

I was not a Jew but did not have the opportunity for adventure and, therefore, did not join. The slightly younger college student dared not partake in the night adventure. It did not matter. It was seen only as a good joke. But since it was a special event, there was a particular need to share the joy and celebrate. The innate spirit of adventure - or the craft itself - resurfaced, though someone may mark it as a mischief. The next day, the village folks saw some posters on the coconut timber and the sidewalls of the provision shop. Caricature records of amphibians, cooking, pottery, and environmental conservation slogans were there.

The frogs marched under one flag and chanted slogans calling for protection on another poster! The performance of the ordinary people in the country is very similar!

In the afternoon, a small group appeared in front of the provision shop. People were in three groups - pros and cons- without joining. The words of some were sharp and violated the boundaries of decency. It was easy for the opponents to trace the poster's origin, as the signs were on blank newsprint paper.

After deciding to give two beatings, looking around for the accused, someone raised his hand. And that was when Chacko Chettan stepped in. He called upon the accused to -"Runaway quick!"

Indeed, it was not a ground-breaking contribution to the genre!

Breaking wrong impressions is sometimes with its straightforward tough-guy style. Who knew it wouldn't continue tomorrow?

"It doesn't matter what the arguments are. The villagers have their own rules and regulations! If politely presented, it may see the light of the day."

After paddy cultivation, a breach is made on the bund of the field, and water is allowed to enter the area and remain there until the next cultivation season. At that time, a small canoe had to be used to get to the houses in the middle of the field. The water will wet the chest and neck if you want to walk with the dhoti loosened. Water in the area is helpful for paddles through the waterlogged paddy field to get to the passage to the river, avoid the curves of the stream, and swim a short distance. When Achayan returned from Ambalapuzha on some days, he would tie the canoe near the south bank of the Maramkunnil site and walk home through the courtyard.

On a Monday morning, Achayan was about to leave for Ambalappuzha when he went to the south bank of the Maramkunnil site and saw the canoe missing. There was hardly any wind or rain the previous night. Could the canoe have been untied, and the wind blew it away? The paddle was not visible at its usual place. But could someone in need get on the canoe at night and go to some island house in the middle of the field? Neighbours, householders, and passers-by knew a little and walked away.

The small canoe was missing. An hour later, someone walking by the Chira (straight plane land) from the east said -

"The canoe is on the east bank. The oar is within the boat." Achayan walked to the eastern end of the Chira, got into the canoe, and went to Ambalapuzha.

Among the villagers who assembled to exchange village talks and news in the evenings on the verandah of the closed shopping complex, some young people who went to catch frogs at night were also there. On Sunday night, when they returned with a few frogs in a bag, they saw a middle-aged man, looking like Kuttiyasan, walking in the waist-high water in the middle of the Kavilpadam behind Maramkunnil. Kuttiyasan's features were unique even in the dim light of the torch! No one asked Kuttiyasan where he went at midnight!

He distributed 250-300 newspapers, each with a monthly subscription of five or six rupees. Every month, it was expected that at least half of the arrears would be received in addition to the regular monthly subscription. After deducting the commission's travel, fare, and distribution expenses, the income from the newspaper distribution became very meagre without getting the arrears and monthly subscriptions as expected.

Libraries waited to receive the annual grants, and the farmers waited for the harvest. The officials waited to get their salary and DA arrears, no matter how trivial. Who else reads the newspaper daily? The newspaper owners were not ready to wait. They were sending reminders every alternate day.

Suppose the bill - issued by those who print the newspaper daily and deliver it is not paid to the bank on the due date. In that case, the newspaper bundle will be blocked, and the daily work will be disrupted. Either way, this business exercise, which has always been the same, the walk on the tight ropes - continued to be on edge for years. It was also found to be only a temporary solution. Therefore, it must have been that he had no formal training for any other occupation or did not have the mind and health to return to the work he had previously done. Achayan continued his life and employment like tidal waves approaching land and suddenly rushing away and crashing back.

When the list of subscribers increased to four hundred or five hundred, at least some started asking for a monthly bill. This was because libraries and other public institutions, such as schools, needed to keep their accounts, demanding the bill. The bill amount will be paid monthly only after getting the statement. The bill copies were printed. Sometimes, I wrote the bill. When registering an account for those in arrears without paying the monthly subscription – I often asked Achayan why they did not pay the exact amount every month. Achayan must have heard many reasons from them. Sometimes, it was a delayed harvest, delayed library grants, or similar reasons they felt. The monthly subscription for the newspaper increased from two rupees to fifteen and twenty rupees over the years. (You know it was Rs.150 in 2012).

At the end of the month, Achayan would sometimes call me and make me sit in a chair on the side of the table to write the bill for newspaper subscriptions and other related publications.

If school holidays and the beginning of the month coincide, he will open the register of subscribers, and the bill book, carbon paper, and pen will be handed over to me and say -

"Sit here and write as I say." Write this so-and-so name, Manorama, Deepika, or Kerala Kaumudi, previous balance, this month's subscription, weekly, special publications, calendar, and diary. How much is the total?

When it's time to go to the library - "Enough for the day today, the rest for tomorrow."

The owners, especially the Manorama management, pushed the weekly and other periodic publications and the calendar to the agents to increase their monthly income.

Sometimes, the tenth grader was asked to help write and organize news and speeches by leaders and send them to the Manorama, especially during the holidays and Sundays. Achayan must have understood and not called me if I was in the study.

The monthly high school fee was six rupees, and we lived a miserable life. Yet, Achayan never told anyone about it. The rigours and hardships of paying Manorama's bill every month show the value of every rupee. How much money do you have due from the subscribers? If you get it all, this will not be a problem. But those who owe money do not pay on time. If you ask them, they may have several excuses, and if you intend to stop the newspaper supply, at least some complain - "Don't you trust me for such a meagre amount?"

Little drops of water make a mighty ocean. Perhaps they intentionally hide it.

Everything is going to happen. Hasn't it all happened so far?

I saw an advertisement in the Manorama daily for a clerical job in the State Bank of India. The minimum educational qualification required was SSLC. Work experience was not needed. Suppose you join, then six months of training followed by job stabilization. I thought It was a fantastic opportunity. I enthusiastically took the advertisement and showed it to Achayan. In this situation, I dreamed it would be an outstanding achievement if I could get a job now.

"Should I send the application? I will get it because I have my first class. If I get a job, then all these difficulties of ours ..."

Achayan gave the reply shortly afterwards.

"Difficulties ..? You don't have to think about it now. Learn as much as you can. There is no need to work and earn now. Learn to grow as much as possible, and that's enough."

It was a decision that would determine not only mine but also the future fate of a family.

The urge to apply for the job, which was soon available, cooled down.

When the desire for a bank's clerical job cools down, one decides to study more and get a better job. Even those who have passed the degree are less likely to get a good job nowadays.

Is there any other way to get a job quickly? A degree is being able to do any good job beyond the subject being studied, maturing for it, gaining the ability to recognize good and evil, work efficiently, and become a better citizen.

First, go to pre-university for one year, then any degree. If it is engineering, it is better. What about a four-year fee, hostel, where and when, and how can all this happen? If you get first-class, you may get a scholarship to study.

I wondered what to do, staring at the road without a clear goal.

Achayan went to Punnapra and met Anthonichan as he always did. He returned with a decision.

You may be able to join us for a study at SD College. Get good marks and pass the first class. It will be easier to study engineering after the pre-university class. That thought led Achayan to go to Punnapra from Ambalapuzha and return on his way home by canoe.

Thambichan also passed SSLC. He was also returning from Ambalappuzha with the idea of studying after meeting his maternal uncle.

Thommachi and Vavachi walked together. They tied the bull to the plough and carried the paddy on their shoulders during farm labour. The two families were almost identical. A slight difference was there now in their employment. Thommachi continued the same occupation for a few more days. Later, he started selling groceries. Vavachi, rowing in a small canoe, distributed the newspaper.

Come on, come on, get on the canoe. Are you going home?"

Thambichan boarded the small boat.

The eldest sons of Vavachi and Thomachi studied together and now passed SSLC together. They both have a lot in common. They are growing up together to support and shade the family—the birds of the same feathers.

"I am sending my son to SD College. What did Thomachi decide?" Thambichan said nothing. Did a few droplets of water fall into his eyes? It might have been thrown from the paddle while rowing. How can drops of water fall on both eyes at the same time?

The waves of distress do disperse when it is washed ashore. Slowly, the waves caress the shore and return. The beach will be relieved. On the way to the coasts, the small waves will scatter in tiny droplets of an obstacle, such as a small boat. It may even fall on the faces of those travelling in the canoe! It can't be wiped out. Even if it is not wiped out, isn't a bit of water providing relief in the summer heat?

Thambichan did not wipe his wet eyes. He just kept looking around.

The birds of the same feathers, let them grow together and fly. That is brotherly love or loving your neighbour. Achayan knew that more than anyone else.

"Tomorrow, you both go to SD College, buy the form and apply. Tell Thommachi that the joining fee is thirty-seven rupees. I will give that to you."

Achayan brought the canoe closer to the house.

Thambichan met his friend, who went ashore to tie the canoe and pick up the oar - He said: "Let's go to SD College together tomorrow morning,"

Both were happy. We both got admission to Pre-University at SD College.

Achayan said while sitting down to eat -

"I just told him that you won the school final examination, and immediately, I don't know why, the elderly soon took out a hundred rupee note and gave. Do you know it was Kavalackal Mathachan - Kurunnappan's father."?

"Let him study well." He spoke. "Yes, you must study well."

"However, when I told Kuriakose, it didn't seem necessary. As the schools re-opened, a rower on the stern of the egg trade boat was lined up with utensils and groceries, full of notebooks, pens, stationery, and school books."

He sat inside the Valapura boat. After taking out two forty-page notebooks in his hand, he stretched them out to me. I said, "No, you do keep it!"

"It does not matter. Some people are like that, and you aren't hostile towards them."

Achayan had moved to the armchair with the Manorama newspaper.

Kannattumadom Family

14. PRE-UNIVERSITY

It was the year the Eleventh Standard was abolished in the state. Kerala University would conduct a one-year course called Pre-University for that year only. After that, the door to a university degree or diploma in Commerce, engineering, or medicine will open. The decision to join SD College was based on that. The purpose was to receive a college education's benefits and prepare for an excellent career-oriented study. That's why I decided to study at the pre-university as an interim relief. I wanted to take Malayalam as my second subject and study language, literature, grammar, and verse. Thambichan chose Hindi as his second language.

The classes began. In the early days, student unions approached us to join them. There were always temptations and propaganda. There were a hundred pupils per class. Male and female students sat separately on either side of the same classroom. There were altogether different classes for students in the school.

There were some special classes in the college. The first thing that comes to mind is Dr Baliga's English classes and Poetry. Some of the synonyms he taught are still remembered. For being defeated – he says conquered, turned the table upon, frustrated, annihilated, exterminated, eliminated, obliterated, wiped out, overwhelmed, overthrew, routed, foiled, baffled, baulked, downfall. It goes like that.

Gopala Krishnan Sir's algebraic classes in which a, b, and c would be replaced by the fruit trees found in Kerala.

Instead of (a + b) 2 = a2 + 2ab + b2, he would read it as

(Chakka + Manga) 2 = Chakka 2 + 2 Chakka Manga + Manga 2; everyone will remember Gopalakrishnan, Sir. Proper Indianness, the study of vegetation mathematics, rural gurukul vidya + practice; Exercises.

I came across the names of the books studied in the Malayalam class that year: Panineeyam, Kavyams, A long list of Poems, and Book Reviews. Shocked. No matter how well educated you are or how well you write, read, or recite Malayalam, if there is no literature in writing or proper grammar, it won't be easy to get marks for Malayalam. With that awareness came the real trouble. The engineering dream will be far away if you do not get first-class marks and pass. Hindi is enough as a second language. Thambichan has selected Hindi. I had 66% marks in Hindi for SSLC. For Malayalam – I had 50 percent, 100/200. I should have chosen Hindi right from the beginning.

Fifty percent was applied, indicating the same reason and the second language was changed to Hindi. The poem by Sumitra Nandan Pant was enjoyable in the first class of a Hindi teacher.

My interest in the Malayalam language and literature has not diminished, and my only goal was to score good marks and pass the pre-university in first class.

Walked early to go to college, and when you reach the crossroads via Pulikkal, your friends will also cross the Pookaitha River. Koolippurakkal Vavachan was studying for the first-year Commerce. Koolippurakkal Thommachan, Puthenpurakkal Josekutty, Vithupurakkal Gopi, Thambichan ... and so on for the Pre-University. Walk through Mathurchira and Poonthuram. Catch a bus from the stop near Kalithattu near UP School Punnapra. It would be time for the classes when you reach.

On the way back, sometimes I was alone. On some days, the voyage was in a single-row small canoe while the water was in the field, and there was a breach on the ridge. You can take a small boat to Ahmed Yusuf's grocery store. I tied the canoe, kept the car in the shop, and walked to the bus stop. Sometimes, I went to Alappuzha to take the student's concession for the bus. That's how the journey started on my own.

A year of pre-university study at Sanatana Dharma College has given me many new experiences.

It was stipulated that all students should join the National Cadet Corps, the youth wing of the Indian Armed Forces. I had to wear Khaki pants, a grey shirt, a brassy two-inch-wide belt, leather boots to wear on the feet (not soft to call them shoes), and a cap with a red flower with a seal on the head. One could eat a single banana fruit or egg on parade days to relieve fatigue when walking left or right. You must take the NCC dress and boots in the small canoe, row up to Punnapra, carry them to the college, put them on in the evening, and prepare for the parade. How comforting it was to have it only once a week!

That year, the NCC camp was at UC College, Aluva. Participating in it was a good experience. I made a tent house and slept in it for one night. I walked from Aluva UC College, carrying all that kit bag, gun, water bottle, everything, and went to Kaladi to camp there for a night. After a night of sleep, walk back to Aluva UC College in the morning. We took plates and mugs from all the places we stayed, bought food, and sat down with our friends in the shade of trees and grass. The art and cultural events held on the last day of the camp, the campfire, were all new experiences. I wore pants and thick boots for the first time and walked with difficulty for so long. Then again, hiking and walking made me feel like it was good. Before the college exams, the dress and boots were returned, and clearance was obtained. The NCC's discipline, appearance, and experience were kept in mind. It was sure to be useful someday.

Before the year-end university exams, internal college examinations were held for all subjects every two to three months.

It was beneficial as an incentive to study subjects accurately and without arrears. As an incentive, an amount equal to a monthly fee was given to all those who got

good marks. Thambichan and I saw such encouragement as great financial aid. Tuition fees were paid only for the first two or three months. The incentive gift received later was paid as fees in the following months, and a receipt was obtained.

Gandhiji's companion, Vinoba Bhave, known for his social work and the Bhoodan movement, came to the college campus one day while passing through the National Highway NH-47. He spoke at a reception hosted by teachers and students. His sermon was in English. How gently and lovingly he had explained things!

Most of the classes conducted before the examination were for the final review of the subjects. There were also many free classes for self-study, or the instructors were otherwise busy. Everyone exchanged autographs—all young women and men. I wrote notes on the memory manuscript with love and mutual respect and added my name and signature.

Some even wrote addresses. The texts in the autograph were mainly selected literary language, a piece of poetry, a 'quote' from any great personality, or a good text that does not feel repetitive and boring. Although there were no apparent expressions of love, some lines revealed unassuming words of love in a few words. I could understand it from the eyes of the young woman who received and read the writing and responded by saying thank you. Although there is nothing hidden in the script, you can read it and understand the bashfulness in the eyes of the young man, who also replied with 'thank you, see you. As a first-year student at the university, I wrote on almost every autograph -

"Blessed are the pure in heart, for they shall see God."

I always felt like just writing that. I do not particularly remember anyone who made it an unforgettable moment. There is no certainty as to where the autograph is resting now.

"മേയ് ദിന മിരുപത്തിയേഴു നാം മറക്കില്ല,

പോയ് മറഞ്ഞിതു നമ്മൾക്കേറ്റവും പ്രിയപ്പെട്ടോൻ"

"We will not forget the twenty-seventh day of May. That was the day we lost our dearest (Jawaharlal Nehru)."

It is the poem of CP Chellappan Nair. The poems were written when Prime Minister Pandit Jawaharlal Nehru (27 May 1964) died. John F Kennedy was assassinated (on 22 November 1963) just less than six months ago. Kennedy and Nehru were our all-time favourites and the world's foremost leaders.

Ammachi had boiled paddy, dried it, packed it in a gunny bag, and loaded it onto our canoe. I paddled the canoe to the mill at the east end of Valayamchira. The mother was a little relieved as the technology advanced to have a machine for de-husking the paddy. Her son grew up taking the paddy to the rice huller (a process of removing the trash (the outer husks of rice grains) in the mill. On my way back, when I reached the front of the library, I heard many people listening to the radio news. I gave my ears for the information. The body of Jawaharlal Nehru has been brought to Delhi and placed for public viewing at the Theenmurthy Bhavan.

It was a big shock for me. My all-time favourite was Chacha Nehru, India's foremost leader who planned and implemented big projects for the growth of the industrial sector, which was doing everything for the progress of independent India. How many books has he written, like The Discovery of India? I received - the merit -cum -means scholarship - that Nehru had implemented at the beginning of that year when I joined the polytechnic. I had great respect for the government and Nehru for that reason alone.

When the sack of rice was brought home, the canoe was tied up, and I entered the house. It was like the sorrowful time someone got separated from the family. I told my mother the news about Nehru passing away by trying hard to stop crying. My mother also found it challenging.

At the condolence meetings organized by the United Public Library and the Vijnanaposhini Library, many laudable things were said and recorded about Nehru. These were condolence meetings organized by the library officials in the library yard in our village.

After I started college, I would wait for the holidays to find time for the children's club, book reading, and ball games. Most of the time, the task was possible. Palathittachira Kuttappan was always there to read books and give me company. We will visit the library and enjoy contemporary literary works, especially novels. Language and storylines became the talk of the town. However, I had read poetry since 'Nirapara,' I was not keen on poetry, which was not part of my studies. However, when CP Chellappan Nair wrote the poems and how they were recited, it made me somewhat interested in poetry. Thomas Sir's Malayalam verse recitation and grammar teaching style increased my interest in poetry. Poems, examples, and വൃത്താലങ്കാര ലക്ഷണങ്ങൾ etc. will always be remembered.

CP Chellappan Nair was a neighbour and a student of Malayalam up to the 7th standard during the 1950s. He survived poliomyelitis on his limbs at a young age. As a means of self-employment, he took up hand-rolling tendu leaves with tobacco to make Beedis and became a professional worker.

He made his little earnings from his black tea. He got some rice and curry from his sister's house when he was starving on some days.

"He wrote poems about 'natural beauty, 'manjeera shinjitham' (sound of foot trinket), and 'Kuttanad is like the portrait of an enchanted art,' etc. Sometimes, he would recite poems aloud. When he got

boredom from repeated beedi rolling, he stretched his hands. He straightened his head, singing "a song of sixpence with a pocket full of rye" loudly and repeatedly. That rye gave him physical relief as bread!

When the newspaper was in hand, he read the news very loudly. When the newspaper arrived at the grocery store, the stretched hands were of CP, sitting very near the grocery store, to which the newspaper was handed over. The shop owners and others saw it as an advantageous welcome move. Because CP reads all the essential news in the newspaper loudly and clearly. Thirty people quenched their thirst for hearing the information together. That must be why the newspaper was not subscribed by many shop owners nearby.

If there was dissatisfaction, boredom, or things he did not like, he adopted Madhavan's style of repeating the words in the same harsh tone, replacing the purity of language. So, in general, everyone, especially relatives, had a love-hate relationship with CP.

He was a differently-abled person and could do nothing except roll the beedis—his desire to publish the poems possible by the Balajanasakhyam through the manuscript magazine.

We published manuscript magazines during the college vacation. Puthenpurakkal Josekutty painted the cover picture. CP wrote poems. Kavalakkal Joy, Nanatt Pachu Pillai, and others wrote stories and articles. Edited, filled in the gaps with jokes, and published a fascinating manuscript. Three copies were made and distributed in the three libraries nearby. It was an excellent cultural and literary training initiative. It lasted for five or six months. Then, everyone was confined to the strings of their learning and life struggles.

My association with CP prompted me to try writing poetry during the holidays. It was launch time for Manuscript magazine during my first vacation in college. Sitting in the armchair of the house, I opened the window on the west side for the west wind, thought of poetry, and wrote a few rhythmic lines. That was the beginning.

After writing three or four poems, I corrected the mistakes and wanted to see them published. Where to publish? I have never seen such poems in Manorama or elsewhere. I came across a children's magazine - Poompatta, published in Thiruvananthapuram. I sent them the first poems and wrote to them -

"Wish to see it published."

Surprisingly, they published it the next month (The date is written at the bottom of the poem) with minor corrections and no significant changes.

A letter came with a parcel containing ten copies of that month's 'Poompatta.' I was delighted to see the poem published in that Poompatta magazine. I gave copies of the magazine to the libraries and some friends. Many friends said that the poem was nicely written. Later, I kept trying to write some more poetry; that way, I wrote eight or ten more poems. Almost everything was printed in Poompatta; copies came, and I distributed them. Such a spring was not repeated during my educational period. During the holidays, when I had to prioritise things like studying, reading, games, library activities, and homework, I could not find the time and patience to write. There was no time to nurture my interest in writing poetry and children's literature, or my focus somehow shifted away from them.

It was known that there existed a branch of literature called children's literature ('Balasahithyam') even before my writing (children's poems) 'Balakavitha' and I came to know the book 'Mayil Nammude Deshiya Pakshi' (Peafowl - Our National Bird) written by D

Balakrishna Kurup, my teacher in UP School, won the Kendra Sahitya Academy Children's Award.

In 1963, the peafowl was declared the national bird of India because of its rich religious and legendary involvement in Indian traditions. The peacock is a large and majestic bird, and it is a symbol of grace, joy, beauty, and love. A peacock is a colourful, swan-sized bird with a fan-shaped crest of feathers on its head, a white patch under the eye, and a long, slender neck.

I have written a letter of congratulations to Kurup Sir. I got his reply almost immediately.

"It's an example that democracy still prevails here, "he wrote.

Sarojini Naidu was a freedom fighter and a companion of Gandhiji who wrote many poems. "The Nightingale of India" is a book about her.

I read that as a supplementary book in English in high school.

I was fascinated by the book, translated it into Malayalam, and sent it to the children's literature competition – I worked on it for a month.

The result of the competition came with a letter indicating the opinion and observations of the judges while returning the manuscript with 72% marks. That was a great encouragement and stimulus for those wanting to write more in children's literature. Three more years - they were just passed without many literary activities.

After the death of Jawaharlal Nehru, the Times of India published 'Nehru in Pictures'. It was a collection of articles and photographs about Nehru from newspapers and magazines - I read them individually and decided to finish 'Kuttikalude Chacha,' the children's book. The intention was to introduce Jawaharlal Nehru to the children, adding as many events, contributions, personal influences, values, and character traits as possible.

It took more than two months to finish the draft. Sir, the first manuscript was given to DB Kurup to read and provide comments and suggestions. He gladly accepted it. A month later, I went and saw him and got back the manuscript. He mentioned to me -

"Well done. You may read more, add more events, expand here and there, and be good for publishing."

That manuscript should be available somewhere, with more events neither added nor expanded and not yet published — Balakrishna Kurup Sir also left this world.

One year of studies in the SD college was quickly over. The grade I got for the Pre-University was only the Second Class – just adequate for

admission to degree classes. I could join the degree class with Chemistry as the main subject and any other branch of science as the subordinate subject. Gopinathan took mathematics and was admitted to the degree course; he planned to go to Bombay. Thambichan also got second class. We started thinking about what next, and whatever it might be, we would not worry about paying hefty fees to study at a distant engineering college.

You must go to college, get a degree, and then find a job. It is not possible to confirm the degree in which branch of science. After studying Botany and Zoology, Anthonichan graduated and worked as a journalist for Deepika and Manorama dailies. He later became the office superintendent of the Polytechnic. What do botany and zoology have to do with such work? Then, learning is about gaining the courage to face life and the maturity to do any job. If it is not a vocational study, the job you get after the search would have nothing to do with the subjects you chose for your studies. Any job can be done if you gain that maturity.

We probed, analysed, and searched for possibilities and opportunities. What are our priorities and chances?

What were the available resources for that?

What are the barriers to a smooth transition?

It would be best to make some decisions to look forward to in life. As Achayan always did, he went to Punnapra and met Anthonichan. He was the one who always gave well-thought-out and correct guidance and suggested the most practical way of achieving the objectives.

He returned with a decision.

After three years of study in college, you may get a degree, but to get a job, you have to continue the struggle; it is not how long. Studying engineering at the Polytechnic gives you an advantage, and the best job you could get would be after three years of study there. Engineering jobs are in great demand those days, and your waiting time for getting an appointment will be hardly a few weeks. No hostel or outstation stay may be necessary. You could return home daily if you get the training at the Polytechnic where Anthonichan worked. All the pros and cons were done, with reasons and possibilities and all-out explorations for a happy life for myself and all my family members. Who else can do this for you other than your parents?

You will get a job soon after the diploma course because it is a technical course. Besides, the first class you obtained for the SSLC is enough for a merit admission there. It would also be a great help to get a scholarship there. Hence, It was decided accordingly.

"Go to Punnapra tomorrow and fill out the forms. Anthonichan will try to get you to Punnapra Polytechnic when he goes to Thiruvananthapuram."

I was happy and contented to foresee our way of life in the future with generally clean, one-lane long and winding country roads, even though it may not be with too many small and large industrial businesses and other businesses lined up on both sides and with six-lane streets everywhere.

Experience, outlook on life, sincerity, and optimism, which our parents shared and helped us decide, was God's will. The rest of our lives should be to fulfill God's will. That was my determination.

"I'm coming to the Polytechnic too - let's go together tomorrow." No matter who he consults, Thommachi is determined to accept what his sincere friend Vavachi has suggested. Haven't the two children studied together for so long? That is what is destined for us. Their parents think alike. The main reason for this was the minds' faith and the family bond's closeness and unity.

The spirit is the one who allows everyone to live and who causes everything to happen, and everyone worships the supreme being.

"Happy, Sebastian." We looked at each other and smiled.

"Sebastian? Isn't that Thambichan?"

"No." We are college students, so is it right to call our nicknames? I have decided not to call that nickname anymore in front of others.

It is the divine decision that we should walk together and that the path of life is the same for both of us!

The long, winding, one-way street will one day reach the highway!

Nothing seemed to have been missed during one year of pre-university study. What skills and ways could I see in that one year? All these are my gains: the effort, the satisfaction, and the optimistic faith that is not lost in difficulties and even failures.

Rowing in the waves, crossing streams and rivers, and walking along the small ridge of the vast paddy field and the large outer bund is a simple lesson of life's struggle. Little dreams come to mind, playful jokes with classmates and friends, causal analysis, etc., opened an excellent gateway to the world outside the home.

Under the nose, the first facial hair appeared to grow, and it formed a moustache. I never tried to uproot it. I did not try to blacken it further in any way. None of my friends commented on it. When I went out to play volleyball wearing only a sleeveless white cotton vest, I saw the masculinity that had developed a little on my chest – some jeeringly laughed. At least some of them touched the seventeen-year-old lovingly. Then it became a habit to wear a shirt whenever I went out!

Until then, I wore only white shirts in school and college. On Good Friday, during Holy Week, after my PUC exam, Achayan brought me a full-color blue shirt for the first time. That's what I wore when I went to church that day.

Before finishing high school, I went to Carmel College in Punnapra. Every year on the anniversary day there, I went to see the play performed by the students and staff members: Plays by Kainikkara Padmanabha Pillai, N Krishna Pillai, and TN Gopinathan Nair. The stage was set at one end of the unfinished Carmel workshop building, chairs were lined up in the large hall, people were invited, and the play was performed. My Kochuppappan (Anthonichan) took me to see the dramatisations. He was a well-known local playwright, social reformer, and founding leader of the library movement. When Kochuppappan was the Alappuzha correspondent for the dailies Deepika and Manorama, Gilbert Achen brought 'Antony Sir' from Alappuzha to Punnapra to establish Carmel College, later to run the college office. Until retirement, he served as the college administrator and assistant to Fr. Gilbert CMI.

On Carmel College's anniversary, I was fascinated by the automatic decoration of bulbs and lights at the front of the college, which depicted the college's emblem. I saw the same Carmel College Emblem hanging on a gold necklace around the neck of my Chittamma (Mrs Antony).

15. SERVICES, NEWS AND ARTICLES

Ettinchira Outhakutty chaired the meeting, and many people, including adults, small farmers, and those regularly coming to the library, attended. Outhakutty stated, "If we worked together, we could set up a hospital in our village. Everyone will benefit from it."

They formed a committee. People outside political ideologies and those interested in public affairs were added to the committee. The committee sought to influence and support from all, particularly the government. Ettinchira Outhakutty bought Nanatt Thundiyil ground for the Hospital, transferred it, and handed it over to the Government of Kerala. No one objected to our playing games there on the ground until the hospital building was built. A primary health centre began operating in the countryside within four or five years. Despite many limitations and difficulties, everyone was happy that the people's desire was approaching fulfillment. Achayan was an active member of the Hospital Establishment Committee.

Accusers of nepotism may say that Achayan prepared a place for his first grandson to be born on earth. Yet, no one would have had the patience to wait fifteen years to prove it. So, no one made any such accusation.

People overthrew the Communist government of EMS through the liberation struggle, and there was the President's rule for some time. Then

Pattom Thanu Pillai's coalition government came to power in Kerala. That was when the locals came forward with a demand for the Hospital. Later, there was the R Shankar ministry.

The Hospital started functioning during the President's rule after the R Shankar ministry was changed. The hospital backyard was used to play volleyball during my high school and college holidays during the evenings. The foundation for the building was laid on the court, and the stones and gravel for the construction were brought and stored there when the structures started.

Then, we relocated the court and continued the games in the backyard.

The Leo XIII Library in Champakulam hosted a volleyball tournament every year. Mallappally Sunny, Mathai, the famous player of the police team, was an excellent attraction for the match then as they used to come there to play. The crowd was controlled through passes for the semi-finals and the games' final. What a great volleyball game was played there! Achayan allowed me to take a pass and watch some of the volleyball games.

Teams from the surrounding wards were invited when we hosted a volleyball tournament during the Onam holidays. It was assumed that Vanchikal Kuttappan, Koolipurakkal Kochautha, Nanatt Pachu Pillai, and Maramkunnil Appachan benefitted from participating in the games. They all later joined the army. For some, like Joy and Chandappan, though they were interested in playing the games, agriculture and homemaking became everything in their life. Their elder brother Mammachan, who later took up contract jobs, was a good volleyball player. Parayanattuthara Kuttapayi, a ballplayer, later became a fish vendor. No one else has excelled in sports. Recently, it was learned that Kuttappayi's son had won a medal in the Asian Games in the rowing competition.

Kavalakkal Joy lived in one part of Nanatt's backyard after the rest of the land was given to the Hospital. He lived there for several years after getting married. He also wrote stories after engaging himself in farming during the season.

The number of Achayan's newspapers increased. People were always waiting for the daily newspaper to read, especially in the library. The polytechnic student was also assigned to distribute newspapers during the holidays.

Sometimes, he had to walk to Kanjipadam at seven in the morning. Then Mathamma would reach in the canoe with a bundle of newspapers. I would wait at Chellappan Nair's tea shop, take over a wad of newspapers, and walk away. Walk fast to deliver to most houses and libraries on the way. To give the newspaper across the ravine, I would roll it up, tie it up with ropes or threads, and throw it to the other side. If the tie-up broke or the newspaper fell into the water, it was a big mistake and caused embarrassment. Sometimes, the incident was reported to Achayan as a complaint that the subscriber got the paper in wet condition or was torn. Unfortunately, there were no rubber bands available in the shops those days. Every copy would have been rolled up and thrown to the subscribers to reach their doorsteps.

As the number of newspapers increased, so did the number of distributors. Someone was specially appointed for the Thakazhy area. Another to Ambalapuzha and Karumady area. Mathamma used to paddle the canoe through water up to North Thaicherry. The business strategy of the newspaper owners for growth was to diversify and publish various publications, such as the weekly edition, calendar, and diary, and mainly distribute them to the newspapers.

The public considered Achayan's comments and opinions, and most of them were generally acceptable. Even if Thuruthichira Appachan comes or Achayan walks around in the neighbourhood and talks to his Aliyan Varghese in Maramkunnil, the topic of conversation would be the national and political issues. Achayan used to participate in various public meetings held within the boundaries of the newspaper distribution. The intention was to attend all parties' conferences and write a report on the influential leaders' speeches. He sent the news to Manorama, Deepika, and Kaumudi.

Achayan gave an impassionate and patient hearing to various ideas and thoughts and understood different political ideologies and governance strategies. It was on one of those days that he determined that -

"I'll only wear khadi from now onwards and forever." He became a member of the Indian National Congress. Thus, as a public figure, librarian, social worker, reformer, and journalist, Achayan occupied many positions that were not so unimportant in some of the committees.

After P .T. Chacko's resignation, the rally held on the National Highway in front of the Carmel Polytechnic College got a big reception.

During R Shankar's rule, the divisions in the Kerala Congress began to manifest on a more communal basis. The Kerala Congress formed a great stir in the countryside following PT Chacko's resignation. The communist movements highlighted the Kerala land reform legislation and wage reforms. Christian groups expressed sympathy for the leadership of PT Chacko. While the SNDP claimed that R Shankar had run a flawless government and the Congress declared that the economic reforms had been successful, the cabinet was embroiled in some corruption allegations. R Shankar was forced to resign (1964) after the Kerala Congress passed a no-confidence motion (led by separatists led by PT Chacko). The ensuing election (1965) was a significant event in the country. I have never experienced such intense publicity and press coverage.

Only after that did I see the enthusiastic campaigning for the 1965 elections. Achayan thought of deviating from Congress and collaborating with the Kerala Congress and the agricultural capitalists at the instigation of the petty leaders of the Kerala Congress.

Achayan decided to consult his son, who showed interest in social work, the press, and the news media. At the end of a lengthy political debate, Achayan liked my quoting the lines from a leader article.

"The Kerala Congress is a separate entity from the Indian National Congress. So far, Congress has been plagued by inefficiency, dirt, and unwanted fat collected over time. It has been separated now for good. Congress has the legacy of the freedom struggle and Pandit Jawaharlal Nehru. Which Indian can replace it?"

The father must have been very proud of his son's national and political thoughts, who began college studies after school. He never highlighted anything in particular. He would sometimes tell his friends in the library, and those friends used to convey their congratulations when they met me.

When asked how they came to know all this - they said, "We discuss information from the newspapers and the newspaper distributors, which are good."

In that election, Aikkarachira Gopalan was a polling agent for the Communist Party and Achayan for the Congress at the Chempumpuram polling booth.

How many local houses did that practical thinker and college student go to, asking them to vote? Some people were curious to see that this little youth, who had not yet gotten the right to vote, was going from house to house, requesting everyone to vote. Adventure, the determination to achieve anything, even if it is impossible to achieve in full, began there.

I have sometimes wondered what motivated me to do so in that election. Adventure, political interest, the beginning of a response, or an objective glance into the future? That 1965 election was so determined and hard-fought.

Or was it gratitude to the central government, ruled by Jawaharlal Nehru, granting a scholarship of Rs 600 per year to study at the

Polytechnic for three years? Partially yes, one merit cum means scholarship. Thambichan only got a loan scholarship, which he has to repay after employment. Not because of that; Thambichan was not as active in politics as I did. The entire tuition fee of the college could be paid from it.

Anyway, after the election, everything was calm and peaceful. Neither party won a majority in that election, and no one ruled. The elected ones did not even get a chance to take the oath of office! President's rule was imposed again in the state.

Those who agreed to vote said they voted but counterargued, "What happened now?" And everybody laughed. The political ambitions of the youth also simmered down.

The 'Thozhilali' daily was also launched, and an agency was registered in Champakulam. Kuttappan, Manorama's agent and Kuttanad representative, became the coordinator and worked well from Champakulam.

Kuttappan met Achayan and asked him to write an article for the 'Thozhilali.' Achayan asked me to write an essay. I wrote a report on the plight of the people of Kuttanad who were facing various hardships under the heading 'Kuttanad Woes' - the increase in water hyacinth that obstructed waterways in rivers and streams, the plight of the people who did not have access to safe drinking water, illnesses, the distance that students have to travel for access to higher education, and the shortage of bridges, the bumpy, muddy sidewalks, the situation where students have to swim across to cut through the breaches in the ridges, not to mention the difficulties of elders in particular. The article invited attention from politicians and authorities to bring forth improvements. There was still a need for more pieces of public interest. Achayan wrote and published more news and articles, all of which were published.

Kuttanad has been known for not having a drop of clean drinking water even when there was a flood and when the river and ravines were depleted due to low rainfall in summer. African algae and water hyacinths thrive in stagnant waters. It was challenging to move the boats or even row the Canoe. Achayan was often asked to write an article that brought together such difficulties and opened the eyes of the political and social leaders who wanted welfare and development. We wrote the news and articles. It was about half a page when printed in the Thozhilali newspaper. Kuttappan also said that the article was fine and wanted more pieces of the kind.

In the following month, I wrote an article about Albert Einstein. I read and learned a lot of information from various sources. It was sent to Deepika and published in the weekend edition. The editor's request also came: "I am hoping for more such good articles."

During my last vacation at the polytechnic, I wrote an article entitled "The Power of the People" about 'democracy' growing worldwide, especially in India, which is about my age. When it was published in the Deepika weekend edition, it was realized that if one reads a lot more, one can write a little, and from the knowledge gained from reading, new thoughts will emerge. They will satisfy the mind to some extent.

Manorama sometimes allowed up to 10 rupees for an inch news column. Achayan used to get retail income by sending local information about political meetings, social issues, or festivals.

Kuriachan, who studied civil engineering, got a job in the railways, and went to Assam, was on vacation for the first time. It was an excellent opportunity for family and friends to rejoice. From the letters that came home, everyone knew some difficulties getting to work and the work done there.

Unable to eat properly, he constantly struggled with the weather and the terrain. He was fatigued, probably because he was in the woods surveying for the NEFA Railways.

But the joy on his face, the smile, the enthusiasm, and the sincerity with which he did everything were incredible. When asked if I was studying for a diploma in engineering at the polytechnic, I did not immediately respond. He reaffirmed that the ultimate fate of all engineering studies would be to live and work in such remote areas and under unfavourable conditions.

He took his unemployed younger brother Kuttappan to Assam on his way back from vacation. Kuttappan was doing nothing after SSLC. Kuriachan's elder brother, Thommikunju, had passed the Hindi Vidwan examination and was trying to get a job. Kuttappan's elder sister Kunjamma Chechi also joined her mother at home after her high school education. Lillykutty, Kuttappan's younger sister, joined St. Joseph's College Alappuzha after SSLC and continued her studies. She lived with Elayamma (mother's younger sister) at Kottaparambil, Thathampally. Thommachan and Aniyappan remained in school at Champakulam.

Among those close to my age in Kannattumadom, Kunjamma stopped studying and did retail farming. Animma and Kunjachan (Dominic) continued to study. They lived in Kannattumadom.

Joychan was in Champakulam High School. Celinamma, Sicily, and Mathukutty were in the lower classes at the school.

Maramkunnil Appachan was studying at SB College, Changanassery. Thommikunju did not want to learn further after SSLC from high school. We worked together in children's clubs and library activities. Once, when I was working as the secretary of the children's club, for some trivial matter - it seemed that the children's club had lost a notebook - I said it was a lie, or something went wrong. Then Thommikunju became silent with me over a word that went wrong. I, too, did not speak to him later.

Can anyone imagine how many years have passed without a look, a word, or even a smile, walking together on the road or coming face to face? From 1963 to 1975 -12 years. Peers and relatives, we were living in the immediate vicinity. I was solely responsible for the silence for about 12 years due to my youthful ignorance or arrogance. Lillykutty of Maramkunnil was also in conversation with me. She always had that charming smile on her face. At least she would speak two words. Lillykutty of Kavalackal and Lillykutty of Maramkunnil were my favourite sisters of my age, like Kunjamma of Kannattumadom and Elsamma of Anjiliparambil.

They were the ones who gave consolation to me due to the absence of a direct sister, a playmate of the same age I had always missed. Leelamma is ten years younger than me! Kunjamma, Thankamma, and Lucy of Maramkunnil were also 10 - 12 years younger than me.

I often regretted that I did not have an older brother. That thought first occurred when Kuttappan Chettan left for his heavenly abode. Then Kuriachan filled up the gap. Kuriachan also went home for work far away and never became a replacement. That's why I always thought every chance to meet Kuriachan was a time of great pleasure and enjoyment. Until this time around, though, there were other seniors for me.

If I had any misdeeds in school, someone might wonder where it all went when I came to college.

Leaving the way of children's poetry, my daily routine continued with attempts at articles, reading in the library, and engaging in children's clubs and volleyball games. When the pre-university exam results came out after the holidays, I had no purpose for life ahead, not knowing which way to go - to the library, newspaper distribution, or news writing.

When I went to SD College and obtained a pre-university certificate cum marks list, I realized why my life had turned a corner. I got good marks in English, Hindi, and other science subjects except biology, which was expected. I got only twenty-seven marks out of fifty for the Biology Examination- Botany and Zoology. Even after the zoology exam, I was in good faith to get twenty-five marks as I had answered nearly perfectly. Biology was well studied. The common questions also came up for the exams. Botany learning, teaching and assimilation, and exam preparation were all not good.

Puthenpurakkal Josekutty later obtained a Master's degree in Botany. Even before the pre-university era, we knew the botanical name of the rice that gives us food - Oryza sativa - as Josekutty told me. And since all four-legged creatures know about botany plants, it is enough to ask why I alone did not study. For Botany, I should have gotten two marks out of twenty-five, which is the usual mercy of any evaluator for inking the answer paper. If I had studied to get another seventeen marks, I would have gotten first-class in the pre-university and been admitted to an engineering degree without any extra cost. That's what life is all about. I did not know what to do.

The marks I got in Botany may be the reason for my indifference toward paddy cultivation. But it seemed more genuine when Achayan later discovered that his farming had led to more losses and borrowing.

16. NEW CIRCUMSTANCES AND LESSONS

Before joining the Polytechnic, I could see the college, its surroundings, and its workshops. There was an annual day function at the end of the first year of college. I saw the play "Two and Two Make Five," in which Kochuppappan performed. The college's emblem was designed by Kochuppappan, who received the prize at the annual day function - a gold locket of one sovereign. Like a pendant for Chittamma's long chain, that locket looked like a proclamation of great honour for her husband and like the turban of pride for a while.

By then, Kochuppappan had stopped working as a journalist at Alappuzha and devoted his entire time to establishing and operating the Polytechnic with Fr. Gilbert CMI.

Before the lathe and drilling machines were installed, the annual ceremony and the plays took place inside the completed workshop building.

When the first year of my diploma classes began, the building complex and offices had new classrooms, new friends, and a new atmosphere. Antony Sir's brother's eldest son lacked self-confidence and support in college. Another uncle also taught English there - AP Kuriakosesee. He was previously a professor at some other college. After settling in Punnapra, he joined the nearby Carmel College and continued his profession.

Before the college re-opened, Grandpa took his grandson to his son's (Anthonichan's) home in Punnapra to stay there and study. Kochuppappan or Achayan must have told about the difficulties of walking in inclement weather, rowing in a small canoe, and getting to the college daily as he did the previous year.

At Kochuppappan's house, Babychan and Mammachan went to school. Molamma was a girl child then. Chittamma was very proud of her job as a school teacher. And she was proud of her family. She was the eldest daughter of Fr. Gregory Kalluparambil. One of the less fortunate grandmothers from home for the aged, attached to the Punnapra Church, was engaged in retail chores, often accompanied by an elderly grandpa from the same home. Anthonichan and his family lived in a large, newly built house on the south side of the church and a white sand field, maidan, on the east side of the house. Across the road to the north of the house, there was a cashew plantation to the church's south side. The church can be reached by walking through the garden corridor. The vicar of the church at that time was Father Sebastian Narakatra. There was a holy mass every day at 6 a.m.

"Go for the mass whenever you get time," said my grandpa.

A small bag brought two or three shirts and dhotis from home.

"When there's no class, go home on Saturdays, wash the clothes, and return to class on Monday morning."

Four or five Para (Para = approx. 8 kg) of paddy was boiled, dried, and de-husked in the mill, and my mother sent it with me in a gunny bag.

"If you go with a free hand, how would Marykutty feel? For the time being, we can send something more next time."

I was carrying rice in a cardboard box prepared by my mother in the small Canoe, and I was wearing the same new blue shirt that Achayan had bought when travelling to Punnapra with my grandpa. Leelamma and Raju stood at the fence and the ghat, respectively, in front of our house.

My mother carried Babychan on her shoulder, came along bidding farewell with tears in her eyes, and encouraged the naughty one to be brave and true.

Since then, the thought that their Kochayan will not be there most of the time to sleep with them or that an adult is leaving home searching for his way of life. When will he be able to return? - What was the meaning of the silence there at that moment? Hope and hope alone were on everyone's faces.

When the Canoe was untied, and the oar was pulled into the water, the water splashed out, and I do not know exactly how it fell into both eyes.

First-year classes started at the Polytechnic. Most of my classmates were from outside the Alappuzha district. More than half of the students stayed in hostels. Regarding all Kerala selections, it was possible to get admission to several colleges in the state, irrespective of where you desired your entry. Chittappan briefly mentioned his efforts to get Sebastian and me access to our chosen college. Since that year, one priest and two friars (brothers) from the early mendicant orders of the Carmelite congregation have joined to study for a diploma in Engineering. Rev. Fr. James was a known priest. He was the younger brother-in-law of Chekkidikkad Elayamma (mother's younger sister). The Brothers were Stephen and Abraham. It was a delight to meet Fr. James. The number of relatives increased in college. Carmelite's father and brothers used the backbench and desk. I was always at the forefront of the class due to my short height.

Kuriakosesee Sir and Mathai Sir were pleased to see me sitting in the front.

Sebastian and Pothakutty came from Muttar and stayed in the hostels, Isaac, Chandrasekharan Nair from Thiruvananthapuram, Sasidharan, Paulose, Vijayappan, and many others, we all became very close.

When I first accessed the Polytechnic, I went to Alappuzha and got new pants stitched. Since wearing pants and shoes for practicals in survey and workshop classes was compulsory, the necessary clothes were purchased and given to Murphy Tailors in Alappuzha. Muppathinkalam Appachan provided the instrument box and T-square to draw me. Appachan studied at the Polytechnic that year, passed the examination, and got a job in the PWD department. So I did not have to buy a new instrument box or T-square. AC Parkinson also obtained engineering drawings from him.

As soon as the grandfather left his grandson with his son in Punnapra and returned home, Chittappan, the head of the household, gave me the training to live away from the hamlet and at his house in Punnapra. Drawing water from the well and collecting water in the bathroom was shown. As a routine hobby, I only needed to water the newly planted coconut saplings, mango trees, and small flowering plants in the backyard. "If only the elderly person from home for older adults had not come, then only you need to do that. "

From the first days, I realized that morning was always a commotion in homes where both parents go to work and drop their children off at school. If a young person in the group needs to get to college on time, everyone will be busy and find a shortage of time. Breakfast should be prepared and served to everyone. The housewife should pack her lunch and get on the bus to school after managing everything in the morning at home.

I was beginning to understand the new world and the living conditions there.

Chittamma has struggled a lot. Before Kochuppappan went to college in the morning, a glass of hot milk and an egg diluted in it was enough as breakfast for him. The boys needed something to eat for breakfast. Even if everyone returns from school and college in the evening, Kochuppappan will not return until late evening. Gilbert Achen gave him multiple assignments in the office.

At the end of the first week of polytechnic studies, I took my small bag and walked home on Friday evening. Before dusk, you must cross the river by ferry, cross the bridge, and go around the temple to reach home. I arrived home just after dusk hours. Achayan had gone to the library. Babu and Raju came to the verandah after their routine games.

I heard it when I woke up on a Sunday morning. The CMS church in the backyard behind Vayalattuthara caught fire!

Achayan had gone there. Going to the back of the house and looking west, we could see fire and smoke coming from the top of the stone-built church. No one had come to church because the fire occurred early in the morning. Despite the efforts of those who arrived, not a single girder was left on the roof without burning, and the whole top was burnt down. All the wooden windows and doors were blazed.

The next day, with the cooperation of the locals, it was decided to renovate and rebuild the CMS church. They elected Achayan (Vavachi) as the head of the church restoration committee. Achayan was already popular in the socio-cultural arena, ran to help in times of disaster for reclamation, and was responsible. It took about a month to raise a good amount of money with the help of the locals. It was possible to renovate the church in about a month and continue the prayers there.

From the village of Kuttanad to the college at Punnapra, there was no motor vehicle facility for about ten kilometres. In Kuttanad, there were no roads even suitable for cycling then. I never had the opportunity to ride a bicycle. I did not even wear sandals at home or travel elsewhere. The only thing not desirable on the sidewalks of Kuttanad pathways was the soft, moist mud, which may spread onto the clothes or legs. It can be washed before entering any building. Isn't it even harder to walk in soil or water wearing pants? I could walk with sandals, but Newton's third law of motion might have painted pictures on the back of my shirt with mud sprinkles.

So, I rowed alone in the small canoe, crossed the ravine and the river, and reached the narrow canyon ending at the village road in Punnapra. I tied the canoe to the dock, dressed in pants and shoes in the nearby Abdul Qadir (Ekka) grocery store, and walked to the college. Sitting and paddling in the small canoe with my pants and shoes on was complicated, which was the reason.

I returned to the shop on my way back, changed my clothes, got into the canoe, and rowed home. On days when there were workshops or survey classes, wearing pants and shoes to college was mandatory as part of safety instructions. Not only that, but Mathai Sir insisted more than anyone else that the shirt must be tucked into the pants when worn. When working in a machine shop, it is best to avoid loose-fitting clothing to ensure safety. Also, wear only shoes that cover the entire foot. In the last 55 years, I have never worn pants without the shirt tucked in, even for a day. Similarly, wearing a shirt, a full-sleeved shirt, and shoes that always cover the whole foot when going to work and out of the house are mandatory. That was the habit that Carmel nurtured in me.

When I started training with NCC in the evenings after college, it became even more challenging to walk to college with other coloured trousers, a belt, heavy boots, and a cap and travel in a small canoe.

17. FEVER DURING THE ONAM SEASON

It was a two-week vacation during the first Onam period of the Polytechnic study. I have participated in all the usual boat races-boat races organized by libraries, then at Thaicherry ghat and Pookaitha river. Regardless of the rain or the cold, I soaked wet, sang, and rowed in the boat. One day, when I woke up in the morning, I felt swelling and pain, and walking was not easy.

"After soaking in the water, walking, and remaining cold for so long... Do you have any idea that you are the one who is going to college?" – Mother rebuked me.

I saw a doctor, K. K. Nair, at his residence in Parappalli, north of Pulikkalkavu. I brought the medicines he prescribed. Thambichan's father ran a grocery store in front of the Parappalli house.

"No fever. It will go away in two days. If it doesn't go away, you must go to Alappuzha or Pathirappally," said the doctor. The swelling and leg pain did not subside on the third day, and the fever appeared again. Kochuppappan took me to Shankar Ram's Hospital at Pathirappally. It has been only four or five months since my grandpa was discharged from there.

Shankar Ram checked me up. His son, who returned after studying abroad, also checked me up.

"Admission is required. Further testing and monitoring are required, after which only the treatment may be prescribed."

For the first time, a night was spent in a hospital room without knowing what was happening. Subsequently, medications were taken, and the date and time were recorded on a graph. Arrangements were made to deliver food from the canteen.

Achayan, Kochuppappan, and a person deputed by Kochuppappan used to see me regularly. Thus, a week has passed.

The fever subsided. The swelling and pain in the legs subsided so much that I could walk.

The hospital bills have already been paid three times. Achayan paid the third bill and saw the doctor, hoping to get me discharged.

"The discharge must be given anyway. If it goes like this, a number of classes will be lost." Achayan did not mention any other difficulties.

The doctor said calmly, "Don't worry, it's better to leave after some more treatment. Look, if it were my son, I would tell him to take bed rest all the time – He may have leg cramps or paralysis at any time - I cannot say anything beyond that. - It's Rheumatoid Arthritis!"

Achayan left, saying he would come back the next day. He must have gone to Punnapra to consult with Anthonichan. Did Anthonichan repeat the doctor's opinion? Loss of educational classes, prolonged hospital stays, and the cost of treatment should all be considered before deciding.

Achayan came on the following evening.

"Let's go home. Take what we need in a bag – the medicines and your dress." Achayan did not say whether he saw the doctor or not. I forgot all the fatigue in the joy of going home, and I went home with Achayan and reached home by nightfall.

There were also medications for two to three days more. After finishing them, I went to Punnapra. Not many classes were missed.

The next day, Kochuppappan took me to a doctor consultant at the Medical College hospital in Alappuzha, realizing that my illness was not completely cured. After going through the results of the tests and the amount of medication taken, the doctor asked me-

"Where do you study?"

I answered. The doctor prescribed the medicine-

"Folveron folic acid, 1tsp x 30 days. No problem, nothing to worry about. Go and study well."

The doctor was smiling when he told us.

Three or four days ago, what thoughts went through Achayan's and Anthonichan's minds?

When there are concerns about their children's health, will it allow the parents to be at peace and get them to sleep? Would the extended stay and treatment at Pathirappally Hospital have caused significant financial and psychological hardships? Did the doctor who treated Grandpa to cure his heart disease succumb to other pressures, thoughts, or temptations?

What a high risk it was when everyone said, "Come on, let's go home"? Yet the loved ones themselves thought of the potential danger. They were willing to face it and bravely mitigated the risks quickly. Today, that hurricane has changed its course.

Isn't it a blessing to make such vital decisions in life?

Such decisions are made of God's love and affection for his children. Isn't that love? Isn't it because I have so much that I can write this now?

When I became active in my studies again, I forgot about the illness. I went to college regularly and studied various subjects with as much attention as possible. Looking for a professional course, like a diploma in engineering, was not like learning in a pre-university class. I collaborated closely with everyone in the class and did all the practicals together. In addition to improving the knowledge about the subjects by reading, asking, and listening, it has been possible to increase collaboration among the individuals and develop a collaborative working style of teamwork.

The first year of the Polytechnic was a period of significant international and national events and attention. In the United States, John F. Kennedy became the President, Jawaharlal Nehru became the Prime Minister of India, and Dr S Radhakrishnan became the President of India. Kennedy's speech at the United Nations General Assembly was the subject of much debate. G Partha Sarathy led the Indian delegation at the UN.

UN Day was celebrated worldwide, and a UN mock assembly was held at the Polytechnic. Two academic year-wise students represented different countries and spoke in the General Assembly. I was commissioned to portray India as G Parthasarathy. It was a speech in English explaining the international issues of the time and India's stand and approach to them. AP Kuriakosesee Sir helped me write the majority of the portions of the speech. Taking the opportunity to address a large congregation of students, I could climb one or two steps of love and affection in the minds of my collegemates. I have spoken in English for about ten minutes.

There was another specialty for that day. I tied a black tie around my neck in front of a white shirt and wore a blazer outside for the first time while dressed up as G Partha Sarathy in the UN General Assembly.

I wore the blazer only while making the speech. Thambichan also wore a tie as part of his clothing. He did not have a blazer to put on. So, I removed my blazer when we took a photo in front of the college yard. Thambichan took a picture of his friend standing with the same camera. Both should be in the album.

Sebastian and I, who grew up together in the same village and attended the same school and class, always had a healthy rivalry. Both of us passed the C certificate examination in the NCC.

The 38th International Eucharistic Congress was held in Bombay that same year, and Pope Paul VI came to Bombay. The Eucharistic Congress was a big event and festival for Indian Catholics. The Eucharistic Congress was celebrated mainly in Carmel because it was a Catholic institution. There was a conference where many dignitaries from the church and other Catholic organizations participated. I had the opportunity to speak on behalf of the students at that conference. AP Kuriakose Sir wrote speeches in English for me again. I wrote an article in a book published as a memoir of the Eucharistic Congress. Its preparation gave me more joy and excitement as it summarized the articles and reports published in many publications in English and Malayalam, including the Deepika, which I have read. The speech summarised my paper during the conference and spoke on "The True Presence of Christ in the Eucharist."

During the first year of study at the Polytechnic, I could not continue to stay at Kochuppappan's house in Punnapra for more than six months. Minor inconveniences to Chittamma forced me to shift from there. Babychan and Mammachan did not pay much attention to their studies, thus causing several disturbances, more discussions, noise, accusations, and mutual blame.

"You came here. Who are you to create discord here in my house? Why did you bring him here? " Chittamma started shouting.

Without making any changes in the written weekly resource provision information list, she declared that-

"All this is only possible in my house," she reiterated.

"Why do you love him so much that you do not have that much to my children?" That was the question to her husband. And she

was shaking whatever she got in her hand, be it a teaspoon, a big wooden spoon, or a pitchfork - holding up something in her left hand, gnashing her teeth, saying something loud, with obvious disgust.

"Reduce your sound. If someone heard you, what a shame," Kochuppappan always tried to appease her. But the melee or orchestra continued unabated for most of the days.

It was a late evening when I was ironing my shirt—Chittamma was walking back and forth in the room, angry, shouting, and blaming someone.

Perhaps she thought that I should pay attention, but she said something in general, a statement I did not like at all, as it was annoying and hurting-

"Why are you not reacting to what I say? Don't you have the sense to obey and respect me? Even after listening to what I say?"

"How can I respect you? Should I be bowing down and making the obeisance like this to acknowledge your superiority and importance? Or should I pretend like the king, with both hands on my right knee and pride...."

"Eda, you ... Have you grown up to that ."?

Dhoti was the dress while acting out as above, and it was folded halfway. It was not usual to wear an undergarment when you were at home. It was not intentional.

"Did you grow up to insult me like this? Just get out now. Out now and go down. You get out of here." She kept shouting in a crazy loud voice, slapping me on the shoulder and back, and hitting me until I came through the front door.

I cried a lot.

Bavichan and Mammachan laughed at me and were amused, pointing their hands towards me and shouting, "Come on, that is what you deserve, come on, that is what you deserve. "

Poor kids, what do they know?

Weeping, I stepped down, crossed the fence, stepped onto the dusty soil, walked east, and sat down in the corner of the sand spread field, where the beach sand had been piled up.

The moans had almost subsided into silent cries.

The laughing light of the day faded into the evening dusk. The darkness of grief was beginning to thicken all around.

What's gone wrong with me? What's wrong with me? So much to rebuke me, be blamed and beaten, and ask me to get out?

It was pitch dark all around, with a bit of light on the roadside and in the market at a distance.

Leaning my head on the heap of sand, my thoughts went astray: what would I do, where would I go, whom would I share my agony with, and what would happen to me tomorrow? Thinking like that, I got exhausted - tired of losing everything, sighing from time to time-

Someone was waking me up by shaking my shoulder. Kochuppappan was standing in front of me when I was looking at him.

"Come on, get up ..." It was not evident in the dim light of dawn what kindness or mercy was on that face.

When I stood up and looked straight ahead, I realized there was no accusation or anger on that face. Or was it the sympathy of helplessness?

It was too cold. I touched my face, nose, and ears to feel. It was cold.

Nothing was said. I followed Kochuppappan and returned to the house from where I had driven out yesterday. Didn't see anyone. No one had woken up. Kochuppappan poured out a glass of water from the jug on the table. I drank it as a glass of cold water and felt blissful as I was too thirsty.

There was a feeling of a significant burden on my mind and head. I went to sleep as I felt like I had a fever all over my body and did not go to college.

In the evening, Kochuppappan came back from college and asked me -

"Pack your bag and books, take them, and come with me ..."

I packed my shirts and books, put them on my left shoulder, with books in my left hand, and walked with the T-square cross in my right hand. I walked behind Kochuppappan. As we walked along the National Highway after the church and the college, I realized the long walk was to the Carmel Hostel.

"Take your cross and follow me," I remember reading that verse.

I went straight to Fr. Gilbert Achen's room.

Achen looked at Kochuppappan and returned a smile.

"There's a false sign I can see by looking at him!"

I got a bed and table in a room in the hostel. One of the other two beds was of Chandrasekharan Nair (a native ofThiruvananthapuram), and the other was Paul from Paravur, who was both a classmate.

We had dinner with friends in the hostel. Many friends were happy to see me in the hostel. In the atmosphere of a new learning life, in the excitement, in the presence of classmates, without overthinking about the past days or worrying about them, I found satisfaction in the unique circumstances that were allowed.

The way to a good goal could be narrow and difficult. Let me stroll carefully.

When I went home for the weekend and put on the information, no one said anything. My grandfather had the last word and the most emotional response.

"Poor Anthonichan !"

Does not everyone have the guidance and consolation of an adult in their journey from adolescence to youth? Do they ever think what they got was adequate? Aren't they suffering internally for family peace, harmony, and cooperation? Are they not forgiving? If you believe small sacrifices can bring significant benefits, why use the occasion for temporary gains and relief? If the mind is ready to obey anything, isn't it better to say and understand the right thing? Is it right to reprimand, punish, and allow the mental peace of the partner to be disturbed? Who is responsible? Is it a measure of age, education, selfishness, power, strength, or helplessness? Shouldn't everyone want a personality that can improve daily with correction and continual improvement? Who doesn't need correction, progress, and advancement? What doesn't need it?

18. THE TRIBULATIONS

Hostel life was good for studying. All students were encouraged to cultivate non-academic aptitudes for success in life and obtain good marks in exams. I occasionally won prizes in the college and the hostel in the English and Malayalam speech competitions. I learned to play caroms. I learned to appreciate the artistic talents of others. Isaac's singing, Sasidharan's paintings, and Thomas Cherian, popularly known as Lakshmi, played basketball games very well. And many others like Easo, who excelled in sports.

Sebastian of Muttar was always there to exchange good words and share excellent behaviour and information. He was compassionate and cordial.

Before the start of study time, the song "Kanna, Karumei Niram Kanna, Unnai Kanathe Kannillayo" from Paravur Theatre used to come through the window panes of the hostel as waves. Though the song has no place in my mind, I used to remember the brother watching me in the eyes and smiling always. I used to call him the devotee of Tamil whenever I heard the song.

I remember Chandrappan, James Kutty, and Thomas Mathew, who were very popular in the hostel for mischief and ragging.

Every day, I could attend the Holy Mass in the chapel of the hostel. Breakfast, lunch, and dinner were just a few things I enjoyed more at home than at the hostel. Likes and dislikes must be thrown somewhere along the National Highway. Laughter and commotion prevailed in the common hall after dinner. Quiet study in the room was compulsory afterward. Sleeping at 11 o'clock, waking up, and repeating the same routine the next day was the norm.

The first-year scholarship was awarded seven months after the first-year classes began. The signed amount was handed over to Achayan when I went home. That made Achayan very happy. When he returned from Ambalapuzha, he brought me a flat HMT wristwatch in golden colour. I started using a watch ever since.

Brother Stephen was very close and loving during our class breaks and in college. Sebastian and Fr. James were close. The unique features that Stephen saw in me were studying well, a particular interest in the class teachers, and being the son of Antony sir's elder brother. Stephen mentioned getting the scholarship as a specialty, which he appreciated. Stephen, who came to study technology with a proclaimed ascetic and frugal lifestyle, took my hand, looked at the lines on my hand, and predicted that my future was bright. He took my home address, wrote to the Goethe Institute in Germany, and obtained some books in German.

"Learn German. Germany offers a lot of opportunities for technical education and jobs." All too often, Stephen and I were seen together by classmates and a handful of teachers, some of whom were keenly watching.

Stephen would talk at length about any subject - academic or extracurricular, local politics, or the story of any book that he has read. He was very talkative. He was among those who boasted a lot and said that he was a great thinker and seeker of knowledge.

The UN Mock Assembly and the Eucharistic Congress celebrations allowed us to interact more closely. Somewhere in the conversations came the situations at home, the last few days at Antony Sir's house, and the case leading up to my reaching the hostel.

Stephen's closeness to me was like that of a close relative who deserved sympathy beyond being a classmate. Someone has vainly imagined that there is something immoral hidden in such a normal friendship. Or why did fate lead me to a great trial and extreme mental torture?

Did all the authorities join together to convict an innocent person? What for? Who was to be blamed?

Truth-seeking is good. Without warning, the pursuit of truth began at a completely unexpected moment.

The call came after the dinner at the hostel with friends gathered in the common hall, and the laughter and commotions were not over.

"Someone is standing outside at the hostel door to see you. Go there," said a hostel friend.

When I went there and looked, it was Kochuppappan and someone else. When I saw his face and expressions, I thought some tragic event had happened at home, and he had come to take me away. Who, what, for whom, what happened at home?

"You come here ..." I walked ten steps from the door of the dim-lighted hostel to the National Highway, following Kochuppappan.

My Kochuppappan turned to me to say something and held me close. And then he grabbed me by the neck! It was a great shock. I was speechless.

"Amme!" I shouted - the sound never came out again. He caught hold of me tight and wrapped my shirt's collar around my neck to choke me. I was being lifted. My legs were not touching the ground. I went out of breath. I tried to catch my breath somehow and let go of the grip.

"What's the relationship between you and Stephen?"

Even in the dim light, I saw the eyes of Kochuppappan opening wide and glowing red.

My neck got relaxed. My legs were grounded. I was comfortable and calm. That is all? The answer was trivial and straightforward.

"Relationship? fondness, friendship"

"Is this a friendship? Didn't you tarnish the family's reputation - I don't want to see you. Go away."

I did not understand anything. I was surprised. The darkness of the surroundings caught my eye. I was pushed into deep darkness as I saw my Kochuppappan and his companion walking by. I stood there for a while, looking at the side of the highway. The repeated sighs subsided.

What wrong did I do? What wrong did Stephen do?

I am not a stupid adolescent girl to do something wrong and tarnish the image of my family. I am not engaged in an unholy relationship with anyone. I did nothing to spoil the manifestation of my family by losing my innocence. I do not remember a word or deed that offended me, nor did I ever offend anyone with such criticism. Am I too pretentious or naughty to live with anyone, anywhere? To have no friends? How? What is the reason? What justice is this? What kind of world is this?

Chittamma kicked me out of their house. "Brought me here to stay, and you are also kicking me out from here so soon ...Why? "

Kochuppappan says - "Go away. I don't want to see you..."

Where will I go? Leaving home for vocational study, going back without anything, shattering all the dreams and without a job - why live with a 'disgrace to the family? How do I look at other people's faces? What was the humiliation?

What wrong did I do? Or what duty did I not do? What responsibility did I not complete?

I looked at the stars. I sometimes opened my hands, pointing towards the heavens like Ammachi did, and sighed, "Can you tell me.... something, please?"

I remembered what my mother often said - "Mone, your star is the star of Lord Krishna. Mone, you might hear many accusations ...! You can often be misunderstood and blamed."

Today was Good Friday in 2020. It was in the message given by the parish priest in the church. People commonly misunderstand endurance when others blame you, such as Jesus suffered. Many are trivial and could be easily corrected. Others, however, are disappointed, especially when all attempts to remove them are in vain.

Why do misconceptions arise? Certain behaviours and habits can lead to misunderstandings. What can I do if others misunderstand me? Now, does what others think of me matter to me?

Instead of reacting logically to specific situations, you may respond emotionally. What was said or done sometimes has different meanings than what was intended. It certainly makes sense when you feel that your intentions have been misunderstood.

Friends need not see or know of anything. It is purely personal.

I wiped my eyes and face, went to my hostel room, got on the bed, and lay covered with the blanket. I waited for sleep, rested well, and woke up for a new morning.

I would not have slept the whole night if I had committed any sin.

The next day, after the classes, I got a call to go to Kuzhiveli Sir's office.

Mathew M. Kuzhivelil - Retired from the Army and ran the NCC unit. He was a serious person and an exemplary teacher in implementing discipline. Kuzhivelil Sir was loyal and obedient to Fr. Gilbert and the Principal. He was also a close friend of my Kochuppappan.

What disgrace did I do to my family by joining NCC? What is the relationship between NCC and Stephen?

What are all these temptations? What is the depth of helplessness?

The door of the Kuzhively Sir's office closed behind me. No one was outside to see me entering the room. Everyone had gone after college hours. Kochuppappan would have been there in the office upstairs. Kuzhively gave me a chair at his office desk, politely welcomed me, and made me sit on it. The status of my mind was calm. He slowly got into the matter-

"Honest, correct answers, if given precisely, I can help you and save you from the embarrassment."

A hundred questions followed. Each one was answered honestly. The intensity of questioning increased. They caused an increase in my blood pressure. The muscles in the body were weakened. My blood became hot, and each word was with a sigh, groan, or whine.

My tears flowed profusely as the questions were false allegations or accusations far from the truth. There was nothing to hide or conceal. Yet, there were accusations of selfishness, enmity, and jealousy attributed to the questions. "I do not know what happened," I said. Again, a hundred questions. If anything was left in the mind or heart, it was washed out and sifted through the questions. Some questions appeared to be nudity, immorality, and the venom of accusation. I did not know what such a word was then.

I can write this today. It was not just immorality that was blamed on me.

The devilish masculine form of homosexuality, with its ugly face, may have been worn by him, or he has partnered for gay sex with someone without realizing the seriousness of such thoughtless stupidity! I was accused of cooperating with such a person, which was equal to smearing the family's reputation.

While God is incredibly forgiving, I knew our world could be unforgiving, especially regarding someone's reputation. I learned that, ultimately, accusations of any level do not matter. God's grace is more significant than any mistake you would ever make. You need to maintain that grace always. False accusations about you will only strengthen you for higher glory.

It has been read repeatedly that 'Blessed are the pure in heart.' It is memorized and gathered in mind. So even though I cried a lot, sighed a lot, and suffered a lot of mental torture, For the time being, it was limited. Yes, it was only temporarily. Further investigations may come. I was ready to face anything. I was confident that one day, I would see God.

At eleven o'clock at night, Mr Kuzhiveli took me back to the hostel on a scooter.

I drank some water without telling anyone - let no one know - without blaming anyone, and found myself exhausted in the lap of God, asking myself why all this was happening to me.

No one could find any evidence against me. If it was there, then only it could be found. None of the allegations could be substantiated. There may be more inquiries, mind you, said me. A fool would discover happiness in repeating the folly. A criminal commits a crime again. He cannot avoid it.

Fr. James came home to Maramkunnil the following week to meet my parents. After the father returned, I reached home.

"James Achen came and went back," Ammachi told me.

I understood that Achan came for an investigation when I was not at home. He came as part of further investigations. My table, books, and things I kept there were checked. The authorities might have authorized and executed that. What material evidence they got is not known.

Achayan and Ammachi did not ask me anything. I never felt that their trust in me had not diminished at all.

My friendly conversations with Stephen were also reduced. Investigations, questioning, and findings were not shared with anyone. That was the instruction. The only thought I had in the theory and practical classes and the remaining time in the hostel was to pass the public examination at the end of the first year with good marks.

The trials and tribulations occurred during the most challenging and complex period I have ever faced in Carmel. The accusations, which questioned my integrity and the essence of existence, their investigations, and findings by the concerned all happened meticulously during that period. I am happy that it proved my innocence in the end.

As a result, at least some people may have lost their original SSLC book from the college archives. Kuzhiveli sir tried to bring everything to light and got me relief. Honourable Chairperson Fr. Gilbert and Principal Zachariah Sir carried out the punishment for the culprit. Assistance was provided so that the affected could recover their records. If I had not said this even after they had attained their salvation, would there not be a gap left somewhere? I also write that my challenges in college have strengthened my professional career and personal life. In any crisis, we must strive to regain confidence without being discouraged and disheartened, and we must move forward by creating a positive attitude that combines sincerity and skill. That is the lesson these events have taught me.

19. WHERE CAN I EARN MY BREAD?

While sitting in the class one day, Kochuppappan said that my maternal grandfather had died in Kainakari. The funeral would be in the evening. "James Achen is coming too. You two should go to Alappuzha and get on the boat to Kainakari."

Achayan and Ammachi would go directly. I must get a wreath made at Alleppey and take that, too.

The boat landed on the Panjimarathinkal jetty at the Kainakari stretch of land. We walked to the Arackal courtyard. What a radiance I could see, how serene, on the face of my grandpa, who was lying decorated amid flowers in a coffin, in the decorated pandal, in the front courtyard!

The same affection for his grandson was evident on his face when I placed the wreath.

Kunchacko could not attend his father's funeral, which was a matter of concern and talk among the relatives.

I returned to the hostel with Fr. James.

"Keep it a secret..." James Achen called me closer and said something.

"Don't tell anyone. Stephen is under the surveillance of the Church and the college. Some decision will be made shortly." I heard that without any emotion.

I left the hostel to attend the festival at the Punnapra Church on a Sunday that year. I heard an announcement through a loudspeaker after the procession as I began to walk back.

"The food for the priests and nuns is served in the pavilion on the south side of the church, and for the rest of the people, it is on the north side."

"Did you hear that ..." It was Kochuppappan when I looked back. He came to the hostel at night two months ago and grabbed me by the neck, and after that, I saw him today. I didn't even have to look for him in the office room in the college, nor did he ever look for me.

"Then the essence is that those who go to the pandal on the north are people, and those who go to the south are not human beings...". He was smiling while talking. Let's go home, have lunch, and then you can go to the hostel ..." Kochuppappan called me while laughing.

Eight months after being beaten up and dismissed from that house, Kochuppappan invited me to their home for lunch! I went reluctantly, even though I had not forgotten anything, but I did not highlight anything particularly. I was silent most of the time.

Without further ado, I returned to the hostel after eating the lunch provided by Chittamma.

The trauma and pain of the mind lasted for some time. When you remember, without overthinking about the causes of situations like this, without worrying about the severity of the pain and the depth of the wounds, if you try to forget them all, over time, everything will fade out. Find the source of the mistakes and improve your personality with corrections. You will not feel hurt and cause no injury to others. The ability to do that can be self-earned.

Adults and those in authority — may not be willing to apologize or admit their mistakes. They will do so in some other way. He laughed, changed the subject without damaging the leaves or the thorns, and said, 'Let it go. It doesn't matter. You don't have to reply for that –' everything is forgiven; it doesn't matter. That's good for both parties. That is what Kochuppappan taught.

Forgiveness is letting go of the past pain that could seep into tomorrow and affect one's well-being. Resist the temptation of reopening that old sore. Healing is a process and a journey.

"When you forgive, it does not mean that you have submitted. It simply means that you have chosen to stop bearing any grudge."– Stephen Richards.

Nothing hidden in infinity shall be retrieved, polished, and whitewashed from the dark corridors of time that have faded. Accept and enjoy everything that life has to offer. Learn from the experience and strive for progress and good.

Without knowing anything about electronics, I tried to learn what it was, read many books and magazines without using any electronic equipment, and wrote a review, an article entitled 'Electronics-Coming of the Age,' published in Carmel College Magazine that year.

The next few days, including the holidays, were to prepare for the board exam. There was a model exam for almost all subjects. That also helped us a lot. Most of the questions in the model exam came up for the board exam. Dove-tail Joint - - was given to me for the practical examination in the carpentry workshop. I could do well.

Ensuring that the first year would pass smoothly, I said goodbye to the hostel and went home to celebrate the holidays (May 1964).

It was good that no project work was suggested during the holidays before the second year of study. Gone are the days with a little bit of piece of newspaper distribution, monthly billing of subscribers, the library, adding information in the book distribution register in the library, the volleyball games and tournaments in the backyard, the anniversaries of children's and youth clubs, boat races and preparations for the cultural events.

Nanattu Pachu Pillai, Puthenpurakkal brothers- Josekutty, Appachan, Babychan; Kuttappan from Palathittachira, Chandappan from Kavalackal Sunny, Keeppada Joy and many others wanted to learn and perform a play. A play that had a reasonable public opinion at that time was chosen. Casting was done according to the characters' suitability and the participants' willingness. The rehearsal began in the library from 7:30 p.m. to 10 p.m. Puthenpurakkal Josekutty and Nanattu Pachu Pillai acted well. Finding a person as a female character was a difficult task. Puthenpurakkal Babychan was chosen, and some days went ahead. In addition, there were many other difficulties, like — raising money and not directing the play well. Nanatt Pachu Pillai was recruited into the Army and went away to join.

Pachu Pillai had a good height. A Towel was tied around his head, and when he shook his head, saying - "Hey, stop," as part of the dialogue, the scene of the towel falling off was good enough to make everybody laugh and deserved applause from the audience.

They all parted ways behind the curtain to prepare cultural activities, saying they were happy to conduct any other musical or art event or district-level volleyball tournament that could be organized.

Shortly after the results of the first-year examination of the Polytechnic, an interview was conducted to select the engineering branch of the student's interest. Almost everyone had passed. Someone had notified me that the mechanical engineering branch would most likely get a suitable job. Most friends said the same thing.

During the interview, the HOD of Civil Engineering requested that I reply favourably. He observed that I had good marks during the first year.

"Take Civil Engineering, learn about building, roads, and bridges. Many railways and PWD job opportunities exist, especially in the native state."

I did not pay heed to such a piece of good advice. I have favoured the Mechanical branch.

Staying in a hostel did not seem necessary for the second year of study at the Polytechnic. First was the extra cost, and then there was no board exam, so learning must not be arduous. In addition to the small canoe used for newspaper distribution, another was purchased for Mathamma's convenience and use. Using that small canoe to get to and from the college could help me avoid the hassles of walking such a long distance through the unfavourable muddy terrain. By the time the floodwaters recede, there will be no loss of time waiting for the ferry. So, I went to college in a small canoe to Punnapra. It would be best to walk to the college—a good and straight road.

You can return a little later in the evening on the NCC days. Uniforms and boots were placed in Ekka's provision shop, where I usually tied the canoe. It was only brought home for washing.

After becoming active in NCC, I passed the B and C certificate examinations. I was then given the power to lead and control a parade. Kuzhiveli sir was a strict officer, as always. But he never mentioned the previous year's adventures or consequences to me or anyone else. He never expressed any doubt about my honesty, integrity, or sincerity. I attended NCC camp and received training to use 0.303-inch (7.62 mm) cartridge rifles and 0.22-inch (5.588 mm) long cartridge rifles.

I went home from college daily during my second year at the Polytechnic. I rowed in a small canoe, hung a shoulder bag, put a T-square on the shoulder, and walked to college. I stayed in the parish priest's presbytery at the Church in Punnapra for six months, nearer to the final examination dates in the third year. Thambichan lived with a relative in Punnapra and came to college as a 'day scholar' for all three years.

I started attending second-year classes. Fr. James chose the branch of Electrical Engineering, and Br. Abraham chose Civil Engineering. Stephen had not arrived. Other important friends - Sebastian Muttar, PT Sebastian, Vijayappan, and Cyriac - were in the same class as I was in the mechanical branch.

Kochuppappan said he knew there were other reasons for Stephen not to come.

Before the end of the first-year exams, I saw a letter on the college noticeboard. It came through the post office. The handwriting seemed to be that of Stephen. No one had sent me a letter to my college address ever since I joined the college. This was the first time. Surprised and skeptical, I stood there and saw Kuzhiveli Sir walk by.

Slowly, I approached him and expressed my doubt.

"Anyway, whoever it may be, I can't stand such headaches anymore," I said to myself, handing over the letter to him.

That little light that God showed me was enough to prove my innocence. That incident and instance was a warning to save my life and save me from the impending disaster -

Kuzhiveli sir, read that letter and advised me the following -

'Do not walk out of the hostel after dusk. Someone should accompany you while coming and going to college. Go with some friends."

Kochuppappan said, "The letter you received and gave to Kuzhiveli Sir that day was written by Stephen himself without indicating his name."

I couldn't understand why.

"An advanced information to you and a warning to the rest was the intention. Anyway, nothing happened." It was a great relief.

"Another thing happened. Unfortunately, it could not be prevented. The principal's room and office were locked in the college, and the keys were handed over to Carmel's House. He took the keys and opened the principal's room and office on holiday. All the certificates and files kept in the steel cupboard were scattered. 12 SSLC books were not found. Your certificate was lost in the group. Burnt pieces of paper and ashes were found in Stephen's room in the house."

I just heard everything and listened in silence. It revealed his criminal mind and retaliation for the events he could not stop.

"The case was not handed over to the police because the principal and Gilbert Achen understood everything. Don't worry; we can apply for a duplicate of the SSLC book. We can apply for it through the school. You will get it in one or two months. It is irretrievably lost - the principal will issue a certificate as such. All you have to do is apply with such a certificate from the principal. "

"Then where is Stephen?"

"Suspended. Mostly, he will be deprived of his religious clothing – a cassock. He will not come here anymore."

A chapter of mental agony and distress ended here. What was gained more than losses was the additional power of the mind to face any adverse situation. It can be said that it has helped me all the time.

Soon after, I went to Champakulam High School and applied for a duplicate SSLC book. Three or four months later, it was received by the school, and I collected it by myself. One of the milestones of life was passed twice!

20. ENGINEERING MARATHON

After Jawaharlal Nehru, Lal Bahadur Shastri became the Prime Minister. Shastri's simplicity and the administrative reforms he implemented under Jai Jawan and Jai Kisan were commendable.

We learned what not to do in a college class when Varghese sir came to our classroom first. An authoritarian attitude - that I am a teacher and that you are all just students. You should listen to what I say; you should read and study and not ask any more questions. I should cause no wrinkles on the ironed shirt as I walk to wear it for the next two days.

He was new. He had been a student for so long and had come to teach us for the first time. So, it may be so.

Someone asked his name -

We got the answer - "Varghese."

"Initial, the surname. Isn't there anything?"

"No, Varghese" – He wrote VARGHESE with white chalk on the blackboard and read it -

"Simply VARGHESE"

Everyone acknowledged and reiterated - "Simply Varghese." Dasappan repeated "Simply Varghese" three or four times. Everyone laughed. Varghese sir was not laughing. The name becomes permanent when Dasappan calls it more than once. Dasappan was the joker in our class, and he made everybody laugh!

He was then known throughout college as "Simply Varghese." Three or four months later, he got another job and graduated.

On the way, he thought that the 'teacher' job was unsuitable for him or that these students were not good enough for his teaching.

Students were elected to positions like the chair, secretary, department secretary, college magazine editor, etc. At the request of some of my friends, I submitted a nomination paper for the role of magazine editor. Sasidharan was another candidate. He had the excellent support of the hostel residents. Muttar Sebastian and PM Paulose spent money and issued notices favouring me for the campaign. The poster/notice was printed in Alappuzha and distributed. I went up to all the classes and preached and campaigned. They called out to "pooh" when they were told that a college magazine was a mirror displaying the face of the college'. The speech ended. When the votes were counted, Sasidharan won with a considerable margin. My enthusiasm for representing students or for being a student leader cooled down.

In my second year, I passed off with various subjects and practicals in mechanical engineering.

Some of the village's educated friends left home searching for work; some went outside Kerala, Josekutty went to Kenya, and others went outside India.

The construction of the hospital building started in Nanatt's backyard. Nothing changed in other conditions in the countryside, progress, travel, and water sources. The development will take years, but in any case, the change will not come soon. The ravine where the small canoe was rowing began to fill up with water hyacinth, making it difficult to travel through water.

As the second-year examination approached, I studied extensively, did more projects, practiced exercises, and did engineering drawing. Finding time for everything became more and more arduous. Kochuppappan met the Punnapra church's vicar and requested that the room next to Achen's room on the presbytery be vacated so the college student could stay there. The vicar of the church was Sebastian Narakatra Achen. When Achen said he was not against it, I reduced the canoe rowing, walked a bit, and settled in the parish priest's presbytery.

"One or two months until the end of the final exam," said Kochuppappan. The food was from Paul's Hotel at the Punnapra market. I went home on Saturdays and Sundays if there were no essential study assignments. When the exams were over, I took the bag and went home.

"Thank you so much, Achen. Shall come and see you again."

At the national level and within Kerala, the political developments of 1965 and the election had minor repercussions on the college, Gilbert Achen, and the students, especially after PT Chacko was felicitated.

The second-year examination results were generally suitable for all, and achieving glorious success in the third year was inspiring.

Third-year classes started early with the syllabus revision, more revisions, practicals, and model exams, believing that more time would be available for study by the end of the year.

As soon as the third-year classes started, Balan Sir took charge as Principal and HOD of the Mechanical Engineering department. He always had a smile and a clean shave and dressed like a pure white dove.

Balan Sir was a good, lean, active, well-spoken, well-educated, loving teacher who wrote down all the subject's essentials on the board neat and orderly and made it clear only once. In a few days, he became the students' favourite teacher in all the college classes. Balan Sir became popular among the teachers and the staff in the office. Balan Sir taught us all subjects except Hydraulics. He said everybody's goal was to study everything well without any worries about the year-end exam, apply what was learned as a problem-solving (application), and make the study a satisfying and enjoyable experience. Everyone benefited from it.

In addition to their studies, the college authorities and teachers helped promote individual talents for every student, build teams in sports and games, and encourage everyone in general, especially those interested in the arts and cultural activities.

By August and September, Pakistan had violated the ceasefire on India's border, and the infiltration of Pakistani troops had intensified. The war lasted from September 6 to 22,1965. The scourge of war - food shortages, rising prices, etc.- lasted long. The peace treaty signed by Lal Bahadur Shastri and Ayub Khan on January 10, 1966, in Tashkent, Russia, fostered an atmosphere of peace and tranquillity. The next day, Prime Minister Shastri died of a heart attack in Tashkent.

Indira Gandhi became the next Prime Minister.

The first three or four months of the third year of study were spent travelling to college from home and back. After the Indo-Pakistan war, I returned to the parish priest's presbytery at Punnapra. It helped me find more time for reflection, reduce travel fatigue, and focus on learning in a quiet environment with no noise from the surroundings.

While in college, I received advice and help from teachers, and the support and love of many friends and classmates started in the first year was further strengthened.

Friends are brothers; true friends are always by my side through life's ups and downs. A friend understands our past, believes in our future, and accepts us as we are.

Every one of my friends had an extraordinary friendship and interest in me.

Some thought, "Thomas is a good student and hard worker."

Some thought, "He is sincere."

Some said - "He did not deliberately harm anyone. He was close to the principal and office superintendent but did not betray anyone.

I represented the college at the district level. I went to Alappuzha on National Unity Day (31 October) to participate in an elocution competition.

Most teachers should have told the office superintendent about the feedback about me. Kochuppappan would occasionally point out something to me.

"Well, Balan Sir liked it," "They told me." And similar statements.

Yes, I never wanted to get out of such controls or supervision and scrutiny by elders and the framework of the discipline.

All teachers taught well for three years. I can not but name at least one person, Balan Sir. A talented young engineer, Balan Sir, came to our third-year class in a gorgeous white dress, smiled, gave us knowledge of engineering subjects, saw us, and won us over. He settled in our minds.

Kochuppappan regularly inquired about PT Sebastian also. Both are on the list of those looking forward to notable success from the course. That is what Balan Sir said. Occasionally, some notes were exchanged, and welfare inquiries were made. The similarities increased with one thing - both are students living and studying away from home in Punnapra.

The practical turning examination was done very early in the machine shop. Study leave was after that. Revision and model tests were conducted. All subjects were given adequate time to study after solving problems. I learned and revised lessons by staying at the presbytery for a few days and then at home. I took a risk by skipping the last thermodynamics chapters (refrigeration and air conditioning), which were challenging to memorise. The probability was that I could study the rest of the portions thoroughly and score well on the rest of the syllabus. I thought I would do well as there were choices in the question paper. That was the risk, but sometimes, some decisions can affect the future. Most friends do that. So did I.

The final examination lasted for two weeks. Perfectly focused attention, enthusiasm, and self-confidence were developed. I was confident that my efforts so far would not be in vain. I was exhausted at the end of the exams; It was as if I had just completed a marathon race. I prayed for good results to come.

25. Separation and Expectations

The grief of parting with friends who had been together for three years was more. Change in the way of life—variation in directions and daily routine. For most friends, it was more than they could afford. But the thoughts such as we'll see again at some point in life, and you'll meet here, remember a lot, and rejoice in all the good moments you shared- were all big expectations. The college had a group photo, a farewell meeting, and a tea party.

I also remember lines from the farewell speech: 'Parting is sorrow, and the time has come for us to part ways and seek our future and prospects anywhere in the world. We wish to come off with flying colours and be united with our Alma mater.

A bit of Kuriakosesee Sir's language and style were there. Some even came with autographs and diaries. Most of the writings in the autographs were signs of friendship. Since no female students were in our classes, there was no mischief, love requests, or frustration.

TK Thomas said- "I will take the certificate and go to Bombay."

"I'm going to Poona," said Jameskutty.

Sasidharan and Chandrasekharan Nair said, "Here in Kerala, anywhere in PWD, an electricity board or road transport is enough - a local job nearby.

PT Sebastian said- "I will be an Apprentice at Cochin Shipyard."

Thomas Mathew said - "I will go to HMT; my uncle is there."

Issacs said, "I have no place to go. ഞാനിങ്ങനെ കടാപ്പുറത്ത് പാടി പാടി നടക്കും." (I'm going to sing on the beach like that. Allegorical to 'Chemmeen')

Muttar Sebastian said, -"പോനാൽ പോകട്ടും.., ബാ - അപ്പാ - വേറെ പണിയൊന്നുമില്ലേ, വരുന്നതു പോലെ വരട്ടെ" (Cinematic allegory: "Let it go, let's go, come on Don't you have another engagement. Let it come as it may)."

Everyone was disappointed and sad about a tomorrow without daily visits, give-and-takes, laughter, and jokes. Yet everyone tried to see that certainty with practical wisdom and live with hope. Isaac's voice was in the air, and the harmonious melody of the music became a sigh. No other friend expressed the grief of parting with such depth and sincerity—separated from the college entrance, looking back, until it disappeared, or until the picture was unclear with water getting collected? And just like that, a memory, with hope and only hope for tomorrow.

I waited for the results of the engineering diploma exam for the next two months. Holiday entertainment, the library, and ball games were all there, as usual, a getaway from the college routine.

I went to Kannattumadom and spent some extra time with Grandpa and Grandma. Kuriachan was on vacation, and we could spend some time together.

He was talking to his brothers about household chores. The marriage proposal for Kunjamma Chechi from Changanassery was finalised. "Let's do it next time when we come on vacation."

The elder brother, who studied survey and civil engineering in Delhi, met his younger brother. The latter just completed the studies for a diploma and took the examinations.

"Hay ... Do you know him? - Listen, Thommachan. He would bite everyone who passes by, wherever he could find a place to do that ."

It would be a mistake to assume that everyone forgot my mischief when I started studying in college. Don't you see this? Some reminders from close relatives.

When Kuriachan was going to Assam, Achayan boarded him to the Kottayam railway station. Years later, I remembered what Achayan had said about a 'Kani' (first sight). When Kuriachan was on his way to work leaving home, he saw a 'kettuvallam' (houseboat) full of coconuts being driven on the ravine. That is - saying, "May he be blessed with prosperity." Coconut fruit is a symbol of all prosperity in life.

"Once the results are available, send your application to RDSO Lucknow with a copy of the certificates. The R&D section of the Railways is there. Let's try."

So, he returned to Delhi after giving him some hope.

I went to Kainakari to meet Kunjunju, who came on vacation. It was his first homecoming after the death of his father. On the way home, standing at the door on the south side of the room, he was sighing and crying.

"I could not see him once," he said.

Gradually, the grief subsided. He turned his attention to everyday things and his friends. He walked with his friends for four or five days to Ayiraveli, Chempil, Panjimarathinkal, etc. There was a volleyball tournament in the courtyard of the Chapel near Chempil.

The 20-year-old does not seem to have discretion, knowledge, or maturity. Then, after four or five days of stay at his mother's house, before leaving, he saw an attractive, striped and coloured shirt hanging in the closet in the south room and was fascinated by it and asked for the same Kunjunju - oh, what a childish question -

He is my uncle, and he has a well-paid job. There is no significant age difference between us. Therefore, I must have longed for love and affection from my uncle -

"Will you give me that shirt?"

"Hey, that, that…." He was searching for words to dissuade me

He did not say no. I should not have asked him!

I should have verified whether the shirt size would fit my slender body.

Has he sufficient savings to buy another shirt for him, or Will he have funds to purchase shirts for all his nephews?

If you give to one, how can you not give to others? How to pay for all? Aren't there two or three others who also may desire the same? I did not think that much.

There was a clouded mind and face as I boarded the boat and headed back. Was it the grief of not getting what I desired?

Was it a pity that my grandpa was not there to receive my 'praise for the Lord and bless me with a kiss on my forehead? Whatever…?

Didn't you hear a no? How would I go back after giving whatever I had? Isn't that right? The reluctance to tell someone about the shortfalls and shortcomings did not start today or yesterday! Why did you not understand? That's all the maturity of a twenty-year-old. Was it asked since I did not have any? Then I was tempted to think only of myself; wasn't that the truth?"

These days were not holidays—the interval between study and work. The result would come soon, and I could wait. After that, I could wait for the job. I did not know how long. So, see this break as a vacation and spend the holidays as I did before, or even better. I was determined. I was waiting.

Kuriachan, who relocated from Assam to Delhi, would occasionally write. In a recent letter, he wrote - "No hardships for me to live alone in Delhi. I am worried about my mother and younger sister, who had to stay in the hospital with all the hardships. Thommikunju is idle after I took him to work somewhere in Madhya Pradesh. I have to bear all the burden. Kuttappan has a small job in a railway workshop in Assam. With a meagre income, he manages somehow. They did not learn anything in school or after school. Aniyappan is trying to join the Indian Air Force."

The information came about the announcement date of results at the end of the wait. In those days, exam results were published in newspapers. You would know the outcome if you called the newspaper office the previous day. PT Sebastian (Thambichan) said-

"If we go to the college, you will know the result. If you call Manorama or Deepika's office, you will know the result before its publication."

"Then, let's go to the college."

We both walked together and went to the college. There were no teachers present. The office room was open. During holidays, Antony sir will also be sitting in the office; that was it. We went and met him.

"The result has not yet come in the college either. We are waiting for it to come sometime today."

In the 1966 mechanical batch of the college, PT Sebastian and I, expecting ranks one and two, respectively, waited for Antony sir to call the newspaper office and ask.

Antony Sir called Deepika's office from Carmel at 5 p.m. and introduced himself. It was apparent that somebody knew him on the other end. A brief smile and a ray of hope spread across our faces. It widened our eyes.

Kochuppappan called out my name and number and told the person on the phone to look at the result and say the result.

The answer came. "Yes, passed. There is first class."

Thank you, and happy. I am not relieved yet.

"There's another number too."

Kochuppappan told Thambichan's number and name to look for and say the result.

We waited and listened. Something came up in response.

"What? It will not be like that; pay attention carefully one more time, " he repeated the number.

The answer came - "No, I do not see." Those words shocked us with the exam results that went over the phone. Not credible news at all! I won. PT Sebastian did not win, repeated the request over the phone, and waited; they must have been tired. The phone would have been cut off. Two students hugged and cried together as Kochuppappan looked down at the telephone.

Thambichan said nothing. The winning student kept repeating.-

"No, it's wrong, it's not. It's wrong somewhere.

"Let's find out more," said Antony Sir.

Beyond the joy of knowing that I had won, the difficulty of not knowing Thambichan's result and the associated sadness had overwhelmed and paralysed us.

And in the corridors of Carmel, the moments that were pushed aside, the hours, were a great crisis in life, truly unforgettable!

I came to the verandah and looked outside, and stood like that. No flowers were seen in the garden, or vehicles ran along the highway. Only emptiness and silence everywhere. We stood like that for a long time, holding hands without saying anything and leaning against the wall on the verandah of the drawing hall at the back of the college. It was getting dark outside. It was like so much sadness and mental anguish covered us like tidal waves from the sea in the west.

Let's call the newspaper offices again and inquire, or the result might be coming to the college soon. Let's see.

"It's just temptations, an experiment, and it will pass." My mind kept on saying. We shall overcome.

Thambichan was restless, staring into the distance, wondering where the light was. The evening is over. The college office is not yet closed. Kochuppappan was sitting there writing something. Kochuppappan picked up the phone again and dialled the number as we walked in.

"Tried two or three times earlier. Didn't get it. Now let's see again."

Aware of the rush in the newspaper office, Antony Sir called again. Someone picked up the phone at the Manorama office.

"From Alappuzha Bureau, I want to know the result of Polytechnic Diploma" - Kochuppappan.

Thambichan's number and name were called to look and tell the result.

The answer came.

"Yes, Passed," he said, continuing for a few more moments. It was all visible on the office superintendent's face and the movement of his hands.

The sweet words of truth came to the lips of Kochuppappan as a consolation to the ears waiting to hear with hope and eagerness!

"Congratulations, both of you have distinction!"

"Thank you, happy .... that's right. Congratulations to both of you! -

Still, the two students hugged and cried with joy.

In the evening, we were in front of Kochuppappan in the office. Otherwise, we would have shouted to the world – Hurray!

Someone must have made a mistake. Kochuppappan called the Deepika office again and gave Thambichan's number and name.

"You have won."

Well, that is it. He thanked him and hung up.

"Thambichan has won twice, and it's twice as sweet."

All the sorrows and hardships went away. We washed our faces, drank water, and walked home. We crossed the school grounds east of the 'Kalithattu' and field. The temperature of the sand after dusk was much reduced.

We walked fast. Before Babychan Anjiliparambil closes the shop, we must cross the Vettikkeri paddy fields and the Mathurchira stretch. There was only one way to cross the river Pookaitha. We must request Babychan to help us. The helmsman on the ferry must have gone home.

If Vavachittappan asks, "Why are you so late?" We will say-

"We both won and had been to college to know the exam results..."

"Well, it's easier to get a job now."

"Yes. We will get it, Engineering job." I wanted to call out to the whole world.

It was dark at night when we came to Kannattumadom house at Maramkunnil.

"We both won. There is a first class. The result will be in the paper tomorrow. We found out by calling the newspaper office.!"

Achayan, Ammachi, Babu, Raju, and Leelamma all keenly listened. They came closer and continued smiling. There was great pride and joy on their faces as they stood next to the Engineers of tomorrow. Achayan and Ammachi were happy. My mother joined her hands and brought them up to her neck, and with her eyes and face, she thanked the sacred heart of Jesus. Her eyes were wet.

"It is very dark at night. How could Thambichan go alone through the flooded field? So Thambichan - you sleep here and go home in the morning, shall we?" Achayan asked. "Well, that's enough," Thambichan said

Our two classmates - two engineering diploma holders with the potential to get jobs quickly, had dinner together and slept in one room on another bed next to Achayan's, on a mat with a pillow and a blanket. The intensities of pleasure and pain, the warmth and flame of the mind, were experienced together in one day, and we slept together. We woke up together when everything was calm.

When I looked at the exam results in the morning and laughed, it seemed that our going to the college to know the exam results the day before was unnecessary. Then, he would not have endured so much grief and hardship. That was a reconciliation. Anxiety is never good for anything; otherwise, how the gold will melt in the heat of a fire to become refined and pure! Waiting with anxiety could not have refined it. It must pass through the process.

Mechanical Engineering Final Year, Batch of 1966

21. FIRST ATTEMPTS FOR A JOB

Fifteen years of education, you have had only one goal. A reasonably good job with a steady income is one if you can work for a lifetime. The more you learn, the better the job you get. The practical plan of good parents is to teach the children as much as possible. No one can predict how much to go forward, how much to invest, and how much to achieve. After all, it is a balanced state of life, effort, and fulfillment of desires. It is safe to say that the blessings of God or the acceptance of parents - the opportunities that come with guidance and direction - play a significant role. It is possible to get more education than you earn. The view that children are the support and shade for the family in the rush of life, and a family living by faith, seeing that any child is capable of work, gives great hope for the future.

It is a condition of the farmer who is happy to see that the paddy blooms and becomes fertile by providing fertiliser, water, proper care, and maintenance while sowing and growing the paddy and seeing in his mind that it can be harvested soon. Optimism is what comes to mind when planting. The hope is that the days of suffering are over, and the days that come will be less suffering. Even so, owning one is still beyond the average person's reach.

Diploma Certificate, Mark List, and Certificate of Character were all received from the college. I put them in a file with other certificates. Copies of all certificates were xeroxed, attested by Principal Balan Sir, and ready to be sent with the applications. Some of the application forms received from the college - those to join as apprentice trainees in state and national-level institutions - were signed. When will campus recruitment be implemented in Kerala, which has many educated job seekers?

Applications began to be sent to the technical institutes that appeared in the newspapers and magazines. Most jobs require at least one year of work experience. How do you gain work experience without starting a career? If you do not have work experience, you are not eligible to be selected for the job!

I used to go to Punnapra regularly every week to send applications. Sometimes, Thambichan and I would go together. Kochuppappan had obtained a certificate stating that I had been under training at a machine shop in Alappuzha for six months after passing the final examination. Six months had passed by then. Still looking for a job...

I received notice that I should contact the Recruitment Center at Ernakulam.

Diploma holders were invited to join the Navy as Artificer Apprentices. This is a job to work on a Navy warship. An Artificer is a job that is based on physical fitness and health. Thambichan also said – "Let us go. Let that be the first step towards a career".

We saw a group of students when we reached the recruitment center in Ernakulam in the morning. Everyone should be a peer, young people and diploma holders. We did not know how many vacancies there were. My classmates Vijayappan, Kamath, Dasappan, and Razak were there. We also joined them.

The health monitoring was followed by physical measurements and fitness tests to run 100 meters. A doctor was sitting in a chair in the middle of a room, watching six young people standing in front. Each one was called and made to sit down next to the doctor, and the doctor examined his chest, back, and pulse. We have checked ENT. All six were lined up in front. The doctor asked us to pull down our pants and undergarments to our lower legs and pull the skin of the genitals back. Despite being friends, we were reluctant to look each other in the face, closed our eyes, and did as the doctor wanted. The only goal in mind was to get a job. Ready to reveal all the truth. To get a job! Out of frustration, we were so reluctant to respond that tests could be done in a room, one by one, respecting the individuals. But the ridiculous procedures went on for hours.

After the test, everyone was told to wait outside.

The result was announced. Everyone would receive a job notification within a month. To help, "The following people should go to Lissy Hospital in Ernakulam today, clean their ears, and bring the certificate."

Thambichan's name was among the names mentioned. We went to the hospital together, saw the ENT doctor, brought and submitted the certificate, and returned home.

Two months have passed.

Thambichan recalled, "There was no order for the job of Artificer (skilled mechanic in the armed forces) from the Navy."

"Thambichan was able to clean his ear, though! I didn't even have that luck."

Achayan had gone to the Manorama office, met the managing editor, K. M. Mathew, and told him about his son getting a job. He wrote a letter to HMT General Manager Yesudas and handed it to Achayan.

"Take it and give this and tell him the requirement. He will help."

Thambichan and I also went together to Kalamassery. We reached Kalamassery the previous day evening. We stayed at a lodge and arrived at the home of HMT General Manager Yesudas early in the morning. He was ready to go to his office but patiently listened to what we had to say.

"Our new Foundry will start soon, and we are taking diploma holders to work in a month or two. You can come," he said lovingly.

The letter from Manorama's managing editor to his dear friend, General Manager Yesudas, remained unmoved in my pocket. The letter had recommended that KT Thomas be hired. Then what would he say to his friend, classmate, and fellow traveller PT Sebastian ?! How can I say that the two of us go together to meet him and request him to give a job only to me? How do I do that? If I go home and tell my father this, he will understand. When friends and brothers try to do something together, it is wrong to act selfishly, prioritising their interests there.

When I returned home that evening, I saw that Thankachan (Kochachan) had come from Kainakari. He talked to Achayan.

"You must go to Champakulam in the morning and go to Kainakari by boat. Thevarkattu Babu has come on vacation. You must see him and tell him about a job for you. He is a big military officer in Poona. He will go back in the morning. Before that, you should get there.

We went quickly to Champakulam, boarded the boat to Kainakari, and got down at Ayiraveli jetty without bothering about the drizzle in the early morning.

We folded the dhoti up to the knee and walked quickly. By the time we reached Thevarkattu, it was 8 a.m. The drizzle continued. The pathways were full of dirt and mud. The shirt and dhoti I was wearing were wrinkled and dull. How will I face the officer in such shabby attire? I was worried a bit. The staff saw us standing at the gate.

"Arackal Thankachan, aren't you? Stay inside, and I can call the elder."

On the veranda, near the closed door of the house, Kochachan stood with his right leg bent and leaned against the wall, tired from walking some distance quickly.

I took the envelope with the certificates, straightened the wrinkles, untied the folds, straightened up to the feet, and brought a smile of courage to cover my face. The aspirant waited. To see that angel of God.

The elder opened the door, and we saw him and wished with folded hands.

"You, Arackal Outhakutty's son, Nga. What's your name? Are you... Job?"

The questions and answers all came one after the other as if we were welcome. The elder is older than my grandpa and was a retired chief secretary in the Kerala government. I understood that he might be the father of the military officer.

"Well, what's up?"

"Yes, I am Job - I came ..to see ... then ... Babu ....."

"Eda, Job... Why are you leaning on the wall and stamping with your legs.... Didn't you make the wall all dirty with mud? Is this politeness, Shame!"

We heard a weary voice of total disgust.

I saw a sudden redness on Kochachan's face, disgust and frustration in his eyes.

I do not know what to say or do. Kochachan tried to say something, but by the grace of God, he swallowed the words.

Three to five seconds have passed in silence. Say something or go back? Didn't you come here, anyway? Is it not the need ours?

"Well, why did you come?" The elder calmed down and politely asked.

"I thought I would see Babu."

"Oh... Babu, he is gone. He has just gone to Alappuzha. He will go to Alappuzha and then to Poona today. So, why do you want to see him?"

"He's my nephew. He finished his polytechnic diploma, but he has no job. There's first-class ..." and a few other descriptions. Relationship with Kainakari, Relationship with Job. The relationship between Job and Babu. The illustrations should have melted the elder's mind. The muddy resentment on the wall and the frustration in his eyes faded away. Gently and calmly, with words of kindness, he was giving birth to hope -

"Job, I'm writing a letter. I am sending a sack of rice and coconuts through a parcel service. I should send him the receipt so he can collect it at Poona. I will also write this matter to him."

The elder went inside. We waited on the porch until the writing was done.

Kochachan - No matter how much you praise my uncle's self-control and patience, it may not be enough. It will always be in my mind as a good lesson taught by my uncle, Kochachan.

There was no trace of Kochachan's wet foot resting on the wall. The sticky, damp dirt and mud had dried and then wiped off slowly by hand; it was gone entirely. It faded from my mind also. Hope was beginning to shine on both our faces.

"Here's the letter, inside the cover. I was looking for the glue to paste it. Paste it yourself and put it in the box at the post office."

The letter was handed over to the candidate, and he was confident it would reach its correct destination.

I bought the letter, put it along with the certificates, folded my hands, and thanked him. Above the water's surface flowing through the river Pampa, I saw some aquatic plants desirous of reaching the shore in front of the house.

It was one day late to post the letter. It was because I got late when I got back home. Everything that happened in the morning was reborn in my mind.

If he sends his son a parcel of rice and coconuts and does not get it, his mercy on me for writing a recommendation letter was far greater than the depression and difficulty I had in my mind! I have the same love for a father's affection for his son, through a letter -

I had also agreed to post the letter. And then why not?

The recommendation was written in his writing. I have read it. Where is my address for his information, my qualifications, and so on so he can act if agreed upon? What does he need to fulfill his father's recommendation? Isn't it my responsibility to make it easy for him?

It was good that it got delayed by one day. I didn't remember any of this well in time. After going to Punnapra and showing humility and address, I typed out in English only what was required for him, about my education, age, training, and job, attached a copy of the certificates within the envelope and affixed more stamps and posted the letter at the Punnapra post office on the same day. Now relax, I will have to wait longer.

After receiving the certificate, I sent a copy as I promised Kuriachan so that he could try to find a job for me at the RDSO in Lucknow. After waiting for more than six months, nothing was written about it. Could it be said that Kuriachan did not push or try and failed? There is no need for extra effort now. In any case, the failure of the RDSO attempt did not appear in the text he had sent. You can always go to Delhi and see your brother, who only gave you love.

22. I GOT A JOB

Thambichan was notified to join the Cochin Port Trust as an apprentice. He would get a monthly stipend, and the training was for six months. It said there was no job guarantee after that. When there is a vacancy anywhere, preference will be given to those trained at Port Trust. After all, it's better that way than to remain jobless.

"I'm going there on Monday to join, "Thambichan said.

Thambichan was happy when I saw him a month later.

"Applications have been sent for other jobs."

"Me too," I added. "But this waiting for a job is horrible."

Technical education was necessary to get a job quickly. The result was known in June. It's October now. Job opportunities in Kerala were very meagre. I was ready to go to any country or state. Someone must call. Was it easy to find a job or employ yourself without specialising in any position? The days went by, and I looked at everything I had learned and not learned without doing anything and prepared for the upcoming interview. How many days will go by like this?

"What? Haven't you got any job?" Many people keep asking! It does not take many days to drain the courage that comes with detachment and frustration. Especially when others, including often-seen classmates, get a job somewhere and go away when you know something like that is still far away.

A week later, Thambichan came back from Kochi. There was no going back, he said. I asked, "Why?"

"I attended an interview for Trainee Engineer in the Port Trust. I got that Job. I must go to Paradip Port in Orissa and join. When the opportunity arises, I can try to relocate to Kochi."

At first, it didn't seem easy to comprehend that such a close childhood companion would go to a place so far away. But he got a job there, and I was so happy to learn that he wanted to go there and join.

"You are going after two days, and I'll come to your home !"

While studying for a diploma and waiting for a technical job, I was almost sure where we would get our job - it was nearly inevitable that it would not be close to home. Thambichan got a job in Paradip, Orissa. It may be possible to relocate to any other port in India. But for the first time, so far away, that too in a state that has not seen much development. It is not a port for cruise ships but for ships carrying iron ore and coal to other countries.

When can we meet again? If it's a good job, Thambichan will not fail to find a suitable one for me - even if he did not say so.

As he had said he would go to Kochi early in the morning and board the train, I went to Ottathyckal the previous evening to give him best wishes.

I walked through the light, narrow range of the paddy field to reach Ottathyckal. The paddy seedlings were dancing in the breeze for flowers. While walking, If the toes are not curled together, you will likely slip and fall to the base of the tendons. If you walk barefoot, you will surely stumble and fall.

Ottathyckal is also a solitary island in the middle of a paddy field—an island surrounded by water on all four sides if the area was not drained before cultivation, just like Kannattumadom. Thambichan's mother just brought a basket full of grass. They owned a cow and a calf. Thambichan was somewhere inside the house.

"Eda Thampa - de, didn't you see who has come?" - A special joy was there at that call.

Thambichan came out. Two or three more heads came out of the porch - Thambichan's sisters. I have seen them- The names were later found as Leelamma, Gracy, and Kunjamma. Thambichan's younger brother was a drop-out from school and ran a retail farm. From inside the house, I heard the voices of small kids calling their elder sisters. It was later learned that it was Mercy and Rosamma. Thambichan's Achayan was operating a grocery store in Parappalli.

The five sisters over the years

Thambichan deserves the best job as soon as possible. Everybody knows that. The giver of the blessings knows the needs of the recipients. Also, it is essential to prioritise their needs.

Thambichan's mother quickly milked the cow, brought coffee, and gave it to me. It was a hot steel tumbler. When I looked inside the stainless-steel tumbler, it was milk, not coffee. The old laziness of drinking milk must have been shown on my face as indolence. How do we plead the same to the host? - "Normally, I don't...drink. Milk as such...."

"Don't say anything, and it doesn't matter... there's only a little. Drink it."

I drank the hot milk like coffee in the sweetness of love and affection. Thambichan was also very happy.

"Happy that you came. You came and saw everyone."

"Pray to get a job as soon as possible. Shall write ..."

Ammachi Ottathyckal was always smiling through her hard work

The sun was setting in the west as I returned after wishing Thambichan all the best for his journey. Care was taken not to slip while walking back up the narrow ridge. When I turned around, Thambichan and his mother kept looking away.

A good morning will come, not too late, i.e., tomorrow. A good morning illuminates everything and shines a light of goodness on all. Let's wait for that good day.

Just after a week, Thambichan's letter came. He joined Paradip Port as a Trainee Engineer. Very happy to receive the good news. Thambichan very much desired that job. God has blessed an entire family with the blessings bestowed on Thambichan. Thank you, God.

Achayan came from Ambalappuzha, and after eating lunch, he was sitting on the leaning chair, and Kochachan walked in quickly. Even before sitting, he said he was coming from Kainakari –

"You have to go to Poona tomorrow and join for work as soon as possible! There was a letter received at Thevarkattu. Maybe it was a phone call. The older adult has sent a messenger to inform me. No sooner did I hear the information than I rushed to here?"

My mother's folded hands went up to the heights with her eyes. Achayan shook his head and raised his head, his eyes twinkling.

So, I got a job, too. Just join—no need to think about what career or salary. Just go and join. Maybe the job will be in his office itself.

There is a train from Cochin to Poona every day in the evening, and if you board it, you will reach Poona in the morning after two nights.

"You just have to go straight to his office. That is what was said."

First train journey.

I have not even thought about a long journey out of Kerala. I never travelled more than ten kilometers alone. I have never travelled by train and never seen a train! What all things to carry? How to carry? Isn't the bag I used to take things to Punnapra very small? Isn't it better to buy a small storage box? There are two or three shirts and two pairs of pants. There are shoes.

I went to Alappuzha and bought a tin box and a bedsheet. The toothbrush and paste were arranged.

"Take a bedsheet. Take one or two of the essential books that you have learned."

"Just go to Kochi. You can tell Kunjomma there to board you on the train. Someone you know will be there, and you won't miss them. It is a train that runs every day ..."

"Go home and get the blessings from Achayan and Ammachi."

Suggestions, advice...

On the way to the library, I told everyone on the way -

"Got a job, going to Poona ..."

I went to Kavalackal and saw my Ammayi and Achan.

Aunty looked at the kitchen as soon as she saw me there and said to her daughter -

"Kunjamma, you just give him a cup of black coffee. Give only that, and that too in the smallest cup". And then a laugh. The laughter hides the meanings. Love was filled in that smile. The Ammayi purposely ordered black coffee for me whenever I met her.

Aunty hugged and caressed my forehead. Twenty-five rupees pushed into the palm of my hand - "Keep it...you are beginning a journey...., will happen to be good. !"

23. A JOURNEY WITH CONFIDENCE

1966 November 28: Along with Achayan, I went to Kochi, and from there, along with Kunjommachayan, we arrived at Cochin Harbour Terminus. The train was leaving in the evening. A few rupees and the ticket were considered part of the preparations for the trip. Certificates and dresses were arranged and stacked in a box. In my head, what I had in mind was just the self-confidence I had gained over the period.

Crowds of people were there on the platform. The train was there on the platform. Too many people have already occupied the unreserved compartment. I must go inside regardless.

The blessing from the Arabian Sea was received through a gentle breeze that flowed. The wind was blowing incessantly. It was the beginning of dusk.

Achayan took the muffler from around his neck and wrapped it around my neck, and he said, "It will be cold at night."

My heart was pounding. I was determined to free my eyes from tears while beginning a journey. With folded hands, I sought blessings from Achayan and Kunjommachayan by saying 'glory to Jesus'. Achayan's face was thick with emotions; he tried not to cry, and no words came out. Tears welled up in my eyes. - "Let me go and come back."

"Only good will come to you," they said in their hearts.

I spent two nights and a day sitting and sleeping in the railway compartment, sitting on the floor and leaning my head on the seat, half asleep. When I was about to reach Poona, I was curious and anxious. I must get off the train at the station, find the bus stand, read the address, and get on the bus to the R&DE (Engrs) office. In the meantime, I decided to change the shirt I had worn for more than two days on the trip, first walking through the hustle and bustle of the compartment and then washing my face.

The train stopped at Poona. I did hang the tin box and went down to the platform. I looked around. Many wore white but very dull dhoti, torn shirts, and Gandhi caps, walking back and forth with others, some running. Those who sell sweets in a cart, tea in a kettle in one hand, and small glasses in the other...

"Thomas ..." someone called. Looking back, I saw VM Thomas, a familiar face. I remember Thomas, who studied as a senior at the Polytechnic.

"Don't you know me, Colonel Joseph Sir said - to take Thomas with me ."

What a relief. All the anxiety has gone.

It started with "Welcome to Poona". It was followed by a procession of inquiries, questions, and welfare, and I answered just by walking along. We arrived at the bus stand and boarded the bus to Vishrantwadi.

When I got off the bus, I saw a desolate area, a long road—three or four small shops near the bus stop. One of them was a tea shop. That's what the bench and the glass cupboard in the shop suggested.

"Did you eat anything, Thomas? Let's go and eat something here, and we have to walk a little to the office."

We had buns and tea. We walked. As there was no extra weight, the tin box was carried by my senior Thomas himself.

We walked down the road, which goes up to Alandi. We arrived at the gate of R&DE (Engrs). I left the box at the gate, so Thomas took me and went straight to Colonel Joseph Sir's office.

I got inside behind VM Thomas -

When I said, "Good Morning, Sir," I first saw Colonel Joseph Sir looking up.

"So. You are Thomas."

I could see a proud, majestic moustache on wrinkled lips. I saw a small smile there—lighter on the face. I kept on looking at that face and was standing motionless. He did not repeat anything.

He opened the table drawer and took out a long envelope –

He stretched it out to me.

"You can come and join tomorrow, Okay -

"Thank you, Sir."

I folded my hands and said thank you.

It was the sight of my 'God'. I needed an occupation. He gave it to me.

I visited the library with Thomas and met another colleague, Jacob Thomas. VM Thomas returned to his office after handing me over and saying he would see me again.

After office hours in the evening, Jacob Thomas took me to Pimpri, where he lived. Jacob Thomas was entrusted with arranging accommodation for me. VM Thomas was responsible for picking me up at the railway station.

I slept that day in the house of Jacob Thomas at Pimpri, where he lived alone. When we woke up early the next day, I went to R&DE (Engrs) with Jacob Thomas and joined for work. It was on December 01, 1966.

My career was from December 01, 1966, to February 28, 2006. A break was announced for the memoirs, thinking I could still write after superannuating from the service. The interval was a little too long.

It has now been 14 years since I retired from official life. To this day, I have been engaged in a more exciting occupation. So, there, I could find no time for writing. Today, yesterday, and the next day, nothing came for the work I had been doing for over three months. It's not going to be that easy in the coming days. This is my chance to start writing again - because I do not know how long my life will last. "The night when no one is allowed to work is approaching."

At the beginning of the New Year 2020, a contagious disease called COVID-19 caused by the coronavirus, which could affect an entire population, began spreading to India. It arrived in India at the end of January. Lockdown restrictions were imposed throughout the country and continued through March. The regulations were eased out step by step except for specific precautions. Yet the crisis continued even after a year.

When I feel like writing about the beginning of my official life, I often think about where to start and when I must write. Before the end of the journey, another journey, through the paths taken, a rebirth, is the reason for the description. Most of it I remember so clearly.

Isn't that like the origin of life? Isn't it like a sapling sprouting from a coconut and growing into a coconut tree? Isn't there innocence, greed, hatred, despair, calmness, hope, and love? Don't forget anything. The tree parable, which lacks freedom of movement and does not express emotions, may not be a proper fit here. How can life be complete without transportation and language for communication?

Man is born and grows, i.e., studying and working; he finds as much perfection and purposefulness in the family as possible in his life on his own and retires - that's life! In my case, the thought of 'retiring from work' never occurred.

Jacob Thomas spoke to Madhavan, who runs a typical Kerala Mess in Kirkee Bazar, and arranged accommodation for me at 155 JA Block. I could always have food from the Mess every day. Gopalakrishnan, Venugopal, Radhakrishnan, his younger brother Prabhakaran, and some unmarried youths lived next to the Mess on the first floor. The Kirkee Bazaar and the bus stand were close by. From there, you could take a bus to Vishrantwadi. You can reach R&DE (E) in a few minutes.

New routines were started in a new place- New friends, unfamiliar situations. Work was never done, and I ate unusual food.

When you leave the living room and head to the veranda, you will find the city streets full of shops on both sides. People walk on both sides of the road. In front of the room, you can see the city and the suburbs from the balcony- bicycles, bullock carts, and wheelbarrows amidst the flow of vehicles on the road. The living room is upstairs, so the noise from the street below does not fully reach the living room. On the opposite side of the road was a four-storey building, the Irani Hotel. On the upper floors, there was a lodge.

It was not difficult to adapt to the new environment. Or, it is correct to say that I was satisfied with the facilities provided there, without any other means. Awareness of where the better infrastructure is outside your own home is something you have not yet experienced.

The transition from fifteen years of student life to professional life has occurred. The six months that slipped into the job quest were a break in between or a long midsummer vacation.

The maximum period of professional life in everybody's life should be forty years. It depends on the job, where it is, the fatigue level that runs throughout, or the happiness you get out of the career. In the meantime, I must start a new life, continue, and live well to benefit everyone at home and in the country.

Most importantly, the family's growth through efforts without over-reliance on anyone, one's life ahead, the happiness of the cohabitants, cooperation, and progress towards the goal are all meant by such a change over time. When you say goodbye to your people and fellow citizens, travel long distances, and join a job won by the mercy of many, when you start living in new circumstances, isn't this what everyone wished you, blessed you, and sent you for?

Eighty-nine days of appointment, the basic salary of Rs.150/- and the allowances accordingly- were the employment conditions. No work was given on the ninetieth day. This type of work arrangement is called 'casual employment. You must register your name in the employment exchanges. The employment exchange will nominate the candidates who must pass an interview to get a permanent job in any establishment. This is the rule for institutions to recruit personnel. Temporary appointments can be made through casual employment to continue working for 89 days. The military officer who handed me the order to join the job could appoint me for casual employment. Suppose you want a permanent position in any institution or establishment. In that case, you must go to the employment exchange, register your name, and wait for nominations. In the first week, I entered the employment exchange in Poona and registered my name there.

My casual employment was in the E&M department at the Defence Research and Development (Engineers) establishment.

There were a few foreign-made civil engineering construction equipment in the inventory of defense services, and none of the foreign-made engines was working. This equipment can be operational by replacing the original engines with Indian substitutes and other maintenance tasks. That was the Job. New fittings were needed when the new motor arrived. The job was done once it was designed, fabricated, and fitted. The rest of the servicing was done, tested, and fully functional. Thus, twenty pieces of equipment were lined up on the office premises.

During off-peak hours, I would go to the Chemistry Laboratory, which operated from the nearby barracks. John was one of the scientists who worked there. Going to John and exchanging pleasantries were regular engagements, and there was rare happiness within the monotonous bureaucracy and government work.

John would say and listen to everything with brotherly love. John lived in a one-room house near the workplace. John's cousin Joy worked in a private company, and he was doing agency work for LIC in his spare time. Joy lived in Khorpuri, Poona. The LIC agency for Joy was an additional source of income, and he was doing it at his convenience. John and Joy belonged to Kangazha, east of Changanacherry, in Kerala.

Our church was searched and found on the first Sunday- St. Ignatius Church. After the prayer, I met many locals and colleagues in the church courtyard. I joined the Kerala Catholic Association - KCA activities in my early days in Pune. Moolakatte Georgekutty was a familiar face I met there, and he was from Kainakari.

I was overjoyed when I got my first paycheque. I sent a money order of Rs 101 to Achayan. After paying the rent, mess bill, and retail expenses, the rest was set aside for the bus ride. I purchased a bed and a pillow to lie down on the floor.

One day after work, when I came out of the R&DE (E) gate, I saw Ayyappan Nair waiting for me at the entrance. He studied with me till the eighth class in Vaishyambhagom and is the son of Gopalan Nair, who ran a grocery and tea shop on the north side of

Pullassery Madam. His elder brother had joined the Army along with Pachu Pillai.

He got off the train at Poona, took the bus, and went straight to meet his friend and find some work. Ayyappan Nair had no money, even for the expenses and travel. He had just a tiny bag. I could not find a way to help him. I have taken him to my room. In the evening, we went out to walk, and we walked down to where some prominent army officers were staying. If you see any high-ranking officer who may be unfamiliar, but if a word will be helpful for a friend, even that is solicitous. If he is hired, that is enough, said Ayyappan Nair. We met Colonel Gupta of R&DE (E) and told him the same. He made a few phone calls and explored the possibilities. We had to return disappointed. After eating dinner together, Ayyappan Nair slept nearby, but perhaps he could not sleep all night. He got up early and was ready to go.

"It's not right for me to stay here, so please do me a favour, give me fifty rupees. I can write to my elder brother to send the money from home to the address here. "

"Where are you going? Isn't it better to go back home?"

"No, I'm not going to return home anyway. My brother's acquaintance is in Madras, and I will search for him ."

"The full salary received in January was paid in the first week of February. I have the cash with me only for this month's bus trip."

Ayyappan Nair got sad. "Let me see," I asked Madhavan, who was running the Mess, for help, and I got 25 rupees. I put fifteen rupees more, and 40 rupees were given to Ayyappan Nair. He was happy and continued his journey to make a living for himself and others in his family.

"That's enough."

It's my birthday on Saturday the 11th, and I knew the desire to dine in any hotel would no longer happen. Two weeks later, Ayyappan Nair's elder brother's money order came, with a note written below in the coupon.

"Sending Rs 40 / -. Good, you helped Ayyappan well. He reached Bombay and got a small job. See you when you come home."

The Money Order was sent back without acceptance, and I felt it was incorrect to receive a charity where I helped someone when he needed it. It was a trivial help without expecting anything in return. I felt a little happy. That is the reward and gratitude I received.

In R&DE (E), I worked on casual employment thrice for 89 days each. I joined the job each time in anticipation of a call from the employment exchange. They shortened the fourth extension to only four weeks. It was the rule. Only nominees from the employment exchange can be hired! The call came from the employment exchange while I was sending applications for other jobs, thinking it would go as it should. A call came in at the end of my third casual employment and halfway through my fourth. It was in another institution. It was also an R&D organisation. If it was engineering equipment at R&DE(E), it was the new establishment's design and development of armaments. It was about ten kilometers away and could be reached by bus. Or make accommodations somewhere close by if you attend the interview and get the job. There was no increase in salary, and if received, the position would be permanent. Will not be divorced every three months. There was no need to reunite. Permanent and secure work was the best. Leaving R&DE (Engrs) and the friends should be considered seriously.

John said, "It doesn't matter. You can get a permanent job. ARDE is just another division of the same organization, and you can move here later if you desire."

I attended the interview. After leaving Carmel, I again met four or five classmates - James Kutty, Vijayappan, Samuel, Kamath, and others from the same batch. The interview was well done. They liked the answer to the question about what I did in addition to my study at Carmel.

"I was in NCC and passed the 'B' and 'C' Certificates examinations, making me more eligible for defense engineering jobs. I have participated in the camps and trained to shoot using firearms ."

What type of guns were used?

"0.303-inch (7.62 mm) and 0.202-inch"

The board chair was a senior Army officer. They considered this man to be good for the design and development of armaments. They gave me the selection and told me to join the job immediately.

After the interview, I laughed with my friends and exchanged pleasantries. I was wondering about something and wanted to discuss it with friends.

When I said I had been trained to shoot with a 0.202-inch gun, the chair smiled at other board members. I did not understand why it was so. The under officer in NCC, Jameskutty Thomas, clarified that the correct caliber cartridge size was 0.22 inches, not 0.202. "You said 0.303 and 0.202 thoughtlessly like a flow of words."

"Even if I were not selected, you would surely be selected, Jameskutty."

They did not forgive my mistake. I was deputed to develop the 0.22-caliber rounds used in police rifles. The slightly sharpened flat end of a bullet made of brass is split in four with a small hack-saw and pressed into a case filled with ammunition on the opposite side. When the trigger pulls, the bullet runs out of the rifle. When the bullet hits, the front will bloom like a lily. A mushroomed shell increases surface area and damages the place it hits. It spreads and becomes a large wound on the affected body part. It does not penetrate deep. Because it is made of brass, it will not rust if stored for a while. It will cause a big wound in the human body. It will not penetrate and kill the person on the other side! The police do not have the power to kill anyone in a riotous mob, but they can cause injury as a deterrent.

Jameskutty and Vijayappan were also selected for ARDE. They were posted in the main office. They let me go and work in the Small Arms Division in Kirkee, near where I stay. I did not have to change my place of stay to attend the office. I worked there for more than two months. That's when another call came in from the employment exchange, this time to attend a job interview at R&DE (Engrs), where I had first worked—having the opportunity to return to R&DE (Engrs) and pass the interview. I took leave, attended the discussion, got selected, and got a permanent job in R&D(Engrs).

I resigned from ARDE and joined R&DE (Engrs). I was then posted to the same department where I had previously worked. Friends like Jacob Thomas, John, and VM Thomas were delighted to see my return as an opportunity to see and interact more closely, often without stipulating 89 days of temporary work.

Aviation, space, and defence are the words engraved on my brain. I believe it may be the lines on my head/ brain (ശിരോലിഖിതം). These are the domains I passed through during my career. I got a job first in defence and my permanent job in defence. I received interview letters from Air India for Trainee Technician, Senior Operator Gde-1 from Lignite Corporation, and Technical Supervisor Grade-III in Inspectorate of Armaments. The mind did not allow itself to take advantage of the opportunities that came with the prospect of getting an excellent job at R&DE, which I thought was good for future progress and the possibility of getting more career prospects. Within four or five months, the desire for a position of any kind had grown into the hope of a job with a promising future!

Thambichan's letter came. After training, he secured an Overseer (Mechanical) job at Paradip Port.

24. JOB AT HOME STATE

In October, I saw an advertisement from ISRO's SSTC in Thumba inviting applications for posts ranging from technical assistants to upwards. The first reaction was that it would be better to end the life of an expatriate and get a job in your state so that you could come home at least once a week or a month. I have been away from home for about a year. What if nostalgia didn't seem so overwhelming and disturbing, but an opportunity like this never came close?

The application was sent. I revised everything I had learned in thermodynamics and workshop technology and was ready to go when called for an interview. After the interview, I could go home for the first time without taking a vacation. It would be even better if the interview date were close to Christmas.

"Hi, the smart one. You are a lucky guy. Haven't you succeeded in all the interviews you have given so far? You will win this one too. How much better it will be there in Kerala than being here in this jungle" - Gopalakrishnan, 'Mash,' the oldest of my roommates - as everyone calls him - wished me well.

The interview letter came for another job before I left for ISRO, Thiruvananthapuram. The Employment exchange might have suggested it. The position is here at the most popular CME nearby. It is the only institution in India that provides knowledge and higher studies in various disciplines to those in the military service. Work as a teacher there and impart knowledge and training to those in service. Good job. Being a college, it only works until three o'clock. You will get paid more than you get now. The basic pay itself is Rs 250 / -. There is time to think. It is enough to go to Thiruvananthapuram after this interview. Anyway, try and choose the best one from what you get.

How long did you wait for an interview call last year? It was more than six months after the results of the diploma examination. Now, two interviews in a month. How many were over this year?

CME is a vast organisation. College of Military Engineering, Pune (CME) is the premier technical and tactical training institution of the Indian Army Corps of Engineers. The interview was in the Faculty of E & M Engg Division, where you must work if selected. I went for the interview with the permission and blessings of Colonel Joseph Sir.

The interview took place in a classroom. There were four or five members on the board. And there were about fifteen candidates. When it was my turn, I was told to go to the stage and teach how a 4-stroke engine worked. Well, I was happy to explain that. As Balan Sir taught me, I spoke. All those minor errors were mine alone. I thought there was no need for high hopes, so I thanked the board members after the interview and left. Most of the other job seekers were born and brought up in Poona. Swamy came from Andhra Pradesh, and Jamakhandi from Gulbarga. In the hope of seeing each other again, everyone wished each other further success and departed.

I went straight to Thiruvananthapuram to face the ISRO interview. It was in November.

When I went to Thumba for an interview, a friend from Kirkee met me and asked, "Who is the one who came from Kirkee?"

He had come to meet me because he once stayed in the lodge attached to the Irani Hotel, opposite where I was staying in Kirkee. He had come to receive me and take me to a motel in Kesavadasapuram to arrange a meal.

I came home after the interview at Thumba. If I got a selection, I thought many such trips as this would be required between Punnapra and Thiruvananthapuram.

It has been a year since I left for Poona, and when I returned home, I saw no significant changes. The list of requirements was long. No one noticed any visible changes. I went to Thiruvananthapuram on leave for three or four days without thoroughly preparing to meet my domestic needs. I should return to my current job immediately after.

Achayan's suggestion was justifiable and reasonable.

"It would be a great blessing to get a job in Thumba. It would be good to come and join soon. That's what everyone here wants. Then do as you desire and appropriate."

Achayan's interest further strengthened my desire to work in my home state.

I returned to Poona, and within a week, the offer of an appointment for work in Thumba came. Join for work in Thumba as soon as possible with a medical certificate. A medical certificate can be obtained from Thiruvananthapuram Medical College.

Everyone was happy for me to get a job in Thumba and go there. I thanked my superior in R&DE, Colonel Balakrishnan Sir, my immediate boss. I got a relieving letter from the office, paid the mess bill and rent, and said goodbye to friends and all the roommates. It was most challenging to say goodbye to Col. Joseph Sir. He was the one who caused me to come to Poona and get a job. I was very emotional. These were the words of goodness that Col. Joseph Sir gave me while parting as a gift of love -

"I have been watching you. Unlike others, you are quite good. Keep it up. You have a good academic record. Do hard work and complete your AMIE. These are difficult times. You are young, 21 years old now. It may not be the case when you are 28 or 30. You must pass through a crucial phase. I am sure you would have achieved a lot if you had been here. But anyway, it is also good. Wish you all the best."

"Thank you, Sir."

I will never forget you. I love and respect you as my father. When I left his room, my eyes and mind were filled with that one thought.

After saying goodbye to Poona, I got on the train. It was the pleasure and happiness of a traveller returning home after his first foreign trip throughout the journey.

The next day, I obtained a medical certificate at the Medical College Hospital. I took a Thumba Equatorial Rocket Launching Station (TERLS) bus to the Space Science & Technology Center (SSTC) in Thumba, later renamed the Vikram Sarabhai Space Center (VSSC), and joined the office. I was assigned to the Electronics development section.

I wrote a 'thank you letter' to Colonel Sir when I remembered him. Of course, I owe him a lot.

At SSTC, they were in the final stages of developing the Rohini RH 75-sounding rocket. There was a project head in the section, four young women- Ammal, Ambika, Radha, and Radhamoni; a young man named Sundar; a middle-aged technician named Raghavan; and me. The job of that section was to develop electronic equipment used in rockets.

It was thought that working in such a section would be a punishment for not showing much interest in the subject of Electrical Engg and its subsidiary Electronics while studying in Carmel. Colleagues have reassured me that everything could be learned along the way. The first thing I did was drill some holes in a small Hylam sheet according to a drawing drawn by someone. Raghavan also said that I did well. The girls soldered electronic parts such as transistors, resistors, and diodes in the holes in the Hylam sheet, tested them with a megger, and made a small device called a radio transmitter for use in rockets. I remember using it on a Rohini

RH 75-sounding rocket. November 20, 1967, was an unforgettable day for ISRO and me. When ISRO launched the first Indian-made Rohini RH 75-sounding rocket into the atmosphere. Tied to the seat and carrier of a bicycle, they pushed the bike forward on foot and delivered it to the launch site of the rocket trunk. The next day, I saw a photo of it in the Manorama Daily and kept it in mind.

That was when a mail carrier came to my office looking for me with a registered letter for the first time. When I read the letter, it surprised me and put me in a dilemma. It took a while for the light of understanding to come through. In hindsight, this letter could only be seen as an act of God doing everything for good. Every interview I attended, I passed. It has been about three months since the discussion at CME. The dream of getting a job there had faded. Only now have they realised that the need for the Indian Armed Forces to acquire engineering knowledge was possible through me, too!

It was like sending my mind on a rocket from Thumba to Poona. What are the conditions under which the body can be brought to Poona? How do you convince your parents that the work-at-home state is enough to get me home once a week? Wouldn't it be better to work nearby in your home state for career advancement? Is the present home our permanent home?

There will be a fifty percent increase in the salary. How long will it take to continue working here to gain that much financial gain? How can I claim an immediate pay raise in an organisation where I have not worked for a month?

'Radha 2 Ambika Ammal' - I used to call all four young ladies together, as they were all sitting side-by-side in a room with me. They could see me as a good friend and colleague within a few days. So, having to leave them was not something they were happy about. The words of consolation would be 'see you again.

I met Kochuppappan on the weekend and sought his advice. He drafted an application and said – "Give it a try."

"Aglow, with feelings of a good relationship, I would like to submit…."

That was how the words in the application began with.

If you give me a slight pay raise, I can stay here, or I would like to return to Poona. Anyway, I've been there for about a year. It is a great place to be, and teaching is an excellent profession.

"Consult your father and do the needful . Only good will come to you". Kochuppappan blessed me.

I gave the application, met Director Murthy, and talked to him. This was the reply he gave.

"Chairman Vikram Sarabhai will come in two days, and we will talk to him and inform you of the decision."

The decision announced two days later was not favourable.

25. ANOTHER START

I resigned from SSTC before Christmas. I received the relieving letter on December 30, 1967. In the evening, I ended my stay at the lodge at Kesavadasapuram and boarded the bus home.

After returning home, I commenced a new journey on the first day of 1968. I boarded the train back to Poona for a new job. All the parental blessings and greetings were with me. No one had come to Kochi to see me off. John had come to receive me in Poona. I went to the same place where I stayed two months ago. No one stopped me from entering there either. My roommates considered me as I had returned from vacation. John at R&DE came ready to take me with him if I could not stay there at Kirkee.

I soon joined CME and joined the workforce. I was assigned to the Faculty of Electrical & Mechanical Engineering for day-to-day work. Refrigeration and air conditioning were subjects taught there for a degree, diploma, and other short courses for defence personnel. I met the authorities and my colleagues and introduced myself. The boss asked me-

"Are you prepared?" I said nothing.

Heat Engines and Thermodynamics are all well-studied in the college. Refrigeration & Airconditioning was a chapter I missed due to a lack of time to explore in detail for the Final Year Diploma Exam. Even if some questions come from that chapter for the diploma examination, there will be nine questions. We were to answer only six of them. It was possible to skip one or two chapters from the study, i.e., to miss three questions so that out of the nine questions, we only needed to do the remaining six questions in three hours!

I skipped reading the (Thermodynamics) Refrigeration And Airconditioning chapters to save time for review before the final exams.

The first thing I was asked to teach during the job interview at CME was the subject taught by Balan Sir. I spoke just like he taught me, and I got the job. Then, the topic my professor assigned me to teach in classes was Refrigeration and air conditioning! My eyes went blank! The professor consoled me by saying there were seventeen books on the subject in the Central Library.

"After reading and studying those books from the library, you will feel confident to take classes in about three months. Only then shall you go to any class to teach!"

That was a military command. At least it sounded so.

I took the books and read, learned the subject, and gained confidence. Since then, I have taught refrigeration and air conditioning in degree and diploma classes for 11 years. The topic I skipped during my studies has become a means of earning my bread & butter for the rest of my life!

This is something that students need to understand specifically. Maybe what we neglect in college is very important for our careers. If we have gained the confidence to work in college, we can succeed in any activity in life, anywhere.

Here are some of the ones I found to be interesting. Even if you have excluded some chapters from the study and exam, the branches left out may become necessary for your professional work.

"Learn more and be ready to teach."

"That's enough," said Anantharaman also, my immediate boss. "Go to the library and pick up relevant books and study. I will give you three months. After that, be ready to engage in any class." He was reiterating what the professor told me.

I went to the library on that day. A vast building with various rooms full of books, multiple subjects, a reading room, and a thousand books on a single topic! The librarian was a Malayalee named Johnny, a lovable person. I felt the dilemma in my mind for a while, like a hungry man standing before a sumptuous 'buffet.' I returned to the office with some books I had picked up. The refrigeration and air-conditioning section of the CME has all kinds of standard equipment, including refrigerators, cold storage, ice manufacturing plants, air conditioners, central air conditioning plants, etc. In addition, the theoretical study included the study of all kinds of equipment and practical classes for maintenance, repair & overhaul. The specialty of this institute was that all the course participants should be trained at the operational level, relating to the routine functioning and activities of the equipment.

Happiness, confidence, and a curiosity for knowledge are the fundamental lessons of duty and discipline learned from Carmel. In addition, mental training, development, and the mercy of the teachers. During the NCC parade, Kuzhiveli sir explained clearly what duty and discipline are, their differences, and the appropriate context. It helped me a lot while working at the CME.

I commenced taking classes on March 20. By the end of the year, I had taken lessons for almost all types of courses and had gained reasonable confidence. When I stepped onto the stage to teach at the College of Military Engineering (CME), I gained tremendous confidence to face the audience.

All those sitting in front were people who had completed their school and college education, had completed military training in the Army, were employed, and received a higher monthly salary than I had. Yet, they did not know what I was talking about. If you say it well, they will give you love and respect like a guru.

Bacteria are present in all foods. Bacterial growth causes damage and depletion of stored food. All food items can be stored intact for more days if the growth of bacteria can be prevented. All you need to do is keep it cool and frozen. Doing so can prevent the growth and proliferation of bacteria. How can food be stored refrigerated and frozen?

"Refrigeration is the process of maintaining a space at a temperature lower than the surroundings."... The class began. Heat transfer, convection, thermodynamics, compression .... Thus, the heat of compression, condensation, capillary, evaporation, latent heat of evaporation, insulation, heat, cool.... So, we progressed and arrived at the air conditioning.

" Refrigeration introduced and implemented family planning method for bacteria!" The audience put a smile on their faces and agreed with the teacher.

The first impression lasts. That's what happened. When on stage with severe body language and conversations, contextual humour sometimes comes up. It will motivate the listeners to pay more attention and join the discussion. Thus, the closeness and love for the students increase, and our confidence increases.

Their discipline does not allow them to show misdeeds, as in academic schools or colleges. Their job was to listen carefully, learn the subject, and gain practical knowledge. This reality has been an incredible blessing for me from the beginning of engaging in classes there. That was the advantage of working in CME. Further, teaching itself has evolved to be a delightful job.

Anantharaman Sir said –

"In a year or two, you can reach the pinnacle of your confidence by reading more books like those you have already read and taking better classes. After that, it is enough to update and develop your knowledge through periodicals, etc..."

True, that is the complete responsibility of a man's career in official life.

I also remembered what Colonel Sir had said.

"You are young. 21 years now. It may not be the case when you are 28 or 30. You must pass through a crucial phase. You should have achieved a lot if you were here."

The curious mind asked itself - But I am in a different establishment and job. I hope I will have a promising future here as well.

Eleven years and two months (1968 January 03-1979 February 28) have passed. I took classes for many different courses from 7:30 in the morning to 3 in the afternoon.

Students can easily understand the basics and learn more about science and technology. That is an excellent method to teach, too. After studying many books, I started all classes with an explanation of the basics. Then, I progressed to the science and technology of the equipment.

Before I started teaching, my head of the department (HOD) assigned me to supervise an examination hall. During the examination, I saw an Army Captain copying something from a piece of paper brought by him. It was an unexpected event. I felt no fear. I seized the answer paper and the extra bit of paper he had brought. I thought it was malpractice.

The horror of my early days-heroism was experienced by the students who were officers - it was a moment of pride for me! I stared at him and did not say anything. The captain looked at me for a while and irritatedly walked out of the hall, not liking it. I reported the suspected malpractice incident and the evidence to the HOD. I did not know what disciplinary action was taken. I did not pursue it further. I did not have responsibility for it.

The same captain was promoted and became a major and a teacher in another department of CME six or seven years later. When I saw him in person, we refreshed our familiarity. The unpleasant memories we had were deliberately kept hidden in a smile.

Many top army officials got their refrigerators repaired, and the opportunity was used to train participants in various courses. The Ice Plant was operated periodically, and ice slabs were manufactured for the military regatta.

Examinations were conducted, and evaluations were done. Many students were taken to Bombay and Delhi's Refrigeration and air conditioning factories for practical training. Many sincerely thanked us for receiving their knowledge and training. Many utilised their expertise and training beneficially for their units and equipment.

I later learned that some established private servicing workshops for equipment, such as self-entrepreneurship, and progressed in life.

What did the career give you in return?

I got paid every month. Money orders were sent home every month. Sometimes, it is a little less; the following month, it fills up the shortfalls. Sometimes, it wasn't easy to reconcile the two ends. Friends helped me all the time. Sometimes, I, too, helped them. Who else but friends can be relied upon when necessary for those who live away from home?

26. OFFICIAL LIFE BEGINS

The episodes of events continue every day. Some days, it gives you happiness. Some days, it brings additional effort and sometimes challenges. Almost all days pass on with a mix of joys and challenges, with many variations. Naturally, it affects us physically and mentally. After all, that is what life we pass through.

In the first year of my working in CME, the local postman one day brought a registered parcel, a tin wrapped in cloth, one day before Easter. I was happy and surprised when I opened it! There were a lot of Avalos Unda (roasted rice powder balls, a traditional Syrian Christian snack from Kerala), along with a letter from my mother. It was full of love and sweetness. The roommates and the boys laughed and enjoyed themselves with the mess members.

One month later, I received a notice from the octroi superintendent of the Poona Municipal Corporation stating –

"You must notify the contents of the parcel you received a month back and pay the duty (octroi) for goods contained in the package - at the office. Otherwise ... "The usual warning of the arrogant, ruling bureaucracy! Because the bureaucracy believes that all those notified are misconstrued as wrongdoers! Therefore, the punishment is first notified before any wrongdoing is confirmed. When will my country improve? When will they act with humility and fraternally and deal with people democratically, assuming that all Indian citizens are law-abiding human beings and that they are all patriots until proven otherwise?

I went to the PMC office and gave an affidavit that "it was the Avalos Undas (rice balls) sent by my mother."

"Okay, eatables.... from home? Pay Rs 0.15 in a challan," the officer ordered.

Octroi paid, and a receipt was obtained. Everyone in the room came together and laughed at the bureaucracy's antics. They stopped laughing while biting the Avalos Undas.

In Poona, March is the month from which the winter season changes to summer every year. In March 1969, I got chickenpox and sought refuge at the Corporation Hospital. The illness usually recuperates within seven to eight days. But after a week, I had pneumonia and a few other complications, so it took me 15 days to return to the residence. My roommate Padmanabhan once came to visit me in the hospital. After being cured of the contagion and returning to my room, I thought of the lonely days I spent in the hospital, staring blankly at the emptiness without any emotions except fear. Not fearing dying but thinking about how many people will have to struggle for a person's obsequies and posthumous deeds. That's the life of an expatriate. Now, it can only be remembered with fear.

John came looking for me after a week in the hospital. John later said I spoke to him like I had lost consciousness when he met me. When I went to CME with a fitness certificate, I was exhausted. After joining the work and writing home, only all at home knew I was in the hospital.

How much more terrible is the Covid epidemic today? How tragic is the fact that the bodies of those who died in the hospital due to infectious disease were not even shown to their next of kin? The dead bodies were wrapped and taken to the cemetery for cremation or burial. Six months after the pandemic started, the government revised its guidelines - 'The face of the dead may be shown to relatives, and specific religious obsequies may be carried out ." We have passed through a terrible period.

Letters were coming in regularly from home, and replies were sent soon to everyone.

Learning more was a dream. I have applied for student membership at AMIE with a copy of my diploma certificate. I should appear for the section 'A' examination. It was learned that a coaching class was being organised at the Ammunition Factory, Kirkee. I paid the fee through my roommate, Padmanabhan, and joined the first Mathematics class. I attempted to complete the AMIE (Section A and Section B) by studying two or three subjects per attempt and not taking more than three years. I commenced my studies. My daily routine was –

Teaching until 2 pm and studying from 4 pm onwards in the room, at least two hours before all roommates arrived. I Wrote the exam. I got three out of four subjects attempted in section A for the first time. The result came on my twenty-fifth birthday. I was happy to start preparations for the next exam without wasting more days. Swamy, my colleague in CME, came to my room to do a combined study. It worked out very well.

I have actively participated in social gatherings & sports events in connection with the anniversary of KCA in the church. I was able to meet and cooperate with many Malayalee Catholics. They gave me more responsibility for conducting the sports. Georgekutty Moolakatte had planned to relocate to Bombay and went to his native before doing that. He would go to Bombay after returning from Kainakari. I had been to the railway station to see him off. I requested him to go to Arackal house and tell my grandmother that her grandson at Poona was fine. "Convey my regards to everyone there. Give this to Ammammachi, and she will be happy." A small amount was handed over to Georgekutty.

Unfortunately, a girl named Raji did not get a good start in the 100-meter race. The girl's mother complained that the starter blew the whistle without ensuring the participants were precisely on the starting line. I was the starter. Manichean, Jose, and many others rushed to my rescue. It was decided not to conduct the same category race again. There was no complaint from Raji. It was later learned that Raji's mother's resentment lasted a month or two. The protest was not that the match was not held again, but that the young man who did the sports event did not consider the graduated girl seriously enough!

After the event, Fr. Kuriani gave thanks and gifted me a book titled 'Life of Christ with a special vote of thanks for conducting the sports.

My cousin Joy started working in a Bata Shoe trading shop in Thane, Bombay. Ammini studied nursing and got a job in Bombay itself. When Joy came to Poona, I took him around in CME and showed him my place of work. Our rapport grew when I went to Thane for the Dussehra holidays.

Appachi's writings from Kainakari were initially about the frustration, uncertainty, and worries of unemployed youth, which are the most common reactions of an educated sibling. No matter how much effort you make to help him, the frustration will continue until he succeeds or reconciles the realities. He later assessed my attempts to get a job for him as indiscreet or negligent as it was getting delayed for good results.

Do you know what he had written? - "I was looking for the scent of some glamorous flowers in Poona." I did not know how to convince a brother, with a poetic sense of interpretation, that I did not realize nor seek the fragrance of any flower at all!

I sent the job advertisements with the application forms obtained from ISRO. I shipped them to my friends and classmates Muttar Sebastian and Isaac as they sought my help for employment. Appachi had a diploma in Civil Engineering.

On the first Easter, I joined John from R&DE and his cousin Joy in Poona. After church prayers, I went with John to Joy's residence.

The three of us sat on the floor and prepared everything for cooking. Joy cooked well, and he bought fish and chicken. He made nice round flat chapatis. Joy brought a bottle from somewhere when the cooking was over and served the food. I read the label - Brandy. That was the first time I tasted alcohol in Poona.

By the time we got back, it was very late.

I watched famous movies with John and Joy, such as The Ten Commandments and The Bible. It gave us an outstanding visual experience in the West End theatre.

Joy had a part-time business running a LIC Agency, a hobby after working in a private company. Business was generally good. When Joy came to my room and met my roommates, he greeted them and had lively discussions with them. Before returning home, he picked up two or three application forms for my roommates to enroll in the LIC. Joy requested me -

"Ask and see if they could join - it's better for them!"

I was able to become a salesperson without much effort. Radhakrishnan and Ramesan Nair, a newcomer to the room, signed the LIC application forms. The following month, on payday, I called Joy and handed over the papers - Life Insurance Business for Rs 30,000 / -. Joy was happy, so he opened his purse, took a note of a hundred rupees, and pushed it into my pocket! Despite my pleading not to give the commission to me!

"When their lives are safe, we can go to the nearby hotel and have a meal, which is a pleasure. The LIC pays so much commission." Said Joy.

The extra income I got was turned into an asset immediately. Suppose I Celebrate and get rid of hunger momentarily and luxuriously. In that case, I must return in the evening, spread the bed on the floor, and sleep in the room. That gave me a chance to rest as my friends did – Sleep on a cot. The food could be eaten from the mess. As usual, that was good enough. I bought a 6 X 3 steel cot for sleeping—the first significant movable property I purchased in Poona.

When it was time to go to bed, the light in the room often bothered Padmanabhan. He used to ask the one who usually slept on the floor - "Why don't you become Earth today? Is there no office tomorrow?"

Padmanabhan would be surprised when I spread the bed on the steel cot without going down 'to earth' tonight. Padmanabhan, belonging to Pattambi would comment with a smile on the corner of his lips and scratching his head's back.

Ramesan Nair started living with us by announcing the sale of his foreign-made Titoni watch. I bought the watch for Rs 125 as it looked attractive. I sent the watch to Achayan as a parcel. The HMT watch that Achayan bought for me when I got the scholarship was in my hand. I was always reluctant to wear gold jewellery. However, I liked the gold-coloured HMT watch Achayan from Ambalappuzha brought me. It had a black strap, and it was nice to wear.

27. TO KNOW MORE

Radhakrishnan's younger brother Prabhakaran was selected for the short service commission in the Army. He went to the Officers Training Academy, Chennai (OTA for training.

There was a large banyan tree to the right of the Irani Hotel in Kirkee. Most trade unions had held public meetings in the shady area beneath. The trade union organisation of thousands of workers at India's largest factory that makes ammunition meets there often. We can hear the leaders' speeches on my living room balcony. I had sometimes seen leaders like George Fernandez preaching there. Vice President VV Giri came one day and laid the foundation stone for a trade union building near the bus stand at Kirkee.

One day, Radhakrishnan's brother Sudhakaran and my classmate Thomas Mathew from Kozhencherry came from Satara. They both work for a Kirloskar Company in Satara. The whole day was spent joking, narrating heroics, and playing cards. When they returned, they invited us to visit Satara and spend time with them. We all went to Satara one day, had an excellent time there, and celebrated the whole day. Despite showing excessive joy or intoxication, it was proved that everyone could maintain discipline and obey unwritten rules of conduct amid the noise.

A forty-year-old man from Thrissur, Porinchu, who must have seen me attending KCA activities at the church, called me one day specifically. He lived very close to the CME. "You have to come home one day and say something significant. It's okay at home. Won't you come? "

I said I would come. The next day, after the office, I searched the house and found a thatched roof shed covered on its sides with tin sheets. Porinchu came down. A beautiful young woman followed him. She appeared to be twenty-two to twenty-four years old, not so tall and tired, but with a prosperous-looking face and a slight smile.

"May come inside."

I was scared! I did not know why.

An unfamiliar environment - I was sitting on a small stool near the door, ready to jump out quickly if required.

"It's my children - I'm shown a girl who looked about ten years old. Three other girls, ages 6, 4, and 2, are standing around their sister. My fears were allayed soon.

"Well, Porinchu - what do you want to say." I meant that I could have gone if you could finish faster.

"Sir, kindly request our parish priest to baptise my children so I can arrange their confession and the holy communion."

It was a great relief. Well, I am too happy to be a missionary. Is that enough? I asked silently. I promised to do all I could to help them and returned, saying I would see everyone at the church next week. I was hoping to get a bumper crop here instead of a soul.

The following week, they came to church. I met the parish priest and talked about them. Father wanted to know the whole history. After arranging to speak to them for a long time, I waited in the courtyard with other friends until the parish priest called me when the discussion was over.

"The flaws in their marriage must be resolved first. After that, everything else is easy. This is what they have been told. Let them think about it and do what they need to. There will be cooperation from the parish."

They went back. I have not had the opportunity to see them since then. Porinchu did not come back looking for me further.

I began to call Sebastian K. Joseph 'Brother' in my first year since I saw him as my most sincere friend at Carmel College. He was kind, compassionate, and of helping nature. He knew about my family and me, including Antony Sir at the college, and my likes and dislikes. He was always willing to cooperate with me for mutual benefit. He had the courage and conviction for all things good, ethical, and moral.

I could seek solutions to complex problems from him, and we were steadfast and stood together when we faced difficulties and passed through stressful periods. We often met in the chapel for the morning mass, at the dining table, and during our free hours at the hostel and college.

Separation on the last day of college was excruciating for both of us. He waited, though he said to let our future come as per His decision. After I, too, went to Poona, there was a lot of delay in getting happy news for him. We were in constant touch through letters.

The same Sebastian Kochuveedu in Muttar came to Poona searching for work. I had received a letter earlier saying that he was coming. No matter how many requests were sent, nothing reached the stage of an interview, and my efforts were not fruitful. Brother has decided to stay with George, his native and neighbour. George and his family lived in the Range Hills quarters of the Ammunition Factory. His wife was employed, and his two brothers and a sister stayed with him.

Sebastian soon got a call letter to interview for a job at the armament lab. The flash of light suddenly came to me was meeting Colonel Sir with Sebastian. Within a month, Sebastian joined the armament laboratory. The classmates often met, got together, went to Vijayappan's residence, and played badminton.

Thomas, a native of Mavelikara who worked for a private company close to CME, used to come to my room at 155 JA Block to see his friends on most Sundays. He was a close friend of Gopalakrishnan Mash and Ravi. He became a friend of mine, too, after getting acquainted. He and his family lived very near to the company where he worked.

Kuriat-Padmanabhan, my roommate, used to broadcast ageless words in the form of satire. It was like how Ravi responded to cricket commentary. The only difference was that the terms of Ravi were on the fence of comedy, separating vulgarity. Still, the words of Padmanabhan were always within the boundaries.

When friends get together and talk about politics, art, literature, or cricket, they criticize me, make fun of me, make me angry, and make the situation worse. Then, for a day, I would quarrel without speaking to anyone. Thomas was the one who helped most to change this behaviour. Thomas once said -

"Take it easy, Thomas, when they laugh, laugh together, make fun of ourselves, and laugh, as we have nothing to lose."

I changed my attitude so that what they said was for my good. I saw their method of criticism as teaching. When I started doing so, I was amazed at the positive change that had taken place. This has helped me to avoid conflicts and to maintain friendships.

One day, when I returned from the office, my friends were standing together and mourning.

"Our Thomas' seven-year-old son - who had a fever - was taken away by God. Their grief cannot be overlooked."

We all went to Thomas' house, shared our grief, and returned the next day after the funeral.

Not precisely three months had passed; Thomas, too, passed away, leaving many more in deep sorrow. He had jaundice or similar liver disease. Thomas' relatives from Mavelikara went home with Thomas' wife.

28. PERSONAL RELATIONS

Most CME colleagues went together to Bhuleshwar (Yavath), which is far from Poona. Pradhan, Jamakhandi, Swamy, Wagholikar and Pankhandi were there. Jayashree and Shobha came with Wagholikar. We got off the train at Yavath station and walked towards the Bhuleshwar temple on the hilltop. We did not feel tired as everyone climbed the hill, exchanging jokes and laughing. There were many granite sculptures and stone slabs in and around the temple. The landscape and farmland were beautiful from the top of the hill—lovely scenery outside the city. After lunch, we turned into two batches and were about to play the cards on the hilltop on the temple grounds. In the second batch, Shobha was along with Wagholikar. Jayashree was in the first batch, which consisted of Swamy and me. After some time, when the card game ended, everyone visited the temple and captured the surroundings on camera.

Swamy and I stood a little apart and analysed the appearance of the Khajuraho-style sculptures.

Instead of visiting the temple, Shobha and Wagholikar laughed and communicated in their world. It was a naughty question to Swamy that I asked about Wagholikar, the reason for Swamy's sudden depression.

"What is the reason? Did I disturb my friend's mind?"

"Sorry, my friend. I was like that until a while ago. I desired so much. At first, we got close. We shared a lot of dreams, and I started loving her."

"Then what happened?"

"Almost six months on, we were on the verge of marriage. She presented the matter to her parents. You know, they are all Marathi

Brahmins. Very orthodox! My parents are from Vijayawada, and they speak Telugu. Her father knows the Wagholikar family. Slowly, she walked away from me. It was zero zones for some time. Now you see! It pains me a lot!

Swamy took a deep breath, and I stared helplessly!

What should I say?

Each such event gives us a unique experience on the other side and teaches lessons.

xxxX

No matter how lonely life is, what jobs, friends, and experiences, no one cares as time passes and months go by. But nostalgia - going home, seeing everyone, parents, relatives, elderly father and mother, the village, the natives, and so on - is all that was needed. A savings account in a bank is a savings account of ten or twenty rupees per month, found every month when calculating the income and the expenses so that it does not become more expensive. It was not possible every month. Sometimes, it was the recovery that happened. How can you be sure that a vacation trip would be enjoyable if you don't have at least a month's salary?

It was the time when land reform was implemented in Kerala. The property owner must pay the tenants five cents of the land to build a house. In Maramkunnil, my tenant's father wrote to me - we have nothing to lose or gain. Peace alone is enough. May we have peace without hearing anyone's curse or lamentation. We can eat bread with sweat on our foreheads. That is the law of God. We will be included in that law, though not in the land reforms law!

Achayan had written another essential thing. That was a question.

"Do you need money to come to see us?"

That said, there was not enough money to go on vacation immediately. At the beginning of March, he had told me to "send all your savings." Then, at the end of March, he asked, "Do you need money to come and see us?" It was not written that way. All the hardships were contained within. It was resolved to take a vacation anyway. I could not have seen my mother's eyes getting wet.

I joined the College of Military Engineering as a staff member, and it has been two years since I joined the College of Military Engineering. The first Easter of the seventies. This question also made the desire even stronger to see everyone on vacation.

"Good morning. Good morning at Paradip Port." Thambichan wrote from Paradip Port. He has asked if it would be possible to come on leave this month. He is going home without many preparations. He needed to return soon.

"If you can make it, try to come soon. The four sisters grow up together at home. The elder one was being allowed to study Malayalam. Those below have no job. Every time I went, I needed to bring at least one to do some work. If they stay home, only the cow gets enough rich food. The girls were all well-trained and were going to mow the grass for the cow. Humans still must search for their food. This time, Gracy is being taken along. I can put them up here at Bhubaneswar and send her for typewriting or shorthand. She must be added for a job somewhere. The purpose of my going home is the family's responsibility of being the eldest son."

Thambichan came home and went back with Gracy. I couldn't take a quick vacation. After two years, I could not see my friend because I had not gone home.

On the Saturday before Palm Sunday, Joy and Ammini, the children of the Kochi Uncle, were travelling to Kochi. I went to the Poona railway station to meet them. They would return from Kochi in three weeks.

If you could reach home before Easter, you could spend time with them. I have decided to go home. Most people who work away from their native state do the same. If you save money and wait to go home with that for vacation, it might not happen.

The next day, I applied for leave. Leelamma, my sister, wrote that a transistor radio was an essential item to bring home with me. After work with Swamy and Jamaghandi, I went to the Deccan Gymkhana and bought a Philips Victor transistor radio. The Malayalam conversation I heard while tuning in to the radio test was- സന്തുഷ്ടിയാണ് നിങ്ങൾക്ക് ആവശ്യം ("you need happiness"). The unnatural sound we hear from the sky, through the transistor, sometimes tells us what we desire most in our minds.

It was the day that the United States launched Apollo 13 into space. After getting a permanent job in Poona, I boarded a train for the first time to go home on holiday.

The joy of seeing siblings and parents eagerly waiting was boundless. The mother said something after a loving kiss. The greatest happiness for the brothers and sisters was that I brought a radio. Raju, Leelamma, Babu, and Babychan said the same thing. Who is there otherwise if their tiny wishes were not fulfilled in any financial crisis? That motivated me to buy a radio and take it with me. That night, after a long night of talking, everyone fell asleep.

After a long year, the health I lost through the diet from the mess, chickenpox, and pneumonia was partly restored, and I was back home. The situation at home is not so good. However, when my parents and siblings slept with me in the environment where I grew up, I said, "Oh, there is no better happiness even in heaven – Let the philosophy be away!" ".......സ്വർല്ലോകത്തും ലഭിക്കില്ലുപരിയൊരു സുഖം - പോക വേദാന്തമേ നീ! (ചങ്ങമ്പുഴ) ".(Changampuzha)

When I landed at Ernakulam, Joy was waiting. Leelamma, Ammini, and Joseph Kutty were there when we went to Thoppumpadi. We arrived in Alappuzha to board the Alappuzha-Kollam boat at 5:30 p.m. We were a little late. The boat left on time, then we travelled by bus to Punnapra, where he walked to my house. Nice words were heard from the locals all along the way. When I got home, it was half past eight at night. Due to the lack of local travel facilities, getting home from Ernakulam takes longer than travelling to Delhi.

I was waking up on Vishu day. I woke up late because I had slept late. After the morning rituals, we had breakfast -It was the Puttu (steamed cylinders of ground rice layered with coconut shavings) or Idiyappam (string hoppers, a culinary specialty of Kerala, consisting of rice flour pressed into noodles and then steamed) made by my mother. After that, I went to see my grandfather and grandmother. This time, I was meticulous not to repeat the mistake of the last time. They were loving and healthy. It was old age. They complained that the children did not dare to fulfill all their desires. I spoke about the new prayers and reforms in the church and repeated the old stories. I was asked about things in Poona. They eagerly inquired about my experiences: I met Joy and his younger siblings, including chittamma's recently born twins. My grandmother says -

That one is like you. All evil deeds, "All the 'subhavams' (idiosyncrasies) are there as it was for you, like that" –

"But he's the replica of our Souriarkunj, passed away long back!

Looking at my grandfather, Grandma said-

"Do you know what he did when playing with Kunjamma, his cousin - jumping onto the top of her? This boy is also jumping like that."

I said, "Yes, boy, keep up our family traditions. Good, I like it."

That smile and play on the children's faces are the semblance of paradise for those old grandparents.

"I heard the elder boy say you brought a song box."

Grandpa was very interested. The next day, Raju took the box transistor radio. He came back after making them listen to many songs and sermons. Modern scientific and technological devices began to be known in the countryside.

The grandfather and grandmother wanted to take photos of the newborn babies in the family. I brought Kuriachan's camera and took some pictures. The copies were sent after the holidays.

Another miracle happened when I came back from my ancestral home. Thommikunju from Maramkunnil, who had been quietly evaded for ten years, has come to the fore. I was the first one to smile at him. Thommikunju giggled and nodded.

Even when we met at several places, we evaded friendship during the last ten years and did not greet or talk.

It was alleged that when he was changed from the secretaryship of the children's club, he misplaced or did not return a notebook or document. Over time, I realized that I needed more training and guidance in my public life and should avoid mentioning trivial things to my friends. We also admitted that only our selfish interests and egos created a smokescreen between us, preventing friendly conversations and interactions.

29. COMPLEXITIES

Kuriachan had come from Delhi. I went to Kavalackal in the afternoon and saw Ammayi, Lillykutty, and everyone else there. Kuriachan's wedding will take place soon. I knew everything was getting ready. Attending Kuriachan's marriage was one of the goals of this trip. We talked lovingly for a while. At five, Isaac Achen, his classmate, came to see Kuriachan. Father Anchil spoke about the changes in the church. We had conversations about beliefs, beliefs, and even devils. After Achen left at five, Kuriachan talked about many things alone, from the planning of the wedding to the circumstances of the day. No one was interested in Kuriachan's desires. That is how I came to Achayan with the request to help him.

Lack of appropriate situations, such as financial or material welfare, affected the negotiations. Due to the timely intervention of Achayan, it was decided that the marriage should be conducted under any conditions. Thus, the Chennithala relations did not raise their heads and passed the certainty. Everyone in the family stared blankly at Kuriachan's love marriage request, who led a dedicated life for his family. No one took the initiative to do the function. When no one came forward to take care of Kuriachan's desires, Achayan led everything and gave necessary instructions.

Achiamma, alias Kunjunjamma Chechy from Chennithala, came to the Catholic Church from the Jacobites, learned catechism, confessed, accepted the Eucharist, consented, and performed the pre-wedding ceremony in Delhi – It was all told by Kuriachan.

"The perpetrators cause some of the problems here. I asked everyone's permission and requested that they write a reply in the return mail.

"Vavachi is the only one you cared about? Aren't any of us like that? .."

Before I could say anything further to calm him down, he told me he had to go to the shop and walk away- Perappan.

However, Perappan suffers the most. Anthonichan and Kunjamma from Valiyaparambil were also there. Achayan complains that Perappan picked them up from the native place and migrated to Punnapra with everything they had.

That is the root cause of non-cooperation. After all, they, too, are suffering more than ever. The health of Kunjamma and her children is deplorable. My sister, beaten up for playing and arguing together, is a mother of two and unhealthy today. When I went and saw her, she had said -

"In your opinion, we decided not to have a third child." Didn't you say that last year? "

Oh, it's just a duty. Problems that arise are only caused by ignorance. Soonamma was a schoolgirl; somehow, she missed this year. Animma sees dreams at home. Kunjachan - my Dominic - is studying and is brilliant. He is helping his father quite a bit. Soonamma was afraid to come before me, saying she had not passed her class this year. Then, I gave her some courage. With a few notes stating that it was for her notebook. Is Peramma reducing her height a little bit as each year passes? The size seems to be reduced again. It was love all the way, and she gave me black coffee.

Kochuppappan was not in good health. Now he is staying in the new house temporarily. Achayan says that Anthonichan's house is a pumphouse. When I came last year, he remained in a leafy hut on the east side of the road. We do not know which house he will be in next year. Some of the backyards in Punnapra are being improved to green, like missionary activities.

"The foundation for a large building has been laid according to Dharaneendran's plan. We need money to raise it. "There will be enough paddy this year," Kochuppappan said. "Milk is used instead of coffee nowadays as the cow gives milk as much as she pleases." We were sipping it.

Chittamma showed affection. There was a fear of being struck repeatedly by the occasional thunderclap. "Last month, it was due to the thunder that my hair started to turn grey. What can be done"?

Even otherwise, what else should we do next? I am superannuating soon. The chances of becoming a principal in the school all faded away.

"But I am the most senior." She raised her left hand and said, "They can't do anything against me"…….

Bavichan's exams were underway. After writing the first one, he said something about lacking confidence. But I think he may win.

"Oh my dear, when the exam approached, I saw his struggle and was upset, too."

Bavichan has grown tall. Maybe growing to maturity - that was obvious.

Mammachan wrote his SSLC this time. He had the belief that he would win. It's a dilemma whether to leave for seminary or college next year. As mentioned earlier, I have given him a pen to write on wherever he may be. It is love that he showed. He said he would come after the tour and write to me. I did not receive any letter from him. Molamma is a baby but very shy. Kunjunjamma and Molamma show so much love that they cannot even leave me for a moment. I have been told a hundred times not to go back home today. Finally, Kunjunjamma came home with me.

After Bavichan's exams, we went to the cinema with Bavichan and his brother Mammachan one day. Chittamma asked if she was not being called. When requested, she said not now. That day in Alappuzha, we all wandered together along with Raju. After the evening show of the film 'Vazhvemayam' in Seematti theatre, we returned to Punnapra and slept there. We ran down and boarded the last bus while returning after the movie. When we reached Punnapra, Raju had no chappel on his foot. One of the pair fell in Alappuzha. I was requested for several days to take them to a movie. It was not possible until that day. When we returned home the next day, Kunjunjamma accompanied us. Walking down the doorsteps, Chittamma wondered, "Oh, there is not even a chain around the girl's neck. You should not go." Jolamma said, "But then I can go." Jolamma had a small chain around her neck.

But Chittamma did not allow anyone to go. "How will you go without a chain, without nice clothes?"

"The road is full of mud, and if you go there, it is an Olappura (palm leaf hut). The water in the stream is dirty." I got boiled all over with irritation.

"Chittamma, the necklace, and the silk dress are unimportant, but the blood relationship will always be. Chittamma, love is much more important and big. There is a lot of it among the children. Why should they be isolated?"

After all, they all parted lovingly. When I went to Poona, I could not see chittamma. Schools were open. All the schools were reopened early that year, i.e., on May 4.

That year, except Babu, everyone else passed the exam. Raju was wise to learn. Leelamma was average. Babychan wants to study. Everyone was told to check well and improve. Everyone was committed to learning. Books and notebooks for their use were bought in advance. The newsprint paper was cut into the exact size for wrapping around the books and notebooks, and all of them were labelled. In the meantime, a conversation that once happened stays in my mind. It never seems to fade.

"Raju"!

"yah"

"Do you like Kochayan?"

Silence, just staring straight into his eyes.

"Tell me, do you like Kochayan?"

Suddenly, those eyes filled with tears, and I watched with difficulty.

"Why are you crying?" A silent cry,

I grabbed him by the arm, staring at my face with only painful eyes and nothing else.

"Why did you cry?"

"Why did Kochayan ask that, then?"

"Or, if you like the same, see you next year. You should bring First Class for SSLC.

Babu has grown up a little, put-on height. He also requires good health. As previously done, the hand-rotating-wheel run is less now-a-days. There seems to be no gossip. He may have matured a bit. That's good. He likes film songs. When he hears English, he is not amused. That's so disgusting. Occasionally, you will listen to little jokes. He is good at swimming in the ravine. He is a swimming expert. He swam with a bet, and I was defeated, a hero if you are also interested in learning, among the radio turning., I wondered. Leelamma did not show much interest in looking after the house.

"I never touched the radio," he says. "Didn't I send the letter?" And yet, I have not reversed it. "

"Nee Podi, I wrote it," said Raju. Until last year, it was known as 'Podi' (go away) Chechi. Today I heard he called Leela!

She checked the suitcase, she took the powder and said -

"You need to buy me a skirt and a blouse, listen."

Raju shows the most love and sentimentality. He will always be there to wake you up, gather, and bathe with you. Babychan tells a much better joke than Raju. He insisted on taking a photo of him alone. He learned to tune the transistor in one day. The entire volume will be left there, and a good song will be searched and found.

If Kozhikode is broadcasting a "children's world" event, he will say while listening - "Ayyodee" That tune has a joke of its own!

Raju and Babychan are inquisitive. They kept on inquiring about many things and learned a lot. They also like to read newspapers. Who knows what level all of these would reach in later life? I want them to grow in my affection, too. No matter how limited my abilities are, it should help them come up.

There has been a new awakening among the public about the library. On the east side of the library building, the caved floor has been demolished, and piles of coconut stems were driven down. The stone foundation was raised, and brick walls were made to the roof. What massive efforts does it take to pile them down?

Sunny, Chandappan, Kuttappan, Vayalaran, and Appachan had swelling in their stomachs. Achayan oversaw everything. It will still rise. They have heard Kurunnappan would give the entire wood necessary for the roof and windows. Everyone can get together for the next vacation.

This time, I read very few books. Probably because I was travelling most days, I read the novel "Vazhiyum Nizhalum" and the memoirs about "Evan Ente Priya CJ." Good style.

I looked at everything that had been written before. I must note, what's next? I wrote some poems for children during the last holiday. This time, not even a line was written. Old stories like those my grandfather told surely touch on the history of the old veteran, Thommy Mooppen. Someone will read and understand the past and the adventures of some of the family members. I could not go to Anjiliparambil at least once. The grandfather there and the grandfather in the Kannattumadom showed us a more profound love relationship than just being brothers.

Kuriachan's wedding was concluded smoothly. (April 30, 1970). I went there on the day before and cooperated in all the preparations. Ambalappuzha Babu, Thommachan, and Vanchikal Baby were the big supporters. He has led the work on pandal and decorations. On Wednesday afternoon, Kuriakose's uncle was present. Didn't see you for lunch. Kuriachan gave a cup of coffee. The grandpa and the grandma came in the evening. It was my father who arranged to send the boat to Punnapra. Grandpa fell from the boat. See how much the elders suffer to make things smooth and solemn. She risks her health to see her children cooperate lovingly. He said he was in pain. He slowly placed on the armchair. Said one wish during dinner. It is said that rice, juice, and fish curry can be given in a bowl. "No, you can sit in the tent and have lunch. That's enough." Thathampally, Aunty had come earlier.

Children should love each other and cooperate sincerely, for which the elders risk their health. He said he was in pain. He was supported onto the armchair. After being comfortable here, he expressed a desire to have dinner sitting in the pandal along with other family members. It was offered that rice, buttermilk, and fish curry could be put in a bowl and served to him. "No, I want to sit with them in the pandal and have food. That's good". Ammayi of Thathampally had come earlier. She immediately arranged everything, and her father's desire was fulfilled.

From Punnapra, Chittamma, Peramma, and children all came by the dusk hours. Didn't see Perappan. It was also heard that the ladies would go only when personally invited by older adults. And then something better came up. Kuriachan's mother went to the ancestor's home and brought her father and mother.

And before it became too late at night, Kuriachan had given a white dhoti and cloth shawl for all elderly men and long cloth for women for their 'chatta and mundu.'

Kuriachan was told to wear pants, a shirt, and a tie to church. He just listened, and nothing was answered. Ammayi was in tears all day, saying that Kuriachan did not receive the golden ring, a gift his sister Kunjamma Chechi gave. Forty-five years later, Kuriachan told me the reason for that. How many teary eyes were seen in those two days?

I was the only one who could bring smiles to the lips of my Ammayi, sometimes just by reiterating the taste of the black coffee she offered me at the wedding house.

The pants and shirt were ironed out and kept ready. Still, why was this adamant nature? The fanfare was unnecessary since Kuttappan and Thommikunju could not arrive on time for the wedding. What a justification! If nothing was necessary, then why were these preparations? How much does it cost?

Thommachan said- "If Lillykutty says ..."

"Are you sure? He would jump!"

Tactically, the message was communicated by Achayan -

Nothing he could answer for some time. He stood there like that for some time.

"No shoes, no socks." Some excuses were barely audible.

Everything was organised and beautified. That was the first time the stubborn attitude was changed to docile. Or was it due to the persistent demands of others?

Kuriachan became the bridegroom from Delhi after wearing a tie, tie clip, and cuff button. The motorboat carried us all to the church at Champakulam. After the wedding, we returned by the same motorboat with the bride and the bridegroom.

I picked up the camera - but the shadow and light played hide and seek in this stranger's hand, and the efforts were wasted.

"He loved his family, had chosen his partner, and nothing would go wrong. Wish him well." Sincere at heart, they seemed telling.

I understood the bride's relatives at the church exit. If Thathampalli Thommachan had not been physically pushed away, he would have shown some high-handedness. Wasn't he a local hero?

They came home as guests for the feast. Ammachi gave them a hearty welcome and sumptuous food. I also went with them to see my grandfather and grandmother at Kannattumadom. The couple offered 'glory and praise to Jesus' through their folded hands, and they blessed the couple.

"Are you going with them too?" Grandpa desired to know.

"We are going on the same day. " I said. They did not tell if they were going to Delhi or the in-law's place, Chennithala.

Then, when I stood next to Grandpa saying 'glory and praise to Jesus', Grandpa said with anxiety and pain-

"What are you looking at—everything you keenly watch and go. God bless you. Next time you come, I don't know, I may be there or not ". It choked his throat.

So much sadness was in my mind, but it was all hidden.

"Appa, Appan told me long back that you will put my son in a small boat and row, and then only… - it's yet to happen. After that, only what you fear will happen. There are many more years to go."

My grandpa stared at me. Do you not remember that?

"Did I say that? Is that so?"

I remember what my grandpa said, and I will never forget that.

"Appa, Give me the oar. You are not well, and I'll row home."

"No, Mone. I can row myself. I'm going to sit with your son and row. Then only I am going back to my heavenly home." Do you remember that?

"I firmly believe that it will happen," I said because no one else in the family today has God's blessing and sincerity as much as my grandpa did.

He prayed for longevity for all.

The grandma sometimes had memory loss. But that would change soon. She felt that she had 'run out of gas' emotionally. When she was under the care of his son at Punnapra, sometimes she thought it was 'Vavachan's wife" who stood there. One day, she asked – "Tell me, Anthonicha, are you not going to Punnapra?" Were they not early symptoms of dementia? Unless adequate care is given to older people, the benefit of their presence in our midst may not be available for long.

Payment of my salary was delayed. When I received it, I thought everyone should benefit from it with some additional clothing. Close relatives got it. I Went to Alappuzha on Monday the 11th. After shopping with Lillykutty, we saw the movie 'Ambalapravu' and gave our daily sorrows a short leave of absence.

We wanted to talk but just looked at each other without saying anything! I went home by boat from Thathampally in the morning. I came to Alappuzha through Punnapra. I met Gilbert Achen, Matthai Sir and Narakatra Achen. They were all cheerful and lovely. I did not investigate the allegation that someone said Narakatra Achan was running a hotel and a toddy shop for the festival. It was not on my lookout, and I never bothered to inquire of his affairs about it.

It was time for me to return to my workplace after the holidays. How quickly the days went by! Meanwhile, where all I went and where all I could not. Achayan and Ammachi said I did not stay home for more time this vacation. Achayan's friends complained that I did not go to Ambalapuzha. I ran about at various engagements but could not see everyone, which was impossible due to limited vacation.

I went to Kainakari one day with Ammachi. Kochachan asked-

"Hey, Eda, Couldn't he get a chance there?" It was about Appachi.

"Be careful what you say". Joy had already warned me that Kochachan was already furious.

"I tried but could not get good results yet. " And there was an explanation of the attempts. Kochachan could not say anything further when I said that the incidence of embarrassing Babu was a little undesirable. He had realised that later. I heard from Appachi the manipulated narrative he gave Babu Sir. Achayan also mentioned it. He came home and rebuked my mother that I had not explained about my hunting job for Appachi. One day, he visited Alappuzha to see Babu and inquire about Appachi's job. He could not see him. When he succeeded in his next attempt, Babu advised him to be patient as an advertisement would come from his organisation. He asked him to write after seeing the ad. The day I went to Alappuzha with Appachi, I met T Chandy Achayan. He was ill and bedridden. The hand that wrote the letter of recommendation for me was paralysed. I had grief and sympathy for the old-timer. There was so much gratitude and remembrance that I prayed for his speedy recovery.

30. BEGAN HIGHER STUDY

I went to Chekkidikkad on the eve of the Edathwa Church festival. In the boat with my mother, the journey went well. I hope to get there by bus next time. The road from Thiruvalla to Ambalappuzha was under construction. Everyone parted happily.

The next day, I went to Changanassery to see Isaac. The black singer was my old friend and has not changed much. He told stories of his love, job search, and the Bombay trip. No matter how many hours we sat in the Hotel Marina, it was the feeling that nothing was said. There was no substitute for the love within that dark-coloured skin. So we had to say bye. The same day, I saw Kangazha John and his wife. Tickets for them to go back to Poona were also booked. Seeing a friend far away from his native place is always special, including special greetings. The language of the eastern mountain ranges was- "that which is"- also remarkable.

I went to Ernakulam itself twice. To send Joy and Ammini away. It was a joy for them too.

"See you in Bombay now".

We saw the movie "Stree" with Kunjommachayan at Vistharama in Ernakulam. I liked the modern theatre that screened the film more than the theatre.

Since I went to enroll Raju in BBMUP school, I met Kurup sir and others there. My 'alma mater, UP school, where I developed the attitude that gave me form and appearance. How many events in my life have this school witnessed?

Even today, those memories are evergreen and live in some corner of my mind. Tahkli, storytelling, Thambi-Gopi alliances, General Secretary, Vellaripravu's romantic antics, questions and answers,

Leelamma Thomas of the lamp-post, boat strike, and everything that happened in those days. One hundred percent for mathematics, the death of Kuttappan Chettan, and trips to Ernakulam, Aluva, and Thiruvananthapuram. Fr. George Kalathra, the parish priest, always had good words for us. He appreciated our making coconut plant guard-fencing for the church property. Organising the 'youth festival' and the play 'Lavakusha' were memorable events. (May I ask you? Did you pay revenge for the question on the romantic antics of 'vellari' doves (Pigeons) and determined to defeat me? You took the same role and performed better than me !). These memories will help me return to my childhood, at least in memory. It gives a lot of satisfaction and comfort.

One holiday ends. The day before, I realised that the holiday was over. I went to see my grandpa and grandma. I went to Ottathyckal. I went to see a friend at Vazhayil. I had lunch with my mother on that day. I visited most of my friends. I was able to drink some toddy with Chennatt Kuttappan. Kuttapayi has in a world of his own. Sunny and Chandappan were patient enough to listen to me for a long time. Vayalattuthara Kuttappan had talked about my work for a long time. I bid farewell to the library. When I saw my Ammayi at Kavalackal, everyone cried - Kuriachan's special message before leaving for Delhi.

"Tears do not taste like sugar candy. You do not understand them," said Kuriachan.

Kuriachan and Chechi were preparing to return to Delhi after their vacation. The absence of something essential created so much trouble. It could be deficiencies or worries. Who can satisfy everyone?

Who gets everyone's love always? How far do we have to travel?

Kuriachan taught me a lot about the realities of life.

"Don't worry, be happy, "I comforted her, wiping the tears on her cheeks and saying goodbye to Ammayi.

My hands knew the warmth of tears on the toothless cheeks. Standing helpless, unable to wipe out, I put her cheeks in my hands. I walked down- quickly, without saying anything, without seeing anything.

Since he knew I was leaving, Raju was silently in tears and pain. Achayan said-

"That's how he can show his love. This love must always be there."

He was reassured that I would be on leave soon and back here.

An open call coming out of the depths of the heart, a request, can be of great value before God. That was done before the journey. I am miles away, and please protect all in my family. Raise this house to prosperity. Get no harm to anyone.

Babu and Leelamma came out into the yard with tears and stared. The journey was intended through Punnapra. Ammachi, Achayan, Raju and Babychan came along. I saw my Perappan and Kochuppappan there at Punnapra. Kochuppappan told me about a chit fund. The kids were inquiring - and they said-

"When Ummachettan comes, he will bring all the sweets and fruits. When this Kuriachan Chachan comes, he will not get us anything. Why was it so?" There was silence for a few moments. And then continued -

"When there was one thousand three hundred in the bank, and when I asked him for some amount, he did not give it. That's why I gave him four hundred now. Let him understand if he can."

After taking a vacation and having a lovely wedding, you must borrow from someone to return to your workplace. All returns of Kuriachan were like that, the uniqueness of expatriate life.

My home and my country are growing. My compatriots can share their joys and sorrows. I live here in Poona with the love of my family and fellow citizens.

Why did I write all this like an entry in a diary? This may help me remember my human relationships over time. Much of what I have written in it may have been thought that would probably never be repeated.

I had begun to study. The exam was approaching.

Join Chitti and draw a plan for a house.

I was a prisoner of thought - or dreams. The movement of the mind, which was often unfocused, was like an ape.

After the holidays, I signed and sent the application to join the Koshamattom Chit Fund in Kottayam and sent the amount of Rs. 200 / -as a money order.

Joy's letter from Kannattumadom - "Hoping to come," announcing the exam results. No matter how interested you are in their affairs, do not expect a response from them.

I did not pay him much during my vacation. How many are waiting with hope like this? Who can behave like Kuriachan, trying to satisfy everyone? Who will be happy like that? Ready to help as much as you can? But shouldn't that be done considering the prevailing family financial situation?

One thing was for sure - I was ready to give if I had adequate resources, whether I received anything earlier or not. Others might not know that. I know how to share if there is enough. I never hesitated to ask those who have. I never thought I could live without anyone's help. I'm more interested in doing what I can to help those who deserve it.

My grandmother in Kainakari went to her heavenly abode on June 2, 1970. Everyone from home went there to pay homage. The funeral and obsequies were all beautiful. There were only prayers left to give to my grandmother. I occasionally prayed for her soul.

While writing about trying for a job for Bavichan of Punnapra, Kochuppappan also informed me about his desire to join the Indian Air Force.

Instead of joining the Air Force as an Airman, I replied to advise Bavichan to learn more and try a better job after graduation or after achieving a technical qualification.

I sent an advertisement to Appachi for technical posts in Colonel Sir's office. He had a small job as a draftsman in the Alappuzha port office.

Attachment training was planned for the CME refrigeration course in Bombay and Delhi, with ten days in Bombay and ten days in Delhi. The confidence to stay with Joy in Bombay and Kuriachan in Delhi helped me overcome other inconveniences. A trip to two major cities in three weeks and the historical monuments you see for the first time are always on your mind. Many thoughts that often ran through my mind were written in the pages of a dream that had yet to be put into practice. This is nothing; everything is yet to be seen in detail!

I have memorised the words of the Mahatma recorded at the north gate of Gandhi Smriti: - "I would like to see India free and strong so that she may offer herself as a willing and pure sacrifice for the betterment of the world. The individual, being pure, sacrifices himself for the family. The latter for the village, the village for the district, the district for the province, the province for the nation, and the nation for all. I want Khudai Raj, which is the same thing as the Kingdom of God on earth. Establishing such a Rajya would mean the welfare of not only the whole Indian People but also the whole world."

When I returned from the tour, I saw Colonel Sir looking for Appachi's job opportunity. I learned that the CIE had asked him to get more certificates from the employment exchange and would be called for an interview soon if he got them. I also wrote to Appachi to see Sir when he reached his home in Alleppey.

31. NEW PASTURES

I met Anthonichayan in Kirkee's churchyard. He belonged to Kainakari, with his house located east of Arackal house on the bank of the river. When he told me he knew everyone in the Arackal house, including my mother, I introduced myself to him, saying that my mother belonged to the Arackal house. When he was told that his son, who had studied in Changanassery and had passed his graduate degree and was looking for a job, was coming to Poona, I only thought that George was another Kuttanad native instead of Moolakatte Georgekutty. Appachi said, "I know - he is also known as Babychan, Kadamattuthara. He is an intellectual!" It was also written that they would get together if they could come to Poona. I believed it was possible.

Jose of the CIE reported that no interview call was sent to Appachi. Then there was the chase. I knew some strings were being pulled, misspellings and distortions somewhere. I thought it was wise to approach the local guardian, who unties all the knots without blaming anyone. I did that.

After that, they sent an Express Telegram to Appachi to come for the interview 24 hours later. I talked about it with Anthonichayan and George until 11 p.m.

Before they left, I received a telegram from Appachi. "Coming for the Tech Sup (Civil Engg) post-interview two days later."

George was also there to receive Appachi at Poona railway station. I brought him to my room, handed over a textbook to calculate the bending moment, and went to CME. George also had a book by Bertrand Russel in hand. George sometimes quotes non-traditional quotes. On the way back from the railway station,

Appachi said, which has become the thought-provoking quotation of the day, engaging us throughout our bus travel.

"People are better known for their writing skills, good administration skills, power, and other abilities. If you cannot become one of them - produce children!"

What to do first? Or do both together, I mean concurrently?

George's favourite subject was philosophy of mind, and he required more books to read. My trying to make his desires come true was not intended to change George's thoughts on life. But George maintained that the book I brought from CME- "History of Western Philosophy" has caused a metamorphosis - not just threw a light - on becoming another philosopher. George had an excellent, sumptuous intellectual and philosophical meal for about two months. George often said that no other book has impacted his later life as the "History of Western Philosophy."

I read many books during that period: good classics, novels, stories, and articles by famous writers in English and Malayalam.

Although Appachi said that the written test and the interview were good, I understood from his body language that he still had to wait for a job in Poona. The local patron reiterated that he could help better at any other time.

I wrote the AMIE (I) examination for the remaining Section-A subjects in November. Decisions were soon made to ensure that those who worked hard would be rewarded. George got a job at HAL Pimpri - India's only antibiotic (Drugs & Pharmaceutical Sector) company. George, who studied chemistry, said- "Explanation about the hallucination experienced by the hippies who smoked LSD helped me get the breakthrough." George accepted the job offer and announced - "On to the battlefield," the battle of life.

Appachi has been called for the Selection Trial for direct appointment as JCO at MEG & Center, Bangalore.

"Go, win, come back". It was a great relief for the family to succeed in a rigorous experiment in which Puthenpurakkal Appachan and many other locals and friends participated. He asked for retail financial assistance during his stay in Bangalore, and I could send it, but he did not receive it in time.

Before joining the MEG & Center in Bangalore, Appachi went to Bombay before leaving for home. I went with Appachi. I met Joy and Ammini, walked around Marine Drive, and met a snake charmer (Pampatti) at the Gateway of India.

KCA Members performed CL Jose's play – "Vedanayude Thazhvarayil " (In the Valley of Pain), renamed "Athmavinte Novukal" (Pains of the Soul). Excellent service was given to the team to perform the play and sell the tickets to raise funds. Sebastian Brother, Appachi, George of Range Hills, and I saw the play together.

After about two months of cohabitation with me, Appachi was sent home by train. Here, he found a way to soothe the pains of so many souls at home! Anthonichayan, George, and the Colonel's son, Alex, were there to board him on the train. In the meantime, the appointment letter for Appachi reached home. The family redirected the letter to Poona. The appointment letter reached Poona when Appachi reached Kainakari. Luckily, I could collect the letter and send it to Appachi immediately.

I had high hopes that at least one of the close relations in the family would work in this area. It was a false hope. As we lay in bed together the evening before leaving for home, I heard the sighs of despair as we parted in a depressing mood. It was a prophecy that I had reassured him that he would be back in Poona in later years to rebuild some military barracks or quarters in the area soon!

Shortly after Sebastian arrived in Poona, Paulose, another classmate in Carmel, moved from the Meteorological Center in Delhi to Poona. Thus, Carmel alumni's membership grew in Poona. When all of us gathered for Christmas, Vijayappan also joined. What else to do? Together we went to a movie of Gregory Peck at the 'Rahul' Theatre - Cape Fear!

1972 provided extraordinary friendships, study opportunities, and career advancement.

I have found that George's different readings and conversational style have considerably affected me. You may find some of their symptoms in some of my texts. The contact with George and the apparent improvement in book reading may show some of the changes I have made over a short period in the following lines. Reading and reviewing contemporary literary works and George's commentary have influenced my thoughts, language, and personal relationships.

Not all the changes that happened to me were for the better. More often, I took things seriously, analysed the future, and presented it more maturely. However, sometimes, I jumped into trouble by giving undue seriousness to things others did not see as much.

I thought that Sebastian (brother) had no chance until then to get to know George as closely as I did. When we friends – George, Sebastian and myself got the opportunity to be together, we went to see an English film. When we returned after seeing the movie, George's sexually explicit speech and comments, which had never happened before, completely changed my attitude toward him. Sebastian didn't take it seriously. But it could be my selfishness, my hypocritical mind, and I was hot. One or two hours later, George walked away without a word. Sebastian said-

"Cool down, change this habit of taking things seriously, listen."

"No one should control me; you can't change my behaviour!"

"That's right, Brother, no one else can change that. Only You Can!"

My mind was filled with many thoughts. On the way back, I saw nothing. We got off the bus at Kirkee and went straight to the park.

I remembered my duties and personal shortcomings. It would be best to change yourself, not take simple matters seriously, deliberate too much on them, and not behave selfishly with others. Give them an outlet and the support they need to keep going. It was then an attempt always to remember the lesson Sebastian, my brother, taught when mingling with friends.

Reading books, tiredness after work, and studying regularly also affected my career. More selfishness in me grew without me knowing it.

The evening in the park was over, and the neon lights were noticeable. There was a lot to learn. I must write the rest of the subjects and pass the May exam. There were moral obligations to reply to the letters received. Achayan was preparing to buy 1.7 acres of land near Thaicherry in the northern field belonging to the Koolippurackal family. Requests for money kept coming from the home. I got up and walked towards my room.

On the holidays, in the afternoon, Kadamattuthara George and his brother Thomas would visit me in the lodge. They both were interested in reading books. We usually went to Manney's Books on Central Street and got immersed for two or three hours in the world of books. The routine was to search, buy one or two books, and return to the lodge. Or go to Sebastian's or Paulose's house and talk about one or more subjects for an hour or two. The tedious repetitions continued until more responsibilities came along for each of us.

32. DIVERSITY IN THE CITY

When I arrived at the office, after confirming in the register that I had arrived at the office, I usually walked to the seat of my colleague, Technician Anthony. Anthony was a senior technician who regularly came to the office with the newspaper - Poona Herald. We used to have an overview of the work on that day. Then, I glanced through the local news.

Anthony has already arrived; by then, he must have finished reading the newspaper. Since we had nothing to plan for work on that day, Anthony got up and walked away. Someone walked toward me, looking at me carefully while I was looking at the newspaper. I knew he was employed in the same institution but did not know his name or details. Quite seriously, I heard a quick question. It must have been to me, as no one else was nearby.

"Are you a Christian?"

I thought for a moment and said, "Yes."

Further inquiring - "Do you believe in the Bible?"

"I read the Bible." I looked at him. He had crossed his hands to his chest and perhaps pretended to be defensive or hostile.

"May I ask you a question?"

I gestured to him with my head to go ahead. My attention shifted from the newspaper I was reading to his face. Who was this, and why did he choose me to question early in the morning? He may have been a Bible preacher or pretended to be so.

"Did God know that Adam would eat the forbidden fruit?"

God is omnipotent, omniscient, past, present, and future. Then-

"Yes, he knew everything."

"Then, did he want to punish the man that way?"

"No, Is it not the freedom without restrictions dangerous? A man may have abused it. Maybe he has done so." After saying that, I remained silent.

"I have not read the Old Testament much; I often read the New Testament."

"Oh," he shook his head, making a careful observation.

"How can you claim to be a Christian?" There was a look of disgust in his eyes. The sound became louder. As a consolation, let the hatred subside, and the noise reduce, I said -

"Beyond necessary communication, I'm not here for a debate. To say that I am a Christian is an answer to your curiosity. I'm not a Christian. There was only one Christ in the world. I do not think there is anyone who can be another Christ. All are trying to be another Christ."

He was eloquent but suddenly became silent. After a few minutes, he said calmly-

"I, too, am searching for the truth. How many religions, how much unrest - everywhere? I am searching for who and what God is."

Recently, I remembered that I went with Gopalakrishnan Mash and listened to Swamy Chinmayananda's Gita discourses. He could see only a slight smile on my face.

He asked another question -

"God has many names in the Bible, beginning with Jehovah (Yahweh). But what is the name of the God you believe in?"

"I do not know names other than Jesus for my God. Many names are called, like Yahoweh, Ram, Rahim, Allah, Guru Nanak, etc. It is all One God Almighty and One religion – Humanity. Are you not seeking, then the God you seek is your conscience! What do you call your conscience? Let your deeds follow that conscience, and then you will meet your God."

He was eager to hear more. The office assistant came and told me that someone was looking for me. Our conversation had to stop there.

When I came to the office and finished my work, I took a sheet of paper, wrote something and put it in my pocket - 'Next time I go to Manney's, I want to buy 'The Present Crisis of Faith' (By Dr S Radhakrishnan). I bought and read the book that month. After that, I did not find the preacher anywhere.

After Appachi left for Bangalore to join the military – Madras Engineer Group (MEG), informally known as the Madras Sappers - James came to Poona searching for work. Soon after James' interview in Paulose's meteorological office, he got a job there. James lodged in the upper room of the Irani Hotel, opposite the 155 JA Block, until he moved near Kirkee Station to stay with a Palakkad Menon who worked for a private company. They used to dine at Madhavan's mess, and I often saw them. James and I sometimes went to Sebastian's house in Range Hills. We went to church together, and during most of the holidays, we spent time together.

As Puthenpurakkal Appachan did not get the job as a JCO in Madras Sappers, he went straight to Hyderabad searching for a civilian job. There, he lived for a year in the foothills of Moula Ali. Some application forms were sent to him, but nothing worked. After he got a job, Appachan wrote to me in Poona to inform me of the news and whereabouts of our friends. He was eager to learn about the country's development and the new books we read.

Wrote letters to Appachan - It has some of the graffiti of the time, the colours, and some of the features of the place - time - and language. Here, I reproduce some of the words while remembering the period.

"After another day of daydreaming laziness,
Flowers in full bloom on Maula Ali Hill
In the twin forests, rice and dal,
The sound of a ball being hit in the shade of the sun,
Which was leaning beyond the 130 paddy field,
Echoes in the corners of the hospital hall,
If you read the mother tongue that arrives weekly,
Lie down in that soil, breathe in the smell of that soil,
And listen to the heartbeat. If you can reconcile,
There are not even two leaves in this desert to bring out the murmuring sound;
The shadows are frozen.
Many human beings are affected by the sorrow of existence.
Some machines only have the boredom of repetition.
They are nothing more than Sartre's theory of survival.
They wander searching for charas, bhang, and hope daru to reach the unearthly realms of experience to change grief and find their form and appearance.
The curse of alienation is a blessing; the curse of lack of purpose is a blessing here.
The city is a forest of neon lights, and there is no loneliness here.
The native has no heartbeat, frozen mind, or dead emotions.
The delicately moving life of the machine.
There is no such thing (CPC Nair) as "Like the portrait of a charming art."
Is it your younger brother Joy's wedding?
The one ahead is behind; the follower is leading.
We still have the taste of the wait, got the roots, the woods, like the banyan tree,
Vayalaran discovered the colour and appearance of his ribs

and, thereby, the truth.
Some time in the loneliness created by the functional vacuum
So that if I can remember the past and forget the dull laziness,
Let me open the doors of curiosity- "

He visited Benny the day before Easter at the Kirkee Military Hospital. He had fallen off his bicycle. Many Muktibahini soldiers were wounded in the 1971 Bangladesh war and were admitted to the military hospital. No one even thinks about their lost limbs, so they sing and walk around telling jokes. Views that evoke compassion!

As I began to attend the passion service on Good Friday, my mind was going through a crisis of faith. A few shattering thoughts. Where am I? If I am a believer, I will be a complete believer. Can I ever be a rebel? The decision was made when I touched the foot of the crucifix.

After the Easter Sunday Mass, the sun was still hotter than usual when we all got out.

Brother had come in the evening. When he asked me to take a photo together, I did not ask to whom he wanted to give my picture. I requested him to share a copy with me. There would be some reason, or he could have asked me for a copy of my photograph! Was it for some other purpose? Whatever it might be, that's what Brother asked. We took a photo in the nearby studio.

It took me a few days to figure out what it was like to be photographed together by fellow travellers in the college.

After Babu's SSLC exam, Raju had a scholarship exam the next day. It was written to me that everyone would pass. Among them were the photos of Bavichan's first holy communion. I could not go on vacation to participate in the celebration. Achayan's resentment was visible in the lovely words he wrote in his letter. The same anger was reflected when I asked about purchasing a paddy field. But it appeared that his concern was about the amount I should gather. He could understand my indifference to agriculture, which might have delayed my timely reply.

The newspaper's income alone was insufficient to cover the routine expenses at home. The property was agricultural land that was going cheaper, comparatively. If purchased, we could make the flooring for a tiny house on the river bank from the paddy field. Achayan had his justifications even though agriculture was a loss-making, troublesome occupation, especially for people who could not do field jobs alone.

You can write the exam again. Home visits during holidays could be changed to Onam season. In the end, Achayan's interest was given priority. Even in another state, putting aside one's necessities and wearing tight pants was nothing new.

"This is everything I could organise, and I am sending the amount. Things are going on normal here." I wrote a reply to Achayan.

Acquiring wealth with savings only - that may be my selfish thought. The practice of lending money from the banks had started. However, all the loans taken must be repaid with interest. How can farming be profitable by borrowing from land acquisition from now on? No farmer in Kuttanad found anything to be happy about in the balance sheet of agriculture. Was it not a practical assessment?

Rare friendships that make you happy and sadness you share from some companies you get from college last a lifetime! The brother went home because of a call he received from home. My college classmate and close friend, brother, was looking for his life partner. If he liked the proposal, he would come back after the wedding. At the Poona railway station, all our friends gave an emotional farewell to the brother who had bought a ticket to a different life journey.

" An Eve as Anne, a red ripe apple, a paradise of Muttar, a voice from heaven, come, eat, eat this fruit. Poor Adam, the punishment for sin is not death – birth! New birth and a new life.

" You might see the hanging bag, the search for a house, the party, and the bondage would be terrifying to man more than death. We are doomed to this life. Judgment arrived in Pune on the evening of the eighth on a train. Adam has been swept away in that flow. Let's wait for the first birthday of the new Adam." - Friends bid greetings to him.

After listening patiently to everything, Brother said lightly in his usual style-

"മണ്ണാങ്കട്ട (Clay-mass)! Come on, let us see when it comes!"

"Tell all your imagination to go, brother. " Then he sang,"

Please accept me. Fill me ... " (കനിവേ ാടെ സ്വീകരിക്കണേമേ .. നിറയുമെൻ)"

A week after he reached there, a letter came from Muttar.

"It doesn't seem to be happening. The girl is not enough."

Brother came back alone. He was unable to join Annie. He said, "Let's see later" when I met him. From Muttar, his parents had already migrated to Gudalur in Nilgiris.

When I visited the IAT with refrigeration & air conditioning course students from CME, I met my classmate James Kutty Thomas and Sebastian's friend Thankachan. They work there.

Just before May Day, Ramachandran joined CME as a new teacher. He came from Palakkad and was employed in Instrumentation Ltd. I realized from my first acquaintance that he was a good friend with similar interests. Ramachandran had given me the same support as John at R&DE (Engrs). He lived in Shirin Lodge in Kirkee. I met Babu when I went to Shirin Lodge with Ramachandran. Babu laid out a leopard skin to sleep, woke up, and worked for a private company on Bombay-Poona Road.

The marriages of two other colleagues - Hanumanth Jamakhandi and PM Pradhan – were held in May. I attended their banquet with Ramachandran.

We occasionally recalled the story contexts in the books we read during discussions with Ramachandran -

"Are you dying for him? she whispered.

"And his wife and child." "Hush! Yes."

"O, you will let me hold your brave hand, stranger?"

"Hush! Yes, my poor sister; to the last." (Quote from "A Tale of Two Cities" by Charles Dickens)

Then Ramachandran asked, "Whose hand did you want to hold?"

"That I will tell you later. Here's your ice cream, the most essential, unique, and solo item in Pradhan Babu's wedding reception!

I desired all my siblings to be well-educated and happy. Babu barely won and reached Standard 10. Leelamma, Raju, and Bavichan studied well, passed, and got the tenth standard threshold. They always understood that the future was only through education.

When I returned from the office in the afternoon, I first remembered to look at Babu's SSLC result. I was curious. I picked up the paper and carried it into the room: 122411, Nos 10 and 12, No 11. I opened the drawer, took an Inland, and kept it above the newspaper, which had the names and photographs of Pankajakshan and David, the children who passed meritoriously. I wrote the address and wrote as below without calling anyone as dear- I did not want my brother to be a David or Pankajakshan. But his name or number could have been included in the list of victorious candidates!

My sorrow was dumb, and my voice trembled.

Achayan's reply letter was all about Babu and his future. He had concernedly announced, "For I have become heir to six feet of land." Though the statement was clearly out of context, Achayan used the figure of speech to express his happiness of owning a little farmland, like his younger brothers. The farmland in the north has been purchased.

I believed that there was nothing to be happy about. But why should I deny that to Achayan if he was pleased?

I remained in Kazakh legend all day. "I'm leaving again from this reborn - nest made of Mandaram leaves."

"Poyya ... nji .. varille, thattanum kolussumitta, kathil chittukalitta Kunjamina .... Ravi lost something as it slipped from his heart -"

"The primitive boy who gives milk to the ostrich, the genius who seeks the soul of the lice."

"Ravi was waiting for the bus to come."

It was considered the most outstanding work of imaginative literature written in Malayalam. Wasn't it the happiest time that I could read it?

My mind was restless. The words and lines of the Kazakh echoed through my mind repeatedly, like a dream I had seen during the daytime.

The dark cloud of sorrow that even the most outstanding literary work in Malayalam could not erase or hide has conquered my mind. Knowing there was no deliverance, I longed for reprieve or salvation.

Finding a pen and paper, I wrote the 'Legend of Kazakh,' legend and O.V, Vijayan, and OV Vijayan. I also wrote many times that he was a winner. Babu won - enrolled in college - must be registered, can learn, can fly.

Family difficulties will be significantly reduced. I kept on writing something like that.

"It's not my fault." Albert Camus wrote The Outsider. I scribbled as such and ended.

The address was written in Malayalam and signed as Babu. Something still needs to be fixed! Ithihasam Ithihasam, Vijayan Vijayan, and Babu Babu were re-written, crisscrossed on the paper, folded, folded at length again, torn in two, and thrown somewhere. When I saw it again today, I wondered what went through my mind while writing that.

In the chains of another disappointment, like a melancholy. Babu is still like a melancholy sound.

Joy Kannattumadom passed Standard 10. The last time I reached home on vacation, no one told me he was serious about his studies. His severe behaviour and talks helped me think he was serious about his studies. Others said it was not mere disobedience, but he felt isolated and treated himself as not belonging to his parents. Others noted that Chittappan did not pay enough attention to his eldest son while he was growing up.

It was the first time I had received such a letter from him. Joy wrote that he had passed Standard 10.

After Chittappan started farming on his land, it was only during nighttime he came ashore from the ridge. In the evening, we would leave the field, go to the library, get home at night, get up in the morning, and go around the paddy field. Joy was not brought to the farm as he was still in school. Occasionally, even if his father told him something, he would do it only if he were interested; he would seldom obey if the grandfather said anything. After recurrence, his grandfather did not ask him anything.

I recently realized that there was a verbal dispute or non-cooperation with his grandfather for something. Joy wrote to me that his father was obstructing his desires. He was not interested in cultivating in the muddy sludge and water of the paddy field. Someone said that if he paid two thousand rupees, he would get a job in military service.

In response to my compliments for his success in the final school class, Joy wrote back- "Which way to go?" He had also sketched a deformed effigy standing at the junction of roads, similar to the one they place in the field to frighten the birds and rodents. Whether he accepted it or not, replying was essential to me. When I wrote my thoughts, I intended that they should be helpful to any tenth grader at any time.

"Dear Joy,

This letter is due to the sketch showing that you were standing helplessly at the intersection of the sidewalks you have drawn, asking aimlessly, 'Which way to go?'. The image does not fade from my eyes soon.

Other reasons are that you write -

- You may be able to join the army if you pay a bribe of rupees two thousand.

- You write that you are 'swimming in the depths of discomfort that creates generational gaps' –

Controlled selfishness within me may bark often, but I can assure you that it may not bite.

How much I hope to tell you, my blood relations about what I know, no matter how small, to read what I have read and gone beyond that into the realm of knowledge and enjoy looking for pearls there.

You are on that path today, at that crossroads.

Who has advised you to wander in the northern borders with an olive green shirt? Without even getting a piece of paper, that is worth highlighting as your qualification! Do you want that as a burden of grief for the rest of your life?

He is your enemy, who does not understand you and your family. He is none for you.

Intellectuals will agree that self-contained scraps of paper are not the standard of knowledge and that their absence is not a sign of expertise.

I see - here, on the one hand, the war-torn Shivaji's fort, the tomb of tens of thousands who died in World War II, and the vast factories that make bombs and ammunition.

Vain study because it is unclear what one is studying for creation or destruction throughout the days.

They ate food only for survival - on a grassy field, a battle without guns and bullets, and a ploughed field after the war.

On the first day of the month, with frozen emotions, standing in the queue with a dead conscience, buying short and less comprehensive notes, moving the money order like a machine, tossing an empty purse over to the corner, and finding his own in the lined charpoy - the sadness of a lost time.

I see - the question that one who wants to achieve a lot forgets to ask himself is, what is accomplished? Did he set out to reach the same place where he left off?

Ask a soldier who comes home with camouflaged pants and a shirt with a big tin box and a big moustache -

"Sir, what's in that box, money or sovereign ?"

"Baby, this box is a collection of heart-wrenching pains."

Ask again -

"Sir, isn't being outside your home state nice?" Hypocrisy may be revealed-"Yes, child, I am fine." Then he does not say, " but don't want to go back"—a sense of loss.

"I had to do something else and wanted to go another way. Go to the top of the barn and even under the barn; not even a single candlelight will burn."

I see -

Many earned flowers to wear on their shoulders - the so-called officers. They are here because they made flowers from the papers collected through their efforts to obtain higher education degrees from colleges. Here they are in the ivory tower; they get a lot of opportunities for career advancements and bright future life.

Which way to go? Decide for yourself.

If you ever feel depressed that you had to go another way, but at least once say to yourself, "But I do not feel like going back to work," will you remember the image you drew, the question, and the answer?

I do not understand what that uncontrollable difficulty of your mind is.

You say you feel lonely in your own home, and why do you think so? What prompts you to be lonely? We cannot be a stranger like that. The generation gap may come in politics but should not be in family relationships.

Aren't we all blessed in that respect? Our fathers were not superhuman beings in another world. They are also not the sort who issued commandments. They are the people who worked directly for the safety and protection of all of us, and they tolerated pain and suffering. They wanted to see us grow up and be satisfied with what they saw as reasonable. They were like colleagues with us in different spheres of life.

How to be a stranger there?

There is a pious body that believes only in the highest level of sincerity, which never extends the scepter of old age to the growing generation, who is loving, who has not even the slightest hint of selfishness, who finds joy only in sacrifice and love, in our home - the grandfather. If there is a paradise on earth, it is there at the feet of that venerable man.

I desire to stay with that saint for some time –I would be blessed by his love, like a rock touched by the pollen of a flower in the magnetic field of his love.

Is this the generational gap you mention? Then Joy, woe to you!

Without finding the truth of peace, your alienation is nothing but darkness, my brother. You are groping in the dark, and the light shines before you.

Appan is the essence of life, permeating every atom of our soul and body. He is the light in every dust in our house, like the sun's rays. How can you be an alien with that ingenuity in the footsteps of that God, in the ashram of that loving, sacrificial deity? Your stubborn, ignorant assertion hurts me. Your existence has no meaning without getting life and blessings from him.

You decide - which way to go. My answer is written.

Life is a bond of obligations. Redemption is the fulfilment of obligations.

Complete your duties. Then you will see the gates of peace opened and the face of the earth renewed.

Lovingly"

The letter was sent along with a letter to Achayan requesting him to give the letter to Joy.

If those words, written in 1972 or so, reflected the circumstances and attitudes of the day, the lack of a comfortable way of life, and the meagre income, then the day's events were responsible. Joy never wrote to me again. I was not worried about that. We always maintained love and spoke well when we saw each other in person. I lived and worked only through assessing the day's circumstances each time.

33. ALL FOR PROGRESS

While talking to Sebastian in the Range Hills, James told us that our friend and classmate, the Rev. Fr. James, came into my room and returned because he had not seen me there.

We all met Fr. James at Carmel House in Ramwadi, Poona. He arrived there and will be in Germany in three months. After passing away from Carmel, James Achen managed various small businesses under the supervision of the church in Chethipuzha. Before serving in Germany, he came to Poona to study German at Max Muller's House.

Stephen's transformation is known only to Achen – What happened, I inquired.

"He left the provincial house with all the valuables. When he arrived in Bangalore, I heard he married a nurse or had some illegal relationship. He soon left that woman. He had advertised in the newspaper that he had joined the Pentecostal church. He published a leaflet, "Why did I leave the Catholic Church," with his photo. It was a way of survival for him. Again, he went on the wrong way - destroying another girl. Now he is in his house in his hometown. His mother is a pious woman who mourns for her son. He is a pervert."

I got the opportunity or misfortune to hear that, too. I saw Fr. James after a long time. He brought back harsh memories that were hard to erase from my college days.

"Where are the day investigation reports and documents, father?" It would contain documents that proved my innocence.

"It was given to the Provincial House in Kottayam. It is not known what happened after the case was closed."

It was just incidental that some harsh memories flashed through my mind a few moments a week ago. Indeed, the few moments enabled and prepared my mind to hear the consequences of past events and move on. Almighty, who knows the beginning and the end, has drawn all this accurately. Why?

Fr. James, Sebastian, James - We saw Meena Kumari's last film, "Pakeeza." After studying German, Fr. James went to Germany for church services. I went to Santa Cruz Airport Bombay to see off Fr. James, accompanied by Joy and James. We returned the next day.

Information received that Kochuppappan wants to go to Bombay via Poona. Bevan might also be there. He said that he had written a letter. But I did not get any letter. The only telegram I received was - "departing as instructed." There was no writing about why he was going to Bombay, the job there, or what he wanted me to do. Assuming that he could tell when I saw him in person, I had to go and see them at the railway station.

Taking a short leave, I walked across the platform where the train would have come; looking for Bevan, I saw Kochuppappan smiling and approaching me from the front. It was a lovely meeting and much fun on the platform. AP Kuriakose uncle was also travelling with Kochuppappan to Bombay. The matter was about a marriage proposal for Maniamma, AP's daughter. The bridegroom was from Kainakari and lived in Bombay. The boy would come to Dadar and take the guests to his place.

"Are you coming with us for a bit of courage for ourselves? This is our first long-distance trip. "

Maniamma, my cousin, was a postgraduate in Marine Zoology. She was teaching at a college in Thiruvananthapuram.

Kochuppappan was going to find a bridegroom for his cousin's daughter. The bride was my cousin too. It is not possible to evade if asked to go along with them.

"I came to the station, taking a short leave from the office. I can return to the office, take a full day's leave, and arrive in Bombay tomorrow."

When I arrived at the bridegroom's residence the next day, I saw a familiar face—Panavalli Baby, a neighbor to Arackal house at Kainakari. I saw him six or seven years ago, I remembered. He learned Commerce at Alleppey College and came to Bombay for employment. Panavalli Baby received us and entertained us.

The next day, I returned to Poona with my uncles.

When the opportunity arose, they inquired about the proposal- "What do you say?"

"Baby, it's hard to say whether he deserves Maniamma, " I replied, looking at them questioningly to know their reaction. Their opinion was not different, they assured.

Kochuppappan was pleased to get down at Kirkee and come to my room on the way back. I took him around in Kirkee to CME and showed him the college surroundings and the market running in full swing. I bought a few souvenirs from Poona General Stores at Kirkee. We met Fr. James at his residence at Max Muller's house before he boarded the train home.

Ramachandran reached the native place before the Onam. When Ramachandran wrote a letter - "Wandering through the minarets of Kazakh - about this nest of reincarnation - no, I do not want to remind that."

The most significant equipment in the college's Refrigeration and air conditioning workshop was the 15 15-ton ice Plant. The authorities decided to demolish it and bring in modern equipment. That task, which was adventurous and arduous, could be completed in a few days without any accidents. This was because of the sincere efforts of Anthony and another young technician, Khanduri, with me.

Congratulations on your effort. I was granted my annual leave of absence from the college for one month. This time, George decided to accompany me on his journey home. Both of our friends had arrived at the station to bid goodbye.

My mind was dripping like small waves. In many events, boat races, and Onam, All men are like one. Eat puncha rice, swim in the river, go to college -

Achen asked if the government was paying the teachers and if there was a need for his presence in the college.

One could sleep well in good darkness unless the giant Petromax lantern and the frog catchers would not come at night.

Holidays that are full of complexity are neither fun nor comfortable. After the holidays, I returned with unforgettable memories of my village and home, including that of my neighbours and my own family. Then came the Dussehra, the days of festivals.

A couple of days before the Dussehra, it was a little painful, and it was like blood was mixed with urine, like the turbid stream of water flowing through the canals of Kuttanad during the rainy season. Calculi in Kidneys? Suspicious, the doctor told me to take an X-ray. Calculi were not found in the x-ray. Subsequent treatment was ineffective, and I went to KEM for specialist consultation and treatment. After a month of treatment, Dr. Wadia concluded, "You have no diamond jewellery in your kidneys!" It was a great relief.

The next day, I got a letter from Achayan.

"A 24-cent plot of land on the north side of Arakkaparambil house can be bought from Kuruppachan's son at Perumaparambil. It was a good offer. We must accept it because all the facilities are nearby. The total cost would be rupees six thousand. Rupees two thousand should be immediately paid, and the rest should be paid in two instalments."

The Brother came when I was worried about where I could find the necessary amount to send home. I had to show him the letter. After reading the text and returning it to me, the Brother said, "I'm giving you five hundred. Look for the rest!" What an encouragement to support the needs of a brother.

Who am I to show me kindness like this? My eyes went overflowing with tears with emotion. A friend in need is a friend indeed ! ... more than that. He is my beloved Brother. So, as always, he has come to the rescue in any crisis.

Just send as much as you can. When I asked Madhavan, he said he would give 200; if he gave another 300, I would have to pay 60% interest. Padmanabhan and James gave me Rs150 each. There were 200 in the bank. I received a salary of Rs 526 for October. So, I bought a draft for Rs 1500 / - and sent it to Achayan.

At the end of the year, I wrote on the balance sheet that for the Gandhi Store and people staying above the Gandhi Store, I owe a total of Rs 1400, which amounts to the salary for three months!

Achayan's reply came, showing his happiness. Could gather at least half of it, and the rest could be arranged next month.

"I could get some reprieve for the delay from Kuruppachan and his son; they are good men as they are merciful. Give it a try for more."

With that hope, there was an imaginative insight into the plan. We need a hut to be raised there on four pillars!

A month later, Achayan wrote again.

"You draw a plan, get an estimate made, get it signed by an Engineer, and send it to me - I'll arrange to apply for a housing loan from a cooperative society here in Thakazhy."

How hard can it be today to live well tomorrow? Aiming for some green light far away, we walk along the hilly terrain and potholed sidewalk in the dim light.

The birth of the new year 1973 marked the introduction of the first examples of many financial crises, worries, and disappointments. Experiences have taught me that. The great need for money alone was unmet despite knocking on many doors. Kerala Kaumudi and Manorama recovered most of the proceeds Achayan got from agriculture. Attempt to offset losses in business by farming! Rupees one thousand sent by Appachi was some relief. The registration for the 24 cents has not yet been possible. Failure to do so early might result in losing advance payment to the owners. With many friends' help, I could buy a draft for rupees two thousand two hundred and send it to Achayan.

What I have written in my diary for the deduction of rupees three by CDA from my medical reimbursement claim reflected the pain of the financial crisis I faced at that time - "Eaten away by rats at CDA: Rupees Three!".

Ravi, who lived in the next room in the block, listened to cricket commentary on the radio while trying to hide his difficulties of not having a job and other problems in his family. The India-England final Test match was going on in Bombay. He felt it was good. He had been trying to get a job for a long time. Lack of support from his home was also an issue. Madhavan helped him a lot by not missing a meal.

Paulose went home, got married, and came back. I did not send a telegram with greetings and congratulations for the wedding. I wrote a long letter, a letter of congratulation for him,

It was a wedding letter that could be born in the boiling blood of modern-day youth. Trailing through Paulose's travels with friends in Poona, past, present, and near-future, and linking them was a humorous wedding letter. When they returned after the honeymoon, Shantamma said, " Yes, we got it, read it, and I have kept it safely at the bottom of the suitcase for further reading."

I don't know if Paulose reads that scripture regularly besides reading the Bible.

I was reading Anand's "Alkoottam" (The Crowd) - Life and complexities of expatriate Malayalees in the busy city of Bombay – a nicely drawn picture.

Raju wrote - he tried to write short stories during the vacation. In part of Raju's story - for example – he had written, "Now there's an influx of people going to harvest here. It was like the water hyacinth floating and flowing through our ravine. They carry some food, stroll, say the domestic matters, and look for work every morning."

Achayan had written about the riots before Gopalan's tea shop on the bandh day. Aikkarachira Gopi became a martyr. Kuriakose uncle's name was ninth on the list of defendants. Attempts to take his name from the list continue. Brotherly love beyond the colours of the flag! When I read about that incident that shook the countryside, it took some time for the tremors to subside.

In the office, Subedar Damodaran was a colleague who was often indifferent and annoying. He was getting transferred.

And I had to take over the responsibilities from him. With so much formality left over from the transfer, I stopped listening to his annoying words and deeds halfway through and got ready to meet my boss. While going to meet my boss, I suddenly recollected the Bible words-

"Leave the sacrificial offering on the altar, and go first and reconcile with your brother."

This meant that before discussing the matter with my boss, I had to try to reconcile with my colleague first. After coming back, this was what I told Damodaran to do -

"If you can do this more peacefully, I can cooperate. If not, I will have to report."

He paused and said, "Okay, agreed. Ready to forget everything."

"Okay, I'm ready to forgive too."

With the winter training of refrigeration and air conditioning students about to begin in Delhi, it was planned that this time, I would visit Kuriachan's home without any prior information from them. It might be a surprise for them, I thought.

So, I got off the train in Delhi in the evening, and when I reached Kuriachan's house in Kirtinagar, no one was there. They had all gone to the airport together. I was surprised. The wife of Kuriachan's close friend flew to the United States in the night. They went to see her off. Without having any other go, I took a blanket and spread it on the floor on the verandah outside the closed room! The cold in Delhi had not yet abated.

I woke up in the morning with a cold touch. The voice stumbled in surprise.

On Palm Sunday, I woke up early, looked at the calm morning, and regained my sense of place. Kuriachan and Chechi came and looked at me while explaining to Lillykutty how I got there. We attended the palm festival at the Gol Dak Khana Church.

My job was to enroll students who arrived on Monday and Tuesday at their training centres. On Good Friday, Aniyappan also came, and everyone attended the prayers together. We saw Connaught Place and the surrounding historical monuments on Wednesday and Saturday. I bought a shirt from Khadi Bhavan and returned in the evening.

When I got back to Poona, I got a letter written by everyone together from home. I was happy as everyone came together to Poona to see me.

In the evening, George and I went to the train station to see George's friend and family's home. OV and other interested parties came to the station. OV had assigned George a special mission.

"I was forced to ask you again, even though I had told him in advance that he should expect a negative answer from you," George said.

"Got it. Two years ago, another friend asked me the same thing of me. At cyclical intervals, the female tigers of the city create their circle of attraction, show their bravery, and attract their mates!"

"You remain an optimist, Aren't you?"

"Yes, I remain an optimist."

Colonel Joseph Sir was promoted, and he was transferred to Delhi. "Let's go, let's go for sure". He was happy when we went and saw him the next day and congratulated him.

The following Sunday, Brother invited me to the Range Hills house the following evening. I asked him what the special occasion was, but he declined.

"Do you want me to bring any presentation? Can I expect a cup of coffee?" It was thought there would be a personal celebration for the Brother or someone closely related to it.

Kirkee's whole heat was drenched in the rain throughout the day. It rained in the evening too until five o'clock. After drinking the coffee given by the Brother, he revealed a business proposal. It was a business he enjoyed every day. Therefore, I encouraged the Brother to have the start-up of the company.

"Don't worry, say something, and don't take it too seriously."

Brother made an introductory statement before saying the next thing -

"Do not bring such difficult matters for my consideration and comments. Is it a marriage proposal for someone?"

"Yes. "

"See, Brother, Brother knows everything about me. I cannot think of anything like that for at least another three to five years. I hoped you wouldn't say anything to me because you can get on the boat only after reaching the river bank. I'm still walking. "

"But what if they're willing to wait for that long?"

"No, Brother. I do not want anybody to wait for me. I do not know who is so much interested in me. I will not be able to handle a proposal for myself. Don't think otherwise; I am not in love with anyone yet. But, Brother, let me ask you, you are an eligible bachelor. Are you not interested in it?"

The Brother said, "No, not at all."

"Then?"

"Just… asked me to ask you, that is all".

For a while, both of us said nothing. Brother reassured -

"Take it off, and I just told you not to take it seriously."

Nothing was said afterward about the business or the proposal. I have heard of some who have created their attraction zone and were attracting their mates. Remember the female tigers of the city.

I bought a piece of paper and a pen and drew a picture no one could understand. I used two or three colours. I wrote "Self Portrait of a Prisoner of Life's Perpetual Confinement" below.

My common sense knew who had given the job to Brother. I was expecting it one day. That day, I arrived early, even before an answer could be found. But Bernard Shaw helped me to respond in time.

"It is the duty of a girl to get married as early as possible and a man's duty to remain alone as long as he can."

George reminded Socrates -

"My advice is to get married: if you find a good wife, you will be happy; if not, you'll become a philosopher."

I was not ready to be a philosopher. My time will come.

There are so many ways to be happy. When deciding to get married, think about that and its happiness.

34. LIFE PARTNER

The letters of Ammachi, Achayan, and Babu came together. Babu has been writing for a long time, quoting a line from the letter I wrote last time - " At a young age, he had a long bath towel hanging behind the shoulder and was tied in front of the neck. He sang the hymns with a book in his hand - must be Syriac - I don't know what they sang. The style, rhythm, and rituals of the priest were repeated."

Today, Babu writes - Did you forget I sang a song for Kochayan then? Another picture came to mind while reading and thinking about the letter today. The fire spread from the overturned lamp onto the hut. A four-year-old boy came out crying. Panicked, he ran out of the house and said, "Oh, run and come, save us from the fire."

Many ran from the neighbourhood, swam across the ravine, and someone doused the fire with water. And then what happened? Time has passed. Today, Achayan has written that the plan and estimate for a house should be sent home as soon as possible. A house suitable for our site has a frontal view towards the east and cooperation to the west. We can take a government-funded housing loan from the Thakazhi Co-operative Society.

How long does it take to put out this fire? Babu, I'm thinking of you. Where and what will you do in ten years? Where do you want to be? Didn't you block your journey forward by writing the compartmental exam for your SSLC? What recommendation should I write? Let God bless you because you've said so many hymns for Him ! "

After advising me not to take it seriously and saying that Brother had no such interest, why did Brother again keep the subject in mind for so long? His body language and evasive replies without answering direct questions raise serious doubts. Of course, there must be pressure coming from somewhere. Paulose said the same thing. Paulose also wanted Thankachan (as Sebastian was called-pet name) not to fall into any trap. We were gathered for Paulose's son's birthday party. We always hosted all of Paulose's parties on different occasions. Even before the matter got more complicated, the Brother was left alone, and he asked him the right thing. The answer was still silence. Brother understood what Paulose and I were saying without directly commenting on it. When he arrived in Bazar two days later, I took Brother for a walk on the banks of the Mula River.

Still, Brother did not open up his mind. Seeing that the only way was to repeat the question, Brother finally broke his silence and began. We got a definite answer. "No, I have decided not to move forward."

It was planned earlier that Paulose would also reach the banks of the Mula River, but it was a little late. By the time Paulose arrived, Brother had already answered. Talking about other things, we stayed on the riverbank until dusk, on the beach in Kirkee, enjoying the cool breeze.

Babu and Leelamma did not pass the SSLC exam. I thought writing something would make them more uncomfortable. Achayan asked for Sebastian's (Brother's) address so we could write directly to each other. He had not mentioned anything. I gave the postal address. I assumed Achayan might ask Sebastian for more time to repay the borrowed rupees. Therefore, I requested him not to do that.

One day, a week later, Brother came with a slightly mischievous smile on the corner of his lip. He had something to tell me. He showed me Achayan's letter, and he read it to me -

They are parents, and they clearly understand their responsibilities. They wished to know my opinion about marriage. They requested

Sebastian to ask me about my interests and requirements and write back to Achayan.

What are the desirable qualifications for the girl, ABCD... and so on? Because of the reluctance to ask directly, Achayan asked Sebastian to find out from me. "What do you say?"

We are making a plan for house construction. The foundation has not been laid. Housewarming (milk ceremony) and a wedding party may be planned together! "After all, no one in the house remains overaged."

That was my sudden reaction. No son should say as such. Parents are always parents. They have certain responsibilities to fulfill when they are alive. It is not suitable for anybody to belittle their views. Brother did not like the joke. He looked at me a little seriously. All I could remember was that Brother's voice didn't come out. I had to admit my mistake and hung my head down to cover my embarrassment.

I liked the Brother for undertaking the mission from my father. I consoled him by saying -

"There is a lot to be done on the path of development. Brother, it will take time. It may take some time and sometimes a few years. I am ready to wait for the development, Brother."

Brother might have written to Achayan. I understood that the dialogue must continue. That's when Brother came back with Achayan's following letter:

Achayan realizes that - "his opinion is for the betterment of the family. However, development is possible only over a long period." Then he uses a particular phrase in Malayalam- "Until then, I do not intend to call him a 'milking cow' for the family. Do not forget to live." Be more persuasive. That was the suggestion to Brother.

There is nothing more to say. That was my answer.

Achayan was revealing his glory and love for me as a father. My love and intimacy with Brother grew more significant.

KCA president Manichan came to my room and climbed the stairs one evening. A Kottayam resident living in Malabar, he works at R&DE. I could not see him in the office because I was in CME. I thought he would suggest that I be more active in the activities of KCA. I was happy that he came to meet me.

As the talks progressed, Manichan revealed the primary purpose of his visit—a marriage proposal to the sister of Manichan's close friend, who was also working in R&DE.

"You know them, and you might have seen them during the activities of KCA. She is in the Govt service. They are from Kottayam and have all seen you and like you.

The hunter's attitude is that if you go down to the forest with a gun, return with at least one rabbit, if not a leopard! That includes the mindset of a group of familiar friends. No one is hunting for their own sake. It is a pastime for them to find more social status and value. That's it. Nothing more. This rabbit is not able to escape from the eyes of the hunters. That was the question that awoke me from my thoughts.

"What do you say."

I understood the meaning of Brother taking a photograph with me. At least a copy may have gotten there in their hands.

"Oh gosh, brother, what am I supposed to say? I'm not thinking about marriage recently. "

I said something else. Manichan was in a dilemma. He came with high hopes. There was no other way for him but to return in despair.

"Okay, I understand. It's a good relationship. Nothing is compelling about it, but is anyone who fits a good alliance in your knowledge? Tell me then. I'll go and see."

Manichan said he understood my situation and was withdrawing from the attempt.

They might have seen the photo of us taken together. After hearing the things from Manichan, Brother appears to be the first person on the probables list. Let them look for the rest. In any case, we can believe that Manichan will not deceive anyone by lying.

I mustered some courage and said-

"I have a friend named Sebastian. We studied together. We all regularly meet him at the church. He worked for a private company. Recently, he has been selected for a job at the Inspectorate of Armaments. He will be joining there soon."

Manichan was happy that the mission had succeeded, although he did not initially hit the target he aimed for. Manichan returned like any other hunter who found another better target before him.

Indeed, it was a defining moment there. I had the grace from the Heavens for mentioning my friend's name, who perhaps got the benefit for a lifetime.

I got a letter from Kunjunju - "Feeling isolated. I did not go on the annual vacation. Where to go?"

"Fools do not know their folly, but people around them know it, Wise know their folly, and people around them do not know it."

I remembered what Kunjommachayan had said about his younger brother Kunjunju. "Our parents are no more. If he had thought his siblings were alive, he would not have taken two months' leave and sat idle in the field! Has he got no place to go? No relatives to meet? " If they had written that 'he took two months' leave and sat idle' to someone, what would they have understood? If he had written the same to his sibling at home, they would have understood and acted as they should have."

A weed grows in the mind when the parents are gone. If there is a partner to share your love with, you can uproot all the weeds and grow a garden of hope there, and a man can enrich his mind by growing plants, flowers, and fruits for the rest of his life. Finally, return in peace.

This is what the elders thought. Before growing a garden, there should be a small house with a clean kitchen. You can't put two pots on one burner! Let's think about it when the construction is over. It is expected to be completed by December. He will also get the annual vacation by then. A hint from home was that Kunjunju's wedding would happen in December. Thankachan said, "Let him come, see the girl, and if he likes it, then only it could be confirmed."

Despite my humble and strong requests, Appachi did not get time to make and send me the plan and estimate of a small house. Pit lazy! He has no time. The Public Works Department of the Defense Services was busy building barracks for their troops. He wrote that he was planning to go on a two-month vacation. I Wrote to Appachi and sent him a telegram -

"George, James, and Joy are coming. The holidays should be there at least until Christmas. Let us all meet together." This get-together was decided while we were together in Bombay for Onam. We went to the airport and received James Achen from Germany. Achen told life stories in Germany.

I drew a plan for our house based on what I saw in a magazine. I got an estimate made and sent it to Achayan.

Suppose Achayan says that all the money earned from the sale of paddy was spent. In that case, it needs to be understood that the

Manorama and Kerala Kaumudi should be distributed regularly, even if the readers delay the subscription payment. Achayan would again point out that we should not forget our existence was due to the support we received from the newspapers.

I was still wondering what excuse he would say to Sebastian. " I can't work in the field as Kuriakose does. I am even considering whether to continue farming or not." Achayan continues to write, "But if we do not regularly contribute to the Kosamattam Chit Funds, they may also go to court!"

Brother considered the business to "Bring a load of ginger from the Nilgiris, and you will get a reasonable price in Poona. One or two lorry loads per week would be adequate for success". Locals are good at weaving dreams without adequately studying market risk and related service processes.

I paid Brother what I got from Fr James as a loan and the money I could save from my salary, thinking it would help his start-up business. The lorry came loaded with ginger. There were too many obstacles, such as summer heat and undue delay on the way. The road journey, which had to be completed in one day, was completed in three days. By then, more than half the ginger had gone rotten beyond use.

35. SARI & DHOTI

Thambichan was my classmate in school and college. He was perhaps the closest in all my activities. I last saw him when he got a job and went to Paradip. The last time he came home, I could not see him. Thambichan bears the brunt of his family responsibilities.

Thambichan had written that he was on vacation, "coming home on holiday, and wanted my sister Gracy to start a relationship like this. I can say more when I come home." Thambichan and his mother wrote from home that Gracy was getting married on November 29.

"So, You should take leave and come to attend the marriage accordingly."

I must book the train ticket for November 24th, only then would it be possible to reach home on time and attend the function. James helped me to go to the railway station and reserve the ticket. From the previous day's evening to the next morning, when the ticket counter opened, he waited in the queue that started in front of the railway reservation counter. James returned at 8:30 in the morning with a ticket for me.

The health problems resolved a few months ago reappeared when I prepared for the trip home. Blood in the urine and the urine flow were like turbid water. There was a little pain, also.

Did one of the corals break loose from the diamond jewellery made by my kidney? Like last year's landslide, did this year also cause another one? It is something that cannot be postponed. A week ago, I could not see my friend, George, who was going home. I went and met Doctor Prabhu Desai. I had some rest, tests, fluids, medication, and four or five days of casual leave, all for good.

I changed my worries into an opportunity, considered that I could study the available time and write the exam for the remaining subjects. Occasional pain helped me to write the exam well. The pain subsided, my confidence increased to pass the exam, and I was happy. I could take leave and go home on vacation!

I went to Alappuzha from Kochi along with Appachi. Achayan and Thambichan were at the Alappuzha boat jetty.

I went to Kannattumadom early in the morning, met Grandpa and Grandma, and had a lovely time with them.

Two days have passed. I was glad to notice that my siblings had checked my suitcase. "I didn't touch anything," - said my mother.

"Isn't all that yours, too?" asked Achayan. In between, he suggested taking all the coloured clothes from the suitcase and giving them to the tailor to make skirts for the girl-children.

"It's not for a skirt, and it's a sari." I had to clarify.

"Why, sari? To whom do you want to give? Nobody started wearing a sari here."

Silence. When Thambichan wrote that he wanted me to attend his sister's wedding, I had determined, "If I were to participate in the marriage, should I not give at least a gift to the bride?"

Textiles, saris, and dress materials were on sale on the ground floor of my residence in Kirkee. Madhavan Mash of the Mess also came down to help me with the selection. You have to find the right design, colour, and people to wear it when you choose. Anyway, what suddenly came to my mind were my cousins. If Leelamma had started wearing the sari, she would have liked any one of them too. If she was to wear a sari, think about it later. I told the shopkeeper to pack three of the saris, and even though it was not limited to the budget I had planned, I did not feel like giving up any of the choices. Bringing Madhvan Mash helped select the wearables and made the shopkeeper agree to deferred payment of the balance amount to the extent that the total cost exceeded my wallet's capacity. It was not intentional, but it was the right one on the spur of the moment.

"Is it not good if I come to know that these are for whoever it may be?."

Unnecessary tension. The resentment at being late to reply could be heard in words.

"It is like this – one sari is for Gracy, the girl getting married next week. One is for Lillykutty of Kavalackal, and one is for our neighbour Lilly."

Then, no one said anything. And so it happened. One day, Lillykutty from Maramkunnil came home asking for Ammachi in the morning when I had just woken up. I called her closer, put the sari in a paper packet, gave it to her, and said -

"It was brought for you, Lillykutty."

My mother also walked over and looked at Lillykutty and smiled. The light in those eyes and the white teeth on the black, oily face together gave me a perfect smile, and I stood watching it without saying anything.

"This is the first time I'm buying a sari. I do not know if it's good."

"Oh, nothing like, that's good. Let me go."

The building on Maramkunnil was nearing completion. I heard that Appachan and Lillykutty's wedding will be held soon. On the day of raising the main frame of the roof, there was a good celebration. Thommikunju was looking after the library. It was such loving daily exchanges from all the family members at Maramkunnil.

I went to the Ottathyckal house to congratulate Gracy as she was getting ready to be a bride. I was also carrying a sari I had brought her as a gift. Thambichan insisted I go to Dindigul along with the wedding group accompanying the bride. I requested he avoid me if essential people were there to accompany his relations. Still, Thambichan came home with me and got permission from Achayan. Our love for Thambichan, our interest in his family, and their friendly attitude were the reasons behind my favourable decision to go with that group.

In the wedding group, the prominent Ottathyckal relatives were Thambichan's Ambalappuzha Karanavar, living in Madras and his wife, Elayamma, Thathampalli Chittappan, Chettan from Changanassery, and so on. Thambichan had reached the railway station earlier and arranged a sitting reservation from Kollam to Dindigul. Thambichan made everyone comfortable and carried on admirably. The cool breeze was relaxed during the journey. Although I did not sleep much, the journey was comfortable, and everyone enjoyed the trip together.

Thambichan's elder sister searched for a blanket, saying it was getting colder during the trip. It was not common for people who had seldom travelled by train to carry a blanket in the bag for the night. When packing my bag, I told Leelamma to keep a double dhoti. When I looked in the bag, I saw that it was there. The new double dhoti was bought from Alappuzha and has not been worn yet. The traditional idea of wearing new clothes when going first to church was kept in mind, like the wedding in Dindigul, which would be held at the church, and I could wear the dhoti there. It did not matter. It was enough to wear pants there in the church.

I took the double white dhoti from my bag and gave it to the girl as a blanket.

Savariar - Gracy's groom - received us at Dindigul station in the morning. We were taken in a horse-drawn carriage to a nearby hotel and accommodated. We did not expect anything other than a shower and a dress change there.

Savariar - we called him Xavier for convenience- was a promising young man with a pleasing face. He was an officer in MMTC and worked in Bhubaneswar. He belonged to a Tamil Catholic family; his mother and siblings lived in Dindigul. That is why it was decided to hold the wedding ceremony at Dindigul.

Gracy studied stenography and started working in Bhubaneswar. Xavier met Gracy, talked to her, and told Thambichan he liked her. Thambichan, in consultation with his family, decided that Xavier would be a suitable groom for Gracy, even though he did not have all the outstanding credentials of a Malayalee Catholic. Looking at the perfect capability and eligibility criteria, many other circumstances may not be favourable. He was good-natured, loving, and had a good job, income, and education. Although it was difficult for Gracy to readily agree on the first occasion by saying that he was Tamil-speaking and black, not only Gracy but no one dared look at Thambichan's face and say anything against the alliance.

In Gracy's eyes, which appeared as always sad, Xavier saw the calmness and modesty of a Malayalee girl. It was Xavier who persuaded his family in Dindigul. Curious, I watched the family as they showed their love and affection for Xavier.

While we were waiting in the hotel, after getting ready, Xavier arrived at the hotel and took us to his house.

Since we planned to go to the church's party hall after the wedding ceremony, there were no other occasions to visit the house.

It was there that we met Xavier's mother and siblings. For those who did not speak English, the Malayalam language alone felt like a barrier to easy access. Except for the Karanavar (uncle) who came with the bride, no one knew Tamil. Because he has worked as a transport bus driver in Tamil Nadu for a long time, now and then, he would forget and join us with an anecdote and joke in Tamil.

It was traditional for the couple's relatives to get together before the wedding. Years ago, an overview of the give and take—Dowry system in the Kerala Christian community. The bride is sent to the groom's family with the daughter's share of money, gold, and land allotted to her from the family. After the ban on dowry, the practice of giving a share was reduced. In Tamil Nadu, although the dowry system was not very strict, giving clothes and jewellery to the bride at the time of marriage was common. After visiting the bridegroom's house, the married couple will be transported in a vehicle with steel or wooden furniture, steel utensils, copper, milk jug, cow and calf, grinding stones, etc., for the bride to use at their new home. Essential items and tools for the new family, starting with the couple! That was the way in Tamil Nadu. Since Xavier lived in Bhubaneswar, no one thought he would need as many hotchpotch sundry items as in the village.

There was a talk of giving and taking at the causal review meeting. No one from Kuttanad at the bride's party knew about the customs and traditions of Tamil Nadu. Those who knew did not open their mouth. The groom intervened, said something in Tamil, and ended the conversation. Something like the youngsters have discussed and agreed on the matter.

No one considered it an issue.

Xavier knew a lot before Thambichan introduced his classmate to him.

"You were a 'Raksha Anusandhan Evam Vikas' scientist who left to launch a rocket in Thiruvananthapuram. You moved on and were teaching in a Military College in Pune. Thambichan has talked a lot about his classmate." Xavier was a man worthy of respect, very lovable, and decent. Thambichan concluded by winding up the short discussions-

"Let's get together when the couple gets to the bride's home after the wedding."

"Yes, We need to meet," Xavier added.

The ceremony was held at St. Joseph's Church, Dindigul, at 6 p.m. The reception was held afterwards in the Parish Hall.

How could one expect Travancore Catholic wedding receptions and tasty Kuttanad cuisines in Dindigul, Tamil Nadu? Someone expressed resentment over it and raised his voice. Cultural differences could be seen between the two races. Didn't this affect the wedding reception at least a little bit? The bridegroom came down from the podium and soothed and comforted everyone. Everyone calmed down.

Shakespeare's words came out with a laugh that disarmed the stubborn complainant as he shook hands and applauded.

"All's Well That Ends Well".

"May Gracy always be your companion and partner. And thereby to Thambichan's family, too. You are always happy, love each other." We parted ways after saying goodbye to both the groom and the bride. The diverse cultural heritage with which they were born and raised should never lead to contradictions in their married life.

After handing over the bride to the bridegroom and his relatives in the reception hall, the wedding party left for the Dindigul railway station. We arrived at the station at midnight and waited for the train. The next day, the train arrived at 4:30 a.m., although it was announced at 2:00 a.m.

Leelamma, Thambichan, Savariar, Gracy

36. SARASWATI YAMAM AT SENGOTTAI

Matters with God's blessings happen during the holy time of Brahma Muhurta. God's decrees are revealed through man's wisdom, knowledge, and experience.

The men were walking back and forth on the platform to keep from falling asleep. The women were catching some sleep lying in the waiting room's corner or leaning on a pillar on the platform. The night was cold, and there was a light breeze. The intensity of light on the railway platform was very low. The other passengers were meagre in number. Narrating jokes, laughing out loud, and the whole rhetoric did not bother anyone. Ambalapuzha Karanavar told Tamil jokes in Malayalam, providing ample opportunity for others to laugh. Changanacherry Chettan laughed loudly, clapped his hands on the shoulder of the nearest, and alerted the whole area.

Thambichan walked away somewhere.

"Edo then, let's change this joke apart. Let's come to more serious matters."....Ambalapuzha Karanavar came nearby, put his hands on my shoulder, and called me -"

"Then, my dear."

" Yes, uncle. " I like serious matters more than mere jokes. I gave all my ears and listened.

"We have a girl next door. Would you like to consider her?" There was a mischievous smile on Uncle's lips. Even in the dim light, it was visible.

I knew those moments were sacred, and what I heard was in Brahmamuhurtha. I knew who that girl was. I understand that without any man telling me. This question has been heard many times in my mind in another form. I knew someone would ask me this someday. I was anticipating. There was no shortage of them in the native land for hunters.

If anyone asks, "Will you be happy for so and so?" I could not give a reply immediately. Who knows when a question will, in reality, affect our lives? Is that the turning point in life? Are these the defining moments?

" Would you like to consider it?"

A further question. A moment can affect a life, a family, and even generations. There did not seem to be any cultural differences. Love, faith, and unity are all beliefs. There was enough time to think, and I wanted to think more. It's funny, but it's worth the answer. That was the essence of being happy. Without being severe, I wanted to give back in the same coin. I told him as if it was a joke!

"Let's see if you can provide the cow, calf, steel utensils, etc., along with the girl; certainly, I shall consider it. We can survive by drinking milk?"

My seriousness went unnoticed in the dim light. I laughed out loud with Uncle and Chettan; the answer made them happy beyond the laughter.

The waves of laughter melted into the sound of the screaming train, the heavy wheels rolling over the rails and breathing steam.

The family of Ambalapuzha Karanavar travelled in the next seat on the train from Dindigul to Kollam. There was the five-year-old child, their daughter, Minikutty, who became the point of all my affection. The child repeatedly asked her mother who this uncle was travelling with within their group because she had never seen me before. With no answer from the mother, she kept looking at me to understand me as if my name or relationship was written on my face. When she looked at me several times, I thought the child would come closer to me to be my friend, but I called her. She only shook her head, showing her reluctance. I just winked my left eye as a friendly gesture towards the child.

Minikutty started laughing.

I repeated the act smilingly.

The little girl could not stop laughing. She loved the winking uncle. She said to her mother, "Here is an uncle winking his eyes - " winking uncle."

Ten minutes later, I closed my eyes again. The little girl burst out laughing and often got giggles. So I travelled on the train smiling for hours. The adult girl sitting opposite me also smiled and kept laughing in her mind most of the time. It was conspicuously visible on her face.

Forgetting the journey's hardships, those kids gifted the joy-sharing moments, the familiar girl sitting in front, and my thoughts.

Isn't this the same girl who came home running last time when I was on vacation and was reading a book on the verandah? The slender white beauty, wearing a half sari, had her hair braided twice, one backward and the other forward. She called my mother, told her she needed water, and went inside.

Did I think, "I could have given her the water of life"? But I did not ask.

Without asking, 'Aren't you Thambichan's sister?' Just like typical etiquette, I looked at her and smiled. Without answering, was she embarrassed or scared, just looking at me, pretending to be the one unfamiliar, and quickly went to my mother and asked for water? Is not that girl sitting in front of me? In front of me, without looking at me, enjoying the surroundings? Sometimes, some concern that was not in her childish mind was reflected in her face.

What if I ask something? She didn't even look right then. Today, there is plenty of time to look straight ahead, see her, and know her. Relatives may be watching over me, too!

She then came home to drink water, returning from the 'Malayalam Vidwan' class taught by Sharma Sar in Ambalapuzha (temple) East Gate. I realized that the girl who regularly walked twenty kilometers to return home after class, to go home to the 'island' in the middle of the field, and so on, was brave enough, hardworking, decent, and willing to take the troubles of a long journey! Is that what the girl calling my mother and running inside, like a rabbit hiding in a ditch in front of it, constantly trembling with fear of being caught by the hunter?

Natural decency with no artificialities. In the beauty of the youth, you can still see the dignity and maturity on the girl's face. Who did not want a married life with a beautiful, decent girl like this? Taking this girl's difficulties far away and going ahead would be like, along with her, having to 'move ashore from the middle of the lake.' That was the thought deep within my mind.

Was it just a joke when I spontaneously reacted that I could consider if the offer came with a cow and a calf? Did anyone make me say that? Did the trumpet sound for the beginning of a glorious event decided somewhere in the 'seventh manvantara' cosmology? Did it light up the wick for the holy matrimony?

What if I ask her something?

What if the question is about our travels? Travel without sleep at night, no. Or else, if the question was about her sister's wedding yesterday? That's not good. Who would want to listen to a controversial talk when she was the elder and was an eligible spinster, and quickly the younger one was married off? When travelling all the time without showing awkwardness and after participating together in that event, ask a question: Is it not more embarrassing than anything else? I thought asking an unnecessary question that led to misunderstandings was wrong.

If I asked her when the examination for Malayalam Vidwan was,

"With so much left to learn, I've gone to send my sibling off in marriage! I tried to say 'no' to travelling together with the family. I had a lot of chapters to study, but Thambichan's piercing look at me did not allow me to open my mouth. If I had said something that would have been sufficient to create unhappiness all around," - That would be the answer. Why, again, this kind of negative talk? Therefore, I could not ask anything. I did not ask anything at all.

The train would stop suddenly if I sang, 'I love you, mankitave (fawn), baby deer is called a fawn....'

'ഞാൻ നിന്നെ പ്രേമിക്കുന്നു, മാൻകിടാവേ ...'

Relatives would not agree with me singing the rest of the lyrics- 'Give me half of your body and half of your mind.' **'മെയ്യില് പാതി പകുത്തുതരൂ, മനസ്സില് പാതി പകുത്തുതരൂ'**

So it is not right to look ahead even for a bed of thorns.

We sat face to face, looking at each other in the seats opposite the meter-gauge train compartment. Our minds were filled with many questions. Our lips were tightly closed to avoid complications by asking or saying something unpleasant. There was no expression on our faces that we wanted to know each other or knew anything about ourselves. When love sprouts in mind, do many questions arise about the consequences? Is it possible to forget the hardships of life's journey, share joys and sorrows, and do so without being overwhelmed by selfless parallel tracks?

The long-lasting darkness in the tunnels at Chengottai slowly descended, and the light after the tunnel reflected off the face of the girl, who had no fear on her face. No, it was a smile! The gift was that I did not intimidate her in the darkness.

When I was about to reach home, I inquired about my dhoti, which was given to Thambichan's sister as a blanket. Someone might have kept it carefully. I needed to get it back.

" Can I wash and return it to you?" asked the blanket user.

Showing the blood stains of the mosquito and the black charcoal dust of the train clinging to the cloth, the girl insisted with compassionate eyes -

I realized that the pleading habit of - "shall wash and then only give it back" was utterly non-existent. If there were any pleading, I would probably have agreed.

"Doesn't matter; I have nothing else to wear at home; I always wear pants!" I paused.

'What will I do then?' Without even saying a word as fun, I comforted her, saying, "It doesn't matter to me; give it to me."

"The girl's mother - Thambichan's mother - was smiling at her daughter. She did not say any prankish words that boys usually do. I could see on her face that she was a mother with a vision and great desire for greener pastures of life for her daughters!

The next day, Achayan, resting in the armchair after dinner, called me and asked.

"Eda, we still have a long way to go for a better life. But should we forget our own lives for our parents and siblings?"

I understood that it was a continuation of the mission entrusted to Sebastian.

"You don't have to wait that long. It is to ask you about a girl. She works in Alappuzha Telephone Exchange. She has a salary of four hundred rupees. The parents said they would give a gift of ten thousand. Kakkazham Chettan comes and applies pressure often. What do you say?"

I did not reply to anything. What is the necessity of rushing it now?

I complained in my mind. I'm not particularly eager to live with a wife who works in an office from 9 am to 5 pm, bargains for a regular income, and gets paid precisely.

"Shall wait for a little longer". Achayan may not be convinced if I say something more.

I felt frustrated, and even the slightest thing seemed like it could set me off. It can feel like anger, or is it a different emotion that defies words but combines anger, frustration, sadness, and edginess?

No one would have seen the anger and the sadness in my mind as I lay on my bed in the annex. Maybe it was due to the surrounding darkness. Achayan was not willing to persuade me anymore. Achayan did not even indicate what the next move would be.

I woke in the morning, went to Punnapra, and met Kochuppappan. Then I went to Chekkidikkadu, where James and Joy were present. They had seen Kunjunju in Kochi, who had come on leave. They mentioned that the preparations were underway for Kunjunju's wedding. We spent time together with everyone. I returned home around 9 p.m.

Early in the morning, my grandfather went to church and came home to drink coffee on his way back. Grandma and Grandpa love coffee prepared by my mother. After drinking coffee, Achayan told his father that some happenings circumscribed Perappan and Chittappan.

I didn't know whether I overheard it correctly.

When distress comes to the mind, Achayan's throat stumbles, and his eyes water. It's because of his love for his siblings, and it's because of his sincerity. He worked to control himself. Achayan took

Grandpa and went into his office room. The two then calmed down and discussed calmly. After a while, Achayan left for Champakulam, saying he wanted to buy fertilizer for the paddy field.

My grandfather called and sat me down, patted me on the shoulder, looked me in the eyes, and asked a straightforward question - the question was sufficiently serious-.

"If I tell you something, will you obey?" - Life's definable - divergent - Like a farmer ploughs the whole land, levels it, and sows seeds for a better harvest - a question of that sort!

From the beginning, it was understood that the correct answer could only be given if the question was carefully considered. I was ready for it, too, while sitting in the presence of my most lovable person. Anything will have to be answered. I listened carefully and looked into my grandpa's compassionate eyes.

"Thambi ... has Thambi told you anything? Something that will affect the future of this family."

"I do not understand, Appa; about what?"

"About a wedding proposal -"

This is it. The same question has been on my mind many times. A question that needs to be answered with reason.

The students at CME were asked a question like the one the UPSC board chairman asked: "Will the room get warmer or cooler when a refrigerator is running continuously in a closed room? The refrigerator door is fully open."

Is this a continuation of that auspicious 'Brahma Muhurtham' moment,

Continuation of those sacred moments?

How fast things were moving! (Brahmamuhurtham is two hours before sunrise - Kerala Culture)

I was hoping someone would ever ask this. I never thought it would come so soon. Awesome!

"No, Appa, Thambi did not say anything, particularly as such. "

Grandpa found it hard to believe.

"Then, this is how it is. Our Leelamma to go to their family and their Leelamma .."

My concern, fear, or anxiety, nothing of it. It was just a fantastic revelation. I, with fear and devotion, listened with obedience.

Yes, here, through the prophet my grandfather, in these holy moments, reveals the determination of God. The father's presence itself is the epitome of a lifetime, the model.

The grandpa then said something - about recognizing the good in the minds of others, about the ultimate purpose of life, about parents planning every move and desire for their children's future. This advantage is the favourable environment, the same cultural heritage, and much more. Everything was heard keenly without asking anything in return.

"Your father and his elder brother, and for me much beyond that, are happy and very positive about this." My grandfather stopped for a while and then continued - "I need to know now; what do you say?."

"Appa, I always obeyed my parents. This is the same for me; it's a happy thing." I did not elaborate further on what was inside – 'It sprouted in my mind; I did not even say that.

I asked Grandpa -"Appa, will Thambi agree to this? Isn't Leelamma too young? How good it would be if it so happened."

Grandpa said, "Oh, of course. This is what came from them. They will like it too. Your father opened up his mind to me."

I did not know that my grandfather had gone back home. My deep thoughts clouded my sight!

In the evening, Achen, my uncle in Maramkunnil – Achayan's brother-in-law in the neighbourhood - called me. A favourite friend and brother-in-law of all the brothers of Kannattumadom, he considered himself the chieftain of the local clan and assumed the most privileged position. He interfered in all matters and would comment and intervene in all issues that came to his knowledge. He was outspoken about what he disliked. His children were afraid to go close to him.

I was called into the west room of the new house. Without any severe expression, Achen asked me, "What is the agreement between you and Thambi?"

I did not feel any fear as I was asked such questions earlier, too. I looked into his eyes and replied.

"No, Acha, there was no agreement in particular."

"Is that right? Aha. Well, then, what's all that I hear."

"I do not know what Achen heard. I have told my grandfather everything I have to say."

The elder has no intention of leaving. That is why I brought the High Court observations to Achen's attention.

"Okay, you can go; let me ask Vavachan."

He might have thought I had learned to look straight and talk without fear. I never spoke like this before. Achan also might have understood that the children have grown up.

Annakutty Ammayi came to talk to Annamma (my mother) in the evening. Before leaving, she approached me and said - " My boy,

Achan, is like that. He will show great seriousness. That's nature, but he very much likes you. He has great regard for you."

After a pause, she continued.

"Do you want to listen? Two months ago, a man named Vellamkulam Chacko came here to see Achayan. He came to the neighbourhood (Maramkunnil) because Achayan was not there. Achen was not there then either."

I understood who it was. It must be one of the hunters. Let me hear it from my aunt. " I am all ears".

"He told me a story."

"What did he say?"

"There's a nurse or somebody related to them in Poona. Then the man said they had decided on all that about their marriage. You should conduct it for good."

I didn't know from where the anger was boiling within me. My anger was burning. I know the predators will go to extremes. Which stupid got this lousy thought? Only he will do it. He was the one who ran around to arrange for the tie-up of a girl onto someone's head. It was said that the girl, another tigress in the city, had a hole or a split physically made or forcefully developed!

You should be able to say, like Kuriachan, "Shall wear the torn, but not the one mended with stitches." It should be like pouring liquid lead into his ears if he hears it.

Aunty continued – "I told this to Achan and Achayan. I knew immediately then that what he said was not valid.

"Achayan said he would let me know if anything is like that. Nothing like that has been written in his writing till now. If that is the case, it is his wish, and I will not stand in the way. Let him tell me. Sister, this can't be right; I don't believe it."

That must have been in Maramkunnil Achen's mind. My eyes went to the highest. God is great! Hearing all this, how much Achayan would have gotten hurt! How kind and admirable was Achayan?

He was a sensible man who had learned the tricks of some people and rejected them all with the contempt they deserved. Achayan, who was full of admirable things and lived in the blessings of peace, has never asked me a word, and he never got angry with me at least once. He wrote a letter to Sebastian in Poona. He got the first chance to talk to me when I came here. He presented a proposal for a girl working in the telephone exchange on behalf of his Chettan in Kakkazham. Perhaps he had wiped out all about the scandal from his mind. Or was it to verify what resided in my mind?

I would have beaten him to death if I had seen that man. I would beat him until he apologized by touching Achayan's feet. How much pain would my parents and relatives, who always loved me, have suffered because of that wicked man? Anyway, nothing happened. In any case, the tricks of the evil did not work. I love my parents and relatives and am ready to sacrifice for them.

When I said I was going to Sebastian's house in Muttar, Achayan gave me a mission. Achayan said he was giving me the task after deliberating with Achen.

"You mention our Lillykkutty. you know them very well." That's right; something crossed my mind as well. My Brother's brother and parents will be there.

Kunjunju and Joy arrived early in the morning. They were happy to know the state of things at home, about the two marriages in my house. Joy also passed a comment – "What the patient wanted and the doctor prescribed are the same."

No, not one, but two. Aren't both two different 'Leelamma's? It is not clear who the patient is or who the doctor is. Let no one be sick.

Lt Gen (Retd) TC Joseph, AVSM, PVSM

37. ARRANGING LIVES

I went to Champakulam alongwith Kunjunju and Joy . Kunjunju went straight back to Kainakary. Joy came with me to Muttar - since he knew Sebastian while visiting Poona.

The bridges on the Alappuzha - Changanassery road were yet to be completed, and there were ferries to cross the rivers at Nedumudi and Kidangara. Therefore, the journey took a long time.

Brother's mother and brother Thomaskutty gave us a warm welcome. I could present the sensitive subject tactfully amidst other matters of welfare and inquiries. They said they would like to come and see the girl the following Sunday. That response gave good hope to the proposal. We came back through Kainakari. By the time we reached Arackal, good news had arrived. Kunjunj's wedding would take place on the 17th of December 1973, before Appachi's vacation would be over.

The next day, there was a get-together and discussion among the family's elders. I could watch over everything from a distance. Some locals also knew the information about the family's weddings that would be held soon. It was clear from their talk and expressions of happiness that it was a relationship that was acceptable to all. They only constantly desired the best for all of us.

Achayan spoke for the first time about the relationship we were about to build with the Ottathyckal family. Before going to bed in the evening-

"It's only going to happen if there are two inter-relationships. I'm going to do only that. It's not going to be just one. What do you have to say, right?"

"Yeah, that's enough."

My mother also joined in the conversation. Achayan said after being silent for a while.

"Thommachi and I have led our life similarly since we were young."

The memory of the years flashed through my mind. Their joint ventures, achievements, and resentments. Life efforts for their children.

The direct consequences of destiny are determined sometimes long ago within the ages of the gods. This is destined to happen sooner or later!

After years, I partook in Sunday's holy mass at the Champakulam church. The Holy Mass liturgy ended with the faithful praying so they may follow God's will daily.

The liturgical celebration of the Eucharist also controlled everything outside the "church" and influenced all areas of our lives. The celebration made it essential and capable of reaching all the areas of our lives: joys and sufferings, rest and work, oneself and one's family. Thomaskutty and his mother arrived and joined me when I finished the mass and came out.

When I reached home with them, Achayan and Ammachi also received and entertained them. Achayan gave a brief presentation on our Ottathyckal relationships. They were happy. Thomaskutty's mother desired calmly -

"Then let's see the girl."

Everyone met and talked to Lillykutty, Achen, and Ammayi.

They liked Lillykutty. Thomaskutty said-

"I am writing to Achayan and Chetan today. They will be coming home for Christmas. We can decide the rest of the things after they come."

I wrote a letter to Brother and Ramachandran explaining all that has happened recently. Kunjunju, Elayamma, and James also came home. James also read my letter written to Brother.

The routine ritualistic negotiations and ceremonies started with a gathering of elders in the family and close relatives. Chitappan from Anjiliparampil, Kochuppappan, and Perappan, who came from Punnapra, were all there. They went to Ottathyckal and returned, where they announced that the relationship had been agreed upon between the two families. Celebrations and functions may be held sometime in October next year.

'Boy's relatives went to see the girl for an alliance, without the boy," the locals might not have said and laughed about it. The reason they knew well. How many times has the bridegroom seen the bride?

And so was the bride, too.

After Kunjunj's betrothal ceremony, senior relatives from the Arackal family also arrived. They had changed the date of Kunjunj's wedding to December 20, 1973.

Thus, a grand gathering of my parents' relatives was rare. Achayan said- "A day like today is too rare. It is one of the happiest days when all the family's elders gather together."

Before returning to Punnapra, I heard Kochuppappan saying to Achayan and Ammachi –"We did not talk about giving and receiving. It didn't seem necessary. Everyone knows, especially regarding girls being exchanged for each family."

Chittamma was ready to introduce another proposal. An only daughter of a well-to-do Latin family, beautiful and well-educated. All Chitamma's dreams have come to naught."

'Leave me to live in peace; I could have replied to Chittamma.- I thought to myself.

"Had not all the developments here happened so quickly? She would feel sad that Marykutty's plans had gone awry. Tell Marykutty that it is all God's will." Achayan closed the subject.

The next day, when Thambichan and I were going to Punnapra on the way to Alleppey, we did not speak much about what had happened in the past few days. The friendly and familiar villagers kept calling out their comments and reactions. They expected a quick feast. We smiled and thanked them, and we walked away.

We reached Punnapra together. Kochappappan and Chittamma were waiting for us after they prepared coffee, snacks, and sweets.

Chittamma's welcome announcement, "Hello, bridegrooms. Do not hesitate to come in, " loudly proclaimed a sense of loss in Chittamma's mind.

When he returned from the office, Kochuppappan brought the papers for the college loan deed that Thambichan had signed. He had paid off all the loan money from his salary.

Kochuppappan smiled and said to Thambichan -

"When I came home with the proposal, Leelamma said as soon as she saw me - that I helped her in her efforts to go to Germany, and her 'bio-data' I had written is still in her hand. I replied to her that her fiance would rewrite it now. Or let both of them write it together. Leelamma ran away, blushing and laughing. "

Thambichan understood. Leelamma wanted to study nursing in Germany. Thomas Achan of Panakkezham had agreed to help her in that respect and did what he could. Leelamma once told me this.

"So if I had been a nurse in Germany, I could have given birth to the fat white babies of a German cypress. No luck with that."

I had replied to her before thinking about the 'poetical fancy' of the ironical comparison (utpreksa).

Kochuppappan's other joke was when we got permission to leave after saying farewell.

"May God pickle you was the wish of an English writer who was not so strict about using the words appropriately for the occasion. Pickle also means save. So let me also say likewise - may God pickle you".

On the way back, I couldn't stop laughing, remembering Kochuppappan's farewell wishes, filled with love and care.

38. MUTUAL RELATIONS

After vacation, Thambichan went back to Cuttack. I was seeing him off. When he was leaving by boat to Alappuzha, there were moments when words were inadequate to express his feelings and thoughts. Everything was in our minds and thoughts, and we knew everything about each other. Still, they said nothing to each other. The words were silent, and he spoke not even a word. After laying the foundation for the relationship and earthly life, he departs for a temporary separation. Soon to come back and rejoin at home, Thambichan left for work to come back again.

Achayan suggested it. I had to go with a coconut climber to the recently purchased homestead for the first harvest of coconuts. We could get 140 coconuts.

My thoughts and focus were on my routines that were about to change. I doubted the philosophies discussed would crash against the rock of practical life. Or did I hear the proclamation of a new dawn that will break out from the heat of the past ages and time durations? Did I see the morning star emerging in the early morning sky as a dazzling morning lantern, emerging into the view from beyond the eastern horizon, like an anecdote in a story to retell...?

How many good examples are there? None decided against the essentials, worrying about future concerns, and everyone has chosen the best way of life, hoping for good results and a bright future while reaching the ultimate goal. Accordingly, they choose routines that are consistent and non-confrontational. Or they prepare themselves for such a way of life.

I watched curiously as the worker carefully moved towards the pinnacle of the tree, the final destination to harvest the fruits. A tree is to be recognized by its fruit. Coconut got the name 'Kalpa Vriksha' because every part is valuable. The coconut tree is capable of sensing human voice and proximity. Coconut grows well where children play and where there is human proximity. That's why people prefer to build their houses mostly in coconut groves.

The four cousins - Appachi, Joy James, and I- gathered at Kainakari to attend Kunjunj's wedding.

It was a rare occasion when four cousins came together. It's time for the long-awaited dream of Kunjunju to come true. We all arrived early for the preparations. Electrification of the house was attended to and completed. We collaborated to put up the pandal and decorate it. Some family members' and relatives' sincerity, resentment, and non-cooperation could be experienced in a particular proportion. Blood relations should be fluid since no one with self-effort achieved it. But financial power often leads to temporary, worldly stability. The justifications frequently turn into arguments, don't they?

After the morning prayer in front of the big picture frame of the house, Kunjunju's eyes were wet with tears as he extended his folded hands for the blessings of his elderly siblings. It may be because of the sacred memory of his departed parents. They did not wait to witness another milestone in their peaceful family life. As they walked to the nearby Chempil Chapel Church, many hearts were filled with sincere wishes for Kunjunju, the youngest member of the generation, to carry forward the family legacy and to have many years of happy and fruitful married life.

I was watching everything that was going on with equanimity. My heart was full of good wishes and prayers for Kunjunju for a long, happy married life.

If the feeling of "I" begins to exist in the mind, it destroys every good thing. First friendship, then equanimity, brotherhood, and so on... Some tried to show their superiority to the newly arrived relatives. All the rest of the formalities were auspicious. I got to know my Aunty during the regular photo session after the welcome ceremony into the house and receptions, even before anyone introduced Aunty to me. The response was unforgettable.

Even though there was an official photographer, I was responsible for handling a Kodak Click 3. Despite not having much experience, the camera worked efficiently in my hands. The proof was seen in the washed-out, black-and-white but good-looking artistic portraits. I snapped at the appropriate time without allowing time to pose or giving specific instructions to smile. When I did, Auntie was in doubt. She asked me - "Got it?"

"Got it. Thank you, Aunty.." I said.

"Hmmm, it's all 'vilachal'" (insolence = rude and disrespectful behaviour)."

She shared her evaluation and understanding of the photographer with her husband. The introduction was great! I would have laughed it off if it were mischief because I was a naughty one long ago!

Elderly relatives returned to their homes. Appachi, Joy, and James spent the night there with me. When the uncle distributed the Tripple x, the leftover of the military quota, he got the bridegroom, wished us all good night, and went to the bridal chamber, saying it was enough for all the kids. All four of us slept in the same grandpa's room on the same floor mat in the same direction.

Even then, my thoughts were about the coming changes. Summer comes, and then the monsoon, then the winter. Again, the same cycle repeats itself, and the seasons move cyclically. Cyclical variations in Earth's climate occur on multiple scales, from years to decades, centuries, and millennia. Human life also goes through similar changes.

Crops grow, and the fruits or seeds mature and then fall off. After that, they germinate and mature, and the seeds return to the soil. That cycle is being repeated.

The next day, Joy and James came home with me. They wanted to meet my would-be bride and get acquainted with her.

James attended his uncle's wedding ceremony without prior permission from his office and deliberately delayed his return from leave. The same went on for Appachi. I had advised them long ago to take leave at least until Christmas. James felt he had a slight fever on the way home, so I reminded him about extending his leave with a medical certificate. Soon after meeting the familiar and experienced doctor at the Govt hospital, they got their medical certificates and reached home.

My sister Leelamma was younger than the sisters of Joy and James. They were not familiar with Ottathyckal Thambichan. Joy and James were happy to learn about Leelamma's proposed marriage to Thambichan. Then, it was all shyness, bashfulness, making fun, and timidity.

We reached Ottathyckal in the evening twilight. Leelamma showed her face outside the house, wondering who the visitors were, even after Ammachi called her twice to the inside.

I saw that face. Like an untouchable, incredibly mesmerizing lavender-colour flower, the Neelakurinji, with a heart-warming smile, was present before me!

"Do not be afraid, and it's me... these are my cousins. They wanted to see you. Do not be shy. Come down here."

No one was showing their hands like a lotus bud. Perhaps they forgot it while looking at the bright, blooming face. Didn't even the Sun forget his evening bath at that time?

Nobody did say anything. Came to make an acquaintance with my bride-to-be, and you became dumb and speechless? Shyness, language, and lack of experience, what made you so?

I started saying to my brothers - "She knows all languages. You come on, speak - Malayalam, English, Sanskrit, Hindi".

"Ngum nghum, no Hindi!" was the damsel's maiden voice.

Although that imminence was strong, I felt not to mention it as a scare. 'Let's go together and learn Marathi. Or what was your intention of getting higher education in Malayalam? Was it for confining yourself to a school or college nearby? Then I too wanted to find a job here.' I wanted to say all that I deliberated in my mind.

The house's mother milked the cow and brought boiled milk for everyone to drink. On the way back, Joy and James cracked a joke by reiterating the same thing.

"That cow there will give milk any time of the day," said Joy.

"If only I were there with you..!" I filled up that. It became the reason for a long laugh while walking in the middle of the paddy field.

Joy and James went back to their homes in the morning. The announcement came when there was no rush that Thambichan's relatives were coming from Ambalapuzha to meet and get to know us all. After attending Kunjunju's wedding, Leelamma got to know the new aunty, became friends, and stayed there. Babu also went to meet the new Aunty.

"Leelamma should also be available at home when the relatives from Ambalapuzha come." Ammachi desired and requested me -

"You go and bring her here."

I went to Kainakari and fetched Leelamma and Babu.

It was after six years that everyone at home prepared Christmas together. It was last done before I went to Pune after I left the Thumpa Rocket office and came home.

'Peace to all men of goodwill ' was the theme of the return. Babu, Raju, Leelamma, and Bevichan prepared the manger as a makeshift crib for the Baby Jesus and the colourful stars.

Raju and Bevichan made jokes and beautified the manger. We had collected miniature animals that came along with the Bianka toothpaste as part of the campaign, and the miniatures were spread in the manger.

A baby bedding crib was also made for the campaign. An electric bulb was lit inside to give good light to the cattle shed.

Ammachi prepared and arranged the unique Christmas dishes. We, along with Grandpa and Grandma, sat together as a family and relished the Christmas dishes. The joyous experiences of that Christmas and the week leading up to the feast gave everyone rare and extraordinary.

Achayan was like that when he was overjoyed -he asked - "What is Christmas? Peace to men on earth. Peace to whom?"

Grandfather said in reply. putting his hands to his chest, he said -

"For the men of goodwill, you know for the men of goodwill, you know it ?" Laughing and very happy, he looked at every face and said to everyone.

Heaven is here, here at this dining table. Here is my good-hearted God at this dinner table, together with us.

Appan, too, was happy after tasting a glass of nourishing coconut toddy offered to him with gratitude.

My brother's reply was what I had written about the marriage proposal. Nothing was explicitly written. He had informed his parents to do according to their desire. When I informed Maramkunnil Achen about it, I was instructed to go to Muttar to inquire further and report the decision to him. I left in the afternoon, thinking that I might be able to meet my brother's parents as well. So, my trip to Muttar was filled with prayers and more hope. 'May the kind God guide us as hitherto was written to the brother. Marriage proposals control that power because we are all its tools. When I went to Muttar, my hopes were dimmed. Brother has not come. Achayan also did not come. A proposal that existed at Poona got further advanced. The girl's family members have visited Sebastian, who consented to the proposal, and some progress has been made. In the meantime, changing your word and coming to your hometown to see another girl is wrong.

Brother's mother said-

~Therefore, Thomachan, do not think anything further about it. Let God's will be done.

Because of the believer's unwavering faith, the joy of victory is said to be a blessing from Heaven, and the incompetent may explain failure as the act of the Supreme power. Failure to think promptly was my inability, or it may have been God's will. Or when classmates were friends who often met while searching for jobs after their studies, why not use a photograph taken together and get a copy? Lillykutty would have been lucky if I had sent a copy without putting it in the album and started a dialogue at that time. Wasn't it a similar reluctance to take the initiative and not to think promptly for the interest of Joy? Or it might have been God's will. Thirty-five years of non-cooperation was its residue. Without the backing of an invisible force, it is safe to say that none of this was ever under human control.

Achayan's detailed explanation has helped Leelamma clarify the events that preceded her. Leelamma, crying and worried that everything had just happened so fast and earlier than expected, could only see my words and attitude as the selfishness of the interested party. That was the reason for Achayan's intervention. Achayan dealt with it promptly. When Thambichan's relatives came from Ambalapuzha the next day, Leelamma's tearful eyes would not be a positive sign for them. If you do not mature by age, there are many consequences.

That day, Leelamma slept somewhat peacefully. The next day, our grandfather's fond approach and dealings gave her more energy. Only those with a lot of life experience will prepare girls for marriage in such situations to face future life. Hours later, Leelamma laughed at her grandfather's joke. Grandpa had insisted that it should be possible before receiving the guests. My grandpa opened his toothless mouth and told an anecdote -

"If I laugh, all the rats will run through my toothless mouth and into the den. After a while, the rats would realise it was not their den ... What will they do next?"

Leelamma laughed.

Relatives came – Chennai's uncle, Thambichan's uncle, Mavunkal Sir and Panakkezhath Appachan.

Mavunkal Sir said – "When I heard about the establishment of the relationship between the two families, I sincerely felt that it was a "double sweet" feeling.

Madras's Uncle took me aside and told me a particular thing - "The little girl liked the eye-winking Kochayan"(elder brother) very much. She sent me here to convey her special regards to you !"

39. A COW THAT GIVES MILK WHENEVER IT IS MILKED

Before returning to Poona, New Year's greetings came with the words, "Come on, get ready quickly, don't we have to go ..."

Yes, we must go a long way to end this journey.

We were facing new experiences with Joy on January 1, 1974. Our journeys began.

Many weddings, preparations, and related ceremonies have occurred throughout the past year. The holiday season was in the shadows of any marriages - Gracy, Kunjunju, Brother, me, Leelamma, and Lillykutty of Maramkunnil.

It was a continuation of the festive season. Elders at home instructed us to visit Kochuparambil for Ammini, Joy's sister, on the way to Chekidikad. The subject was a marriage proposal for Ammini with James of Kochuparambil. We met Outhakutty of Kochuparambil near the library. As soon as he was introduced to Joy, the elder requested that it was a matter of interest and that they could make further progress on that idea through us. At their house, James' mother exchanged matters of welfare. Some decorative materials from the USA exposed the attitude of the people there.

Chekkidikkad James had typhoid, and we thought he would recover before our journey back to Poona. On the way back, I saw a small face shining in the setting sun's rays in Ambalappuzha.

The kid looked at me and smiled. I walked over and picked her up, and when I asked him if she knew me, she shook her head and smiled again, without saying that for her, I am the winking Kochayan.

Anyone in that house was not unknown to me. I could relax for a while in the warmth of that love.

It was thought that Leelamma could stay in Punnapra and study to prepare for her exam. Though I had the support of Kochuppappan, Chittamma said, ' It would be better to stay in some convent or hostel in Alappuzha.' Celinamma and Leelamma were admitted to study at SD Tutorials in Alappuzha.

The holidays were getting over. Only a day was left when, on that penultimate day, Achayan made slight displeasure that - I went to many houses of the relatives but did not go to Achayan's ancestral home - Anjiliparambil, to meet his Varki Chittappan.

I went to Anjiliparambil, where I was told to see my grandfather's younger brother. I met him and sought his blessings. Raju also came with me.

"Seeing you all is the greatest joy for me. And a biscuit is nothing. You came and met me; how long have I wanted to see you!

It was the magnetic attraction of true love. It would have been a significant loss had I not come to meet him.

I saw the wedding photo of Elsamma and her soldier husband (Chackochan) displayed on the verandah. I received an invitation to come and attend the wedding from Pune. It was due to the difficulty that I did not come. Elsamma already said her displeasure. She was looking and laughing at this mischievous one from the photograph. I told her silently,- "Perhaps you know already that I would also be tied up like you. Your dad went and saw the girl for me and told me it was confirmed. See you next year."

When I visited my grandma at Kannattumadom to say goodbye, Kochuppappan came from Punnapra. Grandma's health condition caused us to worry and be emotional. Controlling himself, her son said to his mother –

" Aren't the holy souls die early, Ammachi? When did you do all the virtues to be holy and to say you would die soon? You don't have enough luck for that, Ammachi."

Many images flashed through my mind. My grandma was a lamp that shone brightly and illuminated many children's minds. She was a lamp that shed the light of mercy and love in the hearts of many children. The oil is running low today. I sat beside my grandmother. I took her wrinkled hand, stroked the half-bent little finger, and held it tight. Years ago, she fell and broke her finger while going to church. I tried to fix that little finger. Amma looked at my face and laughed - "Ngha, Iniya...., after all these days, now it's going to be straight!".

When we came, she was reclining. She was lying there until then.

I tried to talk to my grandmother. "Amma, what do you say ?"

"Neeyo. Where are you now and when did you come? Achayan is keeping well, no?"

How many times did she ask so? I felt a shiver in my nerves for every question she asked. There was a murmur in every word of my answer and ambiguity in every sound I produced.

Sometimes, the grandmother reacted completely normally, sometimes as if she was not with a steady mind. The nerves of her memory were beginning to suffer from paralysis.

Once, I asked, "Amma, where is Ummachan?" Amma replied - "Isn't he somewhere in the north?

"Has he come recently, Amma?"

" Ngha, he came last year ",

"Then, who is this, Amma? Look here, Amma ."

" Don't you go away? Do you think I don't know my children? "

Sometimes, Amma asked me If I was not going to school nowadays., What is your mother doing? and so on.

Once again, "Amme, who is this one? Please tell," Amma said, " That one, that is my elder sister's son, there in Aryad, Pulikkattil."

Once she looked at me quickly and smilingly asked me -

"Why you did not bring her also."

Those standing near me all looked at my face and smiled. Though it was painful to watch Amma with a slippery memory helplessly, it was difficult to watch for long.

I replied in my mind, "Yes, Amma, I shall bring her next time; surely, when I come, I shall bring her too." Amma, until then, please wait for us.

This mother's vitality, intelligence, efforts, and prayers gave Grandpa the strength and inspiration to love all the children in the family.

As I bid farewell to my grandma by saying glory to Jesus, placing my face in those wrinkled geriatric hands, and receiving her blessings, electrical waves ran through my veins. How long should I wait to return and be at this august present? Would it be possible?

I always had the sense that it was in this womb, which I could even touch and feel now, that the entire consciousness, soul, and body of the members of this great family have taken shape.

It was the elderly grandpa who used to take care of Grandma in this bed, even though occasionally, children and grandchildren would help with something or the other.

One thing was sure whether it was so or not; Grandpa used to say to me that they would pray for everyone in the evening prayers and the middle of holy Mass. (1973). When Grandpa prayed for me, he said he always dedicated me to Abhiwandya Kuriakosese Elias, then Father, in the intercession of the prayers. Before Father Kuriakosese Elias Chavara was canonised as Blessed (1984) and again as a Saint (2014), Appan had such great faith and devotion towards the holy Priest.

Before leaving for Poona, I felt my responsibility was to go to Ottathyckal again. I was reluctant to go alone. I requested Raju to accompany me.

At Ottathyckal, I saw Thambichan's mother in the courtyard. I had intended to ask something, even before she could ask me, 'What's up that -

'My relatives came here to see a girl... They didn't bring me. I wanted to see the girl. I don't know who the girl is.'

But even before that, the mother declared-

"Leelamma, see your groom has come."

Leelamma came down - "Chechee," - I heard Raju addressing her formally.

I saw Thambichan's mother take a stainless steel mug in her hand and quickly walk towards the cow shed. No matter when I come, a cow here allows them to milk it for me!

It was impossible to say what was in those eyes, vague eagerness or apparent hope. Did you look at me straight? Or still, are you shy? I am unable to define. I am not a poet.

Even then, I looked at the blue sky, where the clouds moved in one direction. I looked at the green paddy fields all around. The unripe ears of grain on it that desire to ripen soon. Look at the birds flying above them. I saw it with my fully open eyes, and I wanted to paint the picture on the wall of my mind - to see it, remember and recollect it for a whole year. You can only see that from tomorrow.

What? Did you say something with your eyes? Are you in a hurry to occupy my heart?

I saw the group photo hanging on the wall and did not ask for it.

“Is there any single photo available?" No answer came quickly.

“Ok, don't worry. I can ask your brother to send me one."

At Kavalackal, Ammayi had only a few sad things to say. Kunjamma Chechi, Lillikutty, and all her sons live in faraway states, and their father was not keeping healthy here, she said with tears. She bid goodbye to me.

"Edee .. the smallest glass there is one here, half full; just give him black coffee .." I listened, wanting to hear that meaningful joke once again. I didn't hear it. It's on my mind.

As I began to pack things in my suitcase, I thought about how quickly the holidays seemed to fly away. A lot of things happened. I have met a lot of people. Many things did not happen. The desire to watch a film together with brothers was thought about. The excursion and all the stories of Raju are to be read. I heard one or two stories, and they were meaningful words. More incentives are to be given to develop his skills. The study should also be good.

Babychan agreed to take only one of the two choices, and it was enough for him to be taken to Ernakulam. He was not going for a picnic. Raju was disappointed. He was also heartily sorry that Kochayan's vacation was over. Ammachi would sit alone and whimper for many days, saying she did not make anything special for her firstborn. She already said the same thing a couple of times.

Everyone at home sat together to have an informal meeting. Achayan said - "Nothing was planned about the impending resource needs until now, and you are going tomorrow - Yes, you have to go; you can't help without. We need to find a good amount of money to make everything happen. Where to find that was all my thoughts about."

If you put every burden on your shoulders, how will you manage? It would help to have a house with minimum household utensils and appliances when you want to start a new family away from home.

Marriage is not a bed of roses. However, if you have a homemaker who understands, is simple and gentle, shares joys and sorrows, and has no complaints. Any marriage will be fruitful and successful if the partner is like that.

Life ahead is unknown. Leelamma should be willing to cooperate for family life. She has to know and understand a lot of things. There is enough time to prepare. The silence of the night outside, shadow, and light are intermingled and almost fixed in the courtyard. It was challenging to segregate. Our minds were similarly analyzing things and searching for possible solutions.

I will be traveling by train and moving away from here tomorrow. I felt very safe and comfortable here with my parents and siblings. But I have to go back to be more robust and mature.

This time, it was different from any other previous holiday. There was incredible silence everywhere. I was thinking about the past few days. How happy I was under the thatched roof, under the parents' wings, in the brothers' proximity, in the warmth of love, free and without any time constraints.

I woke up at dawn, listening to the music of a bulbul singing from the cowshed roof with the sound of house sparrows in the background.

I hesitated to get up and lay on the bed more. The irreplaceable responsibilities, the inevitable journey, the call of the stomach, and the unknown journey of life made me stand up and walk forward through the same path I crossed for so long, from that automatic life to the boredom of living with strangers.

How to eat half-cooked rationing rice? Pouring a tablespoon of namesake sambar, a handful of dal put in kadi water with four or five veggies cut into pieces and boiled for a tasty sambar- and to eat the chapatis, which were like the long ears of buffalo.

"City is a jungle, a jungle of neon lights," and now LED - I need to travel to that jungle. As the city grows, so does the brightness of its lights.

Babychan and Achayan came along with me to Alappuzha. Babu carried my suitcase all the way. Grandpa, who had said -"Shall come in the morning and take," came over and received my 'Praise be to the Lord before my departure.

Ammachi's eyes were filled with tears, and her face reflected the pain of separation. Leelamma was watching everything silently as if her throat was blocked. She stifled her sobs as I walked over and hugged her.

I stood in silence before the Sacred Heart. No words or voice came out of me, but I prayed to protect all. It has always been like that. Silently, I allowed the teardrops to flow from my eyes through my face without wiping them out. It was my experience that the prayers that came from the heart would have wetness but no sound.

“Prayer of the heart” occurs when the prayer moves from merely mental repetition, forced along by your effort, to an effortless and spontaneous self-repetition of the prayer that emanates from the core of your being, your heart.

Mother always gave me a precious gift that can be kept forever after the prayer- it was Mother's kiss on my wet cheeks. I have collected it from time immemorial. I moved forward. While looking back, I saw the mother and her daughter closely following me up to the fence. Mother's eyes were red, but she tried to put a small smile on her lips.

Since I had agreed with Joy in Kochi to travel by train, I went to his house. Ammini's marriage proposal was discussed with Valyachayan (Joy and Ammini's father). Valyachayan decided we should undertake a special mission to confirm it by going to Bombay and talking to Ammini. If she were interested, she should go home soon by train. That was the mission. The elders at home would make different decisions.

Babychan ran about and walked on the Kochi Harbour Terminus railway platform. He travelled to Ernakulam, and his first railway journey was with us. Valyachayan and Achayan travelled with us to Ernakulam. None understood the pleasant and unpleasant aspects of a long railway journey. However, Bavichan liked his first trip, which was not so long. All of them waited on the platform until they could see us off.

When I started boarding the train at Ernakulam, I saw a short man trying to board the train in the next compartment, at the door close to us. He has seen us all. Perhaps that's why he said "hello" to me loudly. A thought flashed in my mind that I should show this man to Achayan at least once. Achayan has not seen him. Here was an excellent opportunity. I called out to Achayan, standing on the platform -

"This is 'the man' - 'Vellamkulam Chako'." After hearing the name, he looked at Achayan, and Achayan could see his pale face.

He asked Achayan - he was trying to hide his embarrassment by asking or saying something. "What... you know about me? Have you seen me ?"

"I have not seen... but I have heard of you. Yes, I have heard about you".

Those words must have struck fear in him, like thunders in his ears.

That was enough to silence the 'Shakuni' and let him have his way. If even a shred of sanity is left inside that bald head, he will not play tricks anymore. Who knows?

The train ran on parallel rails. The dusk hours gave the light until the end of the day, giving way to the night. Or does the Sun travel to the western lands, where they await dawn and light?

Was it the earth holding the maiden of the night gently onto its breast and getting dissolved into the sea?

The train sped off on parallel rails. It was the twilight time. It gave the light till the end of the day and changed its path at night. Or is the Sun travelling to the light-awaiting western lands?

Many images flashed in my mind, and my thoughts were disintegrating. Contexts change over time and merge. Where do I go, and where do I come from? I closed my eyes and tried to calm my mind.

Green paddy fields, waving coconut trees, coconut groves, long footpaths, hill slopes, and plains run back when I open my eyes. The chugging sound of wheels grinding on the tracks and fellow passengers sharing their worries and concerns. Quiet among the waves of sound, busy but alone. I didn't see anything else, and I didn't hear anything else. I didn't even hear Joy calling me to have the food, packed lemon rice and fish fry.

I re-joined the college after vacation. How true was the advice Anantaraman Sir gave? It is enough to read and study thirty books for three years; you don't need to research anything further to take a class on the same subject for ten years. Of course, periodically update, accept, and modify the changes according to the time and necessity. Focusing on the subject closely and systematically with the awareness of the environment becomes a daily practice. A spontaneous rapport arises with the listeners if you demonstrate the essential knowledge practically. Deliver it on time and at precisely planned levels, and the result is that you enjoy your work, which was the reason behind my eagerness to teach.

Moreover, if teaching and learning were taken together, there would be a minimum deviation from the main focus. Knowledge, not power, is the basis for recognition and respectability. This is commonly seen in the field of education.

John went home, got married, and returned with his wife. Joy (LIC) knew that, and he informed me. I went to see John and congratulated him on beginning his new family life.

John described his hasty journeys, marriage preparations, and ceremonies. He showed me the photo album. They prepared a sumptuous feast, and we enjoyed the time together.

As I recounted my adventures at home during the holidays, I saw John's face changing to show disappointment and a sense of defeat at losing something he had anticipated. When asked why it was so, John did not hesitate to tell everything very frankly. What my close friend John said was this.

John's wife was one of the twins, and he had initiated a marriage proposal for his sister-in-law. He contemplated his companion sitting by his side as the first suitable candidate.

"We have talked about this at our home. What could be done now?"

"Dear John, I don't deserve so much of your gracious kindness, favour, and comfort" - I wanted to console him.

"Why? Nothing like that. It was my hope and extreme desire."

Nothing more was said. I have already given my response and described everything that happened at home. The supreme power always plans things well in advance before any man.

John himself broke the silence.

"I'm glad to hear about your marriage. It's a good thing. If the families are cultured, there's nothing wrong with exchanging girls. You know all of them very well. That is rather important."

I said goodbye to John and his wife so that we could meet again.

When our fellow resident in our room, Girijashankar (short Girijan), relocated to Bangalore, we gave him a hearty send-off. This is how he consoled his friend named Suresh - "It is a holiday for intimate friendship. Take it easy."

Girijan's face turned red, and all his sadness of the separation was visible there. "We will see you soon."- we assured him.

After marriage, Paulos had already started staying with his wife at Appukuttan Nair's house in Range Hills as a sub-tenant.

I went to Bombay for the special mission assigned by Valyachayan. From the meeting and talking to their uncle in Bombay, it was made clear to them that they did not want to take any responsibility for Ammini's marriage proposal.

We talked to the hospital matron where she worked and got permission to take leave and go to her parents. When I returned to Poona, James returned home after the vacation.

When Ammini went to the native, I saw her off at the Poona railway station. James had also joined. Ammini's mind was full of eagerness and hope, and she had all the enthusiasm to become a bride.

"It's all because you have asked me. It is not good for me to desist; I can't help but go?" - Ammini said, "Not like that. If you are not interested in moving forward, say no to the proposal. Say you are not interested. We will not go even an inch forward in this regard. None of us has given any word of assurance to anyone. That is the reason you are being sent now. I had agreed with Valyachayan that I was responsible for sending you to Kochi. The moment you reach there, it will be over ." I couldn't do much with the financial help. A small amount was handed over to Ammini.

A quote came to my notice when the betrothal ceremony was happening at Kainakary. "We see with the mind. We hear with the mind. Desire, certainty, doubt, attention, inattention, steadfastness, fickleness, shyness, intelligence, and fear are the mind itself." (Brhadaranyakam Upanishad I.5.3)

Joy came to Poona again to discuss financial difficulties as he had to find resources for Ammini's wedding. Joy discussed this with James and also spoke to Brother. At the same time, Kochuppappan wrote," There was an opportunity to help me." He had decided to purchase some property. Somehow, I had to send some money to Kochuppappan, which I did with some borrowing from relatives and friends. Still, since the amount was less than what Kocuppappan requested, I had to write him a story that "I was in the hospital for two days, and I could not arrange to help him with more amount". Doubts about the emergence of a diamond mine on my kidney and passing it through the urinary tract had been told to Kochuppappan during the holiday.

After Joy returned to Bombay, James got a letter from him falsely accusing me of non-cooperation and a few other allegations. I learned that there was some conspiracy brewing when he met James at the railway station and inquired about my whereabouts, difficulties, and troubles to his cousin. He had some misconceptions - I was not giving him adequate financial help despite my better earnings.

I never knew that someone had directly or indirectly accused my father or me of suspecting our motive behind the proposal of Ammini marrying James of Kochuparambil. Hearing that, they started questioning our integrity and sincere behaviour.

Achayan's letter made things more difficult for me. Achayan and Ammachi were intentionally not invited to Ammini's wedding. Despite that, they were direct relatives and participated in the wedding. That's what my parents were. As a sign of protest to the parents of Ammini, they both did not attend the reception after the wedding and returned home. Achayan wrote that he had done all he could to help them financially and could not help them more by leaving aside our needs. The reasons behind the accusations and the isolation, thus, came to the limelight. Our contributions did not satisfy them, creating dissatisfaction and displeasure among the relatives.

I never thought a younger cousin who lived among the ordinary men in Bombay would have so much hatred towards me, who sincerely helped him to find an alliance for his sister. And that too after conducting that sister's marriage.

The better thing for Joy was to find out occasionally how his sister lived her life after marriage and forget and forgive any unpleasant thing that happened before instead of accusing a few with animosity after the event

My cousins: James, Joy, and Appachi (1974)

40. GET READY, COME BACK TO WIN

My Brother's wedding was on the fourteenth. I sent a telegram wishing him all the best. I sometimes wondered why I did not write a letter to him as I did to Paulose when he got married.

I will never be able to write a letter like that to Brother. Because Paulose is Paulose and Brother is Brother. The brother wrote immediately after the marriage, asking me to arrange a house for him to stay in when he returned. The next day, George from Range Hills came to my room and kept a note because he could not meet me in person. The note said, "I needed money immediately to arrange a house for Sebastian." When pondering where to find the funds, I found a dependable source. I went and met Paulose. Paulose took the gold chain from around his baby's waist, came to Kirkee with me, pledged it, and gave me the amount.

I included what I had on hand and handed over the amount to George to arrange a house for Sebastian. Our cooperation was so profound in emergencies. Brother, what sacrifices did he make for me? It was not a one-way affair; it went back and forth; that was brotherhood. We were all one when the need arose.

The house was a two-room Siporex flat in Range Hills.

We were waiting on the railway platform. After the wedding, the couple arrived, the Brother and his wife. We welcomed the new Adam and Eve to the new paradise. To start a new journey here, you must end the long journey. Brother has gained more courage to face the challenges of life. An old picture came to my mind. On the college porch, he put his hand on my shoulder, looked into my wet eyes, and said in a sad voice -

"I'm scared, brother, to go down into the vast outside world."

It was the last day of college life, and we, classmates of three years, were getting separated. That was many years ago. After that, we were alone in our way of life in the broader world. He did not experience family life and its pleasures and challenges. "Ekakee na ramithe. (loneliness is not good)...". Brother has begun the journey of family life. Not knowing how to console one who was very close and three years later getting separated, I said while embracing Brother -

"We will meet sometime in some corner of the world, sure."

It is this blessing that has brought us here together so soon. How long we walked through the difficult paths, what were the difficulties - at last two of us could come together at this place, that's a matter of great happiness. Let us face this external world together. With all the courage and hope for a new way of life today, Brother, I am determined to do the same next year.

The train had reached the platform. They were coming down. Georgekutty, Chitta, and Paulose were there as we walked towards them. They were also at the station.

Brother walked over, hugged, and introduced his wife - "This is Tharamma."

"Happy to see you."

I did not forget Manichan looking for a suitable groom for this sister, talking to me, and the image of Brother came to my mind as soon as I heard it. So, what could I say except that it was a cause? Imagine that once we hoped, 'We would meet at one place, one day, we met. We determined once that 'each of us would have a relationship with a female partner, which also happened for us. That's what I said: we could face this world together.

"One is lonely; two is a company."

Everyone gathered at Range Hills and shared the snacks the brother had brought and the brother's mother had made at home. My Brother took me along as a trainee while buying the necessary materials at the market. I also went along with him to learn the trick of the trade.

Soon, without warning, Brother and Tharamma came to my room. Nice pair. How quickly and how well you have become one soul. You have begun to step into the realities of life. Paulose was saying the same thing. Sebastian has seen the beauty of Tharamma's mind. And Tharamma, that of Sebastian. Tharamma works in a government office and understands life outside her hometown. She has been a great support to Sebastian. Only one packet of biscuits was kept with me to give to those who arrived unexpectedly. They gladly accepted it. Then, Brother explained the details of their marriage. Only those friends who were so close and loving could say those words that consoled me again without forgetting -

"If your proposal had come a little earlier, it would have been Lillikutty sitting here instead of Tharamma."

"It makes no difference, Brother. Man proposes, and God disposes. Praise be to the God who brought you together. Be happy." How could I say that like a sermon, I wondered?

Challenges were met one by one. How long did we walk in search of kerosene? Sebastien was happy when he saw Thankachi, who took him home and gave him kerosene for his current need from somewhere!

Sebastian knew Thankachi well before Thankachi's wedding. Thankachi has overtaken these steps already.

When they face life's challenges one by one, the reaction of "It doesn't matter" and the cryptic comments that they made "to have a look and learn the tricks" have made my mind more mature.

We walked from the church to the Range Hills after the mass on a Sunday. Two couples - Paulose and his wife, Sebastian and his wife, and James - walked ahead of me. I was a little behind.

I felt a stray thought of loneliness as if I was all alone. I called James, who was walking ahead -

"James... can you stay put and walk with me?"

Everyone who went ahead turned back and looked at my solitude! It was a long laugh for minutes, then the satirical comments followed-

"It doesn't matter. Let it go for a few more months, and everything will be fine by then."

Everyone gathered at Sebastian's house.

I didn't tell anyone that it was my birthday. No one cared to know. I went to the office as usual after praying for those who gave me birth, those who loved me, and those who remembered me. I wished them well and thanked them.

Ammachi had written a letter remembering my birthday. I got the letter when I came back from the office. Ammachi remembers the day I was born on earth. The day I went from the womb's darkness to the world's light. "You gave me a lot of pain." Said Ammachi. "You are the reason......"

"You had seen the light after I had endured much pain..." Ammachi used to say it long ago, especially when my antics and behavior hurt Ammachi. Now that I have remembered all that, I can say how much I have matured. Mother, I sincerely desire to see you happy as long as I live.

When I saw the address outside the wrapped envelope, I realized Thambichan had sent the photo. Satyan from the mess brought it, smelled it, and knew what it contained. I opened the envelope.

"Good girls," Sathyan saw the group photo. "Marry someone like this, Saare."

"Like this? Like whom?"

"De, like this girl."

"Eda, You clever one, good choice."

Then, when I was alone, I was looking at that photo and saying hello to someone. She looked at me and laughed.

Brother came in the evening. I showed him the photo. There was no need to say who was who. He already knew Thambichan. After looking at it for a while, the brother said-

"Well, nice,"

Brother talked about the party he would host, outlined, and walked home to Siporex. With the night's cold breeze, I was thinking on the way back. I must rent a house, repay the loan, pay off the arrears, and lay the foundation for the house in the native. What are my preparations? What are my sources of income? Uncertainties linger on the agenda.

Brother held a post-wedding party. Everyone had come.

After going to the Institution of Engineers, James told me I had passed the Sec-A exam. "Number 9778 was there in the list published." It felt like a great relief.

George took me to Thankachi's house searching for baby food and returned disappointed. His brother-in-law, an IPS officer, was there at Thankachi's house. We talked about many things. I looked at James and closed my eyes as he told me about his relationship with Stephen.

"Rang Daloom?" (Let us spread the colours?) Laughingly, the neighbour - a Gujarati Marwari girl – shot a question. She was amazingly flirty and sensual. She had an appealing, flirty smile.

Yes, we had a chance to play Holi. Last year, Girijan, Kunjan, and Gopalakrishnan were there. We took hours to wash off all the paint and colour powder on my face, hands, and shirt. It consumed four buckets of water to wash and then rinse.

"Abhi nahi, ... bad me" (not now, enough later). I returned the smile. Sathyan and Girijan, without any particular interest, made flirty comments and laughed while waiting for the bucket to be filled with water.

I wrote a reply to Thambichan. "You know why I delayed sending my sister's photo. It is the same as what you know. I don't hesitate to point it out. Because of her attitude, no matter how good the plan was or who planned it, she did not want to get married so early in life. I also think that the attitude has relaxed over this period. I understand things are moving towards a more mature and relenting attitude now than in the beginning. Thambichan will understand that attitude very well since you had seen the same attitude from your sister Gracy last year. They have little understanding of what we do for their better life."

A lot of work can and should not be done alone. It is an excellent idea to outsource the job to someone who does not know how to do it, for example, a tailor or a technician. So, if everything is set aside for other experts, some may be more difficult or costly. So, I decided I needed to learn how to do it right. The motto came to mind.

"A stitch in time saves nine."

I realised that one of the side pockets of my pants had created a gap, allowing my hand to pass freely into one of the body's most sensitive parts. At an unforeseen time, such trespassing is not permissible! Free time should be used wisely.

I searched for a needle and thread to fix it. The pants were loosened and stretched, and the patient was laid on the bed as if on a stretcher.

It was not unheard of that it would be better to entrust this task to a (housewife- homemaker) stay-at-home spouse than to do it alone with a sharp needle (stay-at-home spouse (housewife). But it will have to wait, and allowing this encroachment until then would be dangerous.

I slowly began to sew with all my adventure, skill, and mental strength to face adversity. After about half an hour of careful hard work, I broke the thread, put the needle and thread down, and took a deep breath. Curious to know the outcome of the work, I stretched my pants again.

Damn! The pocket that was there has gone.

All I did was close the open door of the pocket, like a whole barbed wire, and sew it on! Not even a little finger can cross, let alone the complete palm.

The sewing was good, so I preferred keeping the closed pocket intact. There was no problem, but a handkerchief and two or three coins were lying in the bag. That's when I realized the stupidity. My anger and miserableness prompted me to break all the stitches I had done so far.

Is it possible to withdraw after losing? Isn't it a doable job? This is a challenge. Be satisfied and finish the sewing before anyone else comes into the room. At least one palm should be able to pass through; more than that, trespassing and intrusion should not be allowed.

As I repeated the sewing slowly, I inadvertently got two or three needle pricks onto the middle finger in my left hand. I still had no intention of quitting my job. The sewing continued and ended. I was delighted. An inadvertent sigh of relief has also come for the second time.

The only thing I saw, but did not appear reasonable, was that the thread was floating here and there, and there was an inch of missing stitch in one part. The back pocket button was also missing.

It derived no more enjoyment in pursuing the work. I got bored. I thought the rest of the work would be done later; that was enough. It was then that I saw as if, for a while, blood had spread on the middle finger of my left hand. There were blood stains on my hand.

I couldn't help but laugh at how much less trouble Uncle Podger went through trying to hang a picture on the wall. I finally decided not to keep a needle and thread for some time. Wouldn't I have started this adventure because of that? Isn't it arrogant to say you will never do a job like this again?

Once you know you can do the work, but not before that. It is better to give the job to those with relevant training. Try to learn from them instead of doing it yourself, and never pretend you know the work, even when alone! I learned that lesson. The only issue is that we learn after we face the consequences of failures.

Especially tasks requiring fine practical skills, such as sewing, can be performed smoothly and satisfactorily once a homemaker arrives. I could have told my mother if I had been younger and at home. But what do you do when you are away from home in these modern times? Go to the professionals.

Not only that, I would like to rewrite Sartre's words, "Man is alone abandoned on earth...". If alone, man is abandoned on earth. We cannot be a 'vagabond' forever.

No matter how sincerely the desire, the availability of resources is an insurmountable barrier that often stands in the way of great success. How many people can we see who have achieved great success among ordinary people?

Outstanding achievements and successes result from hard work and constant effort to set the path towards clear goals. That may not always be possible. So, in any case, always sincerely strive for small pleasures. And often, we receive success. Rather than an outstanding achievement, we desire many tiny pleasures.

Life at 155 JA Block, Kirkee

41. BEING LONELY IS NOT GOOD

On those days, including holidays, we used to have lunch at Sherin Lodge's mess, where we got boiled rice and fish curry. Babu and Ramachandran were good friends at the Sherin Lodge. After lunch, I came to Thankachi's house, and we could go to the church together to watch KCA's play in the evening. They, too, were coming for the play.

I had a knack for hurting those who loved me. Or why did I act with that silence, sad face, resentment, insensitivity, and anger? Acting, wasn't that the motivation of something? Why did I walk with a tired mind that is still restless today?

Ramachandran once told me- "I should prepare to write a book. It will be successful. In the mid-day sun, I felt solitude and freedom." When I returned from an early lunch, I felt I should visit Thankachi."

"No, he has gone looking for Thomas," - Lilykutty came to the door and said. That was Thankachi's wife. They both work at IAT.

While walking towards my room, there he was in front of me! "Where did you go? I was looking for you !" He expressed his disappointment. He took me to his house and mercilessly executed me with his uninterrupted but exciting discussions.

Played cards, smoked, and drank. I had two meals on the day, the second with Thankachi and his family. They were preparing for an evening to share their friendship.

"You don't have any other job; now where to go, sit here, while I am here, this is freedom. Thankachi's friend Sunny sang well. There were some dramatics during the song where everyone had fun. What fantastic roles each one plays.

Thankachan suddenly asked Sunny-

"Ngah, ngah... Is theren't an old song with these lyrics...? "Thaipuyakavadiyattam, Thangamailpiliyattam...

...... Abhirami, you will walk like that swan.. .. I wish to see your Aramam... I want to...to see ." (Sreekumaran Thambi, Jesudas)

"തൈപ്പൂയകാവടിയാട്ടം, തങ്കമയില്പ്പീലിയാട്ടം..

...... അന്നംപോല് നടന്നുപോകും അഭിരാമീ.. നിന്റെ ആരാമമൊന്നു കാണാന് മോഹമായി.. എനിക്കു മോഹമായി...." (Sreekumaran Thambi, Jesudas)

Then Thankachan asked in a spontaneous flirting smirk, "What is it, Sunny? I want to see it too; where is it?"

("അതെന്താണ്, സണ്ണി .. എനിക്കും കാണണം, ..അത് എവിടമാണെന്നു …"),

Lillykutty said from inside, "It's in the sky ... if you look up, you could see. Enough, man. You should be ashamed to call out whatever you feel... sorry!" (അത് ആകാശം ... മേലോട്ട് നോക്കിയാൽ കാണാം, മതി മനുഷ്യാ, കുറച്ചൊക്കെ നാണം വേണം, വായിൽ തോന്നുന്നതൊക്കെ വിളിച്ചു പറയാൻ... കഷ്ടം!"

Then, a few moments of complete silence. I do not think so. As if suddenly stepped on fire. He looked at the face that had entered the front living room and nodded. Lillykutty did not explain that it was a planted garden! That is the wife. A loving wife will not listen to anyone who mocks or views her husband as foolish. Husband: The wife is the one who must help and bring the guide to the right path when he slips away from the track.

Thankachi wisely told Sunny with a pale face, not making the scene worse.

"Sunny, isn't there a song that says a toy boat is tied up somewhere? I don't know the first line, but it's her favourite song. It's a song. Let her enjoy it, my wife. Let her enjoy it."

ഇളവന്നൂർ മഠത്തിലെ ഇണക്കുയിലേ, മാറിൽ മാറിൽ... ....വീശുവാൻ മേടക്കാറ്റിൻ വിശറിയുണ്ടോ,...

കളിവള്ളം കെട്ടിയിട്ടു പുഴക്കടവിൽ ഞാൻ, മലരണിവാകച്ചോട്ടിൽ മയങ്ങുമ്പോൾ

Where does the wind blow,

I tied the toy boat and went to the riverbank when I fell asleep on the riverbank. (G Devarajan, P Bhaskaran, KJ Yesudas)

Then, a few moments of complete silence prevailed. I thought I shouldn't have laughed. It was like suddenly stepping onto the fire. Looking at that face that entered the living room from behind, you will bow your head.

Lilykutty did not explain that it was a garden with watered plants and flowers! That is the wife. A loving wife cannot bear to hear her husband mocked or depicted as unwise. When the husband slips from the walking path, the wife is the one who has to take his hand and bring him to the right path. She does that.

Thankachi cleverly said to Sunny with a pale face to prevent the situation from worsening.

"Sunnicha,(Sunny more lovingly). Isn't there a song that says a toy boat is tied up somewhere? Even though I don't know the first line, it's her favourite song. Just sing that song… Let her be happy that is my wife; let her be happy."

"Ilavannoor maddathilE InakkuyilE, Maril...

...............veesuvaan medakkaattin visariyundO ....

kalivallam kettiyittu puzhakkadavil njaan, malaranni vaakachottil mayangumpol"

(I tied the toy boat in the river when I was sleeping under the flower decked vaka)

(G Devarajan, P Bhaskaran, KJ Yesudas)

Although that was what Thankachi meant, the style of his speech was wrapped in an unaffiliated and humorous laugh. The silence melted like the snow, and Thankachi displayed an innocent face, playing the role of a husband. Both are correct completely: non-violent, peaceful co-existence; that was their family life. That was what I understood then. Usually, changes would have happened later with time.

Then, in the evening, we went to see the play. How many dramas were seen within the play? What must have crossed Thankachi's mind when he saw a female 'tiger'? There was no fuss.

Chitta of the Range Hills put a number on it - "I saw it was keenly watching ."

So what?

Didn't the judge, who stood firmly for justice, get tired "in the wilderness of sand"?

So, that was a Sunday.

Some preparations were still pending. That's not right. No preparation was done.

"Are you coming? Or let me go. I have some work to do ..."

Just silence.

"Yeah. No time to attend the Lord's feast! I bought a pair of bullocks. I got married,...No time to waste; being busy, I am ...

"Mannankatta, I'm leaving ..."

Where do I stand, coming from the street? Am I the man standing before the master's entrance gate? And then the brother defeated me, saying...

"Didn't you read that someone was pushed out for not having a wedding dress?"

I rarely got Leelamma's letter from home. I was preparing for the exam. Malayalam class teacher asked her-

"Where are you coming from ?"

"My house is in ------"

"Oh, do you know one Leelamma who studied with me and coming from there?"

"Yes, I know". That would be my sister-in-law.

"That girl's wedding, someone working in Poona is the groom, I am told."

"Yes, the man who would marry her is my brother."

"Yah! " She opened her eyes wide.

Didn't you say anything more? What was that? Some more information was hidden in the corners of your eyes!

Radhamani teacher must have understood that smile. When she heard about her classmate's wedding, she might have heard about the one talking to her. It was good to say. The mind and the words rise according to the context. That's good.

Brother came to the room when I was lying down about writing letters. While walking around in the bazaar together, we also met Thankachi. He took me to the Chapel of St. Antony. I hadn't been there earlier. I went with Thankachi, sitting on his bicycle carrier. It's fun to listen to Thankachi's talk.

Talking to Thankachi today, I thought my previous judgments should be clarified. Otherwise, developing relations with Thankachi as a good friend will not be possible.

Thankachi said- "I always walked around with a Kolinos smile plastered on my face until a few days ago."

We arrived at the chapel.

Thankachi continued - "Anything can be asked for here. Lillykutty and I come here regularly. Saint Antony has some special powers.

We spent a few moments of prayer in the serene surroundings there. I prayed - to give peace to all, to bless all.

"If you take a flower from here and give it to my daughter, who is not feeling well, she will be cheerful, and her illness will be cured soon," Thangachi confessed his faith.

On the way back, Thankachi narrated how he got intimate with another girl before marriage and lost his peace of mind by getting involved in tangles and labyrinths. He had to quarrel with many relatives. He also indirectly referred to the evils that plague human relationships due to selfish desires. Today, Thankachi is very happy because he has escaped the tangles. Apart from that, by the grace of God, Thangachi got a good-natured girl as his life partner.

"Taking unnecessary responsibilities on one's shoulders and worrying about their fulfillment, life was somewhat wasted. I am trying to forget all that. Before marriage, love is a lustful feeling, my friend. A good love relationship is possible only after marriage."

Thankachi's interesting conversation was heard till half past nine in the night.

42. LIFE PROBLEMS

I heard the same complaint whenever I saw Ramachandran in the machine shop. “Severe fatigue. This time, with a cold, the cough does not go away. I took the medicine of the local doctor for more than a week, and it is not getting better. I want to meet Dr Pai at the appointed time for a consultation in the evening. Let me go and come back”.

The next day, when I went and met him seeking information, here is the reply that he gave me with a smile, even though he was seen as tired:-

"Sit down; I saw the doctor. Two or three tests were done. The results came soon. I was waiting outside, and he called me inside after a while. Very gently, with a caring and loving expression, he said,-

Chandran, There is a small hole in your heart. It might have been there from birth. Nothing to worry about. We will examine it further and then decide the course of action.”

Chandran was shocked and sweating as if he could see nothing unexpectedly.

When you can touch the trophy and suddenly see it crumble in front of you like the soil is washed away from under your feet, how do you react when success is within your grasp?

It is called a 'mitral valve lesion.'

A mitral valve lesion occurs when the mitral valve doesn’t work correctly, allowing blood to flow backward into the left atrium. As a result, the heart does not pump enough blood out of the left ventricular chamber to supply the body with oxygen-filled blood.

Left untreated, it can lead to serious, life-threatening complications such as heart failure or irregular heartbeats.

Open heart surgery will be required. Chandran became restless and showed concern or anxiety. Even if the operation was not done, you could live like this for some time. But if you are a little older, the chances of survival in operation would decrease. So, the question is whether to take a risk.

Where to do the operation should be decided after consulting the family. The mere knowledge of such a condition is more disturbing than the condition itself. It is a mental breakdown. If you take comfort in the fact that there are no symptoms now and do nothing, it will make life more dangerous and uncertain. Chandran does not like pity. I was searching for words to comfort him.

"Do not be afraid; everything will be fine and happen properly. Just give yourself courage."

KEM Hospital called him for more tests the following week. I promised to go with him to help and always be with him.

Thambichan wrote to me that he got a promotion. Chandran commented- "You, too, should get a promotion immediately. If not, …. Chandran stopped halfway and smiled!

"… Is it not a reciprocal arrangement? If the balance is tilted to one side...?

"In CME, we cannot expect a promotion. We have to look for better prospects elsewhere. It's very much within our reach if we have faith, belief in ourselves, and the will to go the extra mile to realise our dreams. Also, realise that you have the power to make a difference on the road to success. So, the means are as important as the end.

While manufacturing antibiotics at HAL, Pimpri George became closer to his trade union friends by imparting his learned philosophies. He was counted among the leaders.

While I explained the history of our wedding preparations to him, George wanted to see his future bhabhi again. I showed him.

Raju wrote that Ammini's husband, James, was going to Bombay through Poona. He asked me whether he could join him on the journey. "Can I come to Poona and spend a few days with Kochayan? Everyone here has agreed. Now Kochayan's reply is awaited..."

"Of course, come, my dear" - I wrote the reply.

My mother's letter was also included in Raju's letter. She was raising a cow that gave birth to a calf, holding its tail up and running, making everyone laugh.

"You and Jameskutty run and come here to drink milk."

Mother also wrote about Thambichan, and getting the promotion was why Thambichan wrote a letter to Leelamma.

Well, it is fine, and I am happy.

"Raju wrote - "When I was told to come to Poona, I rubbed my eyes and looked...made sure that it was not a dream."

I went to the railway station on the 14th, and it was a holiday on Good Friday. I thought Raju and James would arrive. But they did not come. The next day, I got Raju's letter stating they plan to leave on the 14th from Alleppey.

On the 15th, I received another letter from Achayan stating that Raju may leave on the 14th or the 15th!

Have you ever considered the trouble a text or message of that nature can cause?

"Wake up and be with me for an hour and pray ... Achayan ended his letter quoting from the passage of the Passover - "

And therefore, I became calm.

Went to the station on the 16th. Usually, the train takes 37 hours to reach Pune from Ernakulam. The train was not late. The train arrived on time. But none of the passengers I expected came out. I felt a bit disappointed, and I was angry with myself. There was no phone at home. I reached the office very late.

Went to the station on the 17th. It was expected that they would come. The train arrived on time, but I did not see any of them. A faint shadow of fear fell upon me. What to do? Let me send a telegram to Kunjommachayan in Kochi. When I wrote a telegram and went to the railway telegraph office, they said they would send it to Kochi after giving it to the city telegraph office from here tomorrow. It was all a mess. Why does a telegraph office work like this? I tore the paper on which the telegram was written, threw it away, and reached my office at 10:30. I telephoned James and told him to send a telegram from the GPO. On reaching the room in the evening, Valyachayan's letter said - his son-in-law and Raju were leaving on the 15th evening! The fifteenth?

Then they should have reached today. For ten minutes, I looked outside fearfully and wondered what was happening. The telegram should come, the letter or message should come, or they both would be searching for the location of my address. In half-sleep, I heard the sound of someone talking near the window. I stood up and walked towards it and found none. I did not sleep further at night. There was no information till 7 o'clock in the morning, and no one came.

I got up early on the 18th. I must go to the station. A class was planned for the degree course from 7:30. Which is important? Both cannot be done at the same time. What is important? What is the priority? After requesting James to go to the station, I ran to the bus stop.

At 9:30, James' phone call came. What a relief they have arrived! – Kochuparambil James and Raju. After James gave the phone to Raju, I was speechless. "Raju, Raju," I called out loud, but no sound came out!

When I returned to the room from the office, I welcomed both of them with open arms and a hug. Raju was excited and thrilled. There were moments of great joy, and then there were sweets sent by my mother from home. Raju said-

"Achayan and Ammachi have already foreseen that it would be like this. .... Then, these delicacies were made together with Chechi."

It was all done well.

Kochuparambil James insisted on meeting Ammini on that day. We went to the Shirin Lodge and had lunch. We took James to the station and saw him off the train to Bombay.

I sent Joy the money I had agreed to pay through James Kochuparambil.

Raju described the situation at home. After Kunjunju's marriage in Kainakari, the siblings had regrettable minor issues. Never before had such echoes of disunity been heard from there.

When you see panic and anxiety on your friend's face, you should think that he might be thinking of something meaningful in his life.

"What's up, bro."

"The Missus is not in a good mood."

"What, happy sickness?"

"Yeah"

"Congratulations, brother; you have it! good."

Brother was happy. He knew that preparing to be a dad could mean planning how to manage his work-life balance and making positive lifestyle choices and changes.

The summer rains added warmth to nature and fragrance to the air.

In the evening, Raju and I walked to the bank of the river Mula in Khadgi. Raju's curiosity was growing, and he was inquisitive. That was what I understood with every question he asked. Rows of shrubs, flowers, and cement benches in the park were rare. We walked to St Anthony's Chapel and then to the War Cemetery. It was the burial ground of the soldiers who died in the First and Second World Wars. There was a beautiful lawn that maintained the serenity of the burial ground.

He returned to the War Cemetery with James of Kochuparambil after a month. Where else can you find such a serene, blissful, lonely, evocative, and historical atmosphere? Where else is this heart-touching delight that creates soft movements in the strings of the human mind?

I took Raju to CME one day. I showed him various engineering workshops and machinery. Raju did not show much interest in the engineering equipment.

Talking to James on the phone gave him a big motivation and enthusiasm. One day, James showed Raju the entire observatory and its functioning.

I did not know how to ride a bicycle because of the environment I lived in till then.

I even went to college in a small canoe. However, when James and Raju were with me, I saw it as a golden opportunity to rent a bicycle and learn to ride. In a deserted field, not a single vehicle was running; not even another bike was approaching. James and Raju helped; sometimes, Brother also came forward to help.

Some people who are willing to catch the fallen used to come outside their houses and watch. Some stood there and laughed. I also laughed and got up quickly. Although I fell several times, I learned and became good at cycling with some practice. I cycled to Neto's uncle's house, went to George's house, and cycled with Sebastian and James to Vijayappan's residence on Pashan Road, beyond Chaturshringi Temple. Sometimes, I went to church by cycling.

One evening, I rode a bicycle from Khadgi Bazar to Range Hills. It was dusk hours, and I do not remember there was no street light on. I cycled fast. Later, I realized I could even ride the bicycle in the air for a few seconds. I had fallen! I did not lose consciousness and did not hit my head anywhere. Before straightening the bike, I inspected the area thoroughly. I ensured my hands and feet were safe and moving without pain. When I took the bicycle and reached the road, I realized I was getting out of a big ditch on the side of the road!

When I took the currency notes from my pocket and put them in my purse, Raju asked-

"Did you get paid today, Kochaya ..?"

"Yes, I got it."

"Give it to me. Let me see how is this salary, Kochaya?"

"It looks as rupee notes."

"No, I wish to feel it."

"Here it is."

"May I count it once?"

"Okay"

" This has to be distributed to everyone. Shouldn't ?"

"That's right."

I then wrote a note to whom it should be distributed.

43. CHANDRAN

Raju and I read Achayan's letter together.

"It is good to learn that Raju has reached Poona. Until then, it was like a flame that rose from the bottom of my umbilical cord and exploded at the top, and a hot liquid dripped down through the eyes, flowed down to the cheeks, and finally joined where it should have, by the earth's gravitational attraction. When I got your letter, a physical process occurred, like ice falling onto the burning coal. Everything became normal in about ten minutes. I wonder why you did not send me a telegram!"

Raju should be sent to reach here safely without any damage like a parcel item."

"Leelamma continues to read books and sleeps without much fanfare. Ammachi has her cow, house, kitchen, and household chores throughout the day, such as mend tonic, pills, laundry, etc."

"I am like a wanderer moving aimlessly but chasing a green light in the distance, involved in many things. Though I am not getting much benefit from anything, I do. Still, I am not unhappy, pulling on in anticipation and with the support of hope."

Achayan has written a lot to think seriously. Achayan wrote the philosophy of life with its myriad vagaries.

Ammachi's thoughts were all about Raju. We read the letters for a long time.

I went to Bombay with Raju. We met the recently married couple James and Ammini at Anthonichan's flat in Ghatkopar. In the evening, we walked around Malabar Hill and Chaupathi.

A native friend was waiting for us in the middle of the overbridge in Ghatkopar. He came to know that we had gone on a tour to Bombay. He was determined to see us in Bombay and was expecting us to pass through that way. All the tiredness of walking around all day disappeared when I saw my friend on the way. And then there were the usual complaints about delays in answering letters. All the inaccuracies could be forgiven when I found his health and physical shape apart from the pathetic look. He appeared very tired and sick. He said his fatigue would disappear soon, but he did not elaborate.

The couple was waiting without eating dinner for us to return.

The journey on the local train would never be forgotten. Before the railway strike was declared, only a handful of train services were available. Everyone was in a hurry to get home as soon as possible. And yet we went to see Flora Fountain, Picasso's oil paintings in the art gallery, the Gateway of India, and the Taj Hotel. Raju's favourite and most sought-after objects were seen in the museum, where he has spent most of his time.

Sebastian and his mother came to my room in Kirkee. Sebastian (Brother) told us the news of a tragedy that was a shock.

The tragedy came at an unexpected time. Thankachi and his wife were on their way home with their baby on a special holiday train. On the way to Salem, the baby developed a fever, and a doctor was called in for treatment. By the time they reached Coimbatore, the baby was dead.

It is impossible to recollect how Thankachi and Lillikutty faced this distressing incident. When I heard about it, my eyes were filled with sadness. Geetamol was such a cute baby; that baby was a big attraction in Thankachi's house.

I was covering my face and crying when Raju came and called me. While leaving for the railway station, Lillikutty took the baby from Raju's hands and left. It was a trip to take the first child home and show it to Thankachi's parents. God could have allowed the baby to live for four more hours so that her grandparents would have been delighted to see them! But it did not happen. What comforting words could I say to him when Thankachi returned? When we went to Sherin Lodge for lunch, we read Thankachi's letter to Babu. On our way back, we looked at Thankachi's residence, which appeared like a haunted house. Different thoughts were flashing on my mind's screen! "Gitamol, who laughed and played in my hands - Geetapakshi, did your Srivallabhan come so quickly?". Raju lamented while he was crying. Although he could only give her two days of affection and caress, the news of this tragedy hurt him deeply.

Raju's visit to the antibiotics factory with George taught him a lot.

We walked along the sidewalks of Peshwa Park in Poona. We saw birds and some animals. We climbed to the top of the hill where Parvati's temple is located and had an aerial view of Poona. After seeing the natural beauties, I felt that the memory of this journey should be kept as books as usual, and I bought books by two Russian authors and the Wren & Martin English grammar book for Raju.

Raju wanted to meet George again by going to Pimpri. Suddenly, I got angry for some reason. Raju's face withered, so we waited for the transport bus later. The bus did not come even after standing there for a long time. Then, we had to change the plan. We decided to go to Paulose's new residence. He had started living in a new residence at Sanghvi with his family after moving from Appukuttan Nair's house in Range Hills. Paulose was pleased when we got there. Raju played chess with Paulose. When we were about to return, Shanthamma offered us dinner before going. Once again, Raju was delighted to have the homely preparations of food. Raju ate chapati, the North Indian bread, with enthusiasm for the first time.

We returned and went to bed late but got up early the next day to go and meet George at Pimpri.

We met George because he promised to buy Raju a new watch.

There was a big gust of wind and a tornado when we arrived. There was no sign of declining rainfall until late at night. George gave us an umbrella. We came under one umbrella to the bus stop and from the bus stop to the room. Raju recited a short poem I wrote about the rain, which I had forgotten. Raju could memorize the children's poetry and write short stories.

We were of one mind and one soul under one umbrella in the wind and rain. Raju could speak honestly, a great advantage of being a student.

Raju had an intense stomach ache when he woke up early the next day. It must have started at night. We went and met a doctor. Medications and some tablets were taken only once before I went to the office the following day.

When I returned from the office, I saw Raju's swollen face and black eyelids. Added to that, he had heaviness in the head and drowsiness. We met the doctor again. He said it was due to the allergy caused by the concoction of the mixture taken in the morning, and he advised me to stop the mixture and take another medicine. The doctor assured me the anxiety was misplaced, like seeing the doctor often. The doctor assured me that the anxiety that forces us to see the doctor frequently was misplaced, and everything would be all right the following night. The assurance was found correct, and Raju became normal.

In the evening, George brought us anti-amoebic pills for Raju to use. However, he did not consume it. He took it home to give to Ammachi's cow.

Raju was taken to see CME again, as he had requested. He liked the Central Library. While spending time there, heavy rain came in the middle of the day. When the rain cleared, the CME's clock tower building and the surroundings were well-lit. They appeared beautiful, with uniformly trimmed plants, trees, and walkways. Also, at the main entrance steps, an entrance reserved only for VVIPs, I had never entered even once in seven years. With Raju's courage and honour, we became VVIPs. The entrance gate and its surroundings were very majestic and clean. When he went out and returned, I looked back there several times and preserved that image in my mind.

Sebastian and his mother came to my room again in Kirkee. The Railway strike became a hot topic for our discussion due to the uncertainty it created for travel to natives. Raju read his short travelogue to Sebastian's mother, briefly explaining his travel and holidays away from home. I could only serve them tea brought from the Irani Hotel and played a ploy to cover the embarrassment. That's when Ammachi made an assessment -

"Next time I come, you should be able to serve homemade tea and snacks. Will you?"

"Sure, Mom."

As they walked down the steps, I saw great expectations in their coming here, that I could spend some time with them, and that they would return to my house at a better time. When they came here last time, I couldn't say anything because of the grief caused by Geethamol's demise.

" It completed forty days today."

"How do you know that?"

"I counted."

"Wrong, it's only four days."

Nghum, I looked into his teary eyes. Later, I realized that he was thinking of poetry.

"Forty petals have fallen off the fragrant flower. There is only one or two more."

May the ever-scented 'White Ginger Lily flowers (Hedychium coronarium) (കല്യാണസൗഗന്ധികം) bloom for you, my dear, forever!

"Jesus was tempted forty days and forty nights (Matthew 4:2). There were 40 days between Jesus' resurrection and ascension (Acts 1:3). Which one would you prefer to compare with your vacation? City life is always tough, trying, and demanding."

Raju knows that this cannot be compared to anything like that. That was why he didn't answer me and sat down as if he didn't hear the question.

Achayan had suggested sending Raju back safely. James was returning from Bombay, and Sebastian's mother was returning to her native, Muttar. I was not sure of either. I only thought I would see Raju with someone. He travelled and came with James of Kochuparambil. Raju was not all that interested in going back with his company. There has been some indistinct apathy on James' part.

Joy came in the evening with James on his way back from Bombay. He came since I wanted him to take Raju to the native.

Sitting on the terrace of the Iranian hotel, James and Raju saw a Hindi film shown under the banyan tree. Raju was experiencing his first Hindi film. Whether he liked it or not, I called him back halfway through. Because he was lying next to me the previous night, sighing and crying and occasionally looking at me. When hugged and asked why he was crying, he said,

"Not because of the difficulty of going home, but because I remember the days I spent here."

`Only Appachi did that when he got a job and left. We were all highly emotional beings. Our warm tears fell on the pillow, and it became wet.

We slept in that warmth and woke up in the morning.

Joy slept with James, and James Kochuparambil slept alone.

We made coffee, and Joy came in time to drink it. I had made a cup more, considering that Sebastian had promised to come and tell us about his mother leaving for native. Brother came as expected, and he was cheerful. After drinking coffee, he said his mother, Raju, and James would go together by train on the following day.

Joy returned to Bombay. Paulose had offered to show us around the Observatory's laboratories since the train was in the evening. I also went to the Observatory, thinking I could use my time. We roamed in Sambhaji Park, Cave Temple, and IE (I). The journey and the sights were enlightening and pleasing to the mind, except for James's not-so-cordial indifference. When Raju finishes his inter-state journey, people are at home to ask what he has brought and check the suitcase or bag after the tour. So, I bought and packed some retail items for Raju to carry home. It included a saree for Leelamma, a shoe for Bavichan, a few steel utensils for Ammachi, my watch for Babu, and a small amount for Achayan. Undoubtedly, it was inadequate, but that's all a limited monthly salary earner could do.

Sebastian and his mother were told to get straight to the railway station. When it was time to go to the railway station, Ramachandran came to say bye to Raju.

After praying fervently before the Sacred Heart, Raju boarded the train. It was believed that Raju enjoyed the journey to Poona and stayed there for a few days. Sebastian's mother took Raju to her home in Muttar. Thomaskutty, Sebastian's younger brother, took Raju home the next day and handed him over to Achayan. I got a telegram from Achayan six days later, informing me that Raju had reached home safely.

After seeing them off at the railway station, I remembered another train journey with Raju in Bombay while I was returning. He had written about the local train travel in his travelogue: "The electric trains were running very fast, and the people were flowing, like the tropical water hyacinths." Water hyacinths have become a severe weed menace in the inland waterways in our region, polluting water bodies and preventing water transport.

"Raju, be safe and be confined here," I said, seeing the crowd's movement in the speeding local. I desired that he would always be safe in my arms as long as there would be enough strength. He must have understood what I meant! Or why did he look into my eyes and smile?

And then, when you grow up and become stronger, you should hold me in your hands. So that no one else can break it. Listen, not only me, Achayan, Ammachi, and everyone else. Despite that rush, I looked at the fan's leaves above so that no one could see the wetness in my eyes. Still, a drop fell from the cloud onto the forearm shaft of my hand. I could not even raise it. Joy and James were not even visible in the heavy rush.

Raju wrote that the trip back home was good, except for KJ James's idiosyncrasies and sloppy nature. He didn't even bother sharing some rice with Raju while eating! There was anger and resentment. I never knew these peculiarities before. But now, what to do? I am relieved to believe that such things happen only once. But the wedding was over and done much earlier!

44. TOUR WITH RAJU

If anyone felt that Achayan and I did not show enough prudence - discrimination - while proposing Kochuparambil James as a husband to Ammini, that was not to be questioned. That was not to say that the questioning was wrong. Was it enough to admit that the concerned people did not give the necessary attention? A local acquaintance was suggested with no selfish gains and no misguided motives. But what is the point in accusing someone after the leading lady has consulted her parents and submitted in the church that she accepted someone of her own free will? Can the blame be justified after the expression of willingness? I am not blaming anyone; I am asking myself, do I deserve such a cruel trial, Joy?

Kochupappan had written explaining why Mammachan was late joining the Poona seminary. It was also written that Leelamma, Ammachi, and Bavichan went to Alappuzha via Punnapra to buy Ammachi spectacles. For the journey, Leelamma was wearing Chittamma's sari to please me. It was difficult to contain my emotions after reading Kochuppappan's signature line, "Your ever-loving uncle."

I got a letter from each of Achayan and Raju. Leelamma has passed her SSLC. Babu has not been able to do that yet. A big question remained: how would Babu find a way of life?

I wrote to Thambichan about Leelamma passing her examination. I also sought Thambichan's opinion about sending her to college for five or six months instead of idling her time at home. She had nothing to lose but to gain more knowledge and experience of the world around her.

Raju's writing was very emotional. He mentioned getting his grandfather's blessing before he joined the SSLC class for the first time. After listening to the writings, he could feel the intensity of Grandma's love and affection. He said the word intensity was not enough to reflect Grandma's love. He could realise the significant responsibilities as he entered an essential stage of his life and his desire to follow me, helping me to bear and share the burden of the cross and the prayers -

'Education is not the criterion of ability, brother, but tolerance and love are much more important than that - you know that too.'

I read in my diary that letter I had written down to read when I grew older.

These are the legacies of my youth.

Thambichan's opinion came in a letter, and I was sad when I read it. I would have been happy if he had just written that Leelamma need not be sent to college.

I had determined that without Thambichan's favourable opinion, I would never have decided anything about Leelamma in this life. Then Thambichan wrote -

"Have you any intention of reconsidering the marriage proposals decided by our family?"

No intention at all. What do I gain by keeping you in a predicament? We have studied a poem that says, "If you need my head for your salvation ...." Would you get salvation of that nature?

Another question suddenly came to my mind,

"Brother, what was that you question my sincerity and righteousness? Let me think that, Thambicha, you did not mean it like that and did not think to hurt my pride with such a childish question."

I continued to read.

"If you stick to the idea, there is no need to send Leelamma to college."

I am happy. But now, at least this—I have no fickle mind, then and now. I would try to be like that even tomorrow.

After reading it, I wrote the following poem in my diary because I liked it. I reread it.

"The hurricane swept by, and few of us survived. And many failed to answer friendship's roll call,

Whom shall I call on? Who will share with me the wretched happiness of staying alive? "

(Poet Sergei Yesenin quoted in Cancer Ward, a novel by Solzhenitsyn)

"Farewell, my good friend, farewell. In my heart, forever, you'll stay.

May the fated parting foretell That again, we'll meet up someday.

Let no words; no handshakes ensue, No saddened brows in remorse

To die in this life is not new, And living's no newer, of course."

Ramachandran and his cousin Gopi, who came from Palakkad, slept the entire time India played the fourth innings without listening to the cricket commentary.

When they woke up, India had played for 70 minutes and scored 42 runs. Chandran's cousin arrived to attend the next day at Jahangir Hospital, where tests were being done to pinpoint the damaged part of Chandran's heart. Chandran's cousin reached the hospital the next day. Chandran was given medicine, and his body was sedated. After passing the catheter through the arm veins and checking the valve, getting up for the next eight hours was almost impossible. Chandran slept until 9 a.m. the following day. He woke up just once during the night to go to the bathroom. I had to work hard to support his body weight for some time and distance without falling. I went to the office with the satisfaction of being able to do that for a good friend.

In the college, it was decided to organise an all-India seminar on Refrigeration & Air Conditioning. I had to take responsibility for a large share of its back-end work. I also attempted to present a technical paper during the seminar.

John celebrated the birth of a girl child in his family.

I planned to pay off all the retail debts and pool the maximum resources Achayan wanted me to save for our big event.

In the meantime, Joy came from Bombay with one of his friends.

How quickly did differences and objections appear between us, who were very close in love? He did not even mention a word of thanks nor say a single word of explanation; he took some money from his pocket, handed it over to me, and said -

"Repaying the debt from brother." I did not understand anything for a while. If Brother has given you a loan, you have to pay it back to him. He should have told me if it was to be paid through me.

I did ask him how much this was. This amount appeared to be a bit too much!

Joy explained that half of the amount was to be given to Brother. I further enquired -"What about the other half."

He was silent.

I was sure he was returning the gift I gave Ammini, but he refused to accept the gift. I never wanted it back. I never asked for it.

I knew what I had given was inadequate, and I was unsatisfied. But why didn't you understand that the time was like that?

Is it not denying what was given? In a fit of sudden anger, I said something painfully and threw the money into his face.

He went away. I presumed that this was only a reflection of the attitude his father showed to my father. Why blame the uncles? Why did you not understand the truth of matters, though you maintained a close relationship with me? It would help if you asked me the reasons directly about it. Was it not because I had a shortage that I borrowed money from Brother, who was nobody, and gave it to you? Then, if money were inadequate, love would fall short, there would be no misunderstandings, and if you were given more than necessary whenever you asked, you would be happy. Who feels for our troubles?

James listened patiently. Seeing all this, he was sitting as if he had nothing to do with it. I did not blame him. He was trying to take everyone together with brotherly love! He also knew the inflow and outflow of money.

It must have been the older man's desire to get enough dowry from the girl requesting a visa to the United States of America. Weren't you the one talking about it as a barter deal and dowry?

Let us look at the dowry, often in the Malayalees' thoughts, conversations, and news, and the oppression of women who go with or without it. Doesn't the information and discussions about dowry harassment that come to light occasionally from many parts of the country raise concerns among girls? How often do parents with daughters suffer from depression? How much suffering and mental stress does the girl's family endure when they cannot pay the amount of money and property they agreed to on time? What kind of conflict does a girl face with words and vile, inhuman acts from the house she goes to after marriage? How long will the girls endure the evil-minded criminals who see marriage only as a ploy to seize money, property, and comforts by seeing the girl only as a commodity? How many young women end their lives after giving up everything, raising them, educating them, finding a life partner, and giving it to their parents become an everlasting pain? Isn't asking and giving as much as possible an act that does not respect the rules and humanity? Isn't dowry a robbery or bargaining often done out of ignorance and sometimes out of exploiting helplessness? What guarantee is there that relatives who value the love of young twins who start life by getting married will still love them?

Isn't a daughter who stays home divorced better than a daughter who dies of heartache and body aches in her husband's house after marriage? Dowry givers and buyers do not understand this. Why do parents underestimate the dangers of marriage? Can't you find other ways to reduce the risk? We must discover why the human conscience is so degraded and find peaceful solutions that provide spiritual strength. There is no other way to attain the lasting peace necessary for achieving the desirable life goal of the majority.

All my relatives agreed, or I could not see in their words or deeds that getting or giving dowry was an issue for my parents. However, small gifts have been taken or provided as per the traditional practices, which may marginally infringe against the existing legal provisions. No one discusses it and ties it up as a controversial issue or even as a sound that disturbs the mind most slightly. That was the way it was. Achayan conducted five or more marriages leading from the front during his lifetime. It is also revered in the family as Achayan's legacy. No one has had marital deficiencies or related financial problems to my knowledge till the time I keyed in these memoirs.

Thambichan's letter came, and he regretted questioning my sincerity and hurting my pride. Enough. I passed a small test of human relationships. I opened the diary, took a picture of a girl in it, and she looked at me and smiled. Perhaps she moderated it, saying it was a silly matter that did not deserve so much pondering. I, too, smiled back.

A long letter arrived from Joy in Bombay. I was shocked when I opened it and started reading it. I never expected this much. What he was trying to write in four and five pages are baseless allegations. And some hurtful words and unabated verbal bashing.

It is meaningless; He just wanted to detach me deliberately. It was a slap on my cheeks, both left and right. He trampled me under his feet. Some words and phrases hurt a lot. I am a cheater, and for him, I was already dead. Such a brother is not alive. My father was the main enemy of his family!

The numbness was slowly crawling into my head. I was gnashing my teeth with anger. Then I became sad. I bit down on my sadness and concluded that such thoughts and words deserve no reply. I cried a lot for Joy. But one day, Joy, you'll understand. I know you will come back. I will wait until then.

I showed the letter to James with trembling and teary eyes. James read it with a blank face and did not respond to anything. I did not expect any response from him.

I wrote a long letter to Achayan dealing with all the current issues.

I must tell someone about the conflicts in my mind. That was my thought. I was sure that I would get relief from that. "Don't tell me if it's so annoying," usually, that would be Achayan's reaction.

I desired to write about Joy's allegations. Feeling I had 'run out of gas' emotionally, I hesitated. If no one knew about these allegations, someday, someone would say later that there was no answer from us or that nothing could be answered about the allegations. What if someone who knows us gives credit for this relative's indecent acts? What if someone provides honour to dishonourable actions?

Therefore, to defend myself, I had only mentioned a gist of the allegations that Joy mentioned in his letter.

Achayan's reply was very comforting. He desired to read Joy's letter in its entirety. I had cautioned him not to get disturbed as I believed that time would reveal our good intentions to all concerned.

Wedding matters - Achayan would discuss the weddings in our family with Thomachi and decide on further actions. The date might be sometime in January. That would give us a little more time for resource mobilization. It was determined that Leelamma should not be sent for any higher studies. Achayan hoped that the optimism would be fulfilled with the backing of positive efforts.

45. SEPARATION AND COMPASSION

In Poona, James kept his distance from me for some time. I learned he fought with Menon in the room for some reason. He called his friends and threw a party after getting his promotion. I knew all this but did not ask or comment on anything.

Once, when I came out of the church on a Sunday, Muttar George's sister, 'Lucy,' who stayed with him in Range Hills, came to me and said - "I will get a job in Bombay, and I am leaving tomorrow."

Sebastian (Brother) lived with George in the same quarters before his marriage. When I went there to meet Sebastian, I met Lucy and talked to her every time. She had a small job in a private company nearby and was trying to find a better job in Pune. She had a friendship with me because of our long acquaintance and my being Sebastian's classmate. I thought that was the reason for telling me about the lifestyle change. I could smell something fishy, knowing she had hidden some truth.

I asked - "Aren't George and his wife Chitta going with you? Where will you stay in Bombay?" and so on. She ran away without giving a convincing reply.

In the evening, when they came to Bazzar, Lucy knocked on the door of my room with her friend. I was alone in the room. When I opened the door, I saw the two girls entering my room, and it was a shock and surprise for me. They only wanted to see the photo of the girl I would marry in December. I took out the photo and showed it to them. The girls were happy, and they returned.

I learned Brother's wallet and pass had been lost through pickpocketing at Yerwada. When I went to inquire about it, Brother had not returned. George and Chitta kept quiet about Lucy's trip to

Bombay. They were not interested in talking about it or happy about her leaving. George only said that she was going by the morning train. I did not get a chance to share my doubts with my brother. Like me, she had brotherly love and respect for Brother rather than being neighbours in their native village. There were no unnecessary or illegitimate thoughts or inclinations in our acquaintance either. At least Brother will know why George and Chitta were not interested. They were not happy anyway.

The next day, she left for Bombay alone. Brother, James, and I went to the Kirkee railway station to see her off. She was determined and pretended to be happy while receiving the best wishes from all of us. However, her facial expressions reflected her apprehension of being disobedient to the good counsel of elders and deciding to do something out of her own will and pleasure.

Ramachandran was preparing to undergo surgery at the Railway Hospital in Madras after visiting his native place with his friend Venu from Bombay. Venu also had some heart ailments. Together, we had breakfast and wished them all the best for the travel and the success of the impending surgery.

It was after a week. Brother came to talk, but he was agitated. Maybe there were other friends in the room. Before leaving, Brother said he had something to say to me.

"There was a letter from Lucy, and there was nothing to be happy about."

I also walked down with Brother.

"She lives with one Vasudevan, and they are in a living-in relationship. She never mentioned it to anyone here!"

"Who is Vasudevan? And can I see that letter?"

"I have torn off the writing. I had been angry and sad together."

A slight drizzle came down.

"Here the rain comes. Get back to your room. After all, why should we worry and get frustrated?"

I stood there. This was a shock that I had never anticipated. How many people has she made into a quandary - George, Chitta, and we all? How do her parents endure this? Isn't an injury of their pride? How can they look at someone's face? It has also brought us immense shame. We were friends, and walking together, we did not realize her wrong steps!

When I returned to my room and thought about it, I wanted to shout and say - "Hi, Lucy, life is not about running behind the moving shadows!"

On the first day of July, I lost a brother and a sister on the thirty-first of the same month. I didn't do anything to lose both of them. They went away on their own. When I knew of their parting, I just remembered them in pain.

What can you do? Nothing? What if your sister makes a blunder like this?

If we are sincere and genuine friends and join together, we could do something to help the family in distress. That was my thought, and I wanted to discuss it with George and Sebastian, thinking I could help them to do something.

The ultimate objective and route we reached there needed to be clear and pristine. That was the plan when deciding to go to Bombay. It has to be such a mission undertaken truthfully and without any wrong intentions. In addition to the minor inconveniences of others, I had two well-defined goals while deciding to go myself: to know and analyze the situation. That's it. I conscientiously felt that it was my moral duty to do so.

I was determined not to scrutinize their actions as right or wrong. I wanted to see whether they continued to be happy after their crucial decisions in life, About Ammini's life after marriage and Lucy's inappropriate life. The journey was essential for me to achieve both goals. It was not to hurt or report to anyone specifically but to derive satisfaction with self-control and purity of purpose.

I went to Anthonichan's house in Ghatkopar, where Ammini was staying. Ammini's friends Annie and Susie were waiting for a flight to the USA. I was getting to understand related matters about everybody.

After talking for a while, I kept looking into Ammini's eyes as if seeing them for the first time. The salt-water fountain that was easily generated from the depth of the mind in joy and sorrow obscured my view. Ammini asked,

"Why are you sad?"

"Yeah, with the joy of seeing you," I said silently after remembering Joy's letter. I understood a lot. That mystery alone was not understood. Why accuse me of so many criminal allegations? 'You could have taken a cubit of rope and given it to her; that was better!' he had written to me.

I spoke amicably with Anthonichan, Ammini's maternal uncle. I was told at least four or five times that he had given a thousand bucks for the wedding! Before I reached there, I thought I should leave immediately without drinking the water they offered. But after I reached there, I sat there for a long time, drank coffee, and had lunch with them. Ammini's travel news was heartening. At Kochuparambil, James was planning to return to Bombay on the 17th to take her home. They got visas to go to the USA. When James came, and if she didn't go home with him, he said that he would see her later in New York!

Ammini was practicing freelance. She was getting fifty rupees per day. While waiting for the visa interview, she did not go home with James earlier. To pay the dowry agreed by the parents, the nurse earned income by doing extra work.

Could money buy a never to separate love? After agreeing to pay the requested money, he found it challenging to find enough money to pay. How could he blame the alliance after the crucial event? And after that, how could he call his sister's husband by some new name?

"Crazy, thorny, worthless,"

The correct language is the unique 'dialogue' of some people in Kainakari that Kunjommachayaan used to reiterate - "Does that wretched ('naRhi') know what love is?"

"What did you ask me? - Why didn't I go to Joy?"

"Look here, read this."

When you read it, I could see the reaction on your face.

"This was the reason why I asked you the questions."

"Did you ever think after your marriage that it was a failure? Did you ever feel that he had any physical disability? Did you feel his peculiar habits, features, and eyes lacked something? Did you ever regret that this could have been avoided?"

"No, no, no."

Your brother even asked about the behaviour in your bedroom. Just for the satisfaction of my conscience.

You will lack nothing. You shall have nothing less in life.

My liver pounded, and I held my breath. My Throat got choked. I completed my first mission successfully. On the way back, I called out to outer space -

"I have forgiven you, Joy."

I refuse to carry forward the pain I had

After saying goodbye to her patient, the nurse came with me for the next task I planned. It was an evening walk. It has rained a little. On an ordinary day, in the city where the smoke and dust billows fly, the thin crimson rays of the evening sun penetrated.

There was some anxiety in my mind. The fact that Ammini was with me was a source of strength. The whole thought was to take Lucy strategically with us while looking for the MES quarters and even while walking and getting wet on the muddy and marshy road. Ammini had agreed to accommodate her tonight after taking her along. We could locate the house and carefully observed the surroundings as if we knew nothing. I told Lucy why I had come here with Ammini, my cousin.

"Congratulations, Lucy, on your new job in Pune." It was the bait thrown to attract her attention. I did give short explanations, too.

"You have to join in two days. The letter is in the hands of Brother (Thankachan)."

I thought she fell for the bait.

Vasudevan came in with a bag in his right hand, carrying household essentials and bread wrapped in his left hand.

"Glad to meet you, Vasudevan. We have met in Poona." He, too, agreed by shaking his head.

He said he had some work to do and left without further discussion.

I could see a cash bill for a pair of earrings bought from a nearby jewellery shop, which was found thrown carelessly in the room, two bottles, and some scraps of paper.

So much freedom for a young woman and a young man? I did not deliberate on it as it was not the right time or occasion.

I said - "Come with me to Poona if you are interested. Ammini, my cousin, will ensure your safety."

She came with Ammini. She slept with Ammini at Anthonichan's house in Ghatkopar. We took the train to Poona in the morning and left Lucy at Brother's house in the afternoon. Then, everything in the ploy was revealed. There was no work. Having thrown everyone into a dilemma, hurt their pride, and made their parents and siblings sad, it was not fair for her to run away as such. I came out to help them. We did not have enough strength to see you coming back here crying with some obligations after a year or two. My mission was over. Now, you should make any decision only with their knowledge.

She held my brother's and my hand, cried, and apologized for the wrong done. We dropped her off at George's house and headed back. Our duty was done. We could convey many things and were sure she understood them well. "I have acted according to the call of my conscience. I am happy, brother." I told him.

"Brother, do you know? When we came on the train, she looked out from the Harris Bridge across the Mula-Mutha River, and I thought she would jump out. She didn't. Do you know why? She never deviated from the right path, so she didn't jump out."

The joke made everyone laugh, and the atmosphere calmed down and relaxed.

I asked myself whether I was right to do this before and after taking on the mission. Will anyone agree that the characters in this are such close relatives to risk the mission? People who do not usually know things in detail might conclude that it was unnecessary for me and may be construed as interfering with others' problems. Don't they say that it was unbecoming of me? Anyway, I was not worried about what anyone else would say. Because I believed in myself, I knew well that what I did was out of sincerity and purity of heart.

Even if no one realizes it, behind this adventure, I see some lessons learned on personal characteristics and potential consequences, experiences, and life-related troubles that shall not happen to anyone of our own or closely related. This adventure is done with the prayer that our near and dear ones grow up with unique personalities and that everyone might succeed.

This was not like Thankachi burdening his life by taking on unnecessary responsibilities. There was a difference.

One - Why friendship when there is no mutual love and respect? Is it for crying together? Is it only to borrow money frequently?

Two - Is the one who does not render help in danger a friend? When someone's pride hurts, is it a matter of friendship to say, 'That's his problem. Let him heal the wound,' and 'I do not want to look at it and let me run away. Do what you can and trust the one who controls everything. Isn't that the better and the right way?

A week later, Vasudevan and his relatives came to George's house and officially arranged the marriage. Lucy was determined. She went home to celebrate her marriage with Vasudevan and get her relatives' blessings. Brother said ' that a chapter was over.

Brother's (Bhaiyom)…'Ki Duayen Leti Ja, Ja Tujhko Sukhi Sansar Mile"

(Movie: Neel Kamal Singer: Md. Rafi, Music: Ravi)

53. Investigation and Rescue

Not even a year has passed. "I must have the money which Fr. James gave you by the fifteenth of August, and you must find me a motor to pump water." Chekidikatt Chitappan's letter. It was a show of affection, but it was like adding fuel to the fire when I was thinking about the upcoming family events and trying to mobilize resources. People in need will have less property. Selfish interests overshadow the sight of the plight of others.

Dr. K. M. Cherian and Dr MS Valiathan could make Ramachandran's operation successful. I received Ramachandran's salary and sent it to him. Achayan thought that he could make farming successful by sowing Suhasini seeds. As requested, 75 kg of paddy seeds were purchased from Agriculture College, Poona, and sent to Alappuzha through Patel Transport.

After Onam in Pune, the Mother Mary festival was held ten days at Ignatius Church. Brother Tharamma, Thankachi, and Lillikutty attended the festival every day.

I used to reminisce about the marriage of a sister and the broken sibling relationship that followed with pain from time to time. No longer will I be able to call Joy (did he call me brother?) with an open heart and a sincere smile, to caress and comfort, to bring back my tired mind to balance. No longer will he have any influence on me. I have liberated myself. It was great that I could spend some days at the church festival.

By the time the festival was over, my team had been assigned essential tasks for a seminar being organised in the college on refrigeration & air conditioning. I attempted to write a technical paper but did not get the expected result. The Brother, who was a help and support for everything, too, went to Calcutta for temporary duty for 15 days! He also took my newly purchased watch with him.

When the brother returned, he had brought Rasagula and the Calcutta Special Bara Bazar Peda Sweets. While lovingly presenting my watch to his senior sister-in-law in Calcutta, Brother had two good reasons, which I understood very well. Bother paid nothing in cash for a two-week stay with them. And then, in the name of love and freedom towards her, he gave her the favorite watch she liked very much, even though he did not own the same. I was delighted. It would have been an imperfection and a weakness for me if he had not taken that freedom and hesitated an action he desired at a distant place.

He explained his fishing adventure and the frightening atmosphere of 24 Parganas, which he briefly narrated. Brother, a mechanical engineer, also had much to describe the Howrah Bridge, an example of technical expertise of yester years. I must go to see Calcutta someday. You should also visit Mother Teresa's house and see the Howrah Bridge.

I had temporary duty in Bombay but would not stay with Joy this time. I took the double-decker train every morning from Kirkee and returned by the Deccan Queen. On one of those days, James also came to Bombay. I went to meet Joy at Thane's workplace. I thought that it was a formal duty that I had to perform. A responsibility that he did not execute. What difference does it make if I, too, behaved like him? Whether he comes or not, it does not matter. Still, later, he shall have no room to complain about not being invited personally. He did not inform or ask me to his sister's wedding; Perhaps he had a cloud in his mind. If I were to do so- no excuse, this is not just for my sister alone – I do not want him to be tempted to say that he was not informed of a milestone in my life!

"Joycha, You are specially invited to the two marriages in my house - one of Leelamma and the other of mine. Please come and grace the occasion."

He did not answer and did not forget anything of the recent past, showing a face of disgust. I thanked him and returned. I did not want to keep the face of disgust in my memory. James was just a mute witness to the event. Of course, he can have his opinion and views on these matters. That's all up to him.

I have fulfilled my duty and the formality.

When I woke up late on some snowy November mornings and rushed to the office without even drinking a cup of tea, I remembered my stay at 155 JA Block would end soon. What would be the experiences of the coming new year and the new way of life?

I determined I should write two or three subjects in Section B during this November examination. In addition, preparation to go home was included in my occupations in those days.

After the exam, the primary task was to find a house to stay in after marriage. I have heard enough of the deposits, advances, and deposits figures. My Brother often accompanied me on my bicycle journeys searching for a house. In Dapodi, Sanghvi Gaon, Range Hills, and Kirkee, every finding was rejected for one or more reasons. Or, I must say, what came in hand just flew away. Only Netto Uncle confirmed that he would tell the house allottee where he was staying if there was a new Siporex quarters allotment. We were waiting for the factory management to allocate the quarters, which would happen in time. Often, I went and met Netto Uncle. As I left that house, my mind kept whispering that I would come one day to similar factory quarters to stay. I would not miss an opportunity of that kind.

It has been eight years since I came to my current room in Kirkee. I am now left with fifteen days; after that, I must leave this place before Christmas and go home. Christmas should be celebrated with parents and siblings. The wedding date would likely be at the beginning of the new year. I must bid bye to these walls that have given me refuge during the last eight years, the time it has shaped me. I knew these walls understood my dreams, sighs, frustrations, and occasional triumphs. That's why I love these walls separating me from the other side. I got all the food and nutrients from the mess behind, including sambar and chapati, which perhaps I did not relish much.

My wedding invitation from home came today to James. Achayan's letter was addressed only to James! Their parents did not usually invite the children who were getting married. Maybe because of that, I did not get any letter or information. Both marriages would be happening on the thirteenth of January. It felt like a good joke. Post office staff would also enjoy the joke. I was unaware of my wedding date, and my relatives and friends were invited! Achayan has written to James that the betrothal ceremony will also be held on the 28th of December.

Letter to me would come tomorrow or on Monday. Before receiving the letter, I should write home that I will attend Leelamma's wedding. I did write that and posted it. I received Achayan's letter the next day. I did not want to question the elders' decision but felt pity. After both weddings at church, the reception would be held simultaneously in the bridegroom's house. How would the relatives attend the receptions by splitting them into two groups? I would not be attending Thambichan's party, or he would not come to my house for the party. Why is such an arrangement made?

Even in the modern age, some superstitions linger in someone's mind. Some believed that for siblings' marriages from one family to another, some differences of opinions and obstacles would affect their future lives. However, as John indicated, such issues were not likely to happen in educated and cultured families.

The right decisions were made by elders based on facts about transport and the inconvenience of organising a feast for everyone. Adequate consideration of the tender feelings of the participants might also have been given. Further, it can be discussed later at the appropriate forum.

I wrote to Fr. James to come and attend specifically to be the priest in the celebration and make everything run smoothly. Then there were the days of preparation. All friends were invited to meet them in person as much as possible. Brother, Paulose, Thankachi, Vijayappan, George, Range Hills George (Muttar), Vijayan, Suresh, Mammachan, roommates Padmanabhan, Kunjan, Radhakrishnan, Gopalakrishnan, Ravi, Madhavan, Sathyan ..., many office colleagues and so on.

I heard about a highly respected priest in Vishranthawadi from the brother. The Guru would undoubtedly be happy to know that my long silence was for returning to the faithful's congregation. Then, he would embrace the lost sheep as the father did to his prodigal son, who returned. He would advise you on everything you need for a good Christian family life. And that will be how you end this silence.

I was unaware of any formal premarital counselling programme in the churches then; perhaps it was not there, and the same was introduced much later.

I cycled along the tank road to the hermitage. I crossed the hill, valley, pits, and slope to the Ashram yard.

Like the path I traversed for almost eight years, my way to the Ashram was rough and tough. It might have been the expiation or atonement of my sins. That's why I felt hope and tranquillity when I reached that peaceful garden!

After I rang the bell, I thought about the past four or five years of actions, thoughts, sins, doubts, undevoted faith, scratches, inadequacies, incompleteness, etc. I understood that the person who opened the door was not the Guru. I did inquire.

Guru has gone to serve a community that deserves more service than an individual who has come to seek solace for personal benefits. The individual can wait or seek alternate ways.

When I returned, I was not disappointed. I aimed to wipe out, clean, and restore an appropriate state of mind. Three "actions" were expected from the repentant in repentance: admitting the mistakes, grieving over or atoning for them, and being determined not to repeat them. All of that has been achieved. It's easy now. I went straight to St. Ignatius church.

The priest, wearing a lungi and shirt and taking a rest, received me with stretched arms, told me to wait, went in, put on his cassock, and came and invited me to sit by his side.

I gave a long description. Individuals were not significant. It was just my perceptions, thoughts, mind, and conscience. Everything was the mind. My ego melted away in the light of a revealed and uncovered love. A renewed spirit gave me energy, and a new man was born there. The priest welcomed my decision during the Christmas week.

Relieved, calm, and courageous, I started my journey again. A life-long journey began with a vow to be one in the divinely blessed, intimate, co-existing, sacred marriage relationship.

46. YES, I DO

On the train journey back home, Kadamattuthara George accompanied me and Bertrand Russell's book, 'Marriage and Morals.'

It was the day before Christmas. Thinking that Thambichan would come home, we started the Christmas preparations. Together with Bavichan and Raju, we built a crib with hay stacks and palm leaves. Looking at the morning Sun on the new morning that I woke up in the native house, it seemed that nature was asking the Sun, 'What did you invite him for today? Aren't you beginning a new meaning and new relationship in his life soon? Why are you staring at me by keeping everything hidden from me?

In the evening, along with my brother Raju, I went to Ottathyckal to meet the girl who had agreed to join me in marriage. I did not carry anything in my hand. Wrong! My heart was full of eagerness. And yet! While talking to her brother, Thambichan, I saw the lady walking quickly from the pond quay and going into the house. I was surprised. Surprisingly, this tiny figure was the one that occupied my heart so much and for so long, and she soon disappeared into the house. How can I go away without seeing her closely, without asking her to stop, look, and smile? Without asking about her welfare, how could I ? - I would see the whole of her later, I thought, and it was a challenge, courage, and determination for me.

Wedding preparations were going on at home. One day, I needed to go to the church and recite the church's catechism to the priest. The betrothal ceremony will be there to formally ask about the willingness of the bride and the bridegroom for their married life in the presence of a few witnesses. So the ceremonies were arranged, and the guests kept coming. The preparations and the arrangements have begun already.

Bamboo mats were spread on all three outer sides, and a window was built on the west side for the breeze to enter. This extension was due to the special occasion of two young adults getting married on the same day! Achayan's office table and chair were moved from the verandah to the new room. A cot and bed were prepared there for one couple.

Leelamma liked the watch. She did not like the earrings and the chain she had bought earlier. The jewellery was full of fancy stones and coloured discs, and there was a request from Ottathyckal that it be changed to something better.

I went to Bhima Jewellers, Alappuzha, with Leelamma and Kochupappan. The new chain, earrings and bangles were generally to everybody's liking.

"Tell me, who are the ministers in the sacrament of marriage?

"Wedding Ceremonies, Leelamma and Thambichan."

"Um, no, Kochayan and Chechi"

He was not satisfied. I was still wondering who these workers were. He answered in a hurry to move on to the next question-

"Kochaya, Kochaya, it is wrong to tell the priest is the minister. The ministers in the sacrament of marriage are the wedding couple."

"What is marriage?" Babychan asked questions as he opened the book.

"Say it yourself."

Babychan read, and I listened -

"Marriage is a sacrament of God's grace to love one another and raise children to be good Christians." Then he asked me.-

"Will you tell everything correctly, Kochaya? If you don't tell, you cannot get married!"

How many weddings have you been to? Did all the couples get married after answering all these questions? Who could not answer, and did they get married?

With my religious education and family environment, at least until I left my native place to work, I understood the church's rules, liturgy, and modern views. Still, with the desire to get married and to allow the ceremony to go smoothly and begin auspiciously, I went to the church in Champakulam with Perapan after looking at the catechism portion shown by Raju or Bavichan from the old catechism book.

"You have to tell the answer to everything correctly" -

The loving people of the natives continued to comment as and when the events unfolded.

We reached the Vicar's room at the church. Perappan and I were in the verandah of the vicar's room.

Father came down and stood at the doorstep. Fr. Gregory Kalluparambil, I stepped forward. "Glory to Jesus."

Father was more eager to know-

"Is he the one who works in Poona?"

"Yes," Perappan came closer to the father.

Achan improved his knowledge about CME and other general knowledge, such as my work in Poona.

"Is the church nearby?"

"Yes, Father, there is Sunday mass in Malayalam regularly."

"The seminary is near, isn't it?"

"Yes, the Papal Seminary is nearby, in Yerwada.

Like a shepherd to his sheep –

"Well, then get ready and come on Sunday".

If the father had asked me why marriage was necessary, I could have narrated Bertrand Russell's words, quoting St. Paul. And, as my friends said, some modern thoughts. No. How could I dare to say that?

Anyway, nothing was needed.

Christian marriage instituted by God is a public and common covenant for mutual happiness between man and woman in the presence of God, For mutual help and comfort in prosperity and adversity, and, when God wills, for the begetting of children and their nourishment. Thus, marriage is the most suitable way to achieve the ultimate goal of life. Otherwise, one has to renounce everything and become a monk; who can do that?

Like a student who passed the first entrance exam, I returned home and told them what had happened at the church.

After paying respects by offering Glory to Jesus to Appan, Achayan, Ammachi, Aunt, etc., I went to church the next day with chittapan to declare that I was willing to marry Leelamma and to sign as such in the church register. Hasn't the wedding happened on that day? When I said "I do," wasn't the ceremony blessed by God? Leelamma came to church with Kavalackal Ammayi.

No one told me what to say when I went there to church. "So don't worry about what to say. The Holy Spirit will reveal everything to you as and when required ." I remembered the scriptures. Marriage is made in heaven.

Wasn't the main wedding ceremony of giving the veil over last year? On the train when travelling from Kollam to Dindigul. In the culture of tribal people called Ulladans, an Adivasi group who inhabited the forests in Idukki District, Kerala, the husband is the one who gives the veil to the girl who reaches adulthood! Were we Ulladans?

I did not remember anything like that when I gave my double dhoti to cover her body from the cool breeze. Since I didn't remember that, I can forget all that, and now I can cover her with the mantrakoti. Did nature enforce the unwritten personal rule that essential things in my life were often done twice? So, nothing wrong, nothing unpleasant, nothing more than temporary troubles, has happened.

All I prayed during the holy Mass was the grace we needed for happiness and good family life, all the alphabet probably included. I do not remember which alphabets were left out of the vocabulary. Readers might know what the A to Z of happiness is.

I met Thambichan after the holy Mass. Let me briefly reproduce a blog found on WordPress.com (amarvani) here. "Since happiness is the purpose of life, it can be defined with the alphabet, A to Z (vocabulary) of happiness.

A – Awareness, B- Belief in yourself, C- Conscience, not to cause pain to others, and not to compare.

D – Discipline, a consistent discipline, E- Emotional awareness, E- Exercise F- Family, Friends, G- Grit, Gratitude, H- Healthy, Hardworking and Honest

I – Be Inspired and motivated. J- Be Jovial. K- Be kind,

L – Love and Laugh, M-put money to good use and have mindfulness

N – Newness or Novelty, O-Optimism, P- Passion, Purpose, Persistence

Q – inQuisitive mind, R- Be Resilient, S- be Selfish for your happiness, and (meditate) in Solitude and Stop caring about what others think of you.

T – Nurture Talent, U- Uniqueness, V- Values, W- Work

X – XOXO (Hold on to your tribe dearly), Y - Yearning (deep longing), and

Z – Zest (life energy). That is the A-Z of happiness."

I could notice his complete confidence through his eyes, vitality, and courage. It was just an ordinary event for him. I believed it was the only day close friendships became family bonds and lifelong duties and responsibilities.

My eyes were searching for my girl everywhere. She would be standing behind a church door that was longer and much more expansive than usual. She would probably be shy, self-effacing, and wearing eloquent silence on her lips, like a scared and timid, shy baby rabbit. She might be talking to Leelamma, her sister-in-law. Or, like the heart union between Thambichan and me, they might be standing away from the crowd. Would those girls have the guts to go public like commoners without revealing their new status or inhibitions?

Shouldn't the couple's love, trust, and unity be considered before marriage? Isn't that what mutual consent proclaims? In village-born and brought-up couples, family ties are the predominant considerations in addition to all the above.

"So come on, Oommacha, Thambicha... Achen is coming".

With full consent, the four have said they are ready to marry.

Oommacha, stand aside, here, .. here.

I could see a girl approaching with curiosity - Leelamma!

"Not you. You go and tell Chechi to come here."

I saw Leelamma walking away pale and trembling, and another angel appeared by my side there.

This is for you. This is the one God created for you as a partner. This is what I will have – I said in my mind.

Without having a book in hand, Achen asked me a question -

"Thomas, the one who is standing here, what's your name.....,

Someone said, "Leelamma."

Someone else said, "No, not Leelamma. It is Elsy."

I looked. Is this the same girl I saw? Or what's the name to call my angel? She is every name and all the names for me.

I thought marriage was a relationship that should last till the end of life and joint responsibility in all aspects of life.

"To accept as a wife with full heart.."

"Sure," I replied thoughtfully.

A question to Leelamma.

"Eli, are you willing to accept this one standing here, Thomas, as your husband wholeheartedly?"

Silence...

Years to live! 'All the years' moved fast before her in a second or two? Are you worried about anything? Shyness, fear, the bliss of satisfaction? An uncertain future? The silence was weighty.

"If you agree and mean it, say it.."

She said in haste - "Ngha, okay."

Then we signed the fat book of family relationships of the parish members of the church.

Father asked Thambichan and Leelamma the same way he asked Leelamma and me.

As if they had already arrived at a decision well in advance, they immediately responded to the priest's questions - "I agree."

The betrothed girls returned to their homes with their relatives after thinking of their ceremonious return and the wedding in the same church after ten days.

After finishing the church functions, we did not forget to drink tea on our way back with Thambichan.

"Didn't they both say they were willing for the marriage?" Achayan asked Chittappan. At the same time, everyone had coffee and steamed rice puttu. "Let's see the rest for the wedding function."

A draft text of the wedding invitation had been prepared. I showed what I wrote to Thambichan. He had also prepared one, and he showed me. In the invitation written by Thambichan, he mentioned only his marriage. It was also decided that the name 'Lailamma' should not be used in the school, and the name 'Leelamma' would suffice. "No matter what the written name is, the person will not change," came another assessment, according to Thambichan.

The invitation cards were printed at Alappuzha. By the year-end, various addresses were written, stamped, and sent to the invitees. Achayan also took away the cards he wanted for his colleagues and friends.

1975. No New Year celebrations were held due to the emphasis on marriage preparations. How early the personal and mental preparations had begun! The household's most important practices are inviting relatives and friends, buying wedding dresses and jewellery, arranging comfortable seating for the guests, and arranging meals, including hospitality. As the wedding day approaches, locals and friends often refer to the betrothed as the couple. When the girl and the boy were walking in the countryside for some purpose, they could always hear the friendly inquiries of the natives-

"Did you get a house to stay at your workplace? Are you taking your wife along to the workplace?, Or Leave her here to help your mother?"

"How much dowry did you get? Did you take gold for all the money?"

"When you came for the wedding, isn't the boy a little tired?"

"It doesn't matter; both will get fatter soon!"

All the wedding couples usually hear the same conversations and nigglings, sometimes subtle and sometimes overtone.

In addition to those getting married, it is expected to have their paternal relatives with them to buy clothes and jewellery. That is to keep the cash safe and spend it as planned.

"Eda Kuriakose, look here, I have this much in hand ... I don't need anything. I can buy it later... It is difficult to have enough cash for everything ..." Achayan handed a package to his brother and spoke.

That's when I saw my mother coming to see off the people going for the purchases.

That's when he saw Ammachi coming forward to see off the team going on the purchase mission.

"Ngha, For her counterpart (bride's mother), buy a good 'long cloth' too. Let her not have anything less because I have said so! If you give good, you will also get back the same. Don't forget the mangalsutra (thali) pendant and the wedding ring. You see, everything will come from there also in the same measures."

I bought the required clothes and essential jewellery in addition to the earlier purchases from Mullakkal shops. As my paternal relatives were with me, everything was like a balancing act on a rope. Even though I was looking for an opportunity, I didn't get any to crack a joke or make a witty comment.

I bought a length of fabric for the blouse to match the colour of the wedding saree. "If you give it to the tailor, he will sew it in a day or two," said the textile shopkeeper. It was sufficient to give the body part measurements to tailor the blouse. Thambichan's sister was ready to give the measurements. Someone said it was because of me that my sister was not brought along for the purchases!

Thambichan heard that. Then, Thambichan realised and got irritated over Leelamma not coming to give the measurements, angered Thambichan. Or was it a pre-planned comment? Suddenly, I heard it loud enough -

"In that case, take measurements on his chest!" I turned my face away to a distant object as if I was not attentive.

No one pretended to hear that comment from the bridegroom!

Everyone generally liked the jewellery and the clothes. Expenditures were also within limits prescribed by the elder relatives.

47. THE NEW FAMILIES

13 Jan 1975 I saw the day's morning had a unique brightness and unmatched colours for the new era. It was a procession of rays of light, full of serene beauty, calm and sunny, regal and dignified.

Setting out to get married

Life's journey of joys and sorrows began on that day. I was a "Sensitive Plant in a garden grew, And the young winds fed it with silver dew, And it opened its fan-like leaves to the light...." (PB Shelley) beginning of a family began with love. May every family be filled with God's grace, peace, prosperity, and happiness.

Let the seeds sprout where the warmth of love and the moisture of comfort join together in an everlasting bond. Let our families be a garden full of fruit-bearing trees, an actual orchard.

Family members and relatives had arrived earlier. Friends started coming.

I bathed in the canal in front of the house at the quay, had breakfast at the pandal with the relatives, and wore wedding clothes. Since I was from Kuttanadu, I might have to step in slush, mud, and water while walking, so I had already thought about not wearing shoes and pants. Still, a new white shirt and dhoti were sufficient. White cloth for a new shirt was also bought, and the tailer stitched the shirt within a short time. I had felt a catch here and there when it was worn, and the shirt's collar looked like a dachshund dog's ears. It did not matter to me as I had determined to wear it only for the occasion, once in a lifetime.

I said the prayers. Honorarium to the first Teacher (Gurudakshina) was given to Kochupappan. I bowed and sought blessings from Appan, Amma, Achayan Ammachi, and all elder relatives. I chanted praises to the Lord. I got permission to travel to the church. My sister also got permission to travel after me. We travelled to Champakulam Church by motor boat. The relatives followed the bride and groom into the church in two batches.

James Achan came directly to the church.

Marriages take place in heaven.

Before the presence of God, in the presence of relatives and friends in the church, in a moment full of goodness, without emotional conflicts, in a serene environment, with determination in the heavenly moments-

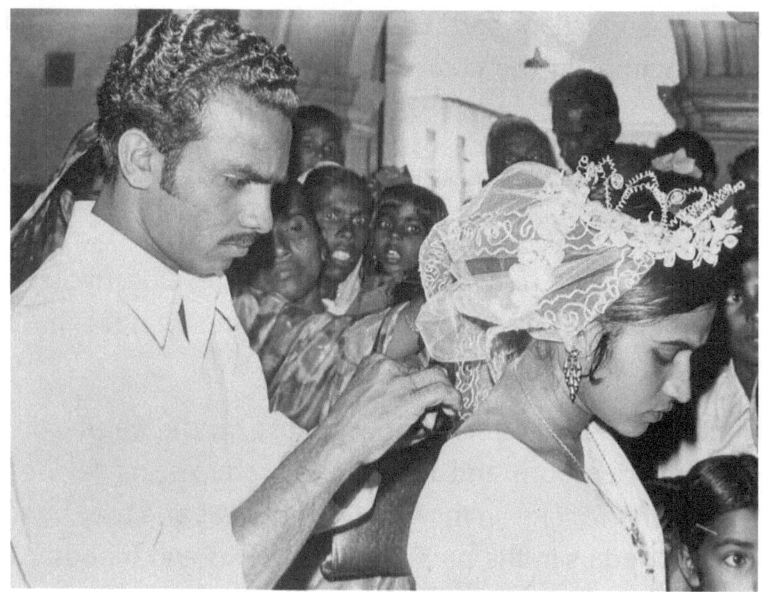

Tying the knot for life (1975)

Putting our right hands upon the Bible and in the presence of the perpetual brightness of the holy spirit, first, we, Thomas and Eli (Leelamma), solemnly vowed -

"From this day until death, in joy and sorrow,

Wealth, poverty, health, and illness,

With mutual love and loyalty,

With one mind to live,

Witness the holy Gospel, we promise.

To live according to this promise,

May God Almighty help us!"

Thambichan and Leelamma particularly witnessed our pledge, along with other relatives.

Then Thambichan and Leelamma (Sebastian and Kathrina registered names in the church) said, "From this day until death." Vowed -

Thomas and Eli (Leelamma) particularly witnessed our vows, along with other relatives.

Thambichan and his wife Leelamma went to Ottathyckal with a batch of relatives. Leelamma and I went home by boat with other relatives; James Achen also came along.

The bride's mother-in-law drew a cross on the forehead of the bride and bridegroom and received the couple inside. We were made to sit on the stage in the courtyard pandal, and they honoured and entertained us in the presence of relatives and friends. Written by my dear friend and poet CPC Nair, read out the matter aloud and presented us with the souvenir printed on art paper.

"കണ്ണിൽ കവിതയും, ചുണ്ടിൽ സ്മിതവുമായ്, കണ്മണിയൊത്തൊരു ഗാനം പോലെ

കൈപിടിച്ചെത്തുന്നു ജീവിതവാസന്തം, കൈവരിച്ചീടുവാൻ നിങ്ങളെന്നും,

ആനന്ദ സാന്ദ്രമാം ദാമ്പത്യ വേദിയിൽ, ആശകൾ പൂവിരിച്ചെത്തിടുമ്പോൾ

പ്രേമമാം വള്ളി നികുഞ്ജത്തിലായിരം, രോമഹർഷങ്ങൾ പുതച്ചുനിൽക്കെ

ആതിര രാവുകൾ വെള്ളിനിലാവുമായ് ആനന്ദ നൃത്തം ചവുട്ടി നിൽക്കെ

മഞ്ഞിൻ കുറിക്കൂട്ടണിയും പുലരികൾ മഞ്ജീര ശിഞ്ചിതം ചേർത്തിടുമ്പോൾ

മന്ദ,സമീരണ ശീതളാ ശ്ലേഷിത, ചന്ദനച്ചാറിൽ മുഴുകിമെല്ലെ സന്ധ്യയാം

ദേവി മദാലസയായെന്നും സിന്ദൂരച്ചെപ്പും തുറന്നു നിൽക്കെ

തമ്പുരുമീട്ടി പവിഴക്കൊടിപോലെ സങ്കല്പ സ്വപ്നത്തിൻ തേരിലേറി

തങ്കച്ചിറകുമായ് മാലാഖമാർ വന്നു മംഗളഗാനങ്ങളാലപിക്കെ

മന്മനോ വീണയിൽ സ്വർഗ്ഗീയാനന്ദത്തിൻ തന്ത്രികൾ പൊട്ടിച്ചിരിച്ചുനിൽക്കെ

മൽസൗഹൃദത്തിന്റെ മംഗളാശംസയാം പുഷ്പങ്ങൾ കൊണ്ടൊരു മാല ചാർത്താം

മൻ മനോ വീണയിൽ സ്വർഗ്ഗീയാനന്ദത്തിൻ, തന്ത്രികൾ പൊട്ടിച്ചിരിച്ചുനിൽക്കേ

മൽ സൗഹൃദത്തിൻറെ മംഗളാശംസയാം പുഷ്പങ്ങൾ കൊണ്ടൊരു മാല ചാർത്താം"

"With poetry in the eyes, with a smile on the lips, like a song with a beloved
The hand grabs life's treasure, and you to grab it,
Ananda Sandramam on the matrimonial stage, when hopes blossom
Premamam Valli Nikunjathilairam, covered with the chill of snow
Athira nights danced with the silver moon in joyous dance
When the morning dew is sprinkled with manjira sprinkles
Manda, Samirana Sheetalashleshita, Sandalwood indulging in Sandhyam
Goddess Madalasa and Sindoorachepp standing open
Like a coral flag, Tamburumi met the dream of imagination
Angels came with gold and sang auspicious songs
Manmano while the strings of heavenly joy burst into laughter on the veena
A garland of flowers can be worn as an auspicious sign of male friendship
Let the strings burst into laughter for heavenly joy on the mano mano veena
A garland of flowers is auspicious for friendship."

My bed in the annex was shown to the bride to rest. There, I breathed a sigh of relief and wanted to open the window for the wind from the west. There, I saw four or five teenage- girls, looking like Nazhi and Changzhi measures, peeping through the window to look at the bride. They have seen a blemishless bride enough and got choked up, tongue-tied, and scrambling for the right words to say but remained there smiling.

A few of my friends remained until late evening, cracking jokes and having fun. They removed the makeshift decorations and helped us to return to our everyday comforts and routine.

My friends wouldn't leave the evening behind without proposing a toast. I had arranged one bottle of golden eagle Scotch. Together, George, Appachi, and Kunjunju held the newly married couple captive and sat around to propose a toast. George quoted from the 'Marriage and Morals, Appachi gave Military Engineer's Salute.

Was it because he heard laughter and noise inside, or did the smell of intoxicating hospitality pervade the surroundings? I was not sure I listened to my grandpa saying to Achayan, - "Vavachcha, let me go home." -

Grandpa walked a few steps; when I understood the situation, I entered the courtyard and looked around. My grandpa was walking and had reached the neighbour's backyard. If I apologise, my grandpa will come back, won't he? What if the eagle flies around again after bringing him back? No. My grandpa will forgive. Wasn't this getting together only for a day?

Who took the bride and the groom out of the pandal stage and put them into the nuptial chamber?

That was much earlier.

The laughter and commotion subsided as the glasses and dishes were cleared away. Everyone looked for a place to sleep. Achayan has already gone to bed. He knew that he had to go to Ambalapuzha early in the morning.

My mother brought a glass of milk and put it on the table. Mother took a blanket and a pillow from the bed, rolled them up, and left. There was a pillow and blanket on the mattress as well. It is never a habit for me to drink milk before going to bed. I knew some of the practices would have to change from this day. It was a ceremony service on the wedding night to serve milk, and I did not tell my mother that she had not given me a second glass because I had heard of such a thing. My mother told me to share everything I get for the rest of my life and go to bed.

On Achayan's office table lay a crucifix, paper, and toys.

Putting everything aside, only the crucifix and the glass of milk were brought to our attention.

Leelamma was amazed at what I was doing. I said-

"Come, come and pray."

We knelt before the crucifix and prayed with words, silent and in mind, what either of us liked. I prayed -

For a good family life, mutual love and peace grow.

In this life journey of joys and sorrows that began today, give me a family based on love. May our lives be filled with God's grace, peace, prosperity, and abundance.

I drank half of the milk and gave the remaining half to Leelamma. She liked it and drank it. Leaving all the bedspreads on the bed, Leelamma was ready to lie on the floor.

Lovingly, I stopped her and coolly said in a low voice -

"No, we can go to bed together forever."

We sat on the bed, prayed briefly, and then lay together. Leelamma appeared shy and was a little afraid of sleeping next to me. I turned off the lights.

I told her not to be afraid. "I am human....not a monkey. A man who has not changed his monkey-like characteristics!"

It did not get there as expected. "If you say it is the same monkey with a tail, but the tail is not at the back... " Yes, she smiled. Was it a little louder, like a laugh? Did anyone hear the laughter?

Silence prevailed for some time. I was not getting sleep by the side of a beautiful girl!

This night should be a typical example of thousands of nights that follow. Expressing love should not be like a beast that bites and eats flesh. I was sure about it in my mind.

I asked her-" Leelam, do you like me?

It was a spontaneous, ordinary call without any specialty like an easy-flowing stream, and the call's name came - "Leelam." Perhaps she was called by that name for the first time. I do not know if anybody else had called her by that short name. There was no possibility. Such short call signs emerge spontaneously only when such a peak of love is expressed. The height of love from the heart and soul resonates with such sweet names.

Silence. This is the same answer she gave when the priest asked her if she would marry me.

"If you like, say you like, Leelam. Do you like me?"

"Yes, I like it."

"Then you must give birth to my children."

There was no response. I could not see her face with an unfamiliar expression because of the dim light peeping through the windows.

She might have been thinking of the enormous pain during labour when it comes! Nobody would think of the bliss that the newborn will bring. She said nothing, and Silence again prevailed. A little smile seemed to emerge in the meanwhile. Nothing was apparent in the dim light of darkness. I asked again.

This time, I asked, keeping her whole body in my hands -

"Leelam, do you like me?"

"Yes, I like."

"Then, you will have to look after my grandchildren."

She must have been thinking, and she did not respond immediately. But she smiled, I know, she laughed; I knew she was laughing and embracing me, and I hugged her close to me."

I got up early. It was a new dawn that I had never seen before.

I realised that I was not alone. My loving wife slept with me and woke up before dawn. She would most likely be with my mother in the kitchen after her short prayer.

When I walked into the inner room with curiosity, There she was! In the kitchen, she was sitting on the floor and eating the pazham kanji (from the previous day's kanji (rice gruel) by hand from an edge-broken bowl.

Embracing the beauty and grace of the countryside, the little native girl looked at me with a calm and beautiful smile. After waving my hand that I would come soon, I quickly brought a camera and captured that extraordinary picture. I have kept it in the album.

The wife would wholeheartedly and confidently accept the deserving love and understanding from the man she loves, thinking there is nothing better on this earth than his love and consideration. It should be understood that the beauty of the body and mind would also increase with the increase in self-confidence.

Improved self-confidence helps the couple to understand each other and makes them fearless. Hugging your partner when they return home from work with a tired mind rejuvenates them by connecting their joys and sorrows with yours. It can console and comfort them whenever they have a terrible day and instantly bring back a smile to their face.

From the next day onwards, we went to relatives' houses for a visit. We used to go in the morning, have lunch with them, and return in the afternoon.

We received numerous inquiries from locals and acquaintances while walking toward the south and the north. Those trips were the first opportunities to build mutual friendships, share thoughts and dreams, and nurture love in our hearts. I got to know my relatives and their relations more closely.

We went to Ottathyckal, where we could meet Thambichan and Leelamma for the first time after our marriage. Everyone was happy and was running about for hospitality and comfort for the visiting couple.

When we went to our wife's house for a party, the newlyweds in that house welcomed us. There were no unfamiliar situations or people. No one felt the need for a formality. That's how everyone got together and found time to sit, talk, and laugh together. Everyone loved songs. I always loved listening to songs. But not all songs. I would try to listen to good songs whenever I had time. If someone asked me to sing one, I might like to leave the place immediately under some pretext. I have never heard Leelamma or Thambichan sing. A lot picked up the order of Singers, and unfortunately, my name came first to sing. I could not run away, so I sat there and sang an incomplete song. After that, I told Leelamma to sing my favourite song - how many times did I request her, and every time she denied it. To sing that song 'ദുഖങ്ങൾക്കിന്നു ഞാൻ അവധി കൊടുത്തു' (I gave off to my sorrows).

"Dukhame ninak pularkala vandanam, ..." (KJ Yesudas).

Everyone started laughing, too. Still, I was singing the same song I loved so much -

The song 'I gave off to my sorrows.' The snow that covered the sorrows of the days will be remembered forever.

'I have given a day off to the sorrows, and I have settled down in a room in heaven, ('ദുഃഖങ്ങൾക്കിന്നു ഞാൻ അവധി കൊടുത്തു, സ്വർഗ്ഗത്തിൽ ഞാനൊരു മുറിയെടുത്തു, വിധിയും ഞാനും ഒരു കൂടു ചീട്ടുമായ്, വിളയാടാനിരിക്കുന്നൂ-വിളയാടാനിരിക്കുന്നു-എന്റെ...)

Destiny and I with a pack of cards to sit and play - to play - my.

(In Ambalapravu, MS Baburaj, P Bhaskaran)

Everyone has forgotten it's the honeymoon evenings – see, someone has come up with a sad song! Everyone laughed again, and the singing was declared enough.

I was expecting that song the other day when I heard songs containing the word 'sadness' on Radio Ceylon. The first and second ones were over. When Yesudas sang 'Dukhame Ninakku' without giving up hope, Sarojini Shivalingam says - Yesudas sang in the movie 'Pushpanjali.' Greetings to you in the morning. '! (MK Arjunan, Sreekumaran Thambi,)

'(ദുഃഖമേ... ദുഃഖമേ... പുലർകാല വന്ദനം, ദുഃഖമേ നിനക്കു പുലർകാല വന്ദനം കാലമേ നിനക്കഭിനന്ദനം, എന്റെ രാജ്യം കീഴടങ്ങി എന്റെ ദൈവത്തെ ഞാൻ വണങ്ങി', ദുഃഖമേ ദുഃഖമേ....കറുത്ത ചിറകുള്ള വാർമുകിലേ, കടലിന്റെ മകനായ് ജനിക്കുന്നു നീ.....)

"Sorrow, sorrow... good morning, sorrow, good morning to you, Congratulations to you, the era my kingdom has surrendered, and I have worshipped my God - sorrow and sorrow... You are born the son of the sea, the dark-winged cluster- cloud."

Some songs are for listening to only once.

Some songs I like to hum, walk around all the time, and always listen to. Which ones? Why should I be so upset and emotional when I hear some of them?

Songs can penetrate deep into the heart and create pulsating sensations and vibrations in the soft areas. Memories of a few moments or a spoken word or sentence in a letter, sent or received. And then-

Had not Isaac written once—

"Bachpan ki muhabat ko dil se na juda karna,

Jab yad meri aai, milne ki dua karna.

What immortal lines. Likewise

I first heard that song in Pazhassiraja on the annual college day, which was sung by that speaker.

"From chutta to Chutala, carrying on your burden, all of you who stand in the pandal of sorrow...

You will see these planted gallows .. you will see."

" ചുട്ട മുതൽ ചുടല വരെ, ചുമടും താങ്ങി, ദുഖത്തിന് തണ്ണീർ പന്തലിൽ നില്കുന്നവരേ .....ഈ രാത്രി ഇരുണ്ടു വെളുത്ത് കിഴക്കുണരുമ്പോൾ ഈ നാട്ടിയ കഴുകുമരങ്ങൾ കാണും നിങ്ങൾ .. കാണും നിങ്ങൾ "

I heard that song years ago and have not heard it again more than two or three times in the whole period. How many times have I longed to listen to it?

Even though I rarely heard the song before leaving the state, one Hindi song that I liked the most and I always longed to listen to, that song which was played many times no matter what the programme was in the college -

"Jo vada kiya voh, nibhana patega,.. roke jamana chahe.."

Even now, whenever I hear it, it appears that the song is flowing from the verandah of the college. There was no other song that had so much of an impact.

Even after going to Pune, I heard so many good songs.

"Rahi manua dukkha ki chinta kyom satati...

"Jeena Yaham, Marna Yaham Iske Ziva...

"Dost Dost Na Raha Pyaar Pyaar ....

"Maine Tere Liye Hee Saat Rang Ke ...

"Woh din yad karo ... Woh chup chup ke milna

"Ab na hum mil sakenge ... tum mujh ko bhool....

"Meri yad me tum ansoo na bahana....

"Kahim dur jab din dhal jaye...

"Chalte Chalte Mere Yeh Geet Yad.....

"Dheere Dheere Meh Chal, Eh Dil Hi Bekar

"Aaj mela he bijade huye...

"Abhi kya sunoge suna toh hasogi...

"Woh Janewalon, ho sake toh...

"Koi jab tumara, hruday thod de tadaptha huaa...

ഈശ്വരനൊരിക്കൽ വിരുന്നിനു പോയി

പ്രേമഭിക്ഷുകി, ഭിക്ഷുകി ... ഏതു സന്ധ്യയിൽ

സുപ്രഭാതം, സുപ്രഭാതം പ്രഭാതം നീല ഗിരിയുടെ സഖികളെ

ഏകാന്തതയുടെ അപാര തീരം ...

("Ishwaran once went to a feast...

"Oh Beloved, Oh beloved ... in which dusk hours

"Good morning, good morning, friends of Neelagiri

"The vast shore of loneliness...)

So, how many more such melodies, and what kind of taste do I have? You will notice that if you check the central theme or salient points. Only couplets of absolute love or sorrow are embedded in those lines

Married on the same day

48. IN YOUR HANDS

I kept my promise to my grandmother that I would bring 'her' the next time I would come. Even though she didn't remember much about what I had said, my grandma came and stayed at home much before our wedding. Grandma was there to receive the praise of the Lord and give us blessings before we went to church for the marriages. The next day after the wedding, Leelamma took out the woven decorated net and crown she had worn for the wedding and put it on Grandma's head to watch her reaction or to get her blessings. Grandma smiled profusely and asked me - "What is it, Mone? It looks good." She further told Leelamma that it looked good on her head, being a young and energetic girl!" I took out the camera and captured the serene and blessed moment as a photograph in the album.

The next time we visited home from Pune, Grandma blessed everyone, slept in the Lord, and went to her heavenly home.

Rosamma, the youngest girl in Ottathyckal, who must have been around eight years then, was always walking by the side of her sister's shadow as a perpetual companion. When her sister 'Chechiyamma' Leelamma came to sleep with me late that evening, Rosamma was still with her. Even though Leelamma told her, "Molu, go inside and sleep with your mother", the girl refused to go. She was determined to sleep with her elder sister only. The married chechi was in a dilemma. She scared Rosamma and sent her away, telling her she would call Ammachi or send her away in marriage as early as possible. Suppose you ask Rosamma, married and with an adult son today, to remember this. In that case, she will run away in shyness and humiliation, bowing her head!

How many days could we stay home like this after marriage without any specific work and having a feast at relatives' homes? How many days could we stay home without work or regular income? Once we reach Pune, I can continue working and get a regular income. Where will you, the happily married couple, stay in Pune? It was a big question, and I lost sleep. There was a temporary relief when I received Brother's letter. If it was not difficult to stay in the living room with my Brother and family until we got a house... Yes, I can reserve the tickets after deciding the date.

I got the telegram for the test and interview at CIE Pune the next day. Better Job, More Salary. Being a family and finding a new place to live, the possibility of getting a job at CIE must be explored vigorously. It may be a great blessing.

Success in life requires a measure of self-sacrifice, dedication, and determination. Marriage is a turning point. New and better work helps to cross that path successfully. So decide - go, and try hard to get it even if you are unsure you will. It is a great relief that Brother will shelter you to stay for now. Must arrive in Poona at least one day before the interview. The date was fixed. However, it was impossible to get a seat reservation on the train. My wife did not experience the hardships of the train journey. Still, I decided to travel without further ado, thinking sharing the difficulties would be a great pleasure. All the necessary packing was done, and we requested permission and blessings from our relatives before the travel.

We prayed together. Everyone in the house was in the pain and grief of being separated from them. My mother and siblings expressed it emotionally. Glory to Jesus was submitted to Grandpa and Grandma. Leelamma did the same after I received their blessings. I overheard Achayan talking to Leelamma-

"Mole, I'm handing this man over to you. Take care."

Family members and relatives came to the railway station to see us off.

The railways had arranged the usual dilapidated and inadequate facilities for the newlyweds- the old-fashioned coach to go to their residence along with other passengers—plywood-lined seats—windows without grills or shutters. There was not enough light at night, and the electric fans did not work. The passengers were crowded, and moving or going to the toilet for essentials was challenging. For the name's sake, the bathroom was a structural enclosure, dirty, loathsome, and did not even have a drop of water to wash my face. The passengers were determined to reach their destinations, facing all troubles and obstacles. No matter what kind of service you do for your country, no matter how proud you are and what condition you live in, no matter how comfortable your life is, if you wanted to realise that you were nobody in India and that you were just a speck of dust in the universe, it was enough for you to travel in a railway passenger coach without reservation (1975).

After standing for a while, someone who felt pity for the newlywed couple, especially the charming lady, offered Leelamma half a seat. Since she was committed to sharing anything, she happily shared half of what she got with her loving partner. It went on for 36 hours like that. Nobody had felt any hunger, thirst, or the dry heat of the day while passing through Andhra Pradesh, and nobody could move away from the unique amenities they occupied.

The train arrived at the platform in Poona and stopped for us to get out. Many of my friends had arrived at the station to receive the newlyweds. No one could walk in or out the coach door as people were sitting or lying on the way. The compartment was full of people going to Bombay.

There was no choice; we had to get out. ! We could see the windows were open, having no grills or shutters. I leaned forward like a trainee acrobat and tried to escape through the window and jump onto the platform. I persuaded my beloved wife to follow me lovingly. She was determined to follow me, as always. My wife, brought in safely by the railways up to Poona, was happily picked up through the window, and I helped her to stand on Poona's flat railway platform. All my friends were watching. After wiping her face, putting on her sari somewhat, and combing her hair with her hands, the bride smiled at my close friends. I introduced Leelamma to my friends. After a courtesy inquiry with everyone, Brother took the newlyweds to his home in Range Hills. We stayed there for a month, enjoying the lovely hospitality.

Commencing our married life with an older brother (Sebastian) could give us much practical experience.

Living in the same house, cooking together, eating together, and caring for a young baby during the day were all practical experiences for the times to come later. After everyone went to work in the morning, Jomon, the son of Brother and Tharamma, spent time playing on Leelamma's lap, sleeping on her shoulders, and drinking bottled milk. The Pattiyamma of the Nilgiris, the help and housemaid at home, told Leelamma several things in Tamil. Tharamma showed her how to light a kerosene stove and cook dal, other pulses, and rice in a pressure cooker. That was the first time she had seen such home and kitchen appliances. She also learned to make chapatis. Jomon was taken to the nearby hospital for timely vaccination against childhood diseases.

Without hurrying to sleep, we often sat in our bedroom, peeked out of the window on the first floor of the building, and enjoyed the moon and the cool white moonlight. All the news and descriptions from the time of going to and returning from work at CME, visits to our friends' houses in the evenings, together with the search for a residence of our own, different locations of crowded homes of the city, sights in the bazaar and so on were the subjects of our talks.

Getting married and living together peacefully as a family always helps fulfill the discharge of duty and work smoothly, serving the country as responsible citizens. Therefore, when I came with my family, I applied and asked the authorities of CME to allot family quarters for us. Considerations in the military establishments were always in favour of the uniformed soldiers. That was the rule of the institution, though the majority of the employees were civilians. The civilian employees would continue to be essential ordinary citizens, no matter how much knowledge, training, and capabilities they showed far beyond the soldiers' capabilities in peace establishments. The positions would always be one step below the civilians according to their qualifications or grades. It was more accurate to say that the uniform-wearing soldiers were one step ahead. Therefore, despite repeated requests, the residential quarters were never allotted to civilians, even when the requirements for solutions under extreme conditions were presented.

Nobody cared seriously about the career prospects, promotion, status, or suitable opportunities a civilian servant deserved. Even in the legal system, such matters were deliberately avoided. Civil servants did not get promotions and honours similar to those of soldiers in the Department of Defence in general and CME in particular.

We visited many friends' homes in the evenings and the house search. Paulose, Neto's Uncle, George, and Narakathra Kuttappan all lived in the surroundings of factory quarters at Range Hills.

Married people jointly celebrate their wedding anniversary. I told my wife that no one would celebrate my birthday after our marriage. Yet, my loving wife decided to celebrate her husband's thirtieth birthday. When I returned from the office in the afternoon, she wanted to serve good rice like the thumba flowers and other accompanying curries. She boiled raw rice in the cooker. The vegetables were chopped to make different curries and prepared.

The raw rice drank all the water, and when she thought it was cooked, she put out the flame and allowed it to cool. In the native, she practiced cooking rice by boiling the water with rice three times and then tilting the pot to drain off the water after closing the pot so that the rice would separate within the pot. In the city, the method she learned was different. She served the rice in a bowl, but the rice was a little overcooked. It appeared, but it looked like a stew when mixed with water! Adding a little sugar would have made it a lovely pudding for the birthday celebration. She was sad and embarrassed, and no wonder she was in a "right old stew" when offering the birthday treat to her boyfriend. It was not like Thumba flowers but like pudding while celebrating her loved one's thirtieth birthday!

Many quarters were built to house the Ammunition Factory workers in the Range Hills. Most of the workers in the factory lived in their limited facilities in nearby villages. Rarely did some come to more comfortable quarters. At the same time, the rest took advance payments and monthly rent from the people searching for rented residences as soon as they got quarters allotted. The old quarters were built during British rule, and later, more new multi-story buildings were created using modern building materials and recent technology.

The quarters would have some greenery and small trees in the area if they were of old construction. However, selecting the appropriate one with a suitable environment and neighborhood was impossible for those in need. You got what you got. It would be a blessing if you got the quarters of your choice and too eco-friendly.

It is a botheration to the occupants that those workers who gave you the quarters on sub-let in this way often ask for money for their various needs. The sub-letting system was officially prohibited, and the authorities, when they knew that the worker had ignored the rule, usually issued notices to evict the occupant. If not, then the employee is punished. The employee would come and plead to vacate the quarters so that he does not lose his job. Those in need see such a risk as a disadvantage of the system. Then it would help if you moved somewhere else. That's it. It was impossible to dream of getting a government quarter allotted out of turn to the employee. Everyone in Poona knew those with 15-20 years of service still lived in rented houses.

There was no other way for an expatriate to come and join for a small job in Poona, and he never got a house from the government. These quarters were always a paradise for those getting married if they were willing to pay ten months' rent in advance and accept the risk. But for people in need, quarters taken on rent from the factory workers were a comfortable sanctuary and a dream world.

As a result of a month's continuous effort, I got one old-type quarter, a forty-year-old army barrack built in haste. The factory worker also seemed gentle and polite. I got it with the combined efforts of my close friends. I took over the quarters in haste without further looking into the quality of construction and the dilapidated built-in facilities.

So one day we moved to the new rented house - the old-type quarters, with only our suitcases. The old vacant quarters and the newly built houses looked alike. There were no furnishings, and no movable furniture was found in the rooms. There was nothing inside the home. I brought my steel cot, the only savings of a bachelor's life from the lodge, 155 JA Block. On the same day, along with Brother, I went to the bazaar to buy the essentials and some utensils for the kitchen. The image of the Sacred Heart was brought from my parents. It was set up, the candle was lit, the milk was boiled, the rice was cooked, and we slept with contentment and thankfulness to the creator, our parents, and friends. A family started living independently in a rented house.

I do not know if what I wrote- slept with contentment- was true. It was not because of the living conditions in Poona, work, or the hardships of married life. Still, I did not know how to give an adjective for a state of perfect contentment. It may take a lifetime to analyse it. Is that enough? As Brother says - "mud ball !" (മണ്ണാങ്കട്ട)!". Such thoughts should not waste life, and Brother said it precisely in one word.

One thing was very pleasing. We had slept together as we were married and slept happily and peacefully. No worries, no quarrels, no guilt. Shortfalls or failures of nobody came into our discussions. In the evening, before going to bed, we used to sit together and read a book. Malayalam books were not available. Most of what we read was classic novels like 'Good Earth.' Les Miserables took several days for us to finish reading. But we finished reading the book and enjoyed it without too many breaks. We exchanged views and comments on significant anecdotes, characters, and their emotional events.

For the parents at home, the older children went to their workplaces with their spouses. After the wedding and the commotion, the whole family became silent as the elder ones left home, and there were other difficulties, too. There were younger children in both families.

Achayan experimented with farming by sowing the Suhasini paddy seeds and caring for and nurturing a new crop in the agricultural field, but it was not so fruitful. He could not harvest enough paddy to take home after paying all the labour costs, pesticides, fertilisers, and other expenses. Achayan wrote to me –

"I see no other way than to get out after selling the agricultural land. If I have long-term dues from newspaper readers, though it may come in the long run, I can not wait longer without paying back the debt due to the wedding expenditures. It must be paid immediately."

It was true that I had no interest in farming. It seemed to me that it was impractical to take on the additional burden of repaying the farming debt, which was increasing yearly. I had no other suggestions or means of providing assistance or financial support to Achayan. Therefore, I accepted the decision to sell the agricultural land and communicated the same to Achayan. He was happy, acted promptly, and got rid of the source of incurring loss and debt.

Although the new family started living independently in Poona, they supported their parents through nominal monthly remittances. It was insufficient; Achayan very much reduced the demands for financial assistance.

The daily expenses of the house were quite burdensome. Babu did not get any job and did not get the required marks to pass the English exam after putting in his best efforts. Not because English is a foreign language but because he could not search for answers and write exams like that. Will it help even if he admitted that it was a deficiency? However, to get a job besides being a labourer, he needed an SSLC certificate after passing all the subjects together or compartmentally. Even if he was brought to Poona, how could he get a convenient job? Local language should be known for such jobs.

Raju joined SD College, Alappuzha, to study for the pre-degree course. (After that, he did a B.Com degree course.) Babychan had not finished high school by then. Babychan passed SSLC in 1978.

The plan and estimates were prepared for a house and given to the Thakazhi Co-operative Society, for the housing loan was sanctioned. Before that, Appan laid the foundation stone to start the construction of the house. Foundation work began. The entire loan amount was received in two or three installments. Work started as per the plan. Even before the job was half over, the whole loan amount for the house construction was received from the society and spent.

The farm loan was repaid with the land sale's proceeds, and the remaining amount was used to build the house. After that, nobody looked at the house's original plan for further work. The house was not finished. Had it been habitable, we could have moved into the completed area. Still, there were no toilets built. Bathing facilities for women were not built outside the house. The inside attached toilets were discarded from the plan to reduce cost. Determined that the rest of the construction would continue as soon as more money would be available, construction was stopped until the pending payments were paid to the carpenters and masonry labourers. Quarterly installments with interest (EMI) of the loan amount were repaid, and a total period of 20 years was fixed for repayment. The interest rate decreases with each payment. The more you pay, the lower the interest rates.

Achayan's monthly letters included regular reminders for the housing loan repayment- "It was time to pay off the loan installment (EMI with interest) to the society in Thakazhi." The longer the delay in payment, the higher the penalty interest became. If we fail three or four times, they will be ready to issue notice to confiscate the property and the house per the loan terms. Achayan went to their office several times, paid a small amount, and got further permission to delay payment. "I will go again next time after your letter arrives."

The financial crisis was making life miserable for everyone.

49. HONEYMOON - THROUGH THE MONUMENTS

We got married, I have salaried employment, and we have a house to stay in, cook, eat, and sleep in. So when you got the freedom, did we, too, feel like celebrating and roaming around like everyone else? With financial hardships always occupied in mind, family life can be disrupted. Things went on, waiting for a good time for each celebration. There came an opportunity when I was required to travel to Delhi for a week's temporary assignment for college work. Thambichan had complained that we could not stay together for at least a full day after getting married in the church at the same time. To find a favourable solution, go to Xavier's and Thambichan's residences and stay with them for a few days. There was a sincere invitation to visit Cuttack, Bhubaneswar, the ships, the seashore, and the port. Seeing this as a good opportunity, I imagined this as a honeymoon trip and got ready. Going to Delhi on duty does not cost much. Travelling and living with a spouse will reduce costs. If you go to Delhi, there is always Kuriachan; in Paradip, there is Thambichan. So there were no extra expenditures. We must find time and take the trouble of travelling in the peak summer through North India.

March is the hottest month in all regions of northern India. Poona - Delhi - Cuttack - Paradip - Bhubaneswar - Kharagpur - Nagpur - Poona, itinerary for a month, relatives, sights, friendships, many experiences. Lots of time we could be together. If our life began to flourish, there might not be another chance to avail like this.

We arrived in Delhi on Holy Wednesday, just before Easter. In front of his house in Kirtinagar, Kuriachan came down with the children and waited on the road to receive us. It has been less than a month since chechi gave birth to their third son. Dennis and Davis were standing to the left and right of Kuriachan, with Diaz lying on his shoulder.

I came to Delhi to see whether the college trainees had reached their allotted companies and whether the training had started properly. I came to Delhi as a honeymoon tourist, but I had to do some work to justify my official responsibility. So, in the afternoon, I went to work.

"Kunjunjamme, when he had been here before, never returned until ten o'clock. Today, you will see him back in not half an hour, in twenty-nine minutes."

Leelamma liked Kuriachan's humour. I was a little late to get up on the Passover Thursday morning, and Kuriachan's inducements woke me up. "Is he going to the office? Is it like this every day, Eda Oommacha? Is 'one of your nine' got closed?"

Chechi served a sweet pudding after lunch. Leelamma was sad that she did not get the 'Passover milk' on the Passover Thursday evening. Kuriachan teased chechi by telling her that she did not know how to boil the

coconut milk for the Passover celebration. Chechi's reply - "Achaya, please get up and go to the urinal. Come and sleep!" made Leelamma laugh.

On Good Friday, we attended the Gol-Dak-Khana Church for the Worship services, prayer, and religious observance of 'The Way of the Cross.

We wanted to go sightseeing on Saturday morning. We went to the New Delhi Railway Station to book the train tickets to Agra. We walked around Connaught Place and the Kamala Market. We saw gardens and groves, a rose garden, astronomical observatories in the Jantar Mantar, the world's tallest brick tower, Qutub Minar, the centuries-old iron pillars, the Rashtrapati Bhavan and the Parliament.

At Qutub Minar

After a long walk around the Teen Murti Bhavan, we came across the Nehru Museum, the Nehru Jyoti, and the Nehru-grown Red Rose Garden, from which he always wore a rose on his coat. To make the visit unforgettable, we took a photograph in front of the house at Teen Murthy.

We got up early. We went to bed early, saying we should see Red Fort and the Samadhis (tombs) in the morning. I woke up on Monday morning to hear Kuriachan ask, "Kunjunjamme; by this time, they might have reached Redfort, have they?"

Connaught place, Gandhi Samadhi, Raj Ghat, Jantar Mantar

On that day, we saw the Red Fort and its surroundings and the banks of the river Yamuna. We visited the final resting places of Mahatma Gandhi, Jawaharlal Nehru, and Lal Bahadur Shastri, the great personalities of Indian politics and history. One by one, we visited their Samadhis (tombs) on the banks of the Yamuna, placed flowers, and paid our homages.

The Sound and Light Show at the Red Fort dramatically presented the Mughal historical events and stories of the Indian freedom struggle with the help of sound and light for an hour. The Red Fort in Delhi is not only a prominent structure of the past but an equally important place even at present. It is the place from where the Prime Minister of India hoists the national flag every year on Independence Day. This has been the tradition since the year of independence in 1947.

We witnessed and participated in the Holi celebrations of Delhi. Women from the neighboring houses came in groups and applied different colours to the bodies and faces of their friends. They went inside the house and applied colours on the face of chechi chechi. They threw water-filled balloons at their friends.

One day, we went to Agra - to see the marble monument of eternal love. Can it be said to be the symbol of everlasting love? It is a tomb built by Emperor Shah Jahan in memory of his wife, who died after she delivered her 14th baby. Nearby was the emperor's final resting place, too. Leelamma and I sat there and travelled through history.

The couple at the Taj Mahal

The pillars were carved in white marble, with a hemispherical dome at the top and the tombs directly below. The calm Yamuna River flowed at the back, a fountain was found in the front, and green lawns were all around. The Taj Mahal is considered by many to be the shrine of eternal love, considered one of the wonders of the world. We also enjoyed its unspeakable beauty and took photos to remember our visit.

Leelam at the Taj

Using the entry pass given by a Member of the Parliament, we saw the Lok Sabha proceedings sitting in the visitors' gallery. Getting the entry pass itself was an extraordinary event. We saw the residences of the MPs while walking on the road; they were lined up, and we were looking for a Malayalee name to approach. The name of Janardhanan was seen in the front of the houses. We went inside the compound, in front of the house, and rang the bell. The door opened, and we saw an older person, an asthma patient. We greeted him and expressed our desire to meet the MP. He called us inside.

"We would like to visit the Lok Sabha during the session. We would like to have a pass?"

"Are you recently married?" He asked, trembling and in a feeble voice.

"Did you come to see Delhi? Well done, come on, sit down! Good that you thought of witnessing the commotion in the house. "

He did not say, ' But you should not do so in your house.'

He agreed to get us a pass for an hour to view the proceedings in the Lok Sabha.

"It is enough that you come to the Parliament reception in the morning, and you can collect the pass from there. I will give it there for you."

That's how we got the pass.

We went into the canteen for the members of Parliament and drank tea. After the security check, we went inside the Parliament and witnessed the house proceedings. We saw leaders and ministers in the house, including Prime Minister Indira Gandhi and many other MPs. Surprisingly, there was no commotion in the Lok Sabha on that day and time.

We went to Krishi Bhavan and bought vegetable seeds. Leelamma needed spinach seeds. We were shown and got seeds for the 'Ladies' fingers and beans. The officials who sold the seeds did not know what the spinach was, even though we said it was black and small and like mustard seeds directly obtained from spinach flowers! Maybe the north Indians knew it as the palak, and only Keralites knew it as the red spinach (cheera)!

Delhi Bird Sanctuary was famous for the presence of various species of birds and animals. The next day, we saw some walking around there. We visited the Birla Mandir, where Mahatma Gandhiji used to go daily for prayer meetings.

The national capital, Delhi, is a popular tourist destination. It is a storehouse of various attractive sights. The old mansions of the Mughal Empire, the Parliament, the South Block, the North Block, the Rashtrapati Bhavan, the city's never-ending crowds, the wide roads, the uninterrupted flow of vehicles on the streets, trees, flowers, fountains, and gardens everywhere. Modern buildings with many floors are the first signs of development, as well as good, clean roads, bridges, double-decker buses, people moving around, historical monuments, areas, and surroundings that stay in mind for a long time.

India Gate is one of the most critical landmarks where any Indian should stand and salute with thoughts of patriotism. It is the largest war memorial in the world, with 13,516 soldiers' names written on the stone walls. India Gate is also the starting point of many major roads in Delhi. The main street, Rajpath, ends at the Rashtrapati Bhavan. The 'Amar Jawan Jyoti' is a flame that always burns and is situated on the side of an iconic inverted rifle and the soldier's war helmet, the symbol of fallen soldiers of 1971, under the stone arch of the India Gate.

We had seen many such sights, but we had not seen enough. Even in the evenings, the day temperature was high and unbearable. We returned home, saying we would later see what was left out.

By the time we came back from the sightseeing tour, we were exhausted. However, we wanted to pack everything so that in the early morning of the next day, we could leave for Bhuvaneswar by train.

Leelamma sat down and opened our suitcase to pack - Kuriachan used to make fun of her squatting position on the floor whenever she was sitting. "Someone is sitting to sell bangles !"

Staying with chechi and Kuriachan for a few days in Delhi was a good training ground for us as we started our family life. How to keep moving on with the days of laughter amid adversity, take care of and raise three children of not much age difference, look after household chores, prepare food for all and make everyone happy, make everyone laugh equally, laugh together, so what kind of training from an elder brother!

The first thing that came to my mind was realising "how to raise three children." No, we never planned that. However, God might have shown all this as an example to follow or imitate in our future life.

One day, Kuriachan's friend 'Oommachan' from Chengannur (Alleppey Dist) came and asked, "Kuriachan, what can I do to stop my child from breastfeeding?"

Oommachan worked with Kuriachan at Rail Bhavan. The two were together earlier in Assam. They are not married, then.

"Eda - then you go .., why are you going too far.... Why don't you go and tie a string tight at the bottleneck? -"

"Are you kidding, Achaya? The child is now three years old. Shouldn't breastfeeding be stopped if we want to have another child?"

Kuriachan thought it over for a while. Then he told him.

"You go to an ayurvedic herbal pharmacy shop - this is the herb shop where you get this "Kadukkai" (in Tamil & Malayalam, "Harad" in Hindi and Urdu), and "Kalkandam" (White sugar rock candy, 'Khadi Sakhar' in Hindi) - go there and buy some 'Chenninayakam' (dried Aloe Vera gum, one of the most bitter-tasting herbal medicines) and apply it on the bottleneck. It is a little hard to grind, and you do grind it because it is like stone. But with bitterness, it will have the desired effect."

Oommachan went to the shop to buy herbal medicine. He drove eight kilometers on a scooter, and when he found the shop, he forgot the name of the herbal medicine. In any case, the shop owner should know, and he ventured in asking. But, -

How do you say 'Chenninayakam' in Hindi?

The shopkeeper in Karol Bagh did not know the Malayalam word. Oommachan was new to this place; it had been only one year since he came to Delhi, and he had not learned Hindi so much. But one must try to communicate well in Hindi-

"ഏ .. ഏക് മാക്‌കാ ദൂധ് ബന്‌ദ് കർനവോല മഡൈിസിൻ ..."

(E… ek maa ka doodh band karnevala davayi)

They did not understand. Oommachan explained.

"കാലാ ഹ, പഥർ ജൈസാ ഹേ, മാ കാ ദൂധ് ബന്ദ് കർണേവാലാ ഹേ..."

(It is black, like a stone. It stops breastfeeding for the baby)

They did not beat him. Nor did they quarrel with him. Oommachan waited for a while. When it was time to close the shop, the shopkeeper told him -

"യഹാം നഹി ഹെ. ഹം ദൂകാൻ ബന്ദ് കർണേവാലാ ഹേ."

(The herb is not here. We are going to close the shop for the day.)

Oommachan should have approached Kuriachayan again to get the prescription for the herb. The herb might have been purchased. That is why Kuriachan and chechi went to the baptism of Chengannur Oommachan's second child!

We all sat down together to say that the trip to Delhi and our stay there were delightful. We thanked Chechi particularly. We shared our experiences. Kuriachan had come to sit on the bed. Everyone ate, put away all the dishes, and washed their faces. Chechi came and sat next to Kuriachan, thinking she could sit and take a rest. That's when Kuriachan made his comment again!

"Kunjunjamme, you move a little away so I can take a breath!

After three deliveries, Chechi had gained some weight.

The train journey from Delhi to Bhubaneswar was less congested. The summer heat was intense. There was nothing worth remembering except the diverse wayside sights and nature.

When the train stopped at a sparsely populated inland railway station, a boy selling rural agricultural produce boarded the train with a load of drumsticks. No one was interested in buying it because they were all long-distance travellers. I just asked about the price. A bundle costs 25 paise and contains about 50 large drumsticks. The boy has the physical capacity to carry a total of four piles. I bought all the bundles for one rupee. The boy happily left. When counted, there were 220, all fresh and had no damage. When we reached Bhubaneswar, I took the bundles of drumsticks (Muringakka) and handed them to Thambichan. Thambichan and Xavier were very happy to share it. Usually, I did not go to the market to buy vegetables. Here, I have purchased more than two hundred drumsticks for one rupee. The matter was the subject of amusing discussion among us for a long time.

Cuttack can be reached by crossing the Mahanadi River through the medium of a three km-long railway bridge. Even for the people of Kuttanad, who have seen many small bridges and streams, the Mahanadi and the bridge had terrific views.

Thambichan and Xavier greeted us warmly at the railway station and picked us up. Gracy and three-month-old Joe were at Xavier's home at first. In the afternoon, a hundred km journey on Bhubaneswar-Paradip Road took us to where Thambichan lived in the Port Trust Quarters. The Port of Paradip was the largest, built since independence, with the main activity being the export of minerals such as iron ore and mined minerals to foreign countries. It has extensive storage capacity, cranes, and docking docks for loading and unloading. The staff was provided accommodation and other essential living facilities such as a school, college, and market.

Cyclones and tsunamis, over some time, have plagued the coasts of Orissa.

The highlight of our first Paradip Yatra was gathering three sibling families at the beginning of their family life, participating in daily activities, sightseeing, and enjoying splendidly for a week.

The summer heat continued to be strong, causing minor ailments for us. One of Paradip's most memorable sights was the Olive Ridley Coastal invasion. Each tortoise weighed up to 50 kg and was the size of a large natural Bamboo-woven coconut basket. The seafront near Paradip was home to the world's largest turtle sanctuary. As the day's temperature slowed, thousands of turtles flocked to the shore from the sea. The tropical climate was the main driving force behind this phenomenon. They came to dig holes in the coastal soil and lay their eggs. Soil-covered eggs hatch in about 70 days, and the young hatch moves into the sea. This phenomenon coincides in harmony with the reproduction of nature. Olive Ridley turtles are an endangered species.

We returned from Bhubaneswar to Poona via Kharagpur. In Kharagpur, we had to walk around the bazaar near the railway station for some time before we changed trains. And we saw the native Bengalis.

Returning to Poona, we straightened out our work and household chores and started weaving dreams of life.

The doctor in Cuttack had expressly advised Leelamma to see a gynaecologist when it was convenient while giving her medications to reduce the urinary tract infection, which started in the day's heat.

Accordingly, we visited the Ruby Hall Clinic, one of Pune's best multispeciality hospitals, and saw the doctor. Dr Sathe announced that a new life had begun to sprout within Leelamma. They were moments of fulfillment—the most crucial and indescribable moment. The focal point of life's mission, vision, and journey begins here. It is the signal of the green light for the smooth path that any man sees in front, especially the family who strive to fulfill life's ultimate mission. It is a moment at which God bestows honor and dignity on the parents' lives while entrusting them with specific duties and noble responsibilities.

Being a mother is one of the most exciting adventures of life. Bringing a new life to the world's light will get you many challenges. You will realize that all these encounters were so precious. Dr Sathe explained everything to Leelamma as if it were the announcement of Archangel Gabriel to Mary, the mother of Jesus.

The joy of a mother begins when that little heartbeat begins inside the baby. It also reminds the mother that she is not alone in facing this life when she gets a pat on the back of the baby's foot and knows the movement. So, Dr Sathe scheduled the first abdominal ultrasound to check for signs of a healthy, developing pregnancy.

50. THE PULSE OF NEW LIFE

In the excitement of being a parent, there were preparations instead of playing fun games and avoiding adventures. Relatives were informed of the good news. Every month, we visited Ruby Hall and received and obeyed all beneficial advice lovingly and caringly given. Friends kept on visiting, and we, too, received their hospitality.

The state of emergency came into effect across the country during one of the most controversial periods in the history of independent India. The state of emergency was imposed by President Fakhruddin Ali Ahmed and promulgated by Prime Minister Indira Gandhi, citing the internal unrest of the nation. It was under Article 352 of the Constitution and remained there from June 25, 1975, until March 21, 1977.

The emergency allowed for the cancellation of elections and the suspension of civil liberties. Most of Indira Gandhi's political opponents were imprisoned. Many old political leaders vacated the festival grounds and retired from public life. Many human rights violations were reported, including a massive sterilisation campaign led by Indira Gandhi's son, Sanjay Gandhi.

Restrictions on democratic practices and the media were strict. Although it did not affect the everyday life of the people, insecurity prevailed throughout the country. Although young Turks were active in the national parties, many suffocated within the emergency walls. In the ensuing 6th Lok Sabha elections, the Janata Party came to power, and Morarji Desai became the Prime Minister.

Tony was commissioned to be born in India when the emergency was in effect. Let the time prove whether it was a birth of any political significance. The Almighty had decided whether the human incarnation would occur in Poona or a government hospital established by his grandfather and friends in our native. Leelamma was familiar with the modern facilities at the hospital in Poona. Sathe spoke about it on one occasion when she went for a check-up. Yet Leelamma repeatedly expressed her desire to go home earlier, saying that her mother's presence during and after childbirth would greatly relieve her.

Only a woman can become a mother. A mother trained more than once can give her daughter the most confidence and wealth of experience. State-of-the-art equipment and scientific knowledge can be emphasised after the mother's presence. Men can do nothing more than make an opinion. It is also the best risk management for your mind. There was nothing but the mother's presence beyond her desire and self-confidence. In light of experience, such decisions may sometimes be questioned and postponed. Yet, when the lack of knowledge becomes an obstacle to understanding future instability, that was the default, and it always remained dependable.

Thambichan and Leelamma decided to do the same, though we had no consultation. That, too, became another driving force. Mothers are the first to find meaning in their existence and achieve ultimate objectives through their daughters. They see the extension of their life through their grandchildren born to their daughters.

That's how we decided to go home in October 1975. I took leave after the pooja holidays in October. At about the same time, Thambichan and Leelamma also reached home.

When a child is born, the rule regarding paternity leave being granted to male government employees did not exist. Therefore, you must take extra leave to stay in the hospital during childbirth. Hence, the male members of the families returned to work. Pregnant women remained in expectation with their mothers for the arrival of the newborns.

I returned to Poona, intending to be in exile for another three months. I cooked myself, slept alone, and went to work. The social restrictions at that time did not allow a young mother to live with her husband for at least 56 days after childbirth. So I planned more vacation days to go earlier than the due date and return much later, hoping she would not return to Poona immediately after giving birth and after Christmas but within that duration.

Before applying for leave, I was unexpectedly instructed to go to Delhi on temporary duty. I had to go for the work-related training of students. Such instructions should not be ignored, especially in military discipline, culture, system, and code of conduct.

The government regularly pays salaries to the employees to keep aside personal matters and to execute the jobs given by the higher authorities under any circumstances. You joined for work, agreeing to that. Any leave would be granted only after considering the individual exigencies; the authorities should feel that the leave is unavoidable for the individual. Leave will be given only if the authorities are convinced that the leave is essential because of personal needs. Therefore, per the rules, leave is not a right or privilege but a desirable employee benefit, advantage, or perk.

Then, if you want to continue working tomorrow, it is better to follow the authorities' instructions without applying for leave. No matter how lovingly and eagerly they wait, those who stay must understand or be made to understand it lovingly.

Narakathra Kuttappan and his pregnant wife are coming to Kirkee MH to deliver their first child. Narakathra Kuttappan had come and informed me that he needed temporary accommodation.

My rented house with two bedrooms, a kitchen, a verandah, and some space outside would be comfortable for them to stay in for as long as there was no one else but me alone. That's what the native understood and asked me. Kuttappan was not the one who had pre-planned accordingly. Everything happens, and the one who controls everything is given complete freedom. We can make wise decisions. Narakathra Kuttappan and his pregnant wife had arrived before I left for Delhi. They could reach MH within 3 minutes when needed. They would have to go to the military hospital in a month. Aren't we obliged to assist the natives when such convenience was available so close?

I went to Delhi after wishing them a peaceful stay and a comfortable delivery when the time came. I had dinner with them on that day.

I went to Delhi and stayed with Kuriachan for a month. When I returned to Poona after work, Appachi and Thankamma Veluthedath came to my house and started living there. Narakathra Kuttappan and his wife moved to MH, and "They had twins," Appachi told me. The next day, Kuttappan came and gave us sweets. Thankamma mainly cooked food in the kitchen. The rest of the time, they were mostly confined to the room where Appachi and Thankamma were limited to writing letters, reading, and conversing. Once they got the quarters to stay in, they moved there. It was convenient for Thankamma to study, apply for a job, and move around occasionally and for Appachi to attend his job at MES.

Those who have adequate ability and have worked for a long time in an organization were not paid enough and were not considered for progress in their career, so they usually try for better jobs in other institutions.

Who doesn't desire so? After working in our establishment for seven to fifteen years, we have submitted petitions to the authorities to make some progress and financial gain in our careers. The authorities did not respond favourably or show any inclination to consider our grievances. Then we, who had worked in the same college for less than ten years, decided with one mind that we could go out and accept any suitable job that gave us career progress, and we began our efforts.

Swamy, who was my colleague, was lucky in his first attempt. Swamy was selected as an Assistant Professor at the Naval College of Engineering, Lonavala. Swamy went away. He got married and lived and worked in Lonavala. I learned that his son became an officer in the Indian Navy after his engineering degree, bought a private flat, and lived there happily.

Ramachandran from Palakkad returned after a heart operation and subsequent rest. Chandran came with two good news.

One – He got a new job as a Senior Engineer at Instrumentation Ltd, Palakkad. Two - He got engaged to a girl from a Coimbatore family, and she was born and brought up in Singapore.

Joe, Tony, Saaji during visit to Pune H-Type Qtrs

Ramachandran also left CME. He was the one who cooperated with me more lovingly than anyone else and shared good thoughts. I experienced a big gap when he went home for the progress of his career and life. I lost contact with close friends in my daily life. Ramachandran left for home, saying he would come to see me whenever he could. After marriage, he would stay in Palakkad. He ordered me like a brother – "You, Nasrani, shall come with your family to my house in Palakkad."

51. LOVE LETTERS

Two or three months was a time of great open-minded hope. Below is a summary of the writings of a prospective father waiting for the arrival of the new generation in the countryside and the child's birth for the expectant mother. It was not intended that the soft feel of men and women would not be reflected in writing; it is only natural that the priorities of those waiting for the new generation would change. Beyond everyday events and spatial and environmental information, letters and testimonials were full of hope and openness to new life. Nothing was wrong if anyone said this was my love letter. Let it be presented here in its original style.

November 01, 1975

This loneliness is brutal.

I went to Kirkee bazaar yesterday and did a great job; He did the remaining of what you did. What did I say? Oh, what a tube light! You didn't realise that – I had my haircut.

I bought a photo frame from the bazaar and put a photo of the girl and her husband in it. I am worshipping with bright marigold flowers, just like the ones in our garden. Maybe I will put a rose flower in it today...

When I come home here, I keep saying something in my mind since I don't have anybody to talk to. A couple of times, I laughed to myself foolishly. You sit in the framed photo and laugh when I look at it.

We both have stomach problems; now, it's food for me. For you, it is ... nghoom!

One day, I went out to a restaurant for food. I stopped going there again. On the second day, I went to the old mess and asked if I could get some rice - "Sir, the rice got over." I went straight to the room after hearing that.

I said I don't need any help from him. I cooked rice and ate; it was three o'clock. The following day, I put water on the stove to boil immediately after I got up. The rice was cooked while I was bathing. "Cool down here when I go to the office until I return." Then I went to the office.

Jomon began to walk. Patti Amma was put on the train to Nilgiris. Your 'Mamma' in the neighbourhood has a fever for a day or two. Thankachi and his family came from the native. Thankachi was hospitalised in Ruby Hall for three or four days with chest pain.

November 08, 1975

Today is Friday.

There were three or four ripe guavas in the guava tree. And I felt to snatch them up.

'I would have had to write that I got my loved one's letter when I was at the top of the guava tree' - If I had done that.

I was waiting for the postman as it was Monday, and the day also ended. Tuesday, I felt uneasy. I was disappointed by the end of the day, Wednesday. By Thursday evening, my eyes began to redden with severe difficulty. I exited the office and determined that if I did not get the letter, I would burn the tubes in the paper pocket and go to bed without dinner. While entering our house, I saw the envelope with the unique stamp on the verandah!

My beloved's first letter was as sweet as the first kiss.

When the postal worker arrives, I should give him Diwali baksheesh. I thought he might be riding a bicycle without seeing me and with letters addressed to me.

When I returned from the office, I did not go to pluck guava from the guava tree or anywhere; I looked at the door and the road, listened to the bicycle bell, and stayed there for four days. If I start plucking the guava, and then if he comes and goes away without seeing me? No, if he puts the letter on the verandah and quickly moves away and leaves -

If Brother asks, "Didn't you receive your sreemathy's letter? When did it come?

Well, Yes, Bother, it came. Shouldn't I say It came while I was sitting on the branch of the guava tree? It is not good. It does not sound well.

I have to put on the shirt, give a rupee note, and receive the letter auspiciously...

I'm writing this with your framed photo in front of me. Even otherwise, my heart and mind are the whole of you!

I can sit like this for as long as you wish.

As for my routine, this is the only possibility. Close both your eyes for some time and walk through the courtyard. Do you feel any difficulty? That's what my routines are now. I am not at home, not in a mess, not in the lodge.

Appachi had come on Tuesday. He brought the wood for the big bed of good width. For the mother and baby to lie down. He slept with me. I said something in sleep, laughed, and preached all night until dawn in the dream and my subconscious mind. I don't know if Appachi heard it or not! Let him know what he may think, probably because your letter came on Monday. But yesterday, nothing of that sort happened.

My usual routine- morning duties and breakfast are over.

I will have tea with the bread added to the Avalos. After pouring the rice, I take the bowl for milk, lock the door, and go to the mamma next door to hand it over.

"Oh, you got the girl's letter, haven't you? I can see it on your face." (She did not say in so many words that – 'I heard the jumps and commotions in the nearby house!)

"Isn't your better half happy and well? Say to her that I'm not in good health. I have a fever and a mild cough. When you write, write mamma's inquiries also."

"I can write, mamma."You also wrote that I am going back to Calicut on the twenty-third.

"Yes, Mamma". Well, the milkman comes late nowadays. I'll buy a little water and add one tablespoon before boiling.

"Well, Mamma, it's time for me to go to the office. " An escape.

When I come in the afternoon, I make the buttermilk and add ginger, green chilies, and curry leaves! (curry stalk) -

Two pieces of fish curry were in a glass bowl – oh! It was a Diwali holiday on Monday. When I saw your Machiwala on the road, I called him to come here – one pomfret. He said - "You don't buy more. Did Bai go home?" I said I did not send her home. I had gone home with her; she wanted to be with her parents, so I left her behind and returned. Not like his wife, who runs away after a fight! "Okay, you go; let me make some fish curry!"

Today, after the exam, when I returned, three letters were waiting on the verandah for me—all in stamped envelopes.

When is the arrival of the new generation? There is someone here who always laughs at anything within the frame. If you ask anything, it will laugh. Glad to know the news from there. My mouth was full of saliva, and why not if you keep saying, ' Duck Curry in a coconut milk gravy! This Kuttanadan style curry makes a lip-smacking side dish with Appam.' Did you ever think about what's going on here?

You said it was attached to the letter! I swept the room entirely and searched for it. I didn't see it. Are you kidding me? Suddenly, I remembered a card game that we played with bets! Who won it?

On Sunday, there were two carpenters, and the work began on making the table and the queen bed. What was my mother running about when there were carpenters in the house for some work - that's precisely happening right here. I made morning tea for them, went to the bazaar, bought fish, made curry, and cooked rice; Appachi and I had lunch. The carpenters had brought chapatis. I gave them fish and rice. Appachi enjoyed the 'fish curry' even though he commented it was not as good as the 'chechi's' curry.'

Are they in the beach hospital at Alleppey, where my sister and mother are? Tell our mother to send a telegram to my residential address in Poona.

Ramachandran's letter was there, saying, 'When writing a love letter to your partner, add Ramachandran's Ramayana too without breaking the rhyme.' He is taking a rest at Palakkad after undergoing a successful heart operation. His relative cousins gave birth to a male child in Bombay and a female child in the native. There were more to come, ...

November 25, 1975

There is a new table and glass on top, and I am looking at your photo and writing this; all these are good fun and allow me to play on the harp!

When I went to church and returned in the evening, there was no electricity, so I sat down and played with Jomon. "Papa," "went away," and "Tata" are the words Jomon spoke, and "Namaste" he showed up.

When I returned home, I was in a good mood to study. I sat down and read for four hours. I wrote the exam this morning. I went there with the thought of returning after collecting the question paper. When I read it sitting there, most of the questions were for the answers I had read the previous day. I wrote for 65 marks.

Saji Mol was born on November 19, Indira Gandhi's birthday. Despite the Emergency, Indira Gandhi was a great, assertive lady. Yesterday, I saw all the joy of being a grandfather in Achayan's letter. I Hope Leelamma and the baby are fine. Double praise to you, oh Lord, for granting the remaining events more beautiful and exciting!

Often, these days, I used to wait for the postman to bring in a telegram. My anxieties and hopes for this waiting cannot be explained in words! I don't know for what. I cry alone and pray emotionally.

Lord, it's only a week more before the due date. My brother asked me when the next Kartika Star day was. You got it? Jomon was born on Kartika, Thambichan's baby girl was Kartika, and the next Kartika is only on 16th Dec. I said - "Let us see if there will be another good day before that"!

Aren't the pills and the tonic all over? You must get it through Babu and drink a lot of milk. How can you tell Babu that you wanted Cadbury chocolate? Who else will buy it? Even if I buy chocolate, will it not melt by the time when I come? The necessity will also be over by then. Well, that's a good question - why do you need chocolate?

That, that .. I'll tell you before your next delivery, okay? You try without chocolate this time.

However, It is sad. You told me to drink fresh, cold water this winter and stay cool and calm! Did Chechi teach you this in Delhi? Let me ask!

Mamma went away on Sunday. She specifically told me to write her inquiry to you. "Mr Thomas, then let me go." She showed her her hand while sitting in the taxi - an exhausted, worn-out, wrinkled hand with long fingers! However, there was a smile and hope on that bright face.

I still shook my head when I washed and put rice in the boiling water. When I looked back, you ran away; you ran and got into the frame of the photo and laughed.

Nowadays, Lata buys milk for me. Lata's grandmother asked me- "Chitti ala ka"?

I said - "Ala, Changli ahe."

"Bur".

What does Achayan say about the horoscope? Isn't Rosamma's first holy communion on the eighth of this month? Did you attach the embroidered band to her knit top dress? Has she got the desired shoes? Hope Mercy is regularly praying the 'Novena of Mother of Perpetual Help!

December 01, 1975

We have a son, my son, our son. It has been four hours since I received the telegram. I was running around; happily, I went to Brother. I went to the bazaar, bought peda sweets, and gave them to everyone. I gave it to you, too, and I ate. After many months of longing, a minor miracle is born, and a new life begins. There is no better thought than to feel like I am a parent. The child is part of us. Another human being with whom we are in a stable relationship in this life. A new human life is generated out of our bodies, and it is a life embodied with our energies. It has an independent mind and soul granted by the creator and a physical likeness to his parents. Congratulations, my congratulations, comrade, a kiss on your cheek, a warm and passionate kiss!

Did you read my letter and set out to deliver the baby? I'm coming soon. This 'Oommachan' is running and coming to provide a thousand ummas to my Leelamma and our beloved child. This is one of the most incredible days of our lives.

The postman came and called out to me, 'Telegram.' I signed for receipt and read the entire content without opening it. I remembered the moment of tying the gold pendant, in which the symbol of the cross is embedded, around your neck. It was hung on a string made from the seven threads of the Mantrakodi. I placed the saree over your head.

Like a solemn prayer and praises to God, I opened the envelope and read. I sent the postman away with a gift and did something with joy and happiness. I felt like announcing to everyone. We are mom and dad!

A mother and a father are born when a child is born and accepted into the family. The birthday of the first child is also the parents' joint birthday. There are no separate birthdays for just any one of us.

It was the happiest moment, the occasion, and the happiest day. Could there be a better or similar time in this human life to think so? There will be, yes, though rarely, shall write anything when it comes to mind. Or when there are more such moments.

December 01 was the day I got a job nine years ago, and it was the day the new generation - our son - was born. It is the inspiration for our future life. Like the sun that gives us the light, a son is born to us; a new light is given to us that inspires the rest of our lives, pointing out meaning, purpose, and quality.

The telegram came as I was getting ready to get under woolen clothes for bed rest due to a severe cold and cough. Isn't it so how men experience labour pains? It would help if you conveyed the 'this father' inquiries to all.

It's been nine years since I got the job on December 01. This is the main achievement of nine years - a baby and a mother, Praise God. Jomon's birthday was celebrated on November 29. Today, I had food at their home, and I came back and am writing this. With love and hugs...

December 10, 1975

The name of this place, Poona, has been changed to Pune.

I got the third Dec letter from there. There was a significant concern. You be a father and be there one thousand five hundred kilometers away, and only then will you know your feelings. When is the baptism ceremony? Who are the godparents? Everything I can visualize, count the hours, and trust in God with great expectations.

I am worried. I will not get leave and go home as I have to go to Delhi with the students. I would have read your letter and been satisfied if I had gotten it. I would be happy if you could sit and write at least four lines. Did Rosamma receive the holy communion? Did she go after confession? Then, did she pray to Jesus for all of us? How are Leelamma and the baby? Who baptized the baby to Christianity?

What is our son doing? Is he sleeping? You can see the mother's habits in him, this siesta or catnap!

You might not be taking salt and sour after childbirth. I remember when I made fish curry and ate food.

As Dr Sathe mentioned, I hope you continue to avoid foods like cakes and fried things, which cause weight gain. Processed foods and drinks like coffee crash dieting and fruit, as well as vegetable-only diets, can affect the baby's development, causing problems like weak immunity or slow recovery after childbirth. So, they must also be avoided.

If you feel sad or empty, it must go away within a few days of giving birth, or depression may come, which is not good. Be cheerful always. We have got a great gift from God.

When Appachi came over the other day, we cooked rice and fried sardines. Lord, cutting and cleaning the sardines was the most demanding job. The whole hand became wet with ghee.

Do you know how many people have congratulated us or sent us loved inquiries and congratulatory messages? If I write their names, the 'Inland' pages might not be sufficient. Everyone we know ....

No letter came during the following fifteen days. Achayan had written in a few words that both the Leelammas who gave birth were ill and were relieved with treatment and prayers. When I went home on vacation, I realized the illness and suffering that Leelamma had undergone. She never wrote to me again anything. The following is what Leelamma told me briefly when I saw her in person.

As the scheduled time for delivery approached, she was taken to the nearby Primary Health Centre. At that time, there were no trained doctors or equipment for intensive care in the hospital. The primary health care center operated without even a trained nurse. She waited for hours in the labour room, tolerating the pain of childbirth - I am told that the pain felt like "extreme menstrual cramps that take your breath away." Twelve hours later – the elders almost decided to take her somehow to the Alappuzha District Hospital, maybe in a Canoe- to be propelled for about 12 km by paddling.

While they were running around to arrange it and while our mothers were singing the praises of the opening of heaven - it was time for the new life to be born. "There should be a song for women to sing or a prayer to recite. But perhaps there is none because there are no strong words to name that moment." A New life was born.

What is that praise of God - something like this - in the language of their hearts, the words that wet their faces and minds, looking up to the heights -

"Silent night, holy night, All is calm, all is bright," bonny boy Thomas, so tender and mild. –"Guardian angels, do not close your eyes ... The baby slumbers in his cradle cloth. .... Oh Guardian angels, .." (Sujatha Mohan, Lyrics AJ Joseph)

On the twelfth day after the child's birth, my cousin Kunjamma and her husband Anthonichan took the child to the church for the sacrament of Baptism. They went to Champakulam by paddling in a Canoe. It took four or five hours to get back after the ceremony. Throughout that time, No one remembered that the baby would be hungry without breast milk.

During the difficult time of hardship, the fact that the baby's father did not go from Delhi to see the baby or even for the baby's baptism ceremony - the naming ceremony justifiably upset Leelamma. There was no one to comfort her. The "baby blues" went away within a few days of giving birth, but postpartum days were an extended time of sorrow and hardships for more than a month.

On the twenty-seventh day after the child's birth, a black or red cotton thread needs to be tied around the waist of the child (Aranjanacharadu)- a custom known in Malayalam as 'Twenty-eighth-day thread.' It was tied around the baby's waist.

Ottathyckal Achayan and Ammachi went on a pilgrimage to Velankanni Church with the Xavier-Gracy family. That night, Leelamma started having a fever, which was intense. There was no one at home even to give food. Apart from fever, swelling and pain in her breasts made breastfeeding the child difficult. Unable to go to the hospital without a boat or a man to paddle the boat, unable to make contact with anyone in the middle of a flooded field, and unable to breastfeed the baby. The Ottathyckal Babichan, too, could not do anything and was upset. He went at night and narrated the difficulties. The next day, my mother from Kannattumadom came and knew the difficulties. She brought the baby and the mother to the hospital for a consultation, bought medicine, and took them home. The pilgrims knew of the events when they arrived after five days. They came to see Leelamma, who was being treated at the hospital again due to the fever and swelling of the breasts. Those were the days of agony, hardships, and great suffering for Leelamma and the baby.

It was that the circumstances were not favourable for us to avoid or reduce the hardships and suffering of my family. I was upset myself. By the grace and goodness of my parents, I did not blame anyone. I thanked everyone for their favours and support.

Leelam kept saying, "I carried a child within my body. I've slept with him on my chest. I kissed his toes and wiped away my tears. I took his vomit and pees on me and spent sleepless nights cradling my child. I would not have it any other way. My body is not perfect for a magazine, but I see a mama in the mirror. And there is no greater joy, honour, love or blessing."

My grandfather came to the hospital and saw the baby and the mother. When he picked up the baby and whispered something to him, the baby caught hold of his scapular (ventinga in Malayalam- is an object of popular piety; it reminds the wearers of their commitment to live a Christian life).

"That's what I've been waiting for, my son," the grandpa said, kissing the baby's forehead. Our Grandpa, a true disciple of Father Chavara Kuriakosesee Elias, who was later canonised as a saint, expired after blessing the firstborn of the fourth generation of his Kannattumadom family. As far as I know, it was my grandfather's last blessing and consolation words for our family. Neither my grandfather nor I have seen each other since then. Yet our Appan lives on in our memory forever! His blessings to our family will continue forever and for all generations. Sometimes, I remember the philosophical words that my grandpa once told me because of his devotion to spiritual things:-

"The less attention and interest we give to material things, the more pleasure we have. That is the truth."

Unaware of the seriousness of these matters at the native, I hoped to take leave and bring the baby and mother to Pune as soon as I returned from Delhi, so I continued my letters home.

December 18, 1975

I think our boy's baptism was celebrated well. I could visualise everything in my mind. May the God of you and me, our parents, our ancestors, and the God of love give our son longevity, health, and a promising future. I pray regularly.

I am going to Delhi on the 22nd. I will be in Delhi for a month and will stay with Kuriachan.

Mamma is coming to see you and the baby. Who will identify her? Someone should locate her with grey hair and white clothes, bespectacled and standing at the Alleppey bus stand. May she be taken home, given all the honour, and sent back safely.

This time, I have made a new design for the Christmas cards, a new handmade project. It uses the leaves and the flowers of the Christmas tree. A small bud and a flower are sent to our son and mother.

I'm looking for a proper name for our son .... I'll make a list, and after asking your opinion, we will decide. Until then, call him any name, whatever you think.

One Hundred sweet kisses.

52. ON THE ANNIVERSARY

January 09, 1976, Delhi

Yes, January 13 is our wedding anniversary. It's not our birthday, but it's our birthday together. It's the day we joined as one soul and one flesh; it is the birthday we celebrate together. From now on, it will be the days born out of us, like Dec 1. It's been a year. Let us celebrate our anniversary with memories, sweet thoughts, love, embraces of last year's experiences, and memories of our blessings. My memories and opinions are all around you. I'll be right back.

Remember January 13, 1975 - For the first time, we looked at each other with the thought that it was my husband, wife, and life partner. You placed your right hand in my hand. I tied the 'minnu' pendant on silk thread around your neck while you bowed your head, and then... then...

Everything that the Almighty predetermined made us experience it. Everything was an experience of goodness and love. They can be grown as evergreens and watered in our heart's garden.

It was early morning, and you were in the kitchen, sitting on the floor and having pazhamkanji. (The previous day's cooked rice soaked in plain water overnight, mixed with butter milk or curd, crushed green chilies, onions, ginger, and curry leaves, and added with enough salt is an excellent breakfast). You got up and looked at me. I came to sit over the storage box and have breakfast. I came to you, kissed you on your cheek, and behind me, you saw my mother coming with breakfast and coffee, looking at you and smiling. And you suddenly bowed your head, smiled, and were shy about looking at me. Do you remember? Do you know why that spontaneous act of romance? "Random acts of love give them that nudge that lets them know you appreciate them. It creates pleasure for the giver, this going-out-of-the-way to show affection, and offers pleasure to the receiver."

Why? Being such a good life partner for giving yourself to me......

Did my mother see and smile, looking at you? Is that so? It is okay; they will understand. I will still indulge in such mischiefs.

Every hug I give you will give an idea of the intensity of love I have for you.

As I was writing this, Chechi came and gave me tea and cut apples, saying - "Write and keep writing, lest you get tired."

I read 'This Stranger, My Son' (By Louise Wilson) in 'Readers Digest.' I liked the story very much, especially the name Tony. Tony's mother tells an unusually heartfelt tale. I was praying that our Tony would not be like that. Tony will grow up to be a unique person with a talented personality. It simply came to my notice then. I thought I would know your opinion and tell you. So we will call our son many names, and let us observe by hearing what name he will smile. What do you say?"

Blessed is every moment that we can serve Appan. Appan is the lamp of our house. That light will never be extinguished. Since I learned that Appan was not well, I was passing through a significant agony and feelings I could not express in words. I want to come home and see my grandfather soon, which would be a great blessing.

My grandfather once told me that he would leave this world only after he could put my son in a canoe, and he rowed the boat. Keeping that in mind, I look forward with hope, faith, and prayer. Appan would see our son grow up. My grandfather never said anything that was not possible. He has kept his word constantly. My grandfather told me that so sincerely and emotionally out of his heart. Take the baby and show him to the grandfather. It would be an excellent relief for Appan. Heaven and peace are at the feet of that grandpa. The blessing of the grandpa will always be upon us forever. It would be best if you went to our grandpa.

On one of these days, Leelamma went to Kannattumadom with the baby, as Appan expressed a desire to see the baby when he was sick in bed. After seeing the baby, Appan caressed and cuddled him on his chest. How happy Appan was!

The father laid the baby on his left side, blessed him by putting his hand on the baby's head, and prayed. As Tony grew up, those blessings from my paternal grandfather became a great asset for him.

Grandfather laid the baby on his left side, his hands on his head, and prayed. When Tony grew up, those blessings from my grandfather became a great asset for him.

While living in Delhi during those days, I found Kuriachan, chechi, their children (Dennis, Davis, Dias), and Thommachan, Kuriachan's younger brother, all very happy. Dias was nearly six months old. I see the image of our son in Dias. I often carry and play with him—what laughter and play he made. And Kuriachan's jokes were sometimes highly amusing.

When your letter came, I read out those portions to him, the portions even if our relatives came to know, there was no harm. It was only information passages for their benefit. Kuriachan joked, "You don't have to read out the whole lot; just tell me the information!"

Kuriachan's three friends gave birth to daughters at the end of December. Kuriachan says, "On these days, only the woodworms that make the exit holes are born." (Do you understand the joke? Where do you know the woodworm 'Paran' makes the exit holes?!

I hope that Gracy, Xavier, Achayan, and Ammachi have all returned from the pilgrimage to Velankanni. I will be coming in late Feb or early March. Be happy.

January 15, 1976

You must have received my letter on our wedding anniversary. That day, I was happy to be in a world of memories.

Appachi went home and returned to Pune, bringing Veluthedath Thankamma with him. He told me before going that he would probably bring her, bring in his responsibility and expenses, teach her typewriting, and get a job for her. I only said that it was entirely his responsibility. He would get his quarters, and until then, they would have to stay in our house. I couldn't say no. They now live in our home, and the boxes and bed have all been brought to our house.

I understand that Narakathra Kuttappan got a posting to MH Kirkee, and after joining, he came to your place. A week before I left for Delhi and before he was leaving for home, having troubled about actual problems he had, he came to me in an afternoon and said, " I'm going home to bring my family. My wife is scheduled to deliver our child to MH Kirkee. I have no place to stay until we get accommodation in MH in February. You must help me by allowing us to stay in your house ."

You see, our house is in great demand! I replied to Kuttappan, "I am going to Delhi, and you can stay here until January 25th." We have been of some help, and It was a relief for Kuttappan. They have come and have been staying here since December 30th.

Achayan wrote about Appan's deteriorating health conditions. He needed money urgently, and the matter was reminded through Babu. Going around with constant prayers for Appan's good health,

I could borrow quickly and send some money through telegram MO. In the letter I received, some matters caused intermittent pain and disturbance to my mind! Perhaps Achayan wrote and posted it before getting my TMO.

I sat in Kirtinagar and cried out until it was dark and cold. My father never wrote anything like this. It was a good gift for my wedding anniversary!

Kuriachan came and read all the letters that came to me. I was consoled by his telling many jokes.

The thirteenth of January that year was a holiday, Muharram. Not because it was our wedding anniversary! I remained silent as usual, without saying a word to anyone, with lots of memories and going out anywhere -

Kuriachan came and interrupted my pensive mood - "Aren't you ashamed to say it's a wedding anniversary and be like this? Edee Kunjunjamme, It is said today is this one's orandu" (first (death) anniversary)!

Even the cruel joke did not bring me out of the enclosure of my melancholic ant-hills (valmeekam).

Kuriachan was not willing to withdraw.

"He's not ashamed anyway, at least don't we need to? Why don't you fry that groundnut? Make some vermicelli pudding (semiya payasam) and tea."

Appachi wrote to me that our mon looks like his father. I am sure he will have the symptoms of his mother, too!

You must go and meet Appan. He will get well soon. The baptism of the daughter of Kuriachan's friend was there last Sunday. The mass was celebrated at his house. I participated and prayed for our son, Sajimol, and our grandpa during the mass. No one saw my eyes getting wet.

I did not expect Joy from Kochi to come there. Well, good, he came. Or why should he be unhappy with my son? While on his way home, he had seen me at the Pune railway station, but he did not come close to me or say a word.

Before I could finish writing this letter, I got Achayan's letter. All those accusations or assertions that disturbed my mind were out of his frustration and hatred. Appan was getting better, too.

What a relief it was when I got it down from my mind!

February 08, 1976

Some bees are nesting among the vines lying next to our backyard house. Right now, it is the size of the chapati you usually make. It is filled with honey and wax between the vines inside. Anyway, the number of occupants in our house has increased. Everyone has high regard for me. Do you know why? I am the head of a refugee camp.

I got into the kitchen very rarely. However, the occupants did not know how to make that special breakfast the church fathers eat. Bull's eye and bread toast, I made it all by myself. I taught Thankamma to hold a hot pan with tongues, make good tea, and burn the kerosene stove.

"This Appachi doesn't know anything. He just learned to light a stove now only." Thankamma said.

The two also went to the Air Force station to see the plane. When I went up to cook rice in the afternoon, the Narakathra couple said – "You can have rice with us."

Last week, when I met our neighbour John, I asked for Mamma's whereabouts. He said she would be back here by the end of March. See, Leelamma is very, very happy, aren't you?

I am happy to know, "While he is lying on the floor, he is kicking with his feet and fluttering his arms vigorously." When I come, will he ask me, "Hello Papa, when did you come?"

Then, if you have sufficient breast milk, you should give it eight times during the day. After three months, we can start giving Glaxo and other baby foods. Then, boil, calm, and pour cow's milk into your mouth. It will go down through the neck and get collected in the breast —that bottle cannot be poured in, but it could be taken out, and the milk in storage would not get spoiled. The milk should be poured into the baby's mouth without opening the cap. When the baby sucks it, the holes will get opened.

And one more psychology - be happy while giving milk to the baby. This is what the doctors advise. If not, it can seriously affect the baby's mood and milk flow. It involves the mental development and intelligence of the baby, too. So do it peacefully and happily. Tab Haliborange can be dissolved in water. Take Adexolin or Becadex drops and give three to four drops twice daily. If you provide it in writing, any pharmacy will deliver it.

All about a name - What sort of labour pain do I feel is for a name? TONY, ROY, SAJU, SANTHOSH, and others are on my office table. The Glaxo book names include Thambi and Thomman, beginning with T. Girls' have sound, reputable names. For that, you did not deliver a baby girl! We will have it later. Why are you getting a smile now?

Before I left for home, the Narakathra couple would move away. The arrival of their baby is scheduled for April 26. How will I tell them to change in the current circumstances? Don't others say that we are Christians? Yet they also know. They have arranged a room inside the MH.

Appachi did not say anything. I hope he, too, understands it.

Are you tired of reading my penmanship? Show my son the letters I have written, give him my love, give him the best out of a thousand kisses, and give him a fresh arrival from Pune.

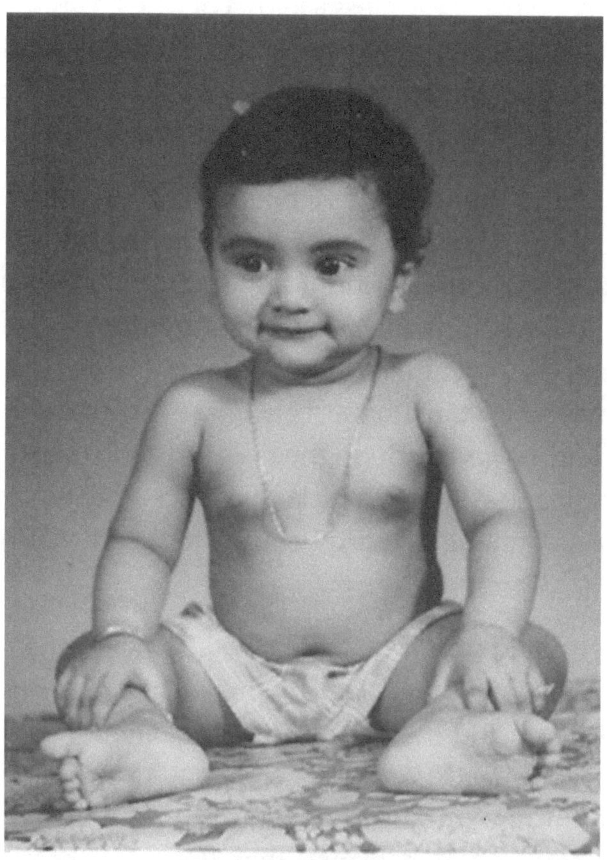

Tony at 10 months

53. SURVIVAL IN THE EMERGENCY

Feb 10, 1976, was the day my grandfather passed away, 70 days after Tony's birth. " ... Unless a kernel of wheat falls to the ground and dies, it remains only a single seed. But if it dies, it produces many seeds...." My grandfather was a wheat grain. We are also wheat grains. That is life. Can we live a life like our grandfather?

None of the grandfather's children felt the need to inform me, nor did they have the time or facility to do so. Kuriachan was not formally notified, and if any such thing had been done, I, too, would have known the information in Delhi. Even after we learned early and spent a large sum of money, we could not have reached on time for the funeral. Leelamma carried the baby on her shoulders and walked through the rice field submerged with water to Kannattumadom to pay her last respects. Leelamma had told Achayan to inform me. The answer was that there was no need for it then.

After returning from Delhi, I reached home for the first time in March. The sight was heartbreaking on reaching there and wanting to see Leelamma and the baby happy. Leelamma was like a weary skeleton covered with skin, like women and children in Somalia suffering from disease and starvation at that time. For the baby, I could understand at a glance that the weakness was due to malnutrition.

I pressed Leelamma close to my chest, kissed her on the forehead and tired eyes. My tears of joy for the baby, my heartfelt thanks to Leelamma for giving birth to my son, the chest-swelling sorrows and wetting pangs I had, the whole thing joined together for a few moments, dissolved into thin air.

No matter how strong-willed they are, seeing their child's plight can break them down. My eyes were filled with tears. Seeing my baby for the first time, I ran, picked him up, and hugged him.

"You will not be an 'Ottaprakkadi' (loner) anyway."

After watching him for some time, some words came from my heart.

The child responded by clapping as he expressed his joy and vigor.

Before explaining the shortcomings and the allegations, I wanted to tell Leelamma about a moment when the boundary had to be restricted. This decision needed not to be explained.

"My dear, it would not be in the native country if you gave birth again."

It was meant to motivate Leelamma to forget the present pain and survive.

The Ottathyckal Ammachi was not only Thambichan's mother and Leelamma's mother but also my mother, just like my mother. And my son's grandmother. All mothers carry and endure the same grief, hardships, and prayers. No pain, no gain. The mothers suffer a lot for a bunch of happiness. This is the experience of all living things in the world.

Ottathyckal Ammachi said sadly -

"She was having a hard time giving birth. She was bleeding."

I understood. I did not blame anyone. No one's fault or shortfall was mentioned. Circumstances and surrounding environments were such that even the most loving people could not do anything right, get it right, repair or fix it. Inadequacy of the system. Why should someone who loves us be saddened or blamed?

"ഇത്രത്തേ ാളം എന്നെ കെ ാണ്ടുവന്നീടുവാൻ ...

ഞാനുമെന്റെ കുടുംബവും എന്തുള്ളൂ (2)

ഇത്ര നന്മകൾ ഞങ്ങളനുഭവിപ്പാൻ

എന്തുള്ളൂ യേ ാഗ്യതാ നിൻ മുൻപിൽ ..."

"To bring me this far ...

What about my family (2) and me

So many good things for us to enjoy

What merit is in front of you ..."

I sang that song only in my mind. I told Leelamma, "I will come tomorrow morning. If you are ready, we can go back."

I did not stay at home for many more days. Thambichan came a week back and went away to Cuttack with his wife, Leelamma, and the baby named Saaji Mol. We also took our Tony-mon to Pune for good. When the young parents went to their workplace with their children, it caused great distress to our older parents. Our homes became desolate and silent all of a sudden. I comforted them by telling them I would bring the baby to show them before the child's birthday or Christmas.

Babu, Raju, and Babychan permitted us to leave reluctantly with sadness in their minds, looking at the uncertain future and wondering how to face the harsh realities of life without their eldest brother present.

All the friends and their families visited our home to see the baby. Appachi and Thankamma came. James and George came. Most of them were friends from the lodge 155 JA block - Kunjan, Padmanabhan, Vijayan, Suresh, and Gopalakrishnan.

Before Christmas 1976, Thambichan and Xavier visited Pune together with their family. They were on their way home, so their stay with us lasted only two or three days. It was a good time to laugh and play together, especially for the three little kids under two. As it was difficult for everyone to travel together, we did not visit any tourist places in Pune.

He returned home in March 1977. Tony was one year old. We took leave before the general election in India. The primary purpose was to move to the new house by the side of Arakkaparambil during this vacation, irrespective of whether the new house construction was completed in full or not.

Although the parents and relatives co-operated lovingly and spoke kind words, our essential needs were beyond their willing minds and capabilities. None of us together as a family or single-handedly could have met the needs of the new premises to begin our stay conveniently. If you want to move from the coconut leaf thatched hut to a brick-walled unfinished house built on our property, pouring milk into a new container to boil was not enough. We must give the carpenter and the masons, who laboured, the respect and love they deserve in addition to the gift. That was the challenge.

So far, we have not pooled the resources, including money, to manage the essential needs. That was why the construction was unfinished and the inability to move into the new house for so long.

It was a challenging year that would end this week, even for the necessary personal expenses. Though the monthly allotment for the parents continued without interruptions, nothing more could be gathered or earned for completing the house.

The arrears of subscriptions from the newspaper readers continued to accumulate. Rarely was there some delay on the part of the distributor in asking for the long pending arrears; the subscriber took it as an indirect advantage. Achayan never wanted to offend them by unpleasantly looking at their faces.

Even when asked, the result was often disappointing. That was the time. Most people had spent on agriculture and other necessities of daily life. They were waiting for the harvest time, thereby delaying the subscription payment. Newspaper corporations and other management will block product releases without asking why there is a delay, and the distributor's work stops.

The reader would be ravenous if the daily newspaper were not received one day. If his appetite were insatiable, he would become a beast and search for prey. Political parties were hotly contesting elections nationwide, especially during the Emergency, and there were many controversial issues. All a commoner wanted was information and a newspaper to read.

Achayan was in such a vicious circle.

Achayan had somehow misunderstood that all business strategies affect human beings' mutual love, beliefs, and morals. Achayan could not help but compromise no matter what anyone said. There will be financial loss; it doesn't matter. Readers cannot be denied access to the newspaper under any circumstances.

Achayan was well aware of the profit and loss of agriculture. Speaking of the commercial aspect of the newspaper job, Achayan would say-

"I had begun with twenty-five newspapers; haven't I raised you all for over twenty-five years? I have not earned and given you anything more, and I have no more time ....." Achayan would groan melancholically.

I could not say anything more.

Because I could not find any other way, the only movable property in the family, I asked for my mother's gold chain and promised to return it without delay. My mother happily gave it to me. I took it to Alappuzha and sold it in a jewellery shop. When we moved house, we gave charity gifts to the carpenter and the masons with the money received.

Although moving the furniture, such as tables, chairs, beds, utensils, etc., to the new house was manageable and started in good earnest. On its completion, I could say that I never had to make such a significant effort while shifting my residences 13 times till then. It is comforting to know that the stains of some original sin have been washed away in the creek's water.

The creek was covered with water hyacinth from Maramkunnil to the Arakkaparambil stretch. Moving a big or small boat using a paddle or a long pushing pole was challenging. I got a medium-sized mooring boat to carry household items. All the goods were collected and loaded into the boat. Chennatt Kuttappan with the long push pole, and I got on with an oar. We were able to leave Maramkunnil at about nine o'clock at night. The warming was planned for 8 a.m. Before that, the essential household items must be carried to the new - unfinished - house. It was an attempt at that. Pushing for three or four hours, pulling up and down, the boat reached in front of the library. At that time, the library was in Valiyaparambil's backyard. We rowed forward, pushed, and tried to pull the rope, but the boat would not move. It was pitch darkness. No one was around on land or water. No one will hear, even if you shout or cry. It was past midnight. Achayan directed and advised each one of us from the library courtyard.

Kuttappan said a ferry was available at this location to cross to the other side. We were not able to move forward as it might have been blocked by the submerged ferry. I got into the ravine in search of the ferry. The rope of the ferry was not found. Slowly, I moved the water hyacinth with my hand and tried to swim across.

I rowed the boat with one hand and then paddled the stick with the other hand, and when he reached the other side, I hit my hand on the ferry. The boat was over the ferry. Alone, I pushed the boat away from the ferry and got into the boat, pushed and shoved, and that way, we could move forward a little bit. At around 7:30 in the morning, the boat approached the dock of the unfinished house at Arakkaparambil. We were all exhausted. Ammachi and my brothers came with whatever belongings they could carry. The carpenter and the master came. Mother prayed; milk was boiled as part of the housewarming ceremony. We started living in a brick-walled, tiled house, though it was unfinished.

While sitting and listening to the radio news about the general election results, we learned about Indira Gandhi's defeat and the Janata Party's victory led by Morarji Desai, who formed the central ministry.

The opportunity we got to eat Pesaha (Passover) at home during the Holy Week that year was after about ten years. My mother could not prepare the traditional Pesaha Appam or Inriyappam (unleavened bread) on Maundy Thursday; instead, she made rice 'puttu' decorated with palm leaves, signifying a cross sign. Babu was boiling Pesaha pal (coconut milk), and Raju and Babychan helped their mother. The brown Pesaha pal is made mainly using jaggery and coconut milk. The meal also includes banana variants such as poovan pazham.

After dinner, the family gathered around Achayan. Achayan prayed, and everyone celebrated Passover together.

The head of the family cuts a small piece of the unleavened bread, or rice puttu, dips it in the coconut milk, and serves it to the other family members.

54. CHANGE OF RESIDENCE

Ezhupathil James had travelled with us to Pune. He was to go to Bombay en route to the Gulf Country for a job he got through his uncle in Bombay. After arriving in Pune, we took James to his uncle's workplace in Juhu the next day. We stayed at that hotel in Juhu for the night and returned to Pune the next day. For us, staying in a hotel was a first-time experience.

The Emergency in the country was lifted, and the people resumed their routine life as usual. Not many weeks passed after we returned to Pune, and we had to face another emergency.

The residence we were staying in should be vacated soon, as the authorities have started checking for unauthorized occupants in the factory quarters.

The factory quarter I got to stay in was allotted to a Maharashtrian worker, and he came home and said - I must vacate the house soon, or else he would lose his job and his family would starve. Usually, the factory workers rented out their allotted houses, spent all their money on liquor, searched for their own homes, and fell somewhere on the way. He was not like that anyway. What he said was true; the quarters should be vacated soon.

For Leelamma, moving out of the house quickly seemed like a shock. Still, when she realized the seriousness, she had to agree to a compromise that would be enough to get a space for her head to rest somewhere.

The search for a house continued. We had to negotiate many conditions put forward by the house owners, such as paying ten months' rent in advance, giving only one room, sharing a bathroom and toilet, not cooking fish or meat in the given space, and so on. We had decided on a compromise: finding at least enough space to lay our heads down without borrowing too much money.

If someone agreed to give me such a place near my workplace, I could do nothing but jump into it. That's how we entered the CME Campus and met one MES guy, George's quarters. We three souls spent two or three months in a single room solitary confinement there. There was no other facility for comfort or convenience except for going to the office and returning.

From daybreak until dark, she was always looking after the baby, making something to eat, not feeling like eating, day and night sleeping or not sleeping, half asleep, and so on for three months!

We faced many such challenges at the beginning of our family life. However, it has not made us feel overwhelmed. We have survived all such challenges. When faced with emotional pain or frustration, it can feel like we will be in it forever. That thought alone can increase the severity of emotions someone is feeling and make it worse.

We were finding happiness in facing every pain or frustration together. For us, the purpose of life was to stay together.

Another MES guy lived alone in Aundh Village. When asked, he said he wanted a place to sleep and would rent the rest to a family. I went, saw, talked about it, and gave an advance for the house. Living in the village is always a happy thing. The house gave us a clear promotion from the occupants of a 'room in the middle of a pathway' facility to another MES quarters, with a cot, bath, a breather area, and a separate kitchen and lots of space in front and behind the house. By that time, I had learned to cycle well. I could reach the office by cycling four or five kilometers. The Bombay-Pune Bypass Road was the main street near the house. There, a bus regularly runs to Shivajinagar. There was no direct bus to the CME.

We moved to Aundh village residence on a Sunday, in a tempo with all the furniture, bed, and utensils we had. Water, milk, the Deccan Herald newspaper, and other essentials were arranged for everyday living. I got up early, rode my bicycle, and went to the office. I returned at three o'clock. Tonymon slept on the floor, woke up, and swam across the room. There was no need to apply 'Chenninayakam,' but we could divert him from breastfeeding to drinking bottled milk. We took Tony to the hospital, where they gave him BCG and other immunizations at the prescribed times.

Everything changes when he starts walking! From creeping and crawling on his chest to dragging his feet along or without lifting them entirely from the ground, navigating and turning sideways, these important gross milestones are the moments parents live for. Once the baby learns how to catch somewhere up to stand, it's only a matter of time before he takes the next little steps forward to see what else is out there in the big wide world.

The mother's laughter and conversation stimulated the baby. By the time he was two years old, he could recognize people. The love and care that the mother imparts with breast milk shape the character and health of a baby. Leelamma, on the other hand, did not hesitate to talk and play with the baby. When the baby started looking at her face, she was cuddling and playing with the baby. The mother develops and best understands the baby's body, intellect, and mind. Tony grew up. He grabbed the chair and stood up. He was walking barefoot like playing dance. Tony stood up with the support of his own hands and clasped. He looked at the newspapers and magazines and clapped his hands. He tried to grab them and took them to his mouth, obviously not for reading, but he laughed. When he heard the song on the radio, he sat on the ground, clapped his hands, laughed, and played. I could spend the evening with Tony when I returned from the office.

It was laughter and fun until the evening, and he enjoyed riding a horse on my back. Colourful, noisy, and moving toys are fun for any child. I could not buy more toys for Tony, which was not intentional.

The three of us rode to the church at Aundh in a cycle rickshaw on Sundays for the holy mass. A Catholic priest from Vidyabhawan, Shivajinagar, used to come to say the mass in a small church in Aundh Village. A few people came to attend the mass there.

The letters from my parents kept coming regularly. I wrote the reply to all the letters. When I gave them the new address, they learned I had changed residence. Despite the monthly relief fund fluctuations, Achayan was relieved and happy that it never stopped. The people at home could see through the letters every stage of the baby's growth, and they wished him full blessings in every letter. Babu, Raju, and Babychan wrote when they had time. Babu got bored sitting at home without any employment or hobby. I thought Raju and Babychan should have given more attention and time to their college studies.

Within a month, two important things happened. This can occur in a busy life, primarily when the person at the top controls everything. Or, for the survival of each life situation, the Almighty sees everything in advance and pulls in the reins for an appropriate daily routine. He gives us only the suitable and the best.

Let the first important thing be narrated first. Leelamma was getting ready to bear a baby again in her womb. We went to Ruby Hall Hospital and met Dr Sathe. It was the same doctor after announcing 'primipara,' caring for Leelamma and the foetus for more than six months, and he had gladly advised us what to do next. It wasn't easy to face him as we had not accepted his advice. Still, he graciously and patiently listened to the hardships and sufferings Leelamma experienced when she went home without going to Ruby Hall for the first childbirth.

"Didn't I tell you you could be healthy if you came here?" That's all that the experienced doctor recalled.

"We will not repeat it, Doctor." I opened my mind to him. The doctor looked up and laughed! And then winked at me -

I said, "We will not do it again." He rightly understood that we were not going home for this purpose again. Still, he immediately seized the opportunity to say a good joke.

"No .., No... I did not mean that. You can have another child after three years!".

Everyone laughed together.

Here is a quote I saw on the front wall of the delivery room when I went out -

"Every child born into the world has a new thought about God, a possibility that is always new and radiant."

We informed our parents about the new expectations of addition to the family.

They explained the things to look out for and their hearty congratulations in the reply.

The following thing is the second one. I was fortunate to see an advertisement in the Deccan Herald, a private company in Shivaji Nagar, asking for training technicians in Refrigeration and air conditioning. It was a part-time job teaching technicians to repair and service the equipment.

Usually, I arrive home from college at 3 p.m. I was required to board a bus to Shivajinagar and return after a two-hour class on the subject I knew well. Even though it was against the government's rules, I went to that private company. I talked, thinking that if I could work for two hours more a day for my family, despite the risks, I would get some extra income and relief from the financial hardships.

Ordinarily, government employees cannot take additional part-time jobs elsewhere unless their employment contract permits. However, I found consolation in the fact that the part-time assignments did not affect my preliminary work, and the employers were likely to be tolerant.

During the first conversation, Sachdeva set aside a part-time job for me. It was decided that the class would start formally in a week. Within a week, Sachdeva arranged all the necessary classroom and workshop facilities, refrigerators, air conditioners, new tools, and replaceable parts and machinery.

I returned from college on a bicycle, had lunch, rested for an hour, and got onto a bus to Shivajinagar. I Came back at eight o'clock. The classroom and workshops were in a nearby school, and practical training was given. There were 20 people in each batch for three months of training. They all understood English. Thus, four or five batches were trained within the next two years.

Every six months, I used to get Achayan's specific directions to give the EMI with interest for the Thakazhy housing loan. A considerable amount was due; therefore, I must send more than the usual monthly subsidy. If we did not pay this time anyway, they would send a foreclosure notice before formally taking action to initiate property confiscation! Who else to tell Achayan's difficulties? My God had already seen this and arranged an overtime job for me. He wanted me to survive with the sweat on my forehead throughout my life! Thank Him.

"By the sweat of your brow, you will eat your food until you return to the ground since from it you were taken; for dust you are, and to dust, you will return." (Genesis 3:19)

The savings from my monthly salary and the extra amount received from Sachdeva were sent as a draft to Achayan. However, it would not have been sufficient to pay the housing loan at Thakazhy Society. That's all I could do.

I planned to buy a toy for my son every month, spending fifty rupees. Despite the extra income, it was impossible; I consoled and comforted myself that it did not matter. Didn't I ignore the fact that doing extra work was not legal? My moral conscience alerted me sometimes that such extra illegal earnings may not come for good for generations.

Ottathyckal Achayan came to Pune. He came to see Tonymon and see our welfare. Achayan loved staying at Aundh Village, which was like the life of agricultural labour in a village in Kuttanad. There was space around the house to walk around. But he did not see the neighbours as friends or greet them. Achayan was unfamiliar with the language used to communicate, except when looking at each other and smiling.

As always, sending students from CME College to Bombay and Delhi for industrial attachment continued. When I went on a trip to Bombay once, I also took Achayan on the double-decker train as he was eager to see the city of Bombay.

Bombay was an unforgettable experience for Achayan. After seeing the Victoria Terminus railway station in Bombay, the continuous flow of people and crowds, the flow of vehicles on the roads, the Flora Fountain, the Museum, the Gateway of India, and the Taj Mahal Hotel. We returned to Pune by the Deccan Queen train in the evening. We both had lunch at a restaurant near the Taj Mahal Hotel. It took about three hours for Achayan to tour the various exhibits in the Museum. In the meantime, I visited the students undergoing training at different establishments to supervise their training. When I returned to the Museum, I saw Achayan walking out of the Museum after finishing his tour. The Architectural design at the Taj Mahal Hotel entrance and the main entrance for the visitors were the most luxurious sights for Achayan in Bombay.

Specifically, he mentioned that -

"Given the property of the richest man in our state, it would not even cost a fortune like this!"

Achayan returned home with enhanced satisfaction.

55. THE ARRIVAL OF ANN NITA

James moved away to the Indian Meteorological Department's head office in Delhi. He sent a letter to me occasionally. He got government quarters to stay at RK Puram. He took his sister to Delhi and found a job for her.

Leelamma decided not to go home for the delivery and started preparations. The prenatal period of three months is when stress and suffering should be minimised or eliminated. It was challenging to look after the baby's interests for all his compulsions and carry him on her shoulder or side. In addition, the mothers realised that it was challenging to do household chores, washing and cleaning, washing in the kitchen, and wiping without help, machines, or tools. Our mothers, who had given birth to five or eight children, understand most of the daily routines of a pregnant lady.

Mothers have innumerable family responsibilities, including housekeeping and outdoor work to protect birds and animals. Those who say they have no time to turn around are always satisfied with their routine and do not share difficulties with anyone else. They never make a complaint. Even if they have health problems, the treatments will continue regularly while they fulfill all their responsibilities. Knowing all this, no loving children should ask them to come and help in our midst away from their happiness and circumstances. Healthy and like-minded mothers do so with their big-heartedness and generosity.

Wouldn't it be like wanting their closeness, help, and cooperation by going there? Is it not better to bring them here and be happy to go through this period smoothly with their services available here? In the present situation where the mothers live, it is more difficult to bring them here for their health reasons. It is not sure if they will get ready for it quickly. Choosing and practicing something like this embarrasses all those who think about it.

Leelamma would get some relief here if she brought her mother, but there would be more troubles at home. There is no one to feed Achayan on time. Raju would go to college, and Babychan would go to school. While at home, Achayan reads the newspaper and writes the news for Manorama or writes on another topic. If there were public meetings, the leaders' speeches would be summarized, and the report would be sent. Manorama likes the news and commentary written by Achayan, who is a local journalist. Retail rewards would also be provided. The library's secretary's secretary's evening duties are until eight o'clock. A task that had been carried out alone for more than 25 years. It had already become part of Achayan's routine.

No doubt it took years, but the country's literacy increased manifold. Reading habits increased. The popularity of political parties, local development activities, political divisions, elections, cabinet reshuffles, and the tumult of some ministries made people more eager to read the news as early as possible. The number and variety of dailies distributed by Achayan also increased. Separate distributors were set up in many areas to deliver the morning paper quickly. Achayan's daily commute, busy schedule, collecting subscriptions, paying the bills to the print media corporations on or before the due dates, recording all the debits and credits of the day, etc., were all restless and heavy work. The children are learning, and the expenses are insufficient for the essentials. The daily income was almost inversely proportional and grew uncontrollably after the two marriages.

Even ordinary people were beginning to understand how to use science and technology to benefit humanity. Science and technology facilities have become very important in all walks of life. As human beings became wiser, life became more contented.

Health, education, knowledge, and training in any technology have helped and motivated all human beings to live happier lives. Life became more difficult for those who had less since the times have changed!

Achayan once again tried the paddy crop by sowing Suhasini. He wrote to me- "No, not again, I stopped... After harvesting this time, I must sell the agricultural land anyway." Each time, after the harvest and threshing, the paddy was sold, and when the field was cleared, the farmer who borrowed must pay off a large sum of money; that was the situation every time.

However, Achayan can be proud of his contribution to journalism and library activities, which made the entire village patriotic and knowledgeable. His children were all so proud. Vavachi's children were loved and respected by the locals.

Our limitations hindered our rapid progress. The inability to grow and become self-sufficient proportional to the times was not due to a lack of willpower but constraints. It will take time to think about it and find a solution. There was no point in blaming anyone and worrying about it. Time is the solution to all limitations.

My mother sometimes said, "Everything is fine; the countryside has improved," .....

She clasped her hands, thanks for whatever little we have received or achieved, which was tremendous and adequate. She pressed them to her chest, looking up and sighing Ammachi, without words to speak, seeing anything or hearing, filling her eyes with tears!

Leelamma will have all the facilities at the hospital for childbirth. But the problem was overcoming the difficulties until we reached that appointed time. Then, Leelamma's sister Kunjamma, who was with Gracy in Madras, came to Pune, accepting her mother's suggestion that she could help her chechi with something.

Kunjamma studied, staying with her sister Gracy and Xavier in Madras, and had treatment for one of her eyes, which was injured at a very young age. The treatment was prolonged. The injury happened when she played with Rosamma at a tender age; a kitchen knife in Rosamma's hand slipped and inadvertently got into Kunjamma's eye. No effective treatment was given immediately. Over time, the wound worsened, and an operation was conducted when her vision was almost lost. Although she underwent one or two more procedures at a famous private hospital in Madras, no progress could be made. Most of the time, the pain and swelling in that eye persisted. As the months passed by, her vision of the eye became worse and irreversible. Kunjamma endured all the pain in her eyes with a smile.

When the famous ophthalmologist Dr Modi came to Pune and conducted a free eye treatment camp, I arranged an appointment to visit the surgeon and met him. After a detailed examination and exploring all the possibilities, Dr Modi told Kunjamma that -

"There's nothing left to do."

Within ten to fifteen years, the vision was utterly lost. But she always laughed and was happy to be engaged in some activity. Kunjamma came to Pune to look after the baby and help Leelamma with her daily housework.

While doing housework without caring for her health condition and forgetting about herself, she paused and looked at me as if to convey that she was smart enough and nothing adverse would happen. It did not matter, which made me angry and invited me to respond immediately. Thinking that I should not spoil the environment by saying more words, all that I said was -

Leelam, look... You know the consequences,... I have scolded you a lot."

Kunjamma looked at me in amazement when she heard what I had said to her chechi. It was so brief and moderate, quite different from the usual way she had heard of some husbands quarrelling with or scolding their wives. And she then talked about it later.

When I told her I could teach her some technical magic to reduce labour pains, Leelamma sneered, saying she did not want to learn anything from an inexperienced teacher. She went to Ruby Hall with a heart full of consolation and a happy mind. Tony was in the care of Kunjamma.

Feb 18, 1978. Nita was born at 6.25 on that day. Leelamma was brought to Ruby Hall around 8 p.m. the previous evening. She was rushed to the hospital and later to the labour room there. I was waiting in the hallway outside, sitting on the bench on the porch, getting up sometimes and walking, occasionally looking anxiously at the labour room door from the verandah till the daylights broke out. I have first-hand experience as an expectant father. Still, I am becoming a father again for the second time. I missed the first experience. But I am petrified to remember the terrifying hours Leelamma briefly mentioned later.

At about six- forty in the morning, the nurse carrying the baby wrapped in swaddling clothes and closely held in her hand opened the labour room door - she said as she approached me that - it was a girl child.

The nurse showed the baby wrapped in a white cotton cloth, and the head, body, or legs were not visible. The baby held both hands close to the face, eyes closed, and the nurse took the child inside so soon. My thoughts turned to the Heavenly Father with indescribable joy, and I thanked Him. After half an hour, the baby and mother were shifted to the room. When I went to the room, Leelamma held the baby. I went closer and touched and caressed the cheeks of the mother and the child. I kissed their forehead – my mind was filled up, and tears of gratitude covered my vision. I stood there, not knowing what to say. There was a need for balance in the family and gender equality. That balance has been achieved.

In those moments - I felt the fullness I had never felt in this life; I said in my mind - I am indebted to you for giving me this moment. Nothing can replace it. Be my favourite daughter, forever. Girls are a blessing that God gives us. All parents have to look after them as they are a God-given gift. As part of us, another human being has poured out embodying our energy, with whom we are in constant contact, and it is in the form of a baby girl. I told Leelam - "She will be a witness to our existence. She will testify that we have lived on this world." Leelamma did not understand.

No one told her, "A sword will pierce your heart." However, Leelamma sang, praising that it must have already been told so and that it was similar to Simeon's prophecy, accepted it with silence, and all was well! I believe the unheard forecast happened 21 years later, and it was for good!

Leelamma was happy, and I saw her face of satisfaction. I had to leave the office at eight o'clock, so I said goodbye and left. All those loved ones were informed, and Barfi Sweet was delivered. In the evening, I went to the institution for a part-time job and returned to the hospital. The mother and baby were waiting in the hospital room.

I arrived at the hospital in the evening with an intense stomach ache.

"This is how labour pain comes to men," I told Leelamma. "Or this is to remember always the daughter's birthday."

After taking one injection and a little nap, the pain in the abdomen subsided. When I woke up, Leelamma said that Brother and Tharamma had come and seen them and went back. That night, I slept on the side bench in the hospital room.

Postpartum care The mother was well cared for with ayurvedic medicines, and the baby was bathed by an elderly Marathi ' aayi' (mother) in the neighbourhood for a month.

Brother and Tharamma came as god-parents and baptized the baby on a Sunday at the church in Aundh Village. When I told the priest to call my mother's name Annamma, the priest suggested that 'Ann' was enough and that the two names were identical. Achayan wrote that she should have a two-letter name to call at home, and Babychan wrote that a name rhyming with Tony was Tessy. There was much searching for a new modern name for the family's first female child of the latest generation. 'Nita Thomas' was a journalist who wrote well-featured articles in the Deccan Herald newspaper, and her articles were knowledgeable and in good language. That's how I came to like the name Nita. I whispered that she was Kathreenamma (Valiyamma of Kannattumadom). Everyone was delighted to have the first girl of the current generation with a face like Kathreenamma's in the Kannattumadom family, Ann Nita Thomas'. Everyone agreed that the name would fit the ponnumol, who brought joy.

Make her lie down in one place, and she will be there without noise or crying; so gentle and calm. Look into her eyes, and you will be rewarded with a heartwarming smile, a baby girl lying on her back and holding her toes, smiling, clapping, pouring joy, or sleeping full-time.

Nita at 1y 3m, Tony at 3y 6m

56. NEW RESIDENCES

We arrived native during the first week of December 1978. Achayan and Ammachi saw Nita and told us she had the same face as Kathreenamma's grandmother in Kannattumadom.

On our way back to Pune, we arrived at Guntakal, and Xavier took us to Hospet. Xavier, Gracy, and Joe were living in Hospet at that time. Tony was three years old, and Nita was ten months old. We were to return to Guntakal at night and leave for Pune by train the next day. Until then, the travel interval was the brake of the journey. It was decided to receive the hospitality of the younger sister-in-law and the co-brother.

Xavier had arranged a visit to the Tungabhadra Dam and Hampi's archaeological sites and temples. Hampi is a UNESCO World Heritage Site. It became a place of pilgrimage for Hindus. It was the capital of the 14th-century Krishnadevaraya, Vijayanagara Empire. It was a rich and magnificent city near the Tungabhadra River, with many temples, farms, and markets. There was a Garuda Temple shaped like a stone chariot in the Vithala Temple courtyard in Hampi. It was often depicted as a symbol of Hampi. Above the chariot was a tower restored at the end of the nineteenth century. In front of the stone, the chariot was a large, square community hall. Most temple complex pillars produce distinct musical notes on knocking, and you can hear them. The stone chariot, the elephant, the animals like Nandi, and the carved architecture are amazing.

During the journey, Nitamol had a slight fever. The baby had a sudden febrile convulsion while returning to the Tungabhadra Dam guest house. The cold wind over the top of the Dam must have exacerbated her fever. The baby's high fever caused us great shock and anxiety.

He quickly returned to the TB Dam Guest House, sought and found a doctor, and the doctor gave her the necessary medication. She was kept under observation till midnight. Realizing that the fever had subsided, we continued our journey to Guntakal at about one o'clock in the morning in the taxi arranged by Xavier. We were to take the early morning train to Pune. Xavier had made a train reservation for Pune. Xavier and his family accompanied us on the four-hour taxi ride.

The taxi was stopped on a deserted road in the middle of the agricultural fields. The smell of coriander leaves pierced our nostrils when we opened the car door. Coriander is widely grown in Andhra Pradesh. The aroma of coriander leaves relieved us of all travel fatigue. Leelamma was squatting on the ground on two legs, like cutting the grass by the edge of the paddy field.

When she got up, I found her holding a bunch of coriander plants! I also saw the increased joy on her face shining in the moonlight. We hoped the farmers would forgive the petty theft from their field at three a.m.

Nita recovered quickly. However, anxiety and worry were present throughout the journey until we reached Pune in the morning.

The coriander leaves plucked directly from the field were wrapped, packed, and taken to Pune. All the curries prepared by Leelamma during the month had coriander's unique aroma and flavour!

It was time to move house again. MES guy Viswanathan was going home to bring his family. We searched for another house, and this time, we got another 'B' Type quarters in the Range Hills, close to Brother's house. All terms and conditions were almost similar for most of the sub-let houses.

What to say to Achayan when he asked me to -

"Take Babu and see if he can get some work there in Pune." Babu did not even clear the SSLC examination or know the language of another state or the national language. Achayan had his justifications - Wasn't it better than simply sitting and stuttering at home?

He was brought. Inquiries and efforts were made to find a job in MES and other establishments. But there was no joy.

Even if he was sent for job-oriented training, how could he understand without knowing the local spoken language? How can I find a Malayalee employer willing to give him a job? Only then can I catch his legs to plead. Babu was not interested in going out alone, talking to someone, or finding a job.

If he had an SSLC pass certificate, he could have obtained any trade training on its strength and would have applied for the job.

Then a letter came from home. The hall ticket for writing his compartmental exam came because Babu had paid the fee to write the exam. Paying fees was a regular activity every six months. There were two weeks left for the exam. Achayan wrote, "Let Babu go home and write the exam." Babu said he had not learned more about writing for the exam. Babu agreed to study further and write the exam six months later. Things only happen when something is determined and acted upon.

It was the need of the hour to do something to improve his way of life. Because Babu got tired of writing in the SSLC exams, he could not cross one hurdle, the hurdle of one paper, the English language. He tried hard to win over the English language. Thirty-two years have passed since Englishmen were sent out. Still, it is considered that schooling is over only when we learn English and pass! Babu was in a vicious circle. And he has not touched his books after leaving school. He Studied ITI in the wireman trade at Alappuzha for some time. No certificate was available for that. I do not know why. Even after coming here, I did not see him reading ABCD in the newspaper. I could have told him if he had read something and asked for any doubt. I don't even know the syllabus he studied. Two decades after SSLC, I am unsure what to ask in an objective-type English examination.

Without any initiative, the examination date was over.

Babu was not interested in going home to write the examination.

Siporex is an autoclaved aerated concrete (AAC) made of lightweight and precast concrete. It was used to build residential quarters quickly. Accommodation in the old Siporex quarters in Range Hills was nothing special. The whole focus was on looking after the two babies. Because Babu also came to stay with us, he was taking care of Tony most of the time. Nita would drink milk regularly and enjoy playing and sleeping. Her cries were seldom heard.

Part-time work in Shivaji Nagar could not be continued after February 1979. Residence changes have always been a problem. Some work had to be done at home, with the kids, or going somewhere for them daily. Moreover, the realization that there were only two or three papers left to pass my AMIE examination equivalent to a degree and that with more sincere efforts, I could study, pass, and get a better job grew ambitiously.

Our parents worked hard to raise their five or eight children fifty years ago. In those days, living facilities and necessities were limited. The available resources and the capability for hard work were adequate to meet the demand. As time went on, the circumstances were again limited. Complications increased, resources reduced, and the necessities and basic needs increased.

My small family was also growing. Needs would become essentials. In that case, the income at the current rates may not be enough. I need a better job with better career prospects and income. Better work is possible only with better knowledge, appropriate skills, and expertise. That is the struggle of life. The correct analysis would be that life priorities have changed.

There is the courage to live with what we get. If the availability of money and resources decreased, we would change our needs and live for the essentials. That was a mature thought. If it is limited, we will find a solution to the limitations when the availability of money increases. Or I can say that this is all I can do, and I am satisfied with this. Efforts for further gains would continue, however, and it continues.

A continuing effort is not just a word; it is not just sitting and ageing. Sweating on the forehead - fatigue - can be caused by overwork affecting parts of the body or the mind. I remember a boss once said a philosophy that "No one gets tired of sincerity and intellectual hard work."

Joseph Scaria, a native of Alappuzha - Thathampally, Mukkam, who studied at Carmel as my senior and worked at GREF (BRO), came on transfer to CME. Working in the harsh living environment, he was mentally and physically exhausted and sought relocation compassionately. It was the result of two years of hard work. For road construction in the border areas, the rations received were bought and spent years in the Himalayan foothills, in tents, and outside. As soon as I got acquainted and started talking, I started seeing the consequences of hard work. Then, whenever he saw me, he would tell me the stories of escaping from there. He came to CME and taught the students how to operate construction machinery.

Occasionally, under extreme circumstances, when he became exhausted and mentally disturbed, Joseph Scaria suddenly developed epileptic seizures, such as falling to the ground with his hands and feet, foaming at the mouth, and fainting after two or three minutes. I happened to see him developing epileptic seizures once in the office. I could only stare at him helplessly. Ten minutes later, he got up and walked to the hospital. There was nothing that could be done about it. In many hospitals, different types of medications were given. Then, the circumstances slowly changed, and when he came to work in a happy atmosphere, it could be said that his illness was almost cured. Three or four years after the marriage, Scaria could live together with his wife after coming to Pune. When they arrived in Pune, they had a baby girl.

Appachi used to come home from time to time. Thankamma studied stenography and was already employed at R&DE (E). Appachi had brought his younger brother Vakkachan to Pune from Kochi, hoping to find a job somewhere. Kochachan and his family had moved to Kochi from Kainakari with the encouragement and enthusiasm of Kunjommachayan and Valyachayan. Kunjunju (Kunchacko) married and stayed in Kainakari for a while during the holidays. After the two brothers married, it became difficult for Kochachan to continue his post-harvest rice milling process in Kainakari. That was how he moved to Kochi. Kunjommachayan, who went to Kochi to run an ice factory, had bought some land in Kochi and settled there. Vakkachan's brother Tomichan and sister Thankamma went to Delhi for employment.

While putting out the lights and lying down, I saw someone walking towards the window in the dim light outside. Leelamma touched me and showed that to me without making a sound. Someone slowly walked towards our bedroom window, covering his head and face with a cloth. It might not be a thief, and even if the window shutters are not closed, thieves cannot enter the room through the window. This was a different situation. This might be the voyeurism of some psychopaths who look for nudity. It must be someone who secretly monitors the deeds of a married couple thirsting for the fantasizing experience!

This was the first such incident I had come across. I slowly got up, approached the window, and shouted, "Who are you?". The fellow quickly left the place. Criminals might be waiting for the opportunity to achieve their desires, and we thought the trial was likely to be repeated the next night, too. Therefore, we prepared early, thinking he might return after the lights were off. It was unknown whether pepper spray for self-defence for women's safety was available in the market then. I took some chilli powder from the cupboard and held it hidden near the window in the room. The person did not come when we waited. I anticipated his visits for two or three nights more. The criminal must have realized that. These pulses were not going to be cooked here. Leelamma feared that if the chilli powder fell on his eyes, he would return to take revenge the next day with complaints of soreness in the eyes!

It became imperative to get a better job, and then we would have a better home where others could not peep in, where you could live without fear, and where you could sleep in peace. Sincere desire - is a prayer from the heart. Almighty, who always hears our prayers, would give results if there was hard work supporting the intentions of prayer. It would happen, sometimes early, sometimes late, but He would never say no.

I was confident when I applied for the Assistant Foreman to CIE (DGI) post in July 78. The written exam was held in October. The interview took place in November. The highest authority in any organization, being very busy in their day-to-day affairs, does not need detailed information about everything happening in the institution. When the interview letter came to me, I wrote to Col.TC Joseph twelve years later, saying it was an opportunity to work with him.

It was also added in my letter to him: "I love to be watched by you always, even though by this time I have passed through the crucial phase you mentioned 12 years ago. "

Frequent residence shifting must have been the highlight of my expatriate life, and of course, I was not the only one affected by it.

When the authorities gave the factory worker a vacation notice, he ran to the tenant. We must pay him money, or we must vacate the house. If you pay, he will spend it and return soon to borrow more. That was a common problem bothering all tenants- the unauthorised occupants of factory quarters.

This time, I got room to stay for only two weeks in the house of another factory worker. Two weeks later, the new Siporex Quarters would be allotted. Then, of course, you can rent a new place. The factory worker cannot stay where he is now for two weeks. So, for two weeks at a time, five men - three adults and two kids - moved in to stay in one room. The shifting house was not as complicated as loading and unloading, as all the household items could only be carried with the family in an auto-rickshaw. A steel bed and movable property, the only increase in property in the last five years after the wedding - One steel folding table and a few utensils –were tied in a sack and loaded onto a cart.

The fact that the stay in that one room did not last more than two weeks was only due to the goodness of the two angels under four years.

In just two weeks, with food prepared and five people sleeping in that one room, I do not remember any other tragedy except the visit of a brother who was hostile to me. Leelamma said that before I returned from the office, Joy from Kochi had come to look at the children and make sure to return. James accompanied him. I was relieved that Joy had seen only me as the enemy.

Like the "invaluable sight in the old tin box of the minister," this memorable experience is written here as a historical record of a fortune I have had. Still, I do not know if anyone will believe it. Babu knows. The door was barely able to open when the folding bed and the table were laid out, and even turning around was difficult. When the window was open, a kerosene stove was lit on that table, and food was served around. Babu would lie down with a blanket on the floor. Both babies could sleep in a cot with their parents on the couch and bed. What sort of new experiences have we had? It isn't easy to describe the experiences that Leelamma and my children went through living with me. Yet we lived; happily, we live - Praise be to Almighty God!

57. NEW HORIZONS AND CHAIN OF SUCCESSES

New Siporex Quarters were allotted to Sudam Vittal Kondwale, a factory worker. Sixteen months' rent was paid in advance, Rs 2000 (@ Rs 125 / pm), and I was permitted to live in the new Siporex quarters D36 / 8. I got it through a long-time friend, Netto Uncle, from Kollam. (September 20, 1979). House number eight was on the first floor. We immediately moved there after washing and cleaning the house, and we started living there. Brother always came along and helped with every move. The rest of the friends often came and went back.

I also wrote the remaining papers for the November AMIE (I) Sec B exam. I was confident I would look for better jobs after receiving the certificate. Better work leads to more responsibilities, income, and living conditions. That is the straightforward path. That's what family lovers do.

This is how I came to understand the meaning of Achayan often talks about how the seeds of the righteous will not ask for bread- ("I have been young, and now am old; yet have I not seen the righteous forsaken, nor his seed begging for bread"- Psalm 37:25). That is why we always work hard. I do believe it so then and even now.

In January 79, I was appointed to the CIE (DGI), Dighi. It was a bit of a hassle to cycle about 5 km up to Dighi while going, but when coming back, it was the happiness to be back home soon. Then I would pedal the bicycle fast, and I never knew the fatigue. What gave me the most happiness was that the most loved and respected Brig (then) TC Joseph was the head of that institution. He was a colonel and was promoted to brigade just two months back.

How fortunate I am to serve the fatherly figure of the new institution with the wealth of experience gained over the last twelve years. In return for the love and compassion he gave, and as a gratitude for all that I have achieved during these years, giving back a tremendous service would be of great satisfaction. 'Services' is only a word of convenience. I was hoping you could read through my contributions to the quality and utility of military engineering equipment. These have been among the best in the eyes of the respective user agencies.

It is more appropriate to say that I served the Central Government that paid me – it was service to my country because each of us is an instrument for service, a tool for the progress and prosperity of the human race.

This change of job and the change of place makes life more meaningful. I changed from my career as a college teacher. It was a great job to ensure the quality and function of engineering equipment used by the Indian Army, ensuring excellent safety and long-term reliability. The main objectives were to ensure safety and smooth long-term operation. If these qualities were guaranteed for equipment used for military purposes, they could gain security and the reliability to operate accurately, when needed, without defects. How many lives could be saved then? In which conflict will the country have to accept defeat?

Any object of great importance will depend on apparently trivial details. Quality is the desired quantity of every feature and information. This word comes in the language of a long proverb about war.

"For want of a nail, the shoe was lost.
For want of a shoe, the horse was lost.
For want of a horse, the rider was lost;
For want of a rider, the message was lost.

For want of a message, the battle was lost.
For want of a battle, the kingdom was lost.
And all for want of a horseshoe nail."

Especially in modern warfare with weapons of the future. Having longed for more than ten years and consistently waited for opportunities to step out, being able to step out of CME was a great event that would change our lives and make a difference.

What unforgettable events in our life happened while I was in CME? It was essential to record in history that the most critical milestone in our life happened when I married while working in CME.

'Duty is a gift from God, and it is like the command of a military commander (to be obeyed first without further deliberations), and Discipline is obedience to the law and the authorities. I learned this from the NCC during my college years. It was strictly followed for twelve long years at CME and became part of life. These lessons have helped me throughout my life. I have also become a good teacher, obtaining work experience from CME.

Although I had participated in the elocution competition and received prizes during college life, in CME, I faced esteemed people who were very much respected and admired, having high ranks and salaries. I could talk about subjects well after thorough preparation because of the confidence I gained from CME. It can only be done by the teachers - those trained in teaching. The confidence gained can be used in any field for a lifetime.

After 11 years (+ 2 months - 2 days) of service, I said goodbye to CME and my colleagues there. I met them later at some point or somewhere because my workplace was not far away, and as I said goodbye to friends at CME, I agreed to keep the contact and friendship. I joined CIE (DGI) the next day and had a new job to do.

Procurement of various compressed air equipment and refrigeration & air conditioning equipment as per demand from the service organisations, arranging delivery to the customer and ensuring their aftermarket operation, usage, maintenance services, and quality till the equipment's end of life - that was the job. Service terminology is Authority Holding Sealed Particulars (AHSP).

I was to be the 'Foreman in Charge' of a department that did these jobs in the office. Doing practical, constructive work on a subject I loved and taught significantly pleased me.

When done carefully, working in the CIE and ensuring the quality of engineering equipment used by the Armed Forces was very interesting. Suppose the user specifications given to the design and manufacturing organisations were written down accurately. In that case, the equipment they manufacture following the specifications would be reliable enough to be used for a long time. The equipment will be of quality. That means quality is designed – the specification is the design output. The job I was given was to write new specifications and test procedures to demonstrate that the equipment manufactured by the manufacturer had the quality specified in the specifications.

It was time for me to start schooling for Tony. We applied to Vidya Bhavan School in Shivajinagar. Tony came to the school enthusiastically for the interview to join the KG class. While preparing for the interview, he learned about the alphabet, colours, names of body parts, and everyday things at home. Being ready to do anything himself started when Tony made his parents sit outside, walk without hesitation, and talk to the teachers who interviewed him. During the interview, we stared helplessly as he put his finger in his mouth. After the discussion, the teacher said, "Smart boy, I'm happy to give him admission. Some parents must come to school every day when school re-opens, as some children cry and make noise."

Tony at Vidya Bhavan Pune

From the day the school re-opened, and the classes started, he used to go and come back by school bus. On the first day, Mommy went to school with Tony. They came back together. Tony did not cry like some other children. In school, he had a lot of friends. There was enough space to play and run around, and the school had loving teachers. He had a green check shirt with a pocket and tie as uniform. Tony always loved going to school.

Since the school bus arrived just before I went to the office, I took him to the bus stop by bicycle. Leelamma went to the bus stop to pick him up when he returned from school in the afternoon.

Tony used to sit on the crossbar before the seat on my cycle, leaving his school bag and water bottle in the bicycle carrier. Most days, while riding the bicycle, he told stories about the games he played, the bus, school, the teachers, colour books, friends, etc. After telling the current stories, Tony once told his daddy about how we would travel in the future -

"When I grow up ... Daddy will get a little smaller and smaller. Then I will ride Daddy on a bicycle."

Tony repeated the story of this progressive future to his mother as he returned home from school. Tony's interest in storytelling and reading began to grow.

One morning, we noticed that Tony had a slight fever. The temperature must have been slightly higher at four o'clock when he had a febrile seizure - a frightening convulsion caused by fever.

I was lying in bed. When we panicked at what we saw, Tony's whole body shook with rapid limb movement and body seizure. A teaspoon was put into his mouth to prevent him from biting his tongue, so his gums or lips got a minor injury, where blood was visible. The baby was brought downstairs from the first floor.

Immediately, Mr Godbole, a Maharashtrian who lived downstairs and returned from the factory, quickly put us on his scooter and took us to the nearest military hospital (MH Kirkee). The doctor in the MI room gave the necessary first aid, provided the injection, and kept him under observation for two to three hours. After that, the doctor said, "I do not see any disease other than fever." Tony was subsequently referred to KEM Hospital for further tests and treatment.

We went to KEM Hospital in the military hospital's vehicle. Tony was admitted, and a lumbar puncture (spinal tap) was done immediately. A needle was inserted into Tony's spine to draw spinal fluid, and the fluid was sent for testing. The test report came just before noon on the next day.

The doctor prescribed some medicine and discharged him, saying nothing was wrong. Tony made us realize how even minor illnesses can cause parents to panic and worry.

The specifications of many engineering equipment used by the Armed Forces have been modified and improved. The authorities, aware of my expertise at CME, believed me and entrusted me with a critical mission for the services.

Sitting inside the control vehicles imported from Russia to launch anti-aircraft missiles into the air was challenging. It caused discomfort and distress for the soldiers to sit inside and work because of the very high temperature (50-55 degrees C) in Northern India throughout the summer season. And more so inside unventilated and closed armoured vehicles with a lot of heat-generating equipment. In any climate, the highest temperature in any part of Russia was not more than 35 degrees C. Bringing and operating the armoured vehicles made for that climate in Russia to India was an adventure and arduous task that required tremendous effort, energy, and crucial technical modifications. None of the soldiers could simultaneously sit inside and control the missile launch and operations for more than three to four minutes. The Army General Staff requested technical assistance for any engineering solution.

The biggest challenge was reducing the cabin temperature to about 25 degrees C from the outside temperature of 50 degrees C. The authorities accepted the proposal to install replaceable air-conditioners on armoured vehicles. I was asked to lead the work. Accordingly, he went to Ambala and stayed for 30 days. With the help of a private company, portable air-conditioners that can be quickly removed when needed were designed, manufactured, fitted to armoured vehicles, and tested in the hottest areas in the North. The Head of the organisation, Brig Joseph, came along to share the joy of victory, which I see as one of the most sacred moments of my life. He sat for about an hour inside the armoured vehicles and operated the controls. The maximum temperature inside the cabins did not rise above 30 degrees Celsius, much to the soldiers' relief.

After completing the assignment satisfactorily, there was also a great reception and appreciation when I returned to the office. The authorities also gave me an award from the Ministry of Defence.

It gives great satisfaction to the family to carry out the responsibilities in any adverse situation. That happiness is for the babies when they will know when they grow up, and I let them grow up knowing it all. I consoled Leelamma. Leelamma had acquired the ability to manage all the household chores and specific responsibilities to the growing-up children, all alone and as required.

My next trip was to Madras. I attended a national seminar, presented a technical paper, and spoke on 'Air Compressors That Gives the Best Service.' On my return to Pune, I saw an advertisement of UPSC for the post of Officer in a Defence Department called DTD & P (Air).

Kuppuswamy, my friend and colleague in the next section, had applied for a similar post per a previous UPSC advertisement, attended the interview, passed, and was awaiting an appointment. The authorities did not hesitate to send my application through the official channel. When I joined the CIE, I realized that Kuppuswamy was very cooperative, a good friend and well-wisher, and a knowledgeable and humble foreman. Kuppuswamy's kind words inspired me to send the application to UPSC.

Appachi used to work in the Pune MES office, and Thankamma Veluthedath in R&DE (E). Appachi came and discussed a marriage proposal for Thankamma. The attitude and relationship of Appachi towards me was of an elder brother. That was why he approached me with a matter they had already discussed and agreed on. He thought my cooperation was needed to conduct the marriage at Pune and use my quarters as the bridal room.

Aby and his brother from Chengannur worked and lived in Pune. They regularly worshipped at St. Thomas Church. According to their wishes, the engagement ceremony occurred in November at the Siporex Quarters, where we stayed, and the wedding was held at the Mar Thoma Church in Pune. Veluthedathu Appachayan, Thankamma's father, also came from Kerala. Aby and Thankamma lived in a rented house at Vishranthawadi.

The interview call came from UPSC for the officer post. Since the job was to ensure the quality of the aircraft, the chairperson, a high-ranking military officer, raised the first question after the introductory salutations between us.

"What do you know about aircraft?"

"Sorry, Sir, I don't know anything about aeroplanes."

"What other subjects do you have experience in?" They didn't think they could scare me away soon. I was relieved.

"I taught Refrigeration & air conditioning at CME for eleven years and ensured the quality of engineering equipment such as Air Compressor for the past two years at CIE."

"A refrigerator works well in a room with all the doors and windows closed. The door to the refrigerator is open. Will the room be heated up or cooled down after a while?"

I smiled, knowing that smiles were more likely to express satisfaction or goodwill. It was a smile of confidence and sincerity.

I asked myself. Would any intelligent person do that? It was the same question I used to ask when I started a class for junior engineers. If you are a mechanical engineer, you must have studied thermodynamics and the dynamic nature of heat energy. The correct answer could be given only when we knew the exact application of the science learning.

"The heat in the room will increase because the heat of compression is added to the heat absorbed from the space ......"

And then, there were more detailed questions and answers. What do you do to ensure the quality of engineering equipment? What was done in the project for Missile Control Cabin and its details, and what is the success story?

The last question came.

"Is it possible to succeed with hard work?

"Achieving success with hard work is not just about physical activity; it requires a commitment to excel in whatever we do. We begin to succeed when we have a good awareness about quality."

"Thank you, and we wish you success."

The interview was over. After seeing Kuriachan and Chechi in Delhi, I boarded the train back to Pune.

I got the intimation two weeks later that I had been selected. The workplace will be announced later. We had to wait for it. From then onwards, we started preparing to leave work and say goodbye to friends in Pune.

Friends in Pune have always been loving and cooperative. The people of Pune are calm, helpful, and gentle. Friends and colleagues at work everywhere cooperated sincerely. There was hope and expectation that many more loved ones would still be in our life's journey.

When I discovered a vacancy in Bangalore, I thought it would be better to go there for work because of the distance from Bangalore to my hometown. And not the distance but the proximity was advantageous. The authorities had decided to send me to Bangalore even before the appointment order was dispatched from Delhi.

Leelamma shared all the joy, and we continued to observe our wedding vow,- "In happiness and sadness to be together in all situations, until death."

I remember having read somewhere. 'Good couples celebrate their partner's success as their own. Success and happiness bring the couple closer together. They are satisfied. The happy family grows. Happiness grows with love. 'Finding love, not money, is the key to happiness.

www.ingramcontent.com/pod-product-compliance
Lightning Source LLC
LaVergne TN
LVHW041007150826
845672LV00001B/7

* 9 7 9 8 8 9 5 4 4 8 0 3 8 *